Rule of Law, Common Values, and Illiberal Constitutionalism

This book challenges the idea that the Rule of Law is still a universal European value given its relatively rapid deterioration in Hungary and Poland, and the apparent inability of the European institutions to adequately address the illiberalisation of these Member States.

The book begins from the general presumption that the Rule of Law, since its emergence, has been a universal European value, a political ideal and legal conception. It also acknowledges that the EU has been struggling in the area of value enforcement, even if the necessary mechanisms are available and, given an innovative outlook and more political commitment, could be successfully used. The authors appreciate the different approaches toward the Rule of Law, both as a concept and as a measurable indicator, and while addressing the core question of the volume, widely rely on them. Ultimately, the book provides a snapshot of how the Rule of Law ideal has been dismantled and offers a theory of the Rule of Law in illiberal constitutionalism. It discusses why voters keep illiberal populist leaders in power when they are undeniably acting contrary to the Rule of Law ideal.

The book will be of interest to academics and researchers engaged with the foundational questions of constitutionalism. The structure and nature of the subject matter covered ensure that the book will be a useful addition for comparative and national constitutional law classes. It will also appeal to legal practitioners wondering about the boundaries of the Rule of Law.

Tímea Drinóczi is a Full Professor at the University of Pécs, Faculty of Law, and a doctor of the Hungarian Academy of Sciences, Hungary.

Agnieszka Bień-Kacała is an Associate Professor at Nicolaus Copernicus University in Toruń, Faculty of Law and Administration, Constitutional Law Department, Poland.

Comparative Constitutional Change

Comparative Constitutional Change has developed into a distinct field of constitutional law. It encompasses the study of constitutions through the way they change and covers a wide scope of topics and methodologies. Books in this series include work on developments in the functions of the constitution, the organisation of powers and the protection of rights, as well as research that focuses on formal amendment rules and the relation between constituent and constituted power. The series includes comparative approaches along with books that focus on single jurisdictions, and brings together research monographs and edited collections which allow the expression of different schools of thought. While the focus is primarily on law, where relevant, the series may also include political science, historical, philosophical, and empirical approaches that explore constitutional change.

Series editors:

Xenophon Contiades is Professor of Public Law, Panteion University, Athens, Greece and Managing Director, Centre for European Constitutional Law, Athens, Greece.

Thomas Fleiner is Emeritus Professor of Law at the University of Fribourg, Switzerland. He teaches and researches in the areas of Federalism, Rule of Law, Multicultural State; Comparative Administrative and Constitutional Law; Political Theory and Philosophy; Swiss Constitutional and Administrative Law; and Legislative Drafting. He has published widely in these and related areas.

Alkmene Fotiadou is Research Associate at the Centre for European Constitutional Law, Athens.

Richard Albert is Professor of Law at the University of Texas at Austin.

Also in the series:

Quasi-Constitutionality and Constitutional Statutes
Forms, Functions, Applications
Edited by Richard Albert and Joel Colón-Ríos

Courts, Politics and Constitutional Law
Judicialization of Politics and Politicization of the Judiciary
Edited by Martin Belov

Judicial Law-Making in European Constitutional Courts
Edited by Monika Florczak-Wątor

For more information about this series, please visit:
www.routledge.com/Comparative-Constitutional-Change/book-series/COMPCONST

Rule of Law, Common Values, and Illiberal Constitutionalism

Poland and Hungary within the European Union

Edited by Tímea Drinóczi and Agnieszka Bień-Kacała

Routledge
Taylor & Francis Group
LONDON AND NEW YORK

First published 2021
by Routledge
2 Park Square, Milton Park, Abingdon, Oxon OX14 4RN

and by Routledge
605 Third Avenue, New York, NY 10017

First issued in paperback 2022

Routledge is an imprint of the Taylor & Francis Group, an informa business

British Library Cataloguing-in-Publication Data
A catalogue record for this book is available from the British Library

Library of Congress Cataloging-in-Publication Data
A catalog record has been requested for this book

ISBN 13: 978-0-367-51213-2 (pbk)
ISBN 13: 978-0-367-51212-5 (hbk)
ISBN 13: 978-1-003-05285-2 (ebk)

DOI: 10.4324/9781003052852

Typeset in Galliard
by Deanta Global Publishing Services, Chennai, India

Contents

List of figures and tables vii
List of contributors viii
Foreword ix
Preface xi
Acknowledgements xviii

PART I
Rule of Law: In context 1

1 **Illiberal constitutionalism and the European Rule of Law** 3
TÍMEA DRINÓCZI AND AGNIESZKA BIEŃ-KACAŁA

PART II
Rule of Law: A common value 43

2 **European values and the Rule of Law** 45
ANDRZEJ MADEJA

3 **'Where the laws do not govern, there is no constitution' – On the relationship between the Rule of Law and constitutionalism** 77
WOJCIECH WŁOCH

PART III
Rule of Law in national practice: Is it a common value? 103

4 **The Rule of Law, democracy, and human rights in Hungary: Tendencies from 1989 until 2019** 105
ANDRÁS JAKAB AND ESZTER BODNÁR

5 **The Rule of Law: The Hungarian perspective** 119
TÍMEA DRINÓCZI

6 **The Rule of Law: The Polish perspective** 133
IWONA WRÓBLEWSKA

PART IV
Rule of Law and supranational struggles: Is it a common value? 151

7 **Rule of Law in Hungary: What can law and politics do?** 153
LÓRÁNT CSINK

8 **Safeguarding the European Union's core values: The EU Rule of Law mission in Poland** 174
SYLWIA MAJKOWSKA-SZULC

9 **Are the EU Member States still masters of the Treaties? The European Rule of Law concept as a means of limiting national authorities** 194
AGNIESZKA GRZELAK

PART V
Illiberal legality vs. European Rule of Law 217

10 **Illiberal legality** 219
TÍMEA DRINÓCZI AND AGNIESZKA BIEŃ-KACAŁA

Index 239

Figures and tables

Figures

0.1 Constitutional development in Hungary and Poland xvi
1.1 The European Rule of Law from the perspective of the national constitutional system 17
1.2 Illiberal constitutionalism in comparison 22
4.1 The Bertelsmann Transformation Index depicted on a diagram, data on Hungary from the period 2006–2018 116
10.1 The European Rule of Law from Chapter 1 222
10.2 Illiberal legality and the European Rule of Law – Hungary and Poland 228

Tables

1.1 Overview of the versions of the Rule of Law 14
1.2 WJP Rule of Law Index Summary table 29
1.3 Indices – Summary table 30
1.4 Number of infringement cases in Hungary and Poland 2011–2018 35
10.1 Overview on the versions of the Rule of Law in Hungary and Poland 226

Contributors

Agnieszka Bień-Kacała, Dr. Habil., is an Associate Professor at Nicolaus Copernicus University in Toruń, Faculty of Law and Administration, Constitutional Law Department, Poland.

Eszter Bodnár, Ph.D., Dr. jur., is an Assistant Professor of ELTE Eötvös Loránd University in Budapest, Faculty of Law, Hungary, and a faculty member in the Master of Electoral Policy and Administration program of Scuola Sant'Anna, Pisa, Italy.

Lóránt Csink, Dr. Habil., is an Associate Professor of Pázmány Péter Catholic University, Budapest, Hungary.

Tímea Drinóczi, Ph.D., DSc, is a Full Professor at the University of Pécs, Faculty of Law and a doctor of the Hungarian Academy of Sciences, Hungary.

Agnieszka Grzelak, Dr. Habil., is an Associate Professor at Kozminski University in Warsaw, Department of International Law and EU Law, Poland.

András Jakab, Univ.-Prof., LLM, DSc, is a Professor of Austrian Constitutional and Administrative Law at the University of Salzburg, Austria.

Andrzej Madeja, Ph.D., is an Assistant Professor at Nicolaus Copernicus University in Toruń, Faculty of Law and Administration, Department of Legal and Political Thought and German Law, Poland.

Sylwia Majkowska-Szulc, Dr. Habil., is an Associate Professor at the University of Gdańsk, Faculty of Law and Administration, Department of Civil Law, Poland.

Wojciech Włoch, Ph.D., is an Assistant Professor at Nicolaus Copernicus University in Toruń, Faculty of Law and Administration, Constitutional Law Department, Poland.

Iwona Wróblewska, Ph.D., is an Assistant Professor at Nicolaus Copernicus University in Toruń, Faculty of Law and Administration, Constitutional Law Department, Poland.

Foreword

These are truly extraordinary times. At time of writing, a health emergency is sweeping the globe in the form of a pandemic which has already led multiple countries on multiple continents to effectively shut down economic and social life for the foreseeable future, with a view to containing and managing the serious health effects of the spreading virus.

Amongst the many unfolding consequences is the emergence of a narrative which suggests that authoritarian or illiberal systems may have managed the initial stages of the outbreak better than democratic systems. The suggestion is that in societies where people have developed habits of obedience to government orders, in which there is a high degree of centralised control even in normal times, and in which restrictions on personal freedoms are commonplace, it has been much easier to implement an effective response to the spread of COVID-19 than in democratic systems. Democratic societies, by comparison, are less likely – at least at first – to tolerate and comply with the kind of severe restrictions on movement, association, and assembly that have been recommended for bringing this crisis under control. The virtues of illiberalism and authoritarianism, in other words, seem to be on display in this moment of global emergency. Needless to say, many voices have been raised to challenge this simple equation, but it is nonetheless true that in previous periods of emergency, many of the civil liberties and constitutional protections of ordinary times have been suspended.

The topic of this book, which concerns the resurgence of illiberalism in Hungary and Poland in recent years, gains fresh and renewed resonance in light of the global pandemic and the apparent opportunities it has created for authoritarian measures. For some years, those concerned with democracy and the Rule of Law have watched with increasing alarm as first Hungary and then Poland have gradually dismantled their constitutional checks and balances, replacing political systems of constitutional democracy with elected 'soft-authoritarian' regimes. Despite a number of interventions by the European Commission and the European Court of Justice, there has been little or no political will, either at the European level or at the collective level of EU Member States, to take any serious action against Poland or Hungary to reverse or prevent the further dismantling of the Rule of Law in those jurisdictions.[1] Hence we now have, at the heart of the European Union and of its institutional functioning, two highly illiberal Member States whose ruling parties continue to capture independent institutions and courts, to commandeer the media, and to suppress and dominate political opposition, including through changes or attempted changes to the electoral rules.

While many observers view what has happened in Poland and Hungary as the dismantling of the Rule of Law and of constitutional democracy, the editors of this volume take a different approach and attempt to challenge some of these arguments and assumptions. They argue that, although Poland and Hungary have certainly rejected the substantive version of liberal constitutional democracy and the Rule of Law espoused and promoted by the European Union, they have nonetheless adopted their own distinctive version of a constitutional system, which the editors call 'illiberal legality' or illiberal constitutionalism. They take the view – contrary to authors such as Wojciech Sadurski and Jan Werner Mueller who have argued that the illiberalism of the Polish and Hungarian governments at present is incompatible with any meaningful notion of democracy despite the presence of elections – that the concept of illiberal democracy is not necessarily an oxymoron. The illiberal legality of Hungary and Poland, they argue, does not amount to fully fledged authoritarianism, even if it is headed in that direction.

Indeed, one of the aims of the book is to spell out the contours of this 'illiberal constitutionalism' as it has been developed in Poland and Hungary. At the same time, even while they make clear that the version of illiberal constitutionalism developed in Poland and Hungary is at odds with the substantive version of the Rule of Law promoted by the EU, the editors argue that their membership of the European Union nonetheless provides some kind of constraint on the political and legal systems in these two states. The various chapters of the book spell out different aspects of these arguments.

The distinctive contours of illiberalism in Poland and Hungary, and its coexistence with a European Union supposedly founded on respect for a substantive conception of the Rule of Law, are matters of grave concern for anyone who cares about the future of liberal democracy and the supposed commitment of the European Union to its protection. This is undoubtedly an interesting and timely book, whose provocative arguments and informative accounts of events in these two EU Member States should make for both interesting and uncomfortable reading.

Gráinne de Búrca

1 For an interesting analysis of why the EU is willing to tolerate the 'soft authoritarian' regimes in Hungary and Poland, see R Daniel Kelemen 'The European Union's Authoritarian Equilibrium' (2020) 27 Journal of European Public Policy 481.

Preface

1. Given the relatively rapid deterioration of the Rule of Law ideal in Hungary and Poland, and the apparent incapability of the European institutions to adequately address the illiberalisation of these Member States in a legal and political manner, the book challenges the idea that the Rule of Law is still a universal European value.

There are several objectives of this monograph – the main goal and some less general purposes. The main goal of this volume is to convincingly argue that the Rule of Law can or cannot be considered (or to what extent it can still be viewed as) a universal European value. Therefore, it focuses on three distinct but interrelated areas in the context of the consolidated Hungarian and Polish illiberal constitutionalism and the different Rule of Law concepts.

As for the context, this book uses the concept of illiberal constitutionalism and introduces the concept of the European Rule of Law. We, the editors, settle for presenting only a summary of our concept of illiberal constitutionalism, which is characterised by an illiberal type of democracy (as opposed to liberal democracy, which implies competitive and repetitive elections, inclusion, respect of political and other related rights, etc.), misuse of the language of human rights (as opposed to the theory of human rights which implies individualism and protection of group rights, high respect of human dignity and equality, inclusion, institutional and procedural protection against the state and any actors having actual power over the individual), and the illiberal version of the Rule of Law, which we propose to call 'illiberal legality'. This book focuses only on this latter component of illiberal constitutionalism in order to answer the question of whether the Rule of Law can or cannot still be viewed as a universal value in Europe.

The book also explores why and how the universal nature of the Rule of Law in Europe could be embodied in the concept of the European Rule of Law. It is argued that the European Rule of Law embraces the context- and culture-dependent nature of the Rule of Law and, therefore, represents its thick version, with which the Hungarian and Polish illiberal legality is at odds, but which still can serve as a weak constraint on the domestic public power.

Against this background, the first area we study is how values can be conceptualised because we are asking if the Rule of Law is still a common value.

Another interrelated area that needs to be highlighted is how the Rule of Law has historically been conceptualised in the European legal theory because it will help us to prove that it has been a universal value. Lastly, we need to have a good recollection of precisely how the Rule of Law has been dismantled in Hungary and Poland and what the wider community, e.g., the EU tried to do to rectify the situation.

Based on these historical, theoretical, legal, and cultural phenomena, we can have a better understanding of how the content of the Rule of Law has been changed, how illiberal legality has emerged, and how it can be conceptualised in Hungary and Poland. When the degree of divergence, the fading away nature of the European Rule of Law, and the emergence of illiberal legality become apparent, the reader will be able to answer the question of whether the Rule of Law is still a universal value, and, if not, what to do with it. This book offers an optimistic, pessimistic, and more realistic assessment, but the final judgment needs to be reached by the reader, which will be a value judgment based on their temper.

There are other, less general purposes of the volume, which we editors think to be its strengths: the first purpose is to invite Polish and Hungarian authors that are experts in their fields in their respective countries but whose views have not yet been generally shared in the international arena. The second purpose is to provide a more comprehensive account about the Rule of Law and constitutionalism, as they are experienced in Poland and Hungary, as compared to other types of edited volumes in the field. Nonetheless, we also wish to offer more diverse but country- or region-specific accounts of ideas, as compared to a monograph. The advantage of this approach is that the book can be read as a monograph (from the first page to the last) and as a volume of collected papers (reading chapters alone or in a deliberately or randomly chosen sequence). This characteristic distinguishes this volume from other books on the Rule of Law or the constitutional remodelling in Hungary and Poland.

2. There are many works on Hungary and Poland, the Rule of Law and democratic decay that cover parts of the subject matter, which this volume aims to partly unite and transcend. All of them, however, are radically different in terms of design and the theory informing them, as none approach the Hungarian and Polish backsliding as comparable, unique among states in democratic decay in the world and, most importantly, constitutional.

This book deals with the Hungarian and Polish illiberal constitutionalism and transformation of the Rule of Law ideal. Even if both Hungary and Poland are affected by the EU law and the inability of European law and politics to address the remodeling of constitutionalism as being contrary to EU values, this volume does not engage in addressing the challenges the EU has in the area of enforcement of its own values and acquis but relies much on the merits of the edited volumes published in this field. *The Enforcement of EU Law and Values* edited by Dimitry Kochenov and András Jakab (Oxford, 2017) and *Reinforcing the Rule of Law Oversight in the European Union* edited by Carlos Closa and Dimitry Kochenov (Cambridge, 2016) are scholarly reactions to the enforcement difficulties the EU has to face due to the different types of crises, including the inability of the EU to be effective in ensuring that all its Member States comply with the principles and values underlying the integration project in Europe.

The *Handbook of the Rule of Law* edited by Christopher May and Adam Winchester (Edward Elgar, 2018) intends to be a bridge between the legal and the common sense of understanding of the Rule of Law in the global arena. Our volume has an admittedly narrower and thus deeper scope as it focuses on Poland and Hungary, as compared to the *Handbook*, which collects different definitions and approaches of the Rule of Law, and investigates its various forms of application and institutions. It is further encouraged by these diversified notions but develops its own understanding of the Rule of Law as it seems to have emerged, evolved and transformed in the countries under scrutiny.

Constitutionalism and the Rule of Law, edited by Maurice Adams et al. (Cambridge, 2017), engages in discussions on the Rule of Law in country-specific settings, including Hungary. It however does not include Poland, and, in his chapter, Attila Gábor Tóth confronts the two types of constitutionalism of Hungary, labelling them Lockian (before 2010) and Hobbesian (after 2010) types of constitutionalism, while rejecting the term illiberal constitutionalism and failing to shed light on what illiberal Rule of Law (the title of his chapter) means. Our book goes much further and ensures a profounder approach than Part II of *Constitutionalism and the Rule of Law* (country-by-country analysis) could achieve: it conceptualizes the term illiberal Rule of Law in the Polish–Hungarian context. The main focus of our book, again, is the remodeled constitutional law of the selected Member States – in this sense it deliberately offers much less than Part III of *Constitutionalism and the Rule of Law*.

Wojciech Sadurski, in his recent book on *Poland's Constitutional Breakdown* (Oxford 2019), focuses on Polish events without making Hungarian insight analysis and sees Polish events as having a mostly anti-democratic dimension rather than transforming the meaning of the Rule of Law. The latter is connected mainly to the anti-constitutional part of Sadurski's concept of anti-constitutional populist backsliding. Polish events, for the author, are gravitating towards populist authoritarianism rather than illiberal democracy. He claims that illiberal and populist actions of PiS are in fact anti-democratic; thus the system that has emerged in Poland cannot be called a 'democracy'. Moreover, Sadurski opines that the Rule of Law is simply breached, but does not assert it a changed content. In our volume, however, we offer a different understanding of the events in both states by providing a theory of illiberal constitutionalism and illiberal legality. We ask rather 'Why?' it was done than how and what was done. By asking 'Why?' we focus on the human factor (value system) more than analyzing tools of state-provided propaganda. The value dimension is the input of our research to the comprehensive picture of Hungarian and Polish constitutional remodeling.

This approach might be similar to the one applied by András Lászlós Pap in his book (*Democratic Decay in Hungary*, Routledge, 2017), but our book goes much further than the Hungarian author, in terms of the covered time period, the depth and breadth of the Rule of law decay, and the methodology used (comparison). *Democratic Decay in Hungary* demonstrates how illiberalism is present in Hungary but does not explain the phenomenon of illiberal constitutionalism and the illiberal understanding of the Rule of Law. It also discusses the reconstituted and re-conceptualized relationship between the state and its citizens but reaches a different conclusion as for the value attitudes of Hungarians.

Our book offers a new, constitutional law-oriented insight and theory of the Rule of Law in illiberal constitutionalism and expands but, at the same time, limits itself to the discussion of the two most renegade Member States of the European Union: Hungary and Poland.

3. Especially because the book is about Hungary and Poland, a summary of the key historical events linking these two states, including a short account of the most critical attacks on the Rule of Law since the beginning of the constitutional remodelling, could serve as a recap and contribute to a better understanding of the arguments presented in this volume.

Both countries transformed their constitutional order to liberal constitutionalism based on European standards, established their new constitutional democracy ruled by the Rule of Law in 1989 and 1990, and joined the Council of Europe (1990–1991) and the European Union (2004). Poland adopted its new and liberal constitution in 1997 (with the Interim Constitution in 1992), while Hungary failed to do so. However, both states passed a series of substantive amendments to their constitutions, which by the end of 1990 added up to substantively new constitutions. The formal and symbolic process of constitution-making to show the abruption from the socialist past, however, was delayed in Hungary. This moment came when, in 2011, the illiberal Fundamental Law was quickly adopted in an exclusive political process and was, in the following years, even more intensively amended. The illiberal constitutional remodelling process started in 2010 when Fidesz won the general election and gained the two-thirds and, thus, constitutional majority in the Parliament. The PiS could not achieve a constitutional majority in the 2015 Polish parliamentary election; nonetheless, right after the election, it too started a similar illiberal remodelling to Hungary, but used unconstitutional measures.

Dismantling the Rule of Law occurred in a series of attacks against the most critical pillars of constitutional democracy; the first victims were the constitutional courts and the ideal of the supremacy of the constitution, as early as 2010 in Hungary and 2015 in Poland. In both states, the process has continued in a non-linear way affecting, among others, the independence of media, civil society, the judiciary, and politically or economically sensitive fundamental rights. In the past couple of years of Hungarian and Polish illiberal constitutionalism, these attacks, both individually and collectively, generated many criticisms, reports, opinions, and procedures. The non-observance of what the reports and opinions delivered by several national, international, and supranational organisations, actors, and bodies (e.g., NGOs, UN, EU, Venice Commission, OSCE ODIHR) has contributed to an almost identical Rule of Law deterioration in both Hungary and Poland. The accompanying populist and nationalistic propaganda widely corroborated with the emotional needs of the population. It resulted in continuous popular support for illiberal populists who could secure a comfortable constitutional majority in Hungary in three consecutive general elections and a simple majority in 2015 in the Polish *Sejm* and *Senat*. The support decreased by 2019 when the opposition could win the majority of seats in the *Senat*, and when the Polish and Hungarian opposition could win several positions in the local election. These, however, serve as quite a weak balance to the power of the central government and its actual populist leader. Today, the procedure envisaged in Article 7 TEU is an ongoing process against Poland (2017) and Hungary (2018); concerned judges, scholars, and citizens demonstrate against Poland's judicial reform, and Hungary has begun to stop executing judicial decisions (segregation of Roma pupils in schools).

An even more concise image is portrayed in the timeline in Figure 0.1 on the following page, and a more detailed description of events and their consequences to the Rule of Law ideal are captured in the chapters.

4. Against this background, and in an endeavour to accomplish the goals set for this book, the first chapter, entitled Rule of Law: In context, supplies a basic overview of the different approaches towards the Rule of Law and the development of illiberal constitutionalism. It introduces the notion of the European Rule of Law, which is viewed as a weak but present constraint on the public power of the Member State, and a certain benchmark that could be used for comparison. It follows that the approach this book takes is a legal, constitutional law perspective, and, as such, it tries to stay in the field of law even though it acknowledges the fact that the Rule of Law ideal has a non-legal, value-oriented, and political understanding as well. In this context, the authors of the following chapters attempt to answer the question of whether the Rule of Law is still a common value in Europe.

The other section of the volume, Rule of Law: A common value, offers a philosophical, historical, and axiological overview of the concept of constitutionalism and the Rule of Law. As the title of Part I – 'Rule of Law: A common value' – indicates, the authors of Chapters 2 and 3 (Andrzej Madeja and Wojciech Włoch, respectively) take a positive view of the Rule of Law.

As suggested by the title of the following section – Rule of Law in national practice: Is it a common value?' – when investigating national and supranational practice in the Rule of Law field the response is more pessimistic. This assessment is palpable in the chapters written by András Jakab and Eszter Bodnár, who give a more general overview on the constitutional developments that have taken place in Hungary over the last 30 years (Chapter 4), Tímea Drinóczi, who offers a more focused analysis on the Hungarian Rule of Law situation (Chapter 5), and Iwona Wróblewska. Chapter 6 explains the fading away feature of the importance of the Rule of Law in Poland. These authors give vivid but quite depressing accounts of the tendencies that could explain experiences in Hungary and Poland from 1989 until 2020.

The next section of the book deals with the Rule of Law and supranational struggles. In its title – 'Rule of Law and supranational struggles: Is it a common value?' – the question ('Is it a common value?') shows the multifaceted challenges that have arisen in realising the Rule of Law as a value and legal concept.

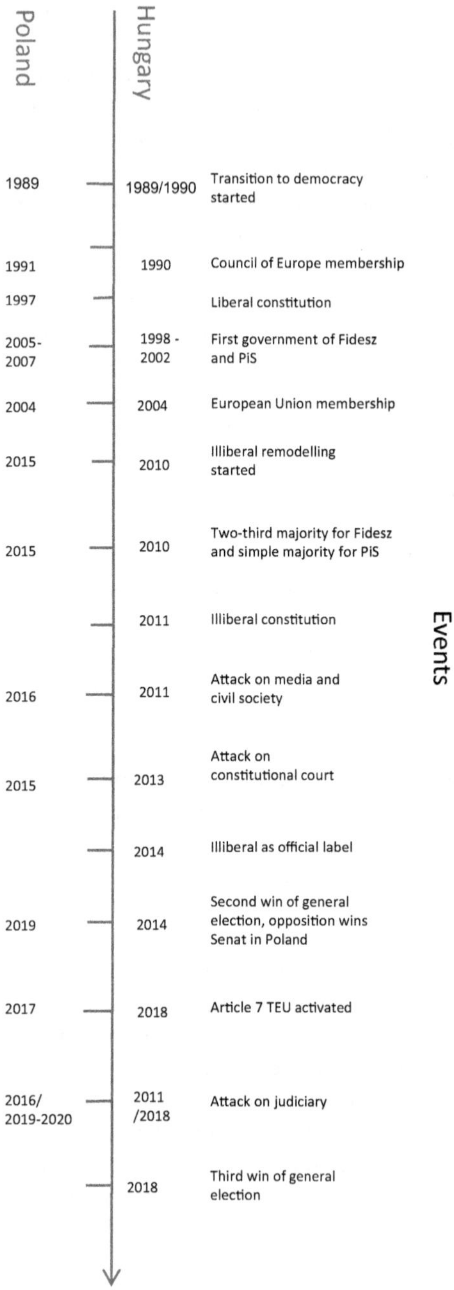

Figure 0.1 Constitutional development in Hungary and Poland. Source: authors.

The obvious challenge is to ensure that the constituent elements of the Rule of Law bind all public authorities in the EU and its Member States. The picture becomes even more complicated and blurred when the Rule of Law is interrogated from the perspective of the success of the Rule of Law mission in Poland (Sylwia Majkowska-Szulc, Chapter 8) and in Hungary, combined with the issue of trust (Lórán Csink, Chapter 7), and as a constraint on the power of national authorities (Agnieszka Grzelak, Chapter 9).

The last section offers an overview within the framework set by Chapter 1, answering the question asked at the beginning of the book from different perspectives. The core finding is that the Rule of Law is still a common, though fading, value, which is still implied in the version of the Rule of Law now found in Hungary and Poland. This version is called 'illiberal legality', and it emphasises the instrumental use of domestic law in both legislation and the application of the law. Another characteristic is the weak constraint that the European Rule of Law poses on the domestic public power because it requires the implementation and application of the EU law, i.e., both the values and the acquis.

Tímea Drinóczi and Agnieszka Bień-Kacała
Pécs, Toruń
February 2020

Acknowledgements

This volume is supported by the National Science Centre, Poland, 2018/29/B/HS5/00232, 'Illiberal constitutionalism in Poland and Hungary'.

Part I

Rule of Law

In context

1 Illiberal constitutionalism and the European Rule of Law

Tímea Drinóczi and Agnieszka Bień-Kacała

1.1. Framework and problem statement: Contested concepts

There are many theories and opinions in the literature concerning the Rule of Law. It is viewed as a national, supranational, transnational or international concept[1] or ideal, or an applicable, and thus enforceable, legal principle or value.[2] There is disagreement on its definition and constituent elements, ranging from a 'thin' to a 'thick' version in a continuum,[3] or from short positive descriptions to negative definitions that list what the Rule of Law does not mean, and on its measurability and suitable methods.[4] One can recall its recognition throughout history as a rule against the arbitrary use of power as summarised by, e.g., Martin Krygier and Wojciech Włoch in Chapter 3.[5] Another conceptualisation of the term is that 'government officials and citizens are bound by and abide by the law' as defined by Brian Z Tamanaha.[6] According to Dimitry Kochenov and Petra Bárd, the concept of the Rule of Law certainly does not extend to human rights and democracy, nor does it mean a mere adherence to law.[7] Scholars interrogate

1 M Adams et al., eds, *Constitutionalism and the Rule of Law* (Cambridge University Press 2017); H Krieger, G Nolte, and A Zimmermann, eds, *The International Rule of Law: Rise or Decline?* (Oxford University Press 2019).
2 J Waldron, 'The concept of the rule of law', 1 *Georgia Law Review* (2008) 59–60; D Kochenov and A Jakab, eds, *The Enforcement of EU law and values* (Oxford University Press 2017); C Closa and D Kochenov, eds, *Reinforcing the Rule of Law oversight in the European Union* (Cambridge University Press 2016).
3 C May and A Winchester, eds, *Handbook of the Rule of Law* (Edward Elgar 2018).
4 See e.g., M Versteeg and T Ginsburg, 'Measuring the rule of law: a comparison of indicators', 1 *Law and Social Inquiry* (2017) 100.
5 M Krygier, 'The Rule of Law: Pasts, Presents, and Two Possible Futures,' 12 *Annual Review of Law and Social Science* (2016); W Włoch, '"Where the Laws Do Not Govern, There is No Constitution": On the Relationship between the Rule of Law and Constitutionalism', Chapter 3 of this book, 77–101.
6 BZ Tamanaha, The History and Elements of the Rule of Law, *Singapore Journal of Legal Studies* (2012) 233
7 D Kochenov and P Bárd, 'Rule of Law Crisis in the New Member States of the EU. The Pitfalls of Overemphasizing Enforcement', *Working Paper No. 1* (July 2018) 20.

the Rule of Law from the perspective of international law and examine the role of international law in a changing global order,[8] while others study it from the perspective of axiology, as Andrzej Madeja in Chapter 2,[9] or in the light of the history of the Western political philosophy on the Rule of Law, as Wojciech Włoch.[10]

Notions such as constitutionalism,[11] to which many adjectives can be added, similarly attract various approaches.[12] The generally accepted view on the term 'constitutionalism' is that it cannot be anything else but liberal, which is why the expression of illiberal constitutionalism is opposed. Another reason is that constitutionalism entails constraints on public power, which is seen in neither Hungary nor Poland.[13] Consequently, when states like Hungary or Poland fail to show the attributes of their former 'liberal'-selves and weaken their former constitutionalism along with their constraints on the public power, they are called (modern) authoritarian[14] or anti-democratic regimes.[15] Others look at the concept differently: they either use other adjectives for constitutionalism (authoritarian) or, while studying the possibility of illiberal constitutionalism, claim that constitutionalism is feasible in the absence of liberal entitlements and democratic processes.[16] For us, illiberal constitutionalism is not only a 'possibility' but a reality, i.e., illiberal constitutionalism has an ever-weakening but still-existing constraint on public power, visible in the Hungarian and Polish constitutional states over this last decade.

This diverse background makes it particularly challenging to conceptualise the deterioration of the Rule of Law in Poland and Hungary. Nevertheless, in the literature, there seems to be agreement on two issues: firstly, that most of these

8 H Krieger, G Nolte, and A Zimmermann, eds., n 1.

9 A Madeja, 'The European Values and the Rule of Law', Chapter 2 of this book ...

10 Włoch, n 5.

11 See e.g., BP Frohnen, 'Is constitutionalism liberal?', 33 *Campbell Law Review* (2011); JM Farinucci-Fernós, 'Post-liberal constitutionalism', 1 *Tulsa Law Review* (2018); A von Bogdandy et al., eds, *Transformative constitutionalism in Latin America. The emergence of a new ius commune* (Oxford University Press 2017); H Alviar Garcia and G Frankenberg, eds, *Authoritarian constitutionalism* (Edward Elgar 2019); M Tushnet, 'The possibility of illiberal constitutionalism', 69 *Florida Law Review* (2017).

12 See e.g., M Loughlin, 'The contemporary crisis of constitutional democracy', 2 *Oxford Journal of Legal Studies* (2019) 446.

13 For a collection of terms used to describe democratic decay and backsliding, see www.democratic-decay.org/.

14 G Halmai, 'Populism, authoritarianism, and constitutionalism', 20 *German Law Journal* (2019); GA Tóth, 'Illiberal rule of law? Changing features of Hungarian constitutionalism', in M Adams et al., eds, *Constitutionalism and the Rule of Law* (Cambridge University Press 2017); KL Scheppele, 'Autocratic legalism', 85 *The University of Chicago Law Review* (2018).

15 W Sadurski, *Poland's constitutional breakdown* (Oxford University Press 2019) 243.

16 See M Tushnet, 'Authoritarian constitutionalism', 100 *Cornell Law Review* (2015); H Alviar Garcia and G Frankenberg, n 11; Tushnet, n 11; T Ginsburg and AZ Huq, *How to save constitutional democracy?* (The University of Chicago Press 2018), respectively. Other alternative views can be found in Frohnen, n 11 and Farinucci-Fernós, n 11.

terms are contested in nature,[17] and secondly, that we have to define first what we want to talk about or, as a matter of fact, measure if we are interested in how a country or the EU is faring in the Rule of Law field.[18] Therefore, in the following sections, we clarify these two contested concepts: the Rule of Law and illiberal constitutionalism.

1.2. Contested concepts: The Rule of Law

1.2.1. *The Rule of Law: What is commonly accepted and shared and what is not*

Christopher May argues that the Rule of Law has reached a status of a global common sense,[19] which seems to be in line with the view of Fallon, who opines that a general theory of the Rule of Law needs to be thin and abstract.[20] Without discarding this interpretation and its use in theory and practice, especially in the Rule of Law measurements and development projects, we, in line with the views of, e.g., Mortimer Sellers and Dimitry Kochenov, argue that there is also a value in viewing the Rule of Law in a thick(er) sense, especially when it is connected to the European constitutional development.[21] Zimmermann observes that the Rule of Law is traditionally connected to classical liberalism, i.e., the power is limited by the individual rights of the citizens. This perspective is embedded in the concepts of *État de Droit* and *Rechtsstaat*,[22] and its Hungarian version of *jogállam* and Polish version of *państwo prawa*. The values that are demanded to supplement the formal or thin understanding of the Rule of Law are usually viewed as liberal values, such as the effective protection and realisation of human rights and governing in a way that promotes a social coexistence in which the state acts for the individual and not vice versa.

In the context of a general theory v. a regional (Western European) concept, and having regard to different political philosophies, scholars differentiate between thin and thick conceptions of the Rule of Law. They also use various

17 Besides the already mentioned sources e.g., in n 1–5, see, e.g., J Waldron, 'Is the Rule of Law an essentially contested concept (in Florida)?' 21 *Law & Philosophy* (2002) 137.

18 J Moller, 'The advantages of a thin version', in C May and A Winchester, eds, *Handbook of the Rule of Law* (Edward Elgar 2018) 32–33.

19 C May and A Winchester, 'Introduction to the Handbook of the Rule of Law', in C May and A Winchester, eds, *Handbook of the Rule of Law* (Edward Elgar 2018) 1.

20 RM Fallon, Jr, '"The Rule of Law" as a concept in constitutional discourse,' 1 *Columbia Law Review* (1997) 7.

21 See also M Sellers, 'What is the rule of law and why it is important?', in JR Silkenat, JRE Hickey Jr, and PD Barenboim, eds, *The legal doctrines of the rule of law and the legal state (Rechtsstaat)* (Springer 2014) 3–6 (the Rule of Law has Western European origin). D Kochenov, 'The EU and the Rule of Law – Naïveté or a grand design?', 5 *University of Groningen Faculty of Law Research Paper Series* 2018, 10 (the EU emerged as a particular type of constitutionalism based on the rule of law through national democracies).

22 A Zimmermann, 'Understanding the rule of law: conceptions and perspective', http://alrf.msk.ru/understanding_the_rule_of_law_conceptions_and_perspectives

terms to express their different views on the Rule of Law, such as formal, procedural, and substantive.

Apparently, the thin and abstract concept of the Rule of Law has been enriched, and there now exists a 'thinnest' and a 'thin' understanding. Earlier, Fuller and Raz (1969 and 1977, respectively) gave a quite narrow definition ('thinnest'), while nowadays, some other principles or elements have been added, and it is suggested to be called 'formal legality'. Both of these thin versions claim that it does not concern itself at all with the content of the law.

The accounts of Fuller and Raz are the prototype of the thinnest concept of the Rule of Law and only contain principles that describe the characteristics of the law. For Lon Fuller, it comprises the following: generality, publicity, stability, prosperity, clarity, consistency of the law, the possibility of compliance with the law, and congruence between rules announced and their actual administration.[23] According to Raz, the principles of the Rule of Law are as follows: reasonably clear, reasonably stable, publicly available general rules and standards that are applied prospectively and not retrospectively.[24] These attributives alone are capable of guiding and, to a certain extent, limiting the exercise of power,[25] which phenomenon seems to be a generally accepted primary function and normative foundation of the Rule of Law in the literature.[26] As Moller comprehensively defines formal legality, this term requires the above-explained characteristics of the law, a power exercised via law (rule by law), the state actions to be subjected to law, and equality before the law.[27]

The advantages of this version of the Rule of Law are its measurability, its capability of investigating causal relationships between, e.g., formal legality and democracy, and if it has any consequences for economic growth and human development. Moreover, the thin concept will not take the researcher to the 'murky waters of the politico-institutional requirements of the rule of law',[28] and ensure that politics do not contaminate the law. Thus, it can be used as a general theory where the law can reflect the common legal grounds of a diverse range of societies.[29] Contrariwise, it also means that this concept of the Rule of Law cannot reflect the characteristics of a particular (legal) cultural context.

As compared to the thin concept of the Rule of Law, its substantive (thick) version[30] emphasises additional elements that are attached to the thin version. These components can be certain values, e.g., that the law shall be 'just', or the need that the law shall bear some specific content or be 'good law'. It can also be

23 L Fuller, *The Morality of Law* (New Haven, Yale University Press 1969).
24 J Raz, 'The Rule of Law and its Virtue', 93 *Law Quarterly Review* (1977).
25 J Moller, n 18, 30.
26 A brief summary is offered by the entry of Rule of Law at https://plato.stanford.edu/entries/rule-of-law/. See also e.g., Zimmermann, n 22, Krygier, n 5.
27 Moller, n 18, 29.
28 Moller, n 18, 30.
29 May and Winchester n. 3, 9.
30 See a summary, e.g., Zimmermann, n 22.

demanded that the law shall dictate the internal form of the realm of power (e.g., to be organised democratically).[31]

Consequently, there is another commonly accepted phenomenon of the Rule of Law. The formal legality, or its variations used by scholars advocating the thin concept, is the core element of any thick understanding of the Rule of Law. It can be seen perfectly in how Tom Bingham and Adrian Bedner depict the thick concept. Bingham adds the following components: the law must protect fundamental human rights, courts must be able to resolve legal disputes, adjudicative procedures must be fair, and states must comply with both international and national legal obligations.[32] For Adrian Bedner, the Rule of Law has procedural elements, including the rule by law (legality and adherence to legal measures), legal certainty, democracy in terms of involvement, substantive elements referring to the fundamental principles of justice and protection of each of the generations of human rights, including group rights, and control mechanisms which are constituted by the independent judiciary and 'other institutions charged with safeguarding elements of the rule of law'.[33] Constitutional texts usually provide all of these components of the Rule of Law. The question is the extent to which these provisions are implemented, or, in other words, whether the constitution is an effective instrument or merely a symbol or façade.

1.2.2. Controversies and uncertainties

There is, however, no agreement on the constitutive elements of the conception of the Rule of Law. It is difficult to determine whether it is possible to exactly demarcate a line between the thin and thick versions, as the Rule of Law can range in a continuum from the thinnest to the thickest end.

For instance, Christopher May narrows down the formal concept even more and claims that the core component of the Rule of Law is predictability, which is in harmony with the concept of the Rule of Law that has already reached the

31 Cf, G Palombella, 'Beyond legality – before democracy: rule of law in the EU two level system', in C Closa and D Kochenov, eds, *Reinforcing the Rule of Law oversight in the European Union* (Cambridge University Press 2016). See also, e.g., A Zanghellini, 'The Foundations of the Rule of Law', 2 *Yale Journal of Law & the Humanities* (2016) 214, Krygier, n 5. Cf also with the works of Friedrich Hayek (FA Hayek, *The Constitution of Liberty*, The University of Chicago Press 1960; connection between the Rule of Law and liberty), Ronald Dworkin (R Dworkin, 'Political Judges and the Rule of Law', Proceedings of the British Academy 1979, 262, www.thebritishacademy.ac.uk/pubs/proc/files/64p259 pdf; connection between the Rule of Law and substantive justice and moral rights).

32 T Bingham, *The Rule of Law* (Penguin 2011); The report of the Secretary-General of the UN on The rule of law and transitional justice in conflict and post-conflict societies, 23/0/04, 4; Rule of Law Checklist (Adopted by the Venice Commission at its 106th Plenary Session [Venice, 11–12 March 2016]).

33 A Bedner, 'An Elementary Approach to the Rule of Law', 2 *Hague Journal on the Rule of Law* (2010) 67, 48; D Boies, 'Judicial Independence and the Rule of Law', 22 *Washington University Journal of Law & Policy* (2006) 60.

status of global common sense. He argues that, if a state is unable to provide a sustained level of predictability, it cannot claim to have implemented the Rule of Law. Predictability is achieved when a predictable legal environment is provided that can guide people's behaviour and regard their freedom and autonomy;[34] it requires even less than the theories of Fuller and Raz. It would result in an even greater proliferation of the adjectives we have to add to the Rule of Law to be able to briefly but adequately express what we mean, i.e., the differences between the thin understandings of the Rule of Law. This difficulty is observable in Table 1.1.

Moreover, the idea that the commonly shared understanding of the Rule of Law, i.e., to prevent the arbitrary use of power, is ambiguous as it depends on the definition of 'arbitrary'. It could imply that the law is not arbitrary if it considers individual liberty, which is already a value that the Rule of Law would demand, which would mean a thick(er) understanding of the term. In contrast, it can also be asserted that, if rulers comply with the characteristics of the law or if they rule with the use of legal measures (rule by law), they cannot act arbitrarily and in unpredictable ways, regardless of how their regulations affect the addressees, including the liberties of individuals. It also brings about one of the disadvantages of the thin(est) concept: the Rule of Law can coexist with systems that are illiberal, authoritarian, and undemocratic.

Along this line, Krygier,[35] when discussing how the Rule of Law gained importance worldwide and how this concept claimed to be a point of reference to the migration of ideas of constitutional borrowing or transplants,[36] warns about the pitfalls of both the thin/thick or formal/substantive approaches. The formal conception would emphasise the importance of institutions and procedures. Authoritarian governments, however, have imported the institutions and procedures essential to the Western understanding of the Rule of Law but could or would not want to operate them properly. Indeed, they would insist on being assessed against formal criteria (the thinnest possible), which is easier to satisfy than the thick, morally demanding ones. Besides this isomorphic mimicry,[37] non-state actors that exercise public power can also be mentioned as they, due to the non-operational procedures and institutions, also can act arbitrarily. Krygier also notes that the substantive concept of the Rule of Law might be meaningless, because 'loading wide-ranging substantive ideals into the concept threatens to melt it into everything else we might like'.[38]

34 C May, The centrality of predictability to the rule of law, in C May and A Winchester, eds, *Handbook of the Rule of Law* (Edward Elgar 2018) 1–7.

35 Krygier, n 5.

36 See e.g., W Osiatyński, 'Paradoxes of constitutional borrowing', 2 *International Journal of Constitutional Law* (2003) 244–268.

37 L Pritchett, M Woolcock, and M Andrews, 'Capability Traps? The Mechanisms of Persistent Implementation Failure', *CGD Working Article* 234, Washington, DC, Center for Global Development (2010), www.cgdev.org/content/publications/detail/1424651; Krygier, n 5.

38 Krygier, n 5.

Opposing this latter view, Ronan Cormacain appreciates the thick concept and acknowledges the duality to the Rule of Law. He explains that 'at one level, the rule of law is a basic principle that we are all subject to the law. At another level, the rule of law is the ideal of the values that a legal system ought to possess'.[39] For him, the mere thin version of the Rule of Law is unacceptable as the Rule of Law cannot be compatible with gross human rights violations, which are indifferent to the thin understanding of the notion.[40] He especially challenges Raz's original view, according to which the content of the law does not matter if certain formal requirements have been met during the law-making and drafting process.

Raz, recently, has offered a new account of the formal concept of the Rule of Law, revising his previous view because that could not guarantee to eliminate the possibility of arbitrary government.[41] He still asserts that substantive matters, such as fundamental rights protection, cannot form part of the concept of the Rule of Law; however, he listed some requirements that might intrinsically entail 'just' elements (which are obviously not considered as such by Raz). Having looked at these elements, Raz's position can be challenged: he claims that the Rule of Law principles 'are not about the content of the laws, but about its mode of generation and application'.[42] Due to the need for acting in the interest of the governed, he added the requirements that decisions have to be reasonable and relative to their declared reasons, and the process shall involve various degrees of representation and hearing to consider relevant arguments and information.[43] Acting in the interest of the governed, representation and involvement in decision-making can obviously be a mere formality, especially in legislation, but if this is so, it does not make much sense, as this process would disregard everything that representation and involvement stands for: hearing the voices of others, avoiding the tunnel vision of decision-makers, and curbing arbitrary actions. Moreover, non-compliance with these elements, depending on their regulatory level and degree, though, should trigger different legal actions, such as the involvement of the judiciary, including constitutional courts as well,[44] which might already be the beginning of the use of a more substantive concept.[45]

39 R Cormacain, *Legislative drafting and the Rule of Law* (PhD Thesis, IALS School of Advanced Study, University of London 2017).

40 Ibid., 22–23.

41 Raz, n 24; J Raz, 'The law's own virtue', 1 *Oxford Journal of Legal Studies* (2019).

42 Raz, n 41, 2.

43 Raz, n 41, 8–9.

44 More about that see P Popelier, 'Consultation on Draft Regulation: Best Practices and Political Objections', in MT Almeida and L Mader, eds, *Proceedings of the 9th IAL Congress Quality of Legislation – Principles and Instruments* [Lisbon, 24–25 June 2010] (Nomos 2011) 140; P Popelier and A Mazmanyan and W Vandenbruwane, eds, *The Role of Constitutional Courts in Multilevel Governance* (Intersentia 2013); H Xanthaki and U Karpen, eds, *Legislation and Legisprudence in Europe. A Comprehensive Guide for Scholars and Legislative Practitioners* (Hart 2017).

45 Raz, n 41, 15.

It is difficult to argue with this above claim of Raz. However, if the Rule of Law in the formal (narrow, thin) sense, i.e., the prohibition of detrimental retroactive legislation, which is the component of the thinnest formal conceptualisation, is not to or cannot be enforced, why should we talk about the Rule of Law at all? Enforcing, e.g., predictability (prohibition of detrimental retroactive legislation) requires a judiciary that is independent of those whose cases it adjudicates or whose legal measures it reviews. An independent judiciary is not bound to deliver 'just' decisions but come up with rulings that are in line with laws and the constitution. In this sense, because modern constitutions are committed to human rights, democracy, and inclusion, even the thin concept of the Rule of Law should not disregard the enforcing mechanism as another constituent element of the concept. Thus, in a constitutional democracy, the Rule of Law has to be 'less thin' or 'thicker' than its 'original' (Raz, Fuller) or 'simplest' (May) conceptualisation.

All of this, however, does not mean that the Rule of Law would be equal to human rights, their protection, or democracy. However, it certainly means that a particular human right or some aspect of democracy may prevail if the principles and the core role of the Rule of Law in the legal system are taken seriously. Enforcement of rights or a constitutional principle can even be supported by the application of the Rule of Law principle.[46] In the process of enforcing and implementing constitutions and international human rights obligations, human rights, democracy, and the Rule of Law are not mutually exclusive but, to a certain extent, overlapping and interdependent concepts.

1.2.3. The Rule of Law: A context-related concept and a common value

1.2.3.1. APPROACHES

Having these approaches, controversies, and uncertainties in mind, Jorgen Moller and Adrian Bedner have collected the advantages of the thin and thick understandings of the concept and came to the same conclusion: the Rule of Law is a context-related concept.[47] The definition of the Rule of Law depends on the purpose of the specific investigation. The thin version is usually supported and used by certain (communist, illiberal, etc.)[48] states, as it is easier to comply with;

46 See e.g., how the social rights are enforced in K Wojtyczek, ed, *Social rights as fundamental rights: XIXth International Congress of Comparative Law/le XIXe Congrès international de droit compare* (Eleven International Publishing 2016); particularly about Hungary and Poland see, T Drinóczi and G Juhász, 'Social rights in Hungary', in K Wojtyczek, Ibid., 171–206; J Trzciński and M Szwast, 'Social rights in Poland', in K Wojtyczek, Ibid.

47 Moller, n 18, 33; A Bedner, 'The promise of a thick view', in C May and A Winchester, eds, *Handbook of the Rule of Law* (Edward Elgar 2018) 41.

48 The thick concept of the Rule of Law, as explained by Gosalbo-Bono, is either refuted in the socialist regimes, or transformed, as it happens in the Islamic law. R Gosalbo-Bono, 'The significance of the rule of law and its implications for the European Union and the United States', 72 *University of Pittsburgh Law Review* (2010), 289. Islamic law is not examined here, as it has been an applicable law neither in Hungary nor in Poland.

some scholars who use the term for analytical purposes; and those who engage with legal-historical, legal-philosophical, and pragmatic research, because they are concerned with the quality of the legal system, therefore they focus on procedural and formal elements. The thick concept is popular among social activists, different (international) organisations, and those who criticise existing authoritarian regimes or states in democratic decay because this version can strongly support their criticism.[49]

Beyond these considerations, it also follows that the Rule of Law can be a political ideal (Włoch), a theoretical construct (Madeja), a constitutional principle or value (other papers in this volume) to be unfolded by interpretation, or a set of quantitative indices (as indicated later in Section 1.4). It also can be noted that its content is historical and geographical context-related, and its interpretation is enabled by a certain tradition in which both the texts on the principle of the Rule of Law and the interpreter participate.[50] That is why, even if we acknowledge that the usefulness and necessity of the idea of the Rule of Law as a universal and, therefore, thin concept, we shall differentiate between legal systems (Western, Asian, socialist, etc.),[51] the scholarly fields in whose framework we are examining it (e.g., political philosophy or law), and its distinct approaches (e.g., formal and substantive or thin and thick) when we are investigating the extent of compliance with the particular Rule of Law concept.

1.2.3.2. LEGAL SYSTEM-ORIENTATION

Different outcomes concerning the meaning and the components of the Rule of Law can be reached if we stay in the realm of political philosophy or consider the jurisprudence of the constitutional courts. Constitutional interpretation contributes to the implementation of the constitution, including many abstractly stipulated constitutional principles such as the Rule of Law. Constitutional court judges may undoubtedly follow a particular political philosophy that they can identify with, but when interpreting the constitutional text they shall be (more) bound by the constitution, the already established case-law, and the rules of constitutional interpretation, however contested and diverse this exercise may be.[52]

49 Moller, n 18, 31–33, Bedner, n 47, 41.

50 Tamanaha, n 6, 247, Zanghellini, n 31, 216.

51 Whichever classification we use, either be based on families (Arminjon, Nolde, and Wolff), multidimensional methodology (Zweiert and Kötz), or be ideologically inspired (Rene David), there is always a clear distinction between 'Western' and 'non-Western' states.

52 On the practices of constitutional interpretation in the USA, Germany, Poland (until 2015), in e.g., DE Finck, 'Judicial Review: The United States Supreme Court Versus the German Constitutional Court', 1 *Boston College International and Comparative Law Review* (1997); DM Beatty, 'The forms and limits of constitutional interpretation', 49 *The American Journal of Comparative Law* (2001); A Bień-Kacała, 'Informal constitutional change' 6 (40) *Przegląd Prawa Konstytucyjnego* 2017, 199–218; T Groppi, 'Constitutional revision in Italy: A marginal instrument for constitutional change', in X Contiades ed, *Engineering Constitutional Change* (Routledge 2016) 218–220.

The Hungarian Constitutional Court (CC), for instance, already in the beginning of its operation, established that it perceives the Rule of Law principle of the Constitution in a formal sense; thus, would not link it to any other existing constitutional provisions, e.g., those on fundamental rights, and yet, it interpreted it widely.[53] In Poland, before 1997 (the Constitution of the Republic of Poland), the Constitutional Tribunal (CT) perceived the Rule of Law in a substantive way linking it with human rights.[54] After constitutionalising most of the human rights in the 1997 Constitution, the perception of the Rule of Law in the jurisprudence of the CT become more formal. The CT, however, still, even though less intensively, links it to human rights. Both courts were also engaged with the interpretation of the Rule of Law when it deemed necessary to decide on the constitutionality of laws.[55]

Scholars taking different perspectives, including the assessment of the jurisdiction of constitutional (supreme) courts, will hardly find themselves on the same page and come to a common understanding of the definition and content of the Rule of Law. Therefore, for the scope of this chapter and the volume, it is more relevant what Michel Rosenfeld notes concerning the conceptualisation of the Rule of Law in Germany during the second half of the 20th century. As opposed to the positivist *Rechtsstaat*, which emphasised legality and predictability, its contemporary version called *Verfassungsstaat* aims at fairness through constitutionalising substantive norms and values.[56] This constitutionalisation and the subsequent jurisprudence of the German Constitutional Court could explain why 'some present day positivists are committed to a substantive conception of the rule of law ideal',[57] whatever its exact content may be. As McDonald observed, it is a misleading simplification to assume that 'that various forms of natural law inspired jurisprudence (such as Ronald Dworkin's) are wedded to "substantive" or "thick" conceptions of the rule of law, whereas positivist theory is committed to a "formal" or "thin" rule of law ideal'.[58]

As said, constitutional courts are usually not concerned with the labelling of what they apply as a benchmark of constitutionality; they consider, among others, the text of the constitutions which usually recognises the particular state as a Rule of Law state, with or without an identifying adjective, and other provisions of the constitution, e.g., fundamental rights or other value-related rules. What

53 A Jakab and E Bodnár, 'The Rule of Law, Democracy and Human Rights in Hungary: Tendencies from 1989 until 2019' and T Drinóczi, 'The Rule of Law: The Hungarian Perspective', Chapters 4, 106 and Chapter 5, 126–127 of this book, respectively.

54 I Wróblewska, 'The Rule of Law: The Polish Perspective', Chapter 6 of this book.

55 Until 2012, neither the CT nor the CC had any power to review the constitutionality of a judicial decision per se, i.e., without focusing on the applicable law.

56 M Rosenfeld, 'Legitimacy of Constitutional Democracy', 74 *Southern California Law Review* (2001) 1313, 1350.

57 Zanghellini, n 31, 216.

58 L McDonald, 'Positivism and the Formal Rule of Law: Questioning the Connection', 26 *Australian Journal of Legal Philosophy* (2001) 93.

constitutional courts interpret as the Rule of Law in a particular country make up the definition and constituent elements of that particular country. The particular texts inform their decisions; if it reads as 'democratic state of the rule of law' [*demokratikus jogállam*] or 'a democratic state ruled by law' [*demokratyczne państwo prawa*], as in the case of the Hungarian Constitution (until 2012) and Fundamental Law (from 2012), and the Polish 1997 Constitution, they might be inclined to give a more value-oriented (thicker) understanding of the Rule of Law, simply because it has received a modifying adjective, i.e., democratic.[59] In the ideal case, the core elements of the domestically interpreted and implemented Rule of Law in the legal sense is in line with the expectations of the supranational (EU) and international community (e.g., CoE) the state belongs to and in whose decision-making processes it participates.

With multilevel constitutionalism, for example, the Rule of Law Checklist of the Venice Commission from 2016, could be used as a benchmark, out of many, when assessing the Hungarian and Polish approaches to the European Rule of Law as a value.[60] The Rule of law Checklist mentions the criteria of equality, non-discrimination, and an independent judiciary, which maintains the constitutional supremacy and legality, legal certainty, prevention of abuse (misuse) power, and access to justice. The Rule of Law concept of the Checklist seems to embrace a more substantive understanding of the Rule of Law, as it fits the European or Western type of (liberal) constitutionalism the EU and the European states have nurtured.[61]

As the Rule of Law is a time- and location-bound, context-related concept, it is worth offering an understanding of the Rule of Law that could be applied in the European region, particularly in the European Union and its Member States.

1.2.4. The European Rule of Law

It is thus proposed that the Rule of Law shall be viewed as a triangle. The two sides adjoining at the top represent a twin legal obligation that stems from

59 They could as well decide to separate these two distinct principles and give a more formal understanding of the Rule of Law. It would satisfy Raz's claim that the law has to possess other different values, beyond the rule of law. Nevertheless, it does not mean that the formerly mentioned interpretation would be unjustified or illegitimate.

60 Rule of Law Checklist, n 32. Undoubtedly, the role and mission of the Venice Commission and that of the EU are different; but as they profess the same values, including the rule of law, they do cooperate. See e.g., the new EU Framework to strengthen the Rule of Law, n 7; W Hoffmann-Riem, 'The Venice Commission of the Council of Europe – Standards and Impact', 2 *European Journal of International Law* (2014) 595. It thus makes sense to use the already available Checklist.

61 Even the ECJ seems to have thickened up judicial independence by the decision on the Polish judicial independence. MA Simonelli, 'Thickening up judicial independence: the ECJ ruling in Commission v. Poland (C-619/18)', https://europeanlawblog.eu/2019/07/08/thickening-up-judicial-independence-the-ecj-ruling-in-commission-v-poland-c-619-18/. This indirectly supports the view on the thick (European) understanding of the Rule of Law.

Table 1.1 Overview of the versions of the Rule of Law

Version	*Source*	*Content*		*Explanation*
Thin/ Formal	Raz (1977)	reasonably clear, reasonably stable, publicly available general rules and standards that are applied prospectively and not retrospectively		Characteristics of the law – what drafters shall observe
	Fuller	generality, publicity, stability, prosperity, clarity, consistency of the law, the possibility of compliance with the law, and congruence between rules announced and their actual administration		
	May	predictability		Core element of the Rule of Law
	Moller	power exercised via law (rule by law) the state actions to be subjected to law equality before the law characteristics of the law (based on Raz/Fuller; above)		Moller calls it formal legality
	Raz (2019)	same as in 1977 decisions have to be reasonable and relative to their declared reasons the process involves various degrees of representation and hearing to consider relevant arguments and information		
Thick	Bedner	Thin/Formal version	formal legality (above)	Bedner calls them procedural elements of the Rule of Law
			independent judiciary, specialised institutions	Bedner calls them enforcement mechanism

(*Continued*)

Table 1.1 (Continued) Overview of the versions of the Rule of Law

Version	*Source*	*Content*		*Explanation*
		Becoming thicker	justice, rights	Bedner calls them substantive elements: the more rights are included the thicker the concept is
			democracy	Bedner calls it procedural element, and if the concept includes it, the Rule of Law understanding is thicker
Thick concept	Bingham	Thin/Formal version	accessible, intelligible, clear, predictable	Characteristics of the law – what drafters shall observe
			the application of the law and not the exercise of discretion is what resolves disputes	
			law applies equally to all	
			conferred power must be exercised in good faith	
		Becoming thicker	attention to human rights	
			means must be provided for resolving disputes without unnecessary delay and cost	

(*Continued*)

Table 1.1 (Continued) Overview of the versions of the Rule of Law

Version	*Source*	*Content*		*Explanation*
			fair adjudication process compliance with international obligations	
	Cormacain	Thin/Formal version Becoming thicker	everybody subject to the law values the legal system have to possess, including human rights with all the implications	Cormacain calls it the duality of the Rule of Law
	Rule of Law Checklist of the Venice Commission	Mixed in each element	constitutional supremacy, legality, legal certainty equality, non-discrimination prevention of abuse (misuse) power independent judiciary and access to justice	

Source: authors.

constitutional rules and the EU law to be observed by the Member States. These are based on a foundation of shared values and political ideals that derive from the common constitutional traditions of the European states.[62] Thus, when the compliance of a Member State to the Rule of Law is examined, the term represents the observance of a unique Rule of Law concept in a particular kind of constitutionalism, namely the Western type of constitutionalism that has been accommodated by Member States (nation-states) and the European Union (supranational community).[63]

Consequently, the twin concept of the Rule of Law is seen as having a core common and intertwined normative meaning for both the EU and its Member

62 Similarly, see G Palombella, n 31.
63 See e.g., D Kochenov, n 21, 10.

States. As a political ideal, which is the foundation line of the triangle, it requires, at least, that no power is exercised arbitrarily. It also implies the demand for the respect[64] and protection[65] of the individual. The Rule of Law also translates to an applicable legal concept, which dictates that law binds all, including the state and the people. The need to obey the law demands that individuals are aware of the law, a prerequisite facilitated by the regulatory state. In this sense, and in order to achieve these purposes, the Rule of Law calls for the fullest possible compliance of state power with the rules of 'formal legality'. Formal legality presupposes the rule by law (power exercised via the law), that state action is subject to law, equality before and under the law, and adherence to specific core characteristics of the law (generality, publicity, predictability, clarity, etc.[66]).[67] Formal legality needs to be enforced by the judiciary, which includes the constitutional courts; otherwise it loses its constraining power. In this process, it is subject to different forms of interpretation and application, such as respecting the legal hierarchy, allowing the necessary time for adjusting to a new regulation (congruence), and respecting legitimate expectations (predictability) (Figure 1.1).[68]

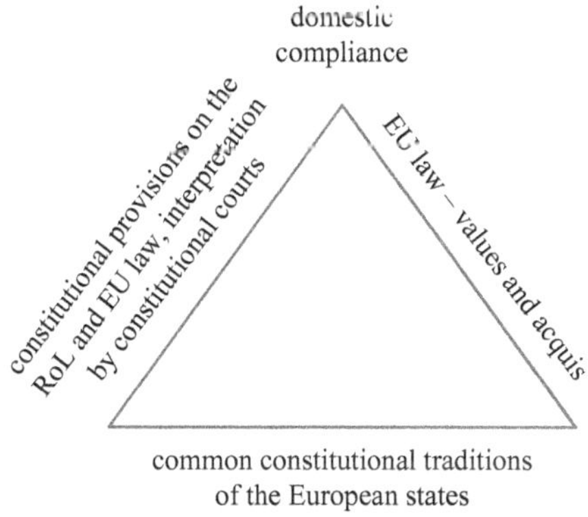

Figure 1.1 The European Rule of Law from the perspective of the national constitutional system. Source: Drinóczi, n 68, 12.

64 Respecting the individual is the underlying idea of limiting power. See Waldron, n 2, 59–60.

65 Protection is an implied component of the prevention of the exercise of arbitrary power, otherwise the underlying idea itself becomes questionable.

66 For this, see L Fuller, n 23; J Raz, 'The rule of law and its virtue' in J Raz, ed, *The authority of law: essays on law and morality* (Oxford University Press 1979).

67 Referring to the theories of Raz, Fuller and Finnis, Moller uses this approach in Moller, n 18, 29.

68 This volume, given its topic, does not make any investigation to the constraint power of the human right documents and human right enforcement mechanism or the rule of law understanding of international or regional human rights law. We are however in agreement with Ricardo Gosalbo-Bono, who calls this phenomenon "European way" of the rule of law,

In domestic legal systems, the national constitutions accommodate EU law and direct state authorities to participate in the EU decision-making process, demanding its enforcement. Suspicion that the Rule of Law is not entirely enforced by a Member State amounts to a violation of, first, constitutional norms on the 'domestic Rule of Law' and the so-called EU clauses, and second, Article 2 TEU.[69] Therefore, the enforcement of these rules and compliance with EU values is the task of national legislative authorities, adjudicative bodies, constitutional courts, and the EU itself. The observance, maintenance, and enforcement of the Rule of Law, as a political ideal, rest with the political community.

The enforcement or non-enforcement of the Rule of Law as a value and legal concept are equally complex and confusing at the EU level. Challenges concerning the observance and enforcement of the value system, including the Rule of Law, democracy, and human rights, on which the European integration project is based, have surfaced in the last decade and have triggered the attention of both EU institutions and scholars.[70] This has been informed by the cumulative effects of the rise of populist nationalism over Europe[71] and the very nature of the contemporary EU, which is neither a community loosely based on economic interest nor a (supranational) federation that could effectively interfere with the domestic affairs of its member states. Therefore, similar to national polities, the EU has been so far ineffective in ensuring that Member States comply with its values and principles. There are many reasons for this: first, the design of the EU is based on the doctrine of delegated powers and mutual trust; second, priority has always been given to the enforcement of the acquis and not to the values.[72] Once a country becomes a Member State, the principle of mutual trust and the presumption that all values and principles are shared, implemented, and enforced internally by the Member States are activated. Therefore, value enforcement has yet to develop effective mechanisms,[73] and to all intents and purposes has not found adequate tools to deal with ideologically induced non-compliance.

as it 'derives from the law of the European Union and from the system established under the European Convention of Human Rights'. Gosalbo-Bono, n 48, 259. For the European Rule of Law concept and its implementation in Hungary, see T Drinóczi, 'The European Rule of Law and illiberal legality in illiberal constitutionalism: the case of Hungary', 16 *MTA Law Working Papers* (2019), https://jog.tk.mta.hu/uploads/files/2019_16_Drinoczi.pdf.

69 See the explanation of the two levels concerning the Rule of Law in a supranational community at Palombella, n 31.

70 See, among others, the books mentioned in n 1, and the different rules of law mechanisms the EU has been experimenting with, such as the rule of law conditionality, the idea of strengthening the rule of law through increased awareness, an annual monitoring cycle and more effective enforcement, and the new EU Framework to strengthen the Rule of Law (COM/2014/0158 final).

71 It had either a weaker or an overwhelming effect on the population of the Member States.

72 Csink deals with the problem of mutual trust between the EU and Hungary. L Csink, 'Rule of Law in Hungary. What Can Law and Politics Do?, in Chapter 7 of this book, 153–173.

73 See e.g., Krygier, n 5; Closa and Kochenov, eds, n 2.; L Pech and D Kochenov, 'Strengthening the Rule of Law within the European Union: diagnoses, recommendations, and what to avoid', *Policy Brief* (June 2019), https://reconnect-europe.eu/news/policy-brief-june-2019/.

The deviation from the EU acquis can also have Rule of Law implications. These include the careless use of law or the random abuse of political power, which, however, can be corrected with time through the available enforcement mechanisms and the functioning of democracy in any given Member State. The same applies to other types of defiance, such as infringing the provisions of the acquis by non-compliance through errors of judgement or interpretation, and incorrect or non-timely implementation of a directive, taking advantage of the fact that there are grey areas in EU economic regulations. None of these non-compliances, however, is confined to a particular regime.[74] The implementation and application of EU law (acquis) have over the years become the daily practice of Member States, including Hungary and Poland.[75]

The European Rule of Law can never be a mere instrument that is misused or abused by a national populist leader. It is also proposed that the European Rule of Law represents a thick(er) understanding of the Rule of Law that has emerged throughout history as a common European heritage, value, and principle.[76] It composes a particular political theory, which demands prevention from any arbitrary use of power with all its necessary preconditions and implementation mechanisms. It also means a legally enforceable concept that is present in the national constitutions and the European legal order and distinctively interpreted by national and supranational courts as per their respective positive constitutional law. Thus, the European Rule of Law, both at the European and domestic arena, is necessarily a less thin (or a thick) concept as it does not only prescribe formal and legal features. It requires the domestic law to bear some specific content, which would make it a 'good domestic law' informed by the political agenda and decisions reached by the EU and, intrinsically, its Member States. The European Rule of Law, as Palombella explained,[77] expresses a limitation on the domestic political decision-maker because there is another positive law (i.e., EU law) that the holder of the domestic rule-making power cannot manipulate and override. No domestic populist leader can hijack the EU law and law-making process in the same way as they could do so with their national legislation and law-making authorities. It would also demand a kind of enforcement mechanism, such as

74 A Jakab and D Kochenov, 'Introductory remarks', in D Kochenov and A Jakab, eds, *The enforcement of EU law and values* (Oxford University Press 2017) 2–3; C Closa, D Kochenov, and JHH Weiler, 'Reinforcing rule of law oversight in the European Union', *EUI Working Paper RSCAS 2014/75 Robert Schuman Centre for Advanced Studies Global Governance Programme*, 4.

75 M Varju, 'A magyar jogrendszer és az Európai Unió joga: tíz év tapasztalata [The Hungarian legal system and the law of the European Union: experiences of ten years]', in A Jakab and G Gajduschek, eds, *A magyar jogrendszer állapota* (MTA Társadalomtudományi Kutatóközpont, Jogtudományi Intézet, 2016) 143–171; Annual reports on monitoring the application of EU law, https://ec.europa.eu/info/publications/annual-reports-monitoring-application-eu-law_en.

76 See also S Majkowska-Szulc, 'Safeguarding the European Union's Core Values: The EU Rule of Law Mission in Poland', in Chapter 8 of this book, 174–193.

77 Palombella, n 31.

the preliminary ruling procedure.[78] This latter requires an independent judiciary with judges of anti-authoritarian attitudes[79] who can serve as national judges of a supranational entity, either as members of the ordinary judicial system or constitutional courts.[80]

These features of the European Rule of Law provide a minimum or thin constraint on the public power of Hungary and Poland. It is precisely this mechanism that makes their systems still constitutionalist. Thus, in this sense, compliance with the European Rule of Law by the Member States should not be restricted to the study of Article 2 TEU (value-level) but the application of EU law as well.[81]

1.3. Contested concepts: Illiberal constitutionalism

1.3.1. Choice of words

Regardless of their differences,[82] Hungary and Poland exemplify the distinct characteristics of illiberal constitutionalism. The use of the term illiberal constitutionalism is intentional: it describes the Hungarian and Polish governmental systems, between 2010 to 2020, and 2015 to 2020, and highlights the paradox that these countries present within the European Union. It is what makes the case of Hungary and Poland unique as compared to authoritarian regimes and any other non-EU Member States in democratic decay: while Member States of the EU, they transformed their constitutional system to an extent that is almost incompatible with the values of the EU.

The choice of the word (illiberal) is based on the speech of the Hungarian prime minister, Viktor Orbán, which was later, contentwise, used by the leader

78 Morten Broberg acknowledges that from a Rule of Law perspective the importance of the procedure is high, although it has not been designed as an enforcement mechanism. M Broberg, 'Preliminary references as a means for enforcing EU law', in D Kochenov and A Jakab, eds, *The enforcement of EU law and values* (Oxford University Press 2017) 111.

79 L Henderson, 'Authoritarianism and the Rule of Law', 66 *Indiana Law Journal* (1991) 396.

80 See e.g., the preliminary ruling procedures concerning, among others, the independence of the judiciary initiated by Polish and Hungarian judges. See more in Majkowska-Szulc, n. 76, this book 186–190, Drinóczi, n 53, 124–125, A Grzelak, 'Are the EU Member States still Masters of the Treaties? The Euroean Rule of Law Concept as a Means of Limiting National Authorities', in Chapter 9 of this book, 210–213. Jakub Kościerzyński edited a volume entitled *Justice under Pressure – repressions as a means of attempting to take control over the judiciary and the prosecution in Poland. Years 2015–2019,* https://ruleoflaw.pl/wp-content/uploads/2020/02/Raport_EN.pdf (2019). In the Introduction, the authors, the Polish Judges, express that 'As judges, we stand guard over the civil rights and freedoms enshrined in the Constitution. We pay a high price for this already, but we are ready to pay even the highest. We do not and will not agree to politicise the courts. We will not allow citizens to be deprived of their right to a fair trial before an impartial and independent court'. Ibid., 8.

81 The following chapters investigate domestic Rule of Law compliance. See, n. 80.

82 See more in T Drinóczi and A Bień-Kacała, 'Illiberal constitutionalism – the case of Hungary and Poland', 20 *German Law Journal* (2019) 1140–1145.

of the PiS (Law and Justice Party), Jarosław Kaczyński, as well.[83] Orbán used the expression of 'illiberal state', referred to the concept that democracy can be illiberal, and later used it to legitimise the constitutional remodelling in his political communication.[84] Thus, the term 'illiberal democracy' described by Fareed Zakaria[85] as another alarming possibility in the path of democratic development,[86] was borrowed and revitalised by the Hungarian prime minister as an adaptable and desirable version of democracy. In our theory, however, illiberal democracy, as a version of democracy, is only one component of illiberal constitutionalism. Illiberal constitutionalism does not only refer to the fact that democratically elected leaders misuse their power. It also encompasses the almost smooth and undisturbed remodelling of the entire liberal constitutional system (constitutional democracy) within a European cultural and legal community represented by the Western ideal of legal and democratic development and appearing under the aegis of the Council of Europe, but most prominently, the European Union. Illiberal constitutionalism is characterised by an illiberal type of democracy (as opposed to liberal democracy which implies competitive and repetitive elections, inclusion, respect of political and other related rights, etc.), misuse of the language of human rights (as opposed to the theory of human rights which implies individualism and protection of group rights, high respect of human dignity and equality, inclusion, institutional and procedural protection against the state and any actors having actual power over the individual), and the illiberal version of the Rule of Law. Based on this and the following chapters, we propose that the illiberal version of the (European) Rule of Law be called 'illiberal legality', which we conceptualise in the last chapter.

Illiberal constitutionalism is not yet an authoritarian system, but it is heading towards that direction. Membership in the EU makes it possible to keep 'constitutionalism', but the actual legal remodelling, legislative, and other legal actions and political behaviours call for the label 'illiberal'. The palpable oxymoron in the term of illiberal constitutionalism, thus, intends to highlight the paradox in which Hungary, Poland, and the EU find themselves. First, the EU, which is built on certain principles, is still having two Member States that keep disrespecting those very same principles. Second, it seems that both the EU, and Hungary and Poland are comfortable with the regime-sustaining and legitimising role of

83 Even if Jarosław Kaczyński has never used the term illiberal democracy, he expressed the will of following Hungarian pattern with words: 'there will be Budapest in Warsaw', www.ft.com/content/0a3c7d44-b48e-11e5-8358-9a82b43f6b2f.

84 Orbán Viktor beszéde a XXV. Bálványosi Nyári Szabadegyetem és Diáktáborban 2014. július 26. Tusnádfürdő (Băile Tuşnad). www.kormany.hu/hu/a-miniszterelnok/beszedek-publikaciok-interjuk/a-munkaalapu-allam-korszaka-kovetkezik.

85 "Democratically elected regimes, often ones that have been reelected or reaffirmed through referenda, are routinely ignoring constitutional limits on their power and depriving their citizens of basic rights and freedoms." F Zakaria, The Rise of Illiberal Democracy, 6 *Foreign Affairs* (1997) 22.

86 Ibid., 24.

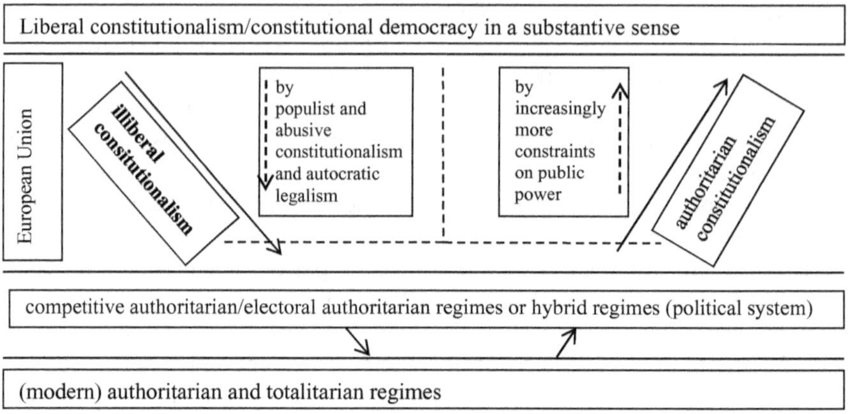

Figure 1.2 Illiberal constitutionalism in comparison. Source: Drinóczi, n 68, 10.

the EU.[87] Third, the populist leaders of Hungary and Poland act like children testing the boundaries of their actions and keep pushing as far as they can. Furthermore, Poland and Hungary have been slowly sliding from their previous constitutional democracy status to authoritarianism, but have not reached it yet. In their degradation, the matter of degree becomes a matter of kind. The uniqueness of the Hungarian and Polish illiberal constitutionalism rests on these phenomena.

In order to remain within the scope of the book, we will focus solely on how illiberal constitutionalism has emerged and what distinguishes it from other systems (Figure 1.2).[88]

1.3.2. Emergence of illiberal constitutionalism from substantive constitutional democracies

Illiberal constitutionalism has emerged through the populist capture of constitution and constitutionalism. The 'capturing' mechanism appears in the manner in which the constitutional changes are implemented, political and legal constitutionalism is theorised, and constitutional/national identity interpreted. It is also present in the relativisation of the Rule of Law and human rights, the constitutionalisation of populist nationalism, identity politics, new patrimonialism,

87 These functions are borrowed from A Bozóki and D Hegedűs, 'An externally constrained hybrid regime: Hungary in the European Union', 7 *Democratization* (2018) 1174.

88 All other issues are discussed in Drinóczi and Bień-Kacała, n 82; T Drinóczi and A Bień-Kacała, 'Extra-legal particularities and illiberal constitutionalism. The case of Hungary and Poland', 4 *Hungarian Journal of Legal Studies* (2018); T Drinóczi and A Bień-Kacała, 'Illiberal constitutionalism in Hungary and Poland: the case of judicialization of politics', in A Bień-Kacała, et al., eds, *Liberal constitutionalism – between individual and collective interests* (Wydział Prawa i Administracji/Faculty of Law and Administration, Uniwersytetu Mikołaja Kopernika w Toruniu/ Nicolaus Copernicus University in Toruń Toruń, 2017) 73–108.

clientelism, and corruption. Illiberal constitutionalism is viewed as the functioning of a public power that upholds the main constitutional structure but, while it lacks normative domestic constitutional commitment to constraints on public power, to a certain extent, it remains within the boundaries set by EU law and politics, as well as international minimum requirements. In these states, all elements of constitutional democracy, such as the Rule of Law, democracy, and human rights, are observable, yet none of them prevails in their entirety.[89]

Illiberal constitutionalism has emerged peacefully from the constitutional democracy that has found its first contemporary manifestation after the 1989 and 1990 transition in the Central Eastern European (CEE) region. After the transition, constitutional democracies in the CEE pursued compliance with, or, depending on their national needs even exceeded, the minimum standards laid down by the Rule of Law, human rights, and democracy requirements in Europe, under the aegis of the Council of Europe and the European Union.[90] For our region, therefore, a constitutional democracy is not only a constitutionalised form of democracy but also a constitutional regime in which the Rule of Law and the protection and promotion of human rights as such prevail.[91] Constitutional democracy embodies constitutionalism (in which no power can be exercised without constraints) and democracy (rule of the people) at the same time; they cannot be mutually exclusive or competing factors neither at a constitutional design level nor in terms of constitutional interpretation. The reason for this is that a constitutional democracy, as established after the transition in the CEE region, required a written constitution, in a legal sense, that encompasses all of its essential principles. These principles include the Rule of Law, human rights, and democracy – in the form in which they have arisen during (Western European) constitutional development, as the core values of modern societies and political systems. As a counter-effect of the former socialist regime, legal procedures and legal constitutions were preferred in the CEE over any political considerations and approaches to the exercise of public power. These constitutions, based on the Kelsenian tradition and relying on the very notion and function of the legal understanding of a constitution, were seen to be senseless unless defended and enforced. Insofar as these instruments focus on the defence of individual human rights, a complying state could be called 'liberal', as this is the politico-philosophical stream that has raised human beings to the forefront of any public action. Nevertheless, we also believe that if a state is a constitutional democracy

89 Instead, some flaws may even be remedied, removed, or even smuggled back in and proudly announced that they are national traditions and, as such, belong to the identity of Hungary and that of Hungarians. See e.g., the treatment of churches and the changing constitutional content of family and marriage, the constitutionalised constitutional identity in Hungary. See e.g., T Drinóczi, 'Hungarian Constitutional Court: The Limits of EU Law in the Hungarian Legal System', 1 *Vienna Journal on International Constitutional Law* (2017) 139–151.

90 On these impacts in general, see RR Ludwikowski, 'Supreme Law or Basic Law? The Decline of the Concept of Constitutional Supremacy', 9 *Cardozo Journal of International & Comparative Law* (2001) 253–296.

91 For a definition, see Drinóczi and Bień-Kacała, n 82, and T Ginsburg and AZ Huq, n 16, 224

in today's Europe, though, theoretically it does not need any adjective to express its commitment towards the Rule of Law, human rights (including not only civil and political rights and liberties) and democracy.

States undergoing a democratic backsliding change from their 'original state' to something new, which is perceived to be worse. Democratic decay, however, has been seen to affect constitutional democracies.[92] Some of these states face significant economic and financial crises; others struggle with migration challenges and the threat of terror. Populist politicians tend to amplify each of these challenges. Even where the results of populist influence are undeniable, there are remarkable differences among states in democratic decay. These appear not only in terms of institutional and structural mechanisms,[93] but also due to the circumstances of their emergence as constitutional democracies, which is usually referred to as the third wave of the democratisation process. As is well known, this has led to three results. The first was a constitutional democracy, which still has not shown any sign of regression.[94] Second, it resulted in an authoritarian (re)consolidation, which, according to Steven Levitsky and Lucan Way, is not to be viewed as a democratic rollback.[95] Third, democracy in some other states has reverted to a more or less authoritarian form, as Alina Rocha Menocal and others observe relying on Latin-American[96] and African experiences. While the authoritarian (re)consolidation (the second result) does not typify the CEE states, because those in power in the regime from which the democratic transition emerged (the communist-socialist party) differ from those that hold power now (right-wing parties, conservatives), the authoritarian form (the third result) could fit the CEE context[97] regardless of the label we attach. The reason is simple, as stated by Menocal et al. about the countries in which they are interested: the

92 See e.g., TG Daly, 'Diagnosing democratic decay', www.academia.edu/34052302/Diagnosing_Democratic_Decay

93 Compare, for example, the unpopularity of Brazilian politicians and the new role of the judiciary in fighting against corruption (see e.g., FJ Gonçalves Acunha and JZ Benvindo, 'Democratic decay in Brazil and the new global populism', https://iacl-aidc-blog.org/2017/06/06/democratic-decay-in-brazil-and-the-new-global-populism/) with the continuing popularity of the Fidesz Party in Hungary or the popular support of PiS in Poland. Further, while in Hungary and Poland the judiciary, including the constitutional courts, has apparently been compromised, the US continues to enjoy an uncompromised judicial system. For more, see Drinóczi and Bień-Kacała, n 82.

94 See e.g., the Baltic states, especially Estonia.

95 S Levitsky and L Way, 'The myth of democratic recession', 1 *Journal of Democracy* (2015) 46–48.

96 In this Introduction, we do not wish to contrast the Latin American new constitutionalism with the European illiberal constitutionalism; in our view, point II offers sufficient context for understanding illiberal constitutionalism.

97 AR Menocal, V Fritz and L Rakner, 'Hybrid regimes and the challenge of deepening and sustaining democracy in developing countries', 1 *South African Journal of International Affairs* (2008) 15–30.

leading political players, forces, and institutions do not accept democracy as 'the only game in town'.[98]

We partly disagree with this view because, as argued below, we contest the categorisation of Hungary and Poland as authoritarian states. We see the events as depicted in Figure 1.2: since 1989–1990, a vector of changes led towards a fully fledged constitutional democracy; since 2010 (in Hungary) and 2015 (in Poland), this vector turned 'down' and now points towards authoritarianism. It also means that in Hungary and Poland, due to the constitutional and historical development of the European states, constitutionalism, the Rule of Law, the ideal of democracy, and the European Union, constitutional democracy and multilevel constitutionalism should be the only game in town. This playfield, however, seems to be taken seriously by Hungarian and Polish actors only in one case. It occurs when they have already 'hit the wall' and receive immediate or prolonged political and legal reminders about the extent of the boundaries that are still tolerated by the political and legal actors of the European Union.

1.4. Illiberal constitutionalism and the Rule of Law

1.4.1. Constraint on domestic public power?

As we know, the domestic political community in Hungary and Poland could not resist populist nationalism and remains in support of the anti Rule of Law politics, which have successfully remodelled Hungarian and Polish constitutionalism.[99] As a result, constitutional courts, which in theory are charged with protecting constitutional principles and other constitutional institutions, actually aid in promoting the anti-Rule of Law political agenda. Nevertheless, in fact, despite the 'business-as-usual-non-compliances' and the systematic Rule of Law value infringements by the public legislative and regulatory powers, EU law is still applied every day by both the Polish and Hungarian ordinary courts. Moreover, the annual transposition deficits do not outstandingly deviate from the EU 28 average.[100] Moreover, in some cases, the constitutional courts uphold their former Rule of Law interpretation[101] and, in others, they expand it.[102]

98 Ibid., 31. See also von Bogdandy et al., eds, n 11.
99 Drinóczi and Bień-Kacała, n 82, 1140–1166.
100 Varju, n 75; Annual reports, n 75.
101 See the chapters by András Jakab and Eszter Bodnár, and Iwona Wróblewska in this book
102 See e.g., decision 45/2012 (XII. 29) of the Hungarian Constitutional Court (CC) [the principle of constitutional legality of the Fundamental Law, which is deduced from the Rule of Law provision, (Article B), binds the constituent power as well]. In the case of the National Council of Judiciary [20 April 2017 (K 5/17)], printer v. LGBTQ [26 June 2019 (K 16/17)] or the pardon of the PiS politician who is also Minister of the interior and administration [17 July 2018 (K 9/17)], the Polish Constitutional Tribunal (CT) misused the previous understanding of the Rule of Law to serve political intentions. See also I Wróblewska, Chapter 6 of this book, 146–148.

Other constitutional actors, such as the ombudsman,[103] ordinary judges,[104] the corruption agency, or the state audit office[105] are successfully attempting to maintain some core tenets of constitutionalism, including the observance of the Rule of Law.

It is undeniable though that the systemic changes in Hungary and Poland are pointing towards authoritarianism, and there are warning signs of authoritarianisation,[106] albeit to a different extent, which is due to their five years' difference since the beginning of regression. In recent years, there have been many reasonable accusations concerning both Hungary and Poland because of non-compliance with the Rule of Law. The Venice Commission issued numerous opinions in which it did not applaud many of the constitutional changes and legislative reforms. The Article 7 procedure was triggered for the first time against Poland in December 2017 by the European Commission after dialogue based on the Rule of Law Framework (2016).[107] The Sargentini report, which alleged that Hungary has seriously violated the principles on which the EU is based, was approved by a comfortable majority of the members of the Committee on Civil Liberties, Justice and Home Affairs against Hungary, and the Article 7 procedure was initiated in September 2018. Besides, according to the WJP Rule of Law Index and other indices (EIU Democracy and Freedom House), neither Hungary nor Poland are doing well as compared to other EU Members or Western countries.

The overall picture on the Rule of Law compliance and its effect on our understanding of constitutionalism is thus puzzling. In our view, it cannot be oversimplified by using the binary code of (liberal) constitutionalism v. authoritarianism, because this might be ill-suited to describe and explain the Hungarian and Polish

103 The Hungarian ombudsman's petitions to the CC have been considered admissible and the Court concurred with the ombudsman concerning the unconstitutionality of the restrictive use of the concept of marriage and family, and the extent of criticism politicians, among others, have to endure in the interest of unfettered democratic public opinion. See decisions 14/2014 (V. 13.) and 6/2014 (III. 7.) of the CC respectively. Conversely, the Polish ombudsman ceases cases (already diverted to the CT) and withdraws already logged ones (e.g., on the Prosecutor General's competences in 2018 or the status of civil servants in 2019) due to the changes in the adjudication panel of the CT. The panel is composed of judges irregularly appointed by *Sejm* to the CT, which raises doubts as to the independence and impartiality of the CT and the constitutionality of its decisions. Nevertheless, the ombudsman is quite vocal in his public speeches about violations of the Polish Rule of Law.

104 Both Polish and Hungarian judges use the possibility of preliminary ruling procedures extensively. See e.g., Varju, n 75, and Sadurski, n 15, 211–213.

105 In 2018, these Polish authorities have expressed concerns about the use of public money, which triggered investigations and sanctions, which turned out to be flawed, https://freedomhouse.org/report/freedom-world/2019/poland.

106 Authoritarianisation is a gradual erosion of democratic norms and practices by democratic leaders, elected at the ballot box through reasonably free and fair elections. E Frantz and A Kendall-Taylor, 'The evolution of autocracy: why authoritarianism is becoming more formidable', 59 *Survival: Global Politics and Strategy* (2017) 57.

107 See e.g., Grzelak, n 80, 201–203 and Majkowska-Szulc, n. 76, 178–182.

constitutional remodelling. When trying to understand the democratic decay in Hungary and Poland, one should not forget that sometimes the matter of degree (what is indicated by different types of indices) is a matter of kind. Not to mention the fact that Hungary and Poland are still members of a regional community that is built on democracy, the Rule of Law, and human rights. Insofar as both parties, i.e., the EU and the two renegade states, maintain this membership, Hungary and Poland should be considered as having a constitutionalist structure, which implies some constraints as well. These Member States remain constitutional democracies even if both are flawed or can momentarily only provide for a thin or formal version of the term.

1.4.2. *Constraint on domestic public power in a comparative perspective*

As already mentioned, there are many contested concepts, and their categorisation sometimes leaves us with more confusion than clarity. Despite these classifications, and even though Hungary has recently been labelled as partly free by the Freedom House (while Poland still retains its free status), in our view, the democratic degeneration of the systems of both countries has not reached the extent of that of Turkey or Russia – the two countries Hungary and Poland have been mentioned with as examples of authoritarianism or modern authoritarianism.[108]

Quantitatively, according to different indices, neither Hungary nor Poland are in as bad a shape as Turkey or Russia, but, admittedly, they are doing worse than their European counterparts. As stated at the beginning of this chapter, all concepts used here are contested, and so are the methods of measuring the Rule of Law. There is, however, some agreement among scholars relating to this issue, too. The first is that there is no definite way of interrogating the Rule of Law, and, before measuring anything, we have to define what we are going to measure. The second is that the measurement of the Rule of Law is far less developed than that of democracy, but the WJP Rule of Law Index, notwithstanding its imperfections, produces more definitive and authoritative measures of the Rule of Law across the globe.[109]

Based on the WJP Rule of Law Index, we can detect some distinctive differences between Hungary and Poland on the one hand, and Russia and Turkey on the other. According to the WJP Rule of Law Index (Table 1.2),[110] the overall

108 GA Tóth, 'Authoritarianism', *Max Planck Encyclopedia of Comparative Constitutional Law*, February 2017, A Puddington, 'Breaking down democracy: Global strategies, and methods of modern authoritarians', https://freedomhouse.org/sites/default/files/June2017_FH_Report_Breaking_Down_Democracy.pdf June 2017.

109 Moller, n 18, 2–24, A Bedner, n 47, 41; May and Winchester, n 3, 11, 15; Versteeg and Ginsburg, n 4, 101.

110 See directly at https://worldjusticeproject.org/our-work

score of Hungary and Poland has been decreasing since 2015,[111] but has never reached below 0.5, while Russia and Turkey have stably stayed within the range of 0.42 and 0.47. The overall score for Hungary has firmly decreased from 0.58 to 0.53, while for Poland, it is the same but within the range of 0.72 (2015) and 0.66 (2019). The WJP measures the Rule of Law in eight categories, but for now, we only focus on the sub-category of constraints on government power. Steady decrease can be seen in the case of Hungary and Poland, while Russia scores around 0.4, reaching 0.45 in 2019. Turkey produced a backsliding from 0.37 (2015) to 0.32 (2019). In the region, Hungary, with its score changing from 0.49 (2015) to 0.41 (2019), was ranked 23rd out of 24 for three years (2015–2018) and fell to the last position in 2019. It is notable that it scored 0.63 in 2012–2013. Poland fell back 0.2 points since 2015: in that year, it scored 0.77 and reached 0.58 by 2019. Simultaneously, its regional rank dropped from the 15th to the 18th place.

Qualitatively, Hungary and Poland accommodated (liberal) constitutionalism for a while, unlike, for instance, Singapore or Venezuela – another set of countries with which they are usually mentioned together. It seems difficult to dismantle a substantive constitutional democracy completely, as it must take time. Besides, there is a weak but tacitly existing constitutional constraint on public power, which is EU law, even though it has partly failed, as its value defence mechanisms have not worked so far. The mere existence of EU law with its admittedly flawed implementation at the legislative level, but its everyday application by adjudication bodies (see point 1.4.3 below) may influence and prevent illiberal politicians from leading their countries into authoritarianism even faster (Table 1.2).[112]

Conversely, Singapore, which features authoritarian constitutionalism, obviously performs better at the WJP Rule of Law Index but, according to the EIU Democracy Index and the reports of Freedom House (Table 1.3), it does not do the same in other fields. The reason is that in authoritarian constitutionalism, liberal freedoms are protected at an intermediate level, elections are reasonably free and fair (but without genuine party competition), and there is a normative commitment to constraints on public power. Against this background, Tushnet differentiates between the abusive constitutionalism of Hungary and the authoritarian constitutionalism of Singapore. He speculates that the 'normative commitment to constraints on public power', which he extracted from the 'description

111 We have chosen 2015 as a baseline for two reasons. First, the reports are more comparable from 2015 despite the fact that they include more and more countries to be measured: it increased from 102 (2015) to 126 (2019) while in the years 2016–2018 the number of the studied countries was 113. Second, Polish deterioration started in 2015, when the Hungarian one was already ongoing.

112 Venezuela is not indicated as it finds itself at the bottom of the lists with its overall score of 0.32 in 2015 and 0.28 in 2019. Corrales argues that Venezuela's shift from competitive authoritarianism towards authoritarianism has been facilitated by authoritarian legalism. J Corrales, 'The authoritarian resurgence: autocratic legalism in Venezuela', 26 *Journal of Democracy* (2015) 38.

Table 1.2 WJP Rule of Law Index Summary table

	2015		*2016*		*2017–2018*		*2019*	
	Overall score	*Constraints*	*Overall score*	*Constraints*	*Overall score*	*Constraints*	*Overall score*	*Constraints*
Hungary	0.58	0.49	0.57	0.46	0.55	0.44	0.53	0.41
Poland	0.71	0.77	0.71	0.68	0.67	0.61	0.66	0.58
Russia	0.47	0.39	0.45	0.4	0.47	0.39	0.47	0.45
Turkey	0.46	0.37	0.43	0.32	0.42	0.3	0.42	0.32
Singapore	0.81	0.76	0.82	0.75	0.8	0.7	0.8	0.69

The rating ranges from 0 (weaker adherence to the Rule of Law) to 1 (stronger adherence to the Rule of Law)

Source: authors.

Table 1.3 Indices – Summary table

	EIU Democracy Index	*Freedom House 2019*			
	2006–2016 (from–to)	*Aggregate score (.../100)*	*Political rights 1–7 (1=most Free, 7=least Free)*	*Civil liberties 1–7 (1=most Free, 7=least Free)*	*Freedom rating 1–7 (1=most Free, 7=least Free)*
Hungary	7.53–6.72	70	3	3	3
Poland	7.3–6.83	84	2	2	2
Russia	5.02–3.24	28	7	6	6.5
Turkey	5.7–5.04	41	5	6	5.5
Singapore	5.89–6.38	85	4	4	4

Source: authors.

of how constitutionalism operates in Singapore, might be a truly distinguishing characteristic of authoritarian constitutionalism'.[113] This claim is supported by the WJP Rule of Law Index: Singapore's overall score is around 0.8, and in the sub-category of constraints on government power it scores around 0.7 (with a range of 0.77 and 0.69), which makes it a better performer than Hungary and Poland (Table 1.2).

Moreover, if we take a look at the other indexes measuring democracy and human rights, Hungary and Poland still perform better compared to other countries (Table 1.3). According to the EIU Democracy Index (2006–2016), which designates countries as full democracies if they score between 8 and 10, Hungary and Poland are flawed democracies,[114] Turkey is a hybrid state,[115] Russia transformed from hybrid to authoritarian (2011), and Singapore has gradually upgraded from a hybrid to a flawed democracy (2014). In the measurements of Freedom House, Hungary and Poland score 70 and 84 respectively, while the aggregate scores of the other countries are: 20 (Russia), 31 (Turkey),

113 M Tushnet, n 16, 72.

114 A flawed democracy respects civil liberties, and free and fair elections but has significant weaknesses in other aspects, such as media freedom, low participation and problems in governance.

115 In hybrid regimes, there is a certain degree of pluralism but with frequent harassment of journalists, a non-independent judiciary, and substantial electoral irregularities, including government pressure on opposition parties.

51 (Singapore). Hungary and Singapore are labelled as partly free, Poland is free, while Russia and Turkey are not considered to be free states.[116]

Without going into details about how the party system looks like (e.g., in Singapore and Russia), how elections are manipulated not only by regulatory means (Russia and Turkey), how free speech is infringed by harassment, bringing criminal charges based on bogus allegations and using violence (Singapore, Russia, and Turkey),[117] it seems evident that there is not only a quantitative but a qualitative difference between Poland and Hungary, on the one hand, and Russia, Turkey, and even Singapore, on the other.

Nevertheless, it is also true that the Singaporean type of 'normative commitment to constraints on public power' is, to a certain extent, missing in Poland and Hungary. The systems of Poland and Hungary have been consolidated or are about to consolidate, however, must respect, to the desirable extent, EU law, which functions as an internal and implied constraint. If we consider EU law as part of the legal system of Member States, any constraint imposed through its daily application and possible influence on the populist agenda need to be seen as internal constraints. These types of constraints only exist within the EU. Thus, it follows that the new systems in Hungary and Poland could be labelled neither (modern) authoritarian regimes nor authoritarian constitutionalism.

1.4.3. Constraint on domestic public power in illiberal constitutionalism

We also assume that illiberal states emerging in Europe are still constitutional democracies, which are shaped peacefully by populist politicians from a more substantial form of constitutional democracy that prioritises (liberal) constitutional values through the use of the above-mentioned methods (populist style of governance, abusive constitutionalism, and autocratic legalism). In our cases, the minimum requirements of a constitutional democracy, such as the Rule of Law, human rights, and democracy, have been defectively worded in a constitution, or poorly implemented or enforced.[118] These states are still constitutional democracies in a formal or thin sense. Each still has a constitution, which is more than the formal (façade) constitution of an autocratic system as it, for example, maintains and allows the functioning of constitutional review mechanisms to a certain extent. Besides, both the constitution and the system are far less oppressive than in 'real' authoritarian regimes. The constitution 'locks in' the European

116 https://freedomhouse.org/report/countries-world-freedom-2019.

117 https://freedomhouse.org/report/freedom-world/2019/singapore, https://freedomhouse.org/report/freedom-world/2019/turkey, https://freedomhouse.org/report/freedom-world/2019/russia.

118 Drinóczi and Bień-Kacała, n 82; Similarly, see M Plattner, 'Populism, pluralism, and liberal democracy', 1 (21) *Journal of Democracy* (2010) 91.

law and international minimum standards.[119] Therefore, after mentioning it so many times above, we are now investigating the actual practice of the operation of EU law in Hungary and Poland and the way it could be seen as a constraint on public power.[120]

Since their accession to the EU in 2004, the application of EU law has become daily practice in the ordinary courts. Regardless of transformative reforms, EU law could have slowed down the degradation but, as Bozóki and Hegedűs observe, it is not easy to demonstrate through examples how the constraining function of the EU works in practice.[121] This is primarily because, first, recent research has focused only on the actions made against the EU and international obligations, and second, we might have never known about the original plans of populist leaders and the reason why they gave them up.[122] What we can note here is that there are some examples when the Hungarian and Polish decision-makers backed off.[123] Conversely, there are scholarly analyses and annual reports of the European Union available on how constitutional systems have accommodated EU law in the last 15 years. The Rule of Law, both as a principle and a legal norm, requires that laws are obeyed, i.e., it demands compliance, implementation, and enforcement. For the Member States, this means that they have to comply with domestic as well as EU law. Since EU institutions, as we claimed before, make EU law, 'no populist leader can hijack the law-making process in the same way as they could with their national legislation and lawmaking authorities'.[124] Nonetheless, this European Rule of Law does not mean that it is powerful enough to circumvent any misuse of non-EU related domestic law or law-making process, or prevent the populist national decision-maker from trying to avoid compliance with EU law.

From a quantitative perspective, an overview of the Annual Reports of the EU on monitoring the application of the European Union law between 2015 and 2018[125] makes us realise that neither Hungary nor Poland is the worst in terms of compliance among the EU28. The Annual Reports on the EU28 differentiate between new infringement cases by the Member States on 31 December of a particular year and the number of infringement cases by that time. The latter

119 T Ginsburg, 'Locking in democracy: constitutions, commitment, and international law', 38 *New York University Journal of International Law & Politics* (2006) 757; A Moravcsik, 'The origins of human rights regimes: democratic delegation in postwar Europe', 54 *International Organizations* (2000) 243–244.

120 Grzelak, n 107, 213–215.

121 Bozóki and Hegedűs, n 87, 180.

122 For instance, there were rumours that, when writing the new constitution, the Fidesz wanted to abolish the CC and relocate the review function to one of the chambers of the Supreme Court.

123 This happened with certain reforms regarding the decision-making process at the CT, the retirement age of the judges of the Supreme Court in Poland and the introduction of the administrative court system in Hungary.

124 Earlier in this chapter, page 19.

125 Annual Report, n 75.

is further divided into infringements for incorrect transposition and/or bad application of EU laws and late transposition infringements for the years 2015 and 2016. Since 2017, the new late transposition infringement cases are shown separately, and in 2018 the total infringement cases are broken down not only to the incorrect transposition and/or inadequate application of EU laws and late transposition infringements but infringements for regulations, treaties, and decisions as well. In neither of these categories can one find Hungary and Poland at the end of the diagram. If we divide the EU28 into four quarters in the diagram used by the Annual Reports (running from the least to the most number of cases), Hungary is placed, with some exceptions,[126] either at the end of the second or the beginning of the third quarter. Poland is different: it has had more cases than Hungary and finds itself more often in the last than in the third quarter. It is worth noting that, when it comes to the new category (infringement of regulations, treaties, and decisions), both states are placed at the beginning of the second half of the scale.

This observation needs to be coupled with some qualitative analyses, while not forgetting the fact that there is an ongoing Article 7 procedure against both Hungary and Poland. Nevertheless, when studying Hungarian EU law compliance up to 2015, Márton Varju[127] found that the degree of compliance has generally been appropriate, even if the data concerning adjudication is scarce. He detected technical problems at both the law-making and adjudication levels, which include late implementation, paying less attention to the details of implementation, and errors in court judgments. More substantial issues mainly related to the field of economic regulation, where the opportunities offered by the grey zone of EU economic policies are profoundly taken advantage of. Varju is hesitant as to whether Hungarian non-compliance is a trend, systematic deficiency, or simply inadequacy. He acknowledges, however, that there are many examples of Hungarian regulatory opportunism, regulatory bad faith, and obstruction of compliance with EU obligations. In his view, in many cases, it is not the regulatory goal that is to be criticised but the methods of its achievement and the further consequences of the enforcement of the particular regulation. There is often bad faith in how the infringement procedures are handled: the postponement of compliance facilitates the maximisation of the advantages originating from the violation of EU law for personal gain. He opines that the outstanding performance of the Hungarian judges in the field of preliminary ruling procedures, especially after 2010, is due in particular to the embeddedness of EU law in the Hungarian legal system. He suggests that it could also be due to the non-compliance of the lawmaker. This latter opinion, however, does not seem to be supported by the statistics provided in the Annual Reports. The number of cases has shown great variability in none of the categories between 2011 and 2018.

126 New infringement cases in 2016 (beginning of the last quarter of the diagram); new late transposition cases in 2017 and 2018 (in the first quarter of the diagram), late transpositions in 2017 (with the second least cases).

127 Varju, n 75, 142–164.

The number of infringement cases open at the end of the year ranged between 54 (2011) and 50 (2018) with a peak of 57 (2016); the least number of cases was 37 (2013). The number of new late transposition infringement cases ranged between 70 (2011), which was the peak, and 11 (2018), which was also the least number of cases. A drastic drop was observed in 2012 (number of cases: 26). The number of late transposition infringement cases ranged between 16 (2013) and 17 (2018), with a peak of 32 (2016); the least number of cases was 13 (2015).

Poland's compliance in 2015 was generally not satisfactory, but the country was not the worst performer, as it was among the last five or six Member States. Jacek K Sokołowski and Dariusz Stolicki suggest that the particularities of the governmental drafting stage of the legislative process could be blamed for the late transposition, but they do not exclude other possible reasons either. They submit the following explanations for delayed transposition: political reasons, i.e., no acceptance of the solutions imposed by the directive to be transposed, the complexity of the subject matter, and organisational failure.[128]

We can note that the number of infringement cases has shown considerable variability in each of the categories between 2011 and 2018 (Table 1.4). In infringement cases and new late transposition infringement cases, the trend seems to be a decrease. The number of infringement cases open at the end of the year varied between the peak of 95 (2011) and 70 (2018); the least number of cases was 68 (2013). The number of new late transposition infringement cases ranged between 44 (2011), which was the peak, and 16 (2018); the least number of cases was 15 (2013). The number of late transposition infringement cases ranged between 20 (2013), which was the least number of cases, and 33 (2018), with a peak of 39 (2016, 2017). Despite the growing numbers in this category, Poland does not perform worse here than in the other categories. If we compare the country's performance with that of the EU28, we find that Poland, since 2015, has been at the beginning of the last quarter in the category of number of infringement cases as of 31 December. The figures concerning new infringement cases are unsteady, and the country fluctuates between the beginning of the third and the beginning of the last quarter. There is a slow deterioration in the number of new late transposition cases, but Poland remains in the third quarter (it dropped back from the beginning of the third quarter to the end of it).

128 JK Sokołowski and D Stolicki, 'Przyczyny opóźnień w transpozycji dyrektyw europejskich do polskiego porządku prawnego w świetle analizy ilościowej krajowego procesu legislacyjnego [Reasons for delays in the transposition of European directives into the Polish legal order in the light of quantitative analysis of the national legislative process]', 2 *Przegląd Politologiczny* 2017, 39–54.

Table 1.4 Number of infringement cases in Hungary and Poland 2011–2018

		2011	*2012*	*2013*	*2014*	*2015*	*2016*	*2017*	*2018*
Infringement cases open as of 31 December	HU	54	42	37	44	38	57	48	50
	PL	95	82	68	79	78	76	70	70
New late transposition infringement cases	HU	70	26	21	26	17	36	13	8
	PL	44	18	15	18	22	36	21	16
Late transposition infringement cases	HU	–	–	16	18	13	32	15	17
	PL	–	–	20	23	30	39	39	33

Source: authors, Annual Reports, n 75.

1.5. Conclusion

The chapters of this book show how the Rule of Law, in the context of this investigation, is perceived as a specific political philosophy and an enforceable legal value. It has become clear that the (Western) European states and the European Union have adopted and nurtured a distinct kind of constitutionalism, which entails a particular understanding of the Rule of Law. The importance of trust[129] underlines the argument that, when it comes to the assessment of the Rule of Law situation of particular European states that belong to a wider supranational and international community, reduction of the examination of the thin version of the Rule of Law cannot bring a satisfactory result.

Hungary and Poland stand out among states in democratic decay and are noticeably different from existing authoritarian regimes. This does not mean that no increasing authoritarian tendencies can be observed in both countries. What is argued here is that Hungary and Poland are not there yet, mainly because they are still members of the European Union, which, notwithstanding its failures, imposes particular political, albeit rather weak, legal constraints on the Hungarian and Polish political leaderships – the European Rule of Law, to a certain extent and varying intensity, is still operational.

The latter is something that can be measured and reported on and can inform the overall Rule of Law assessment of Member States. How to measure, what type of Rule of Law observance to measure, which kind of indices to use and what conclusions to draw from them, and whether the results should be interpreted alongside those of other states or not, can also be puzzling. There are measurements and reports that indicate the obvious Rule of Law deterioration, and there are views claiming that Hungary and Poland have already deviated from a state of constitutionalism towards authoritarianism. One of the central claims of these views is that the Rule of Law has ceased to constrain the exercise of public power and that authoritarian legality has replaced its understanding.[130] As opposed to these views, we used indices and reports that challenge the authoritarian claim and places Hungary and Poland somewhere in-between, sliding down on a slippery slope towards authoritarianism.

The above leaves us with three implications. First, the European Rule of Law as a value will be viewed as a thick Rule of Law notion; in this regard, both the Member States and the EU have failed so far in its enforcement. Second, the European Rule of Law in its thinnest legal sense means the already explained formal legality, which necessarily includes the regulatory and judicial enforcement of EU law. Third, the fact that compliance with the value aspect cannot be secured because of noticeable ideological differences between the actors (which led to the Article 7 TEU procedure against both states) does not mean (yet) that the particular Member State does not comply with EU law at all, thus disregarding the compliance aspects of the European Rule of Law. This feature of the European Rule of Law is proposed to be called illiberal legality, which is further examined in the last chapter.

129 Csink, n 72, 168–173.
130 See e.g., Halmai, n 14; Tóth, n 14.

Bibliography

Maurice Adams, Anne Meuwese, Ernst Hirsch Ballin, eds, *Constitutionalism and the Rule of Law* (Cambridge University Press 2017).

DM Beatty, 'The forms and limits of constitutional interpretation', 49 *The American Journal of Comparative Law* (2001).

Adriaan Bedner, 'An elementary approach to the Rule of Law', 2 *Hague Journal on the Rule of Law* (2010).

Adriaan Bedner, 'The promise of a thick view', in Christopher May and Adam Winchester, eds, *Handbook of the Rule of Law* (Edward Elgar 2018).

Agnieszka Bień-Kacała, 'Informal constitutional change', 6(40) *Przegląd Prawa Konstytucyjnego* (2017).

Tom Bingham, *The Rule of Law* (Penguin 2011).

Armin von Bogdandy, Eduardo Ferrer Mac-Gregor, Mariela Morales Antoniazzi, Flávia Piovesan, and Ximena Soley, eds, *Transformative constitutionalism in Latin America. The emergence of a new ius commune* (Oxford University Press 2017).

David Boies, 'Judicial independence and the Rule of Law', 22 *Washington University Journal of Law and Policy* (2006).

András Bozóki and Dániel Hegedűs, 'An externally constrained hybrid regime: Hungary in the European Union', 7 *Democratization* (2018).

Morten Broberg, 'Preliminary references as a means for enforcing EU law', in Dimitry Kochenov and András Jakab, eds, *The enforcement of EU law and values* (Oxford University Press 2017).

Carlos Closa and Dimitry Kochenov, eds, *Reinforcing the Rule of Law oversight in the European Union* (Cambridge University Press 2016).

Carlos Closa, Dimitry Kochenov, and Joseph Weiler, 'Reinforcing rule of law oversight in the European Union', 2014, *EUI Working Paper RSCAS 2014/75 Robert Schuman Centre for Advanced Studies Global Governance Programme.*

Ronan Cormacain, *Legislative drafting and the Rule of Law* (Ph.D. Thesis, IALS School of Advanced Study, University of London 2017).

Javier Corrales, 'The authoritarian resurgence: Autocratic legalism in Venezuela', 26 *Journal of Democracy* (2015).

Lóránt Csink, 'Rule of Law in Hungary. What can law and politics do?, Chapter 7 of this book.

Tom Gerald Daly, 'Diagnosing democratic decay', 2017, www.academia.edu/34052302/Diagnosing_Democratic_Decay.

Tímea Drinóczi, 'Hungarian Constitutional Court: The limits of EU Law in the Hungarian Legal System', 1 *Vienna Journal on International Constitutional Law* (2017).

Tímea Drinóczi, 'The European Rule of Law and illiberal legality in illiberal constitutionalism: The case of Hungary', *16 MTA Law Working Papers* (2019), https://jog.tk.mta.hu/uploads/files/2019_16_Drinoczi.pdf.

Tímea Drinóczi, 'The Rule of Law: The Hungarian perspective', Chapter 5 of this book.

Tímea Drinóczi and Agnieszka Bień-Kacała, 'Extra-legal particularities and illiberal constitutionalism. The case of Hungary and Poland', 4 *Hungarian Journal of Legal Studies* (2018).

Tímea Drinóczi and Agnieszka Bień-Kacała, 'Illiberal constitutionalism – The case of Hungary and Poland', 20 *German Law Journal* (2019).

Tímea Drinóczi and Agnieszka Bień-Kacała, 'Illiberal constitutionalism in Hungary and Poland: The case of judicialization of politics', in Agnieszka Bień-Kacała, et al., eds, *Liberal constitutionalism – Between individual and collective interests* (Wydział Prawa i Administracji/Faculty of Law and Administration Uniwersytetu Mikołaja Kopernika w Toruniu/ Nicolaus Copernicus University in Toruń Toruń, 2017).

Tímea Drinóczi and Gábor Juhász, 'Social rights in Hungary', in K Wojtyczek, ed, *Social rights as fundamental rights: XIXth international congress of comparative law/le XIXe Congrès international de droit compare* (Eleven International Publishing 2016).

Ronald Dworkin, 'Political judges and the Rule of Law', 64 *Proceedings of the British Academy* (1979).

Richard M, Jr Fallon, '"The Rule of Law" as a concept in constitutional discourse', 1 *Columbia Law Review* (1997).

Jorge M Farinucci-Fernós, 'Post-liberal constitutionalism', 1 *Tulsa Law Review* (2018).

Danielle E Finck, 'Judicial review: The United States Supreme Court versus the German Constitutional Court', 1 *Boston College International and Comparative Law Review* (1997).

Erica Frantz and Andrea Kendall-Taylor, 'The evolution of autocracy: Why authoritarianism is becoming more formidable?', 59 *Survival: Global Politics and Strategy* (2017).

Bruce P Frohnen, 'Is constitutionalism liberal?', 33 *Campbell Law Review* (2011).

Lon Fuller, *The morality of law* (New Haven, Yale University Press 1969).

Helena Alviar Garcia and Günter Frankenberg, eds, *Authoritarian constitutionalism* (Edward Elgar 2019).

Tom Ginsburg, 'Locking in democracy: Constitutions, commitment, and international law', 38 *New York University Journal of International Law and Politics* (2006) 757.

Tom Ginsburg and Aziz Z Huq, *How to save constitutional democracy?* (The University of Chicago Press 2018).

Fernando José Gonçalves Acunha and Juliano Zaiden Benvindo, 'Democratic decay in Brazil and the new global populism', 2017. https://iacl-aidc-blog.org/2017/06/06/democratic-decay-in-brazil-and-the-new-global-populism/.

Ricardo Gosalbo-Bono, 'The significance of the rule of law and its implications for the European Union and the United States', 72 *University of Pittsburgh Law Review* (2010).

Tania Groppi, 'Constitutional revision in Italy: A marginal instrument for constitutional change', in X Contiades, ed, *Engineering constitutional change* (Routledge 2016).

Agnieszka Grzelak, 'Are the EU Member States still masters of the treaties? The European Rule of Law concept as a means of limiting national authorities', Chapter 9 of this book.

Gábor Halmai, 'Populism, authoritarianism, and constitutionalism', 20 *German Law Journal* (2019).

Friedrich Hayek, *The Constitution of Liberty* (The University of Chicago Press 1960).

Lynne Henderson, 'Authoritarianism and the Rule of Law', 66 *Indiana Law Journal* (1991).

Wolfgang Hoffmann-Riem, 'The Venice Commission of the Council of Europe – Standards and impact', 2 *European Journal of International Law* (2014) 595.

András Jakab and Eszter Bodnár, 'The Rule of Law, democracy and human rights in Hungary: Tendencies from 1989 until 2019', Chapter 4 of this book.

András Jakab and Dimitry Kochenov, 'Introductory remarks', in Dimitry Kochenov and András Jakab, eds, *The enforcement of EU law and values* (Oxford University Press 2017).

Dimitry Kochenov, 'The EU and the Rule of Law – Naïveté or a grand design?', *University of Groningen Faculty of Law Research Paper Series*, 2018/5.

Dimitry Kochenov and Petra Bárd, 'Rule of Law crisis in the new member states of the EU. The pitfalls of overemphasizing enforcement', *Working Paper No. 1* (July 2018).

Dimitry Kochenov and András Jakab, eds, *The enforcement of EU law and values* (Oxford University Press 2017).

Jakub Kościerzyński, ed, *Justice under pressure – Repressions as a means of attempting to take control over the judiciary and the prosecution in Poland. Years 2015–2019*, https://ruleoflaw.pl/wp-content/uploads/2020/02/Raport_EN.pdf (2019).

Heike Krieger, Georg Nolte, and Andreas Zimmermann, eds, *The international Rule of Law: Rise or decline?* (Oxford University Press 2019).

Martin Krygier, 'The Rule of Law: Pasts, Presents, and Two Possible Futures', 12 *Annual Review of Law and Social Science* (2016).

Steven Levitsky and Lucan Way, 'The myth of democratic recession', 1 *Journal of Democracy* (2015).

Martin Loughlin, 'The contemporary crisis of constitutional democracy', 2 *Oxford Journal of Legal Studies* (2019).

Rett Ludwikowski, 'Supreme law or basic law? The decline of the concept of constitutional supremacy', 9 *Cardozo Journal of International and Comparative Law* (2001) 253–296.

Andrzej Madeja, 'The European values and the Rule of Law', Chapter 2 of this book.

Sylwia Majkowska-Szulc, 'Safeguarding the European Union's core values: The EU Rule of Law mission in Poland', Chapter 8 of this book.

Christopher May, 'The centrality of predictability to the rule of law', in Christopher May and Adam Winchester, eds, *Handbook of the Rule of Law* (Edward Elgar 2018).

Christopher May and Adam Winchester, eds, *Handbook of the Rule of Law* (Edward Elgar 2018).

Leighton McDonald, 'Positivism and the formal Rule of Law: Questioning the connection', 26 *Australian Journal of Legal Philosophy* (2001).

Alina Rocha Menocal, Verena Fritz, and Lise Rakner, 'Hybrid regimes and the challenge of deepening and sustaining democracy in developing countries', 1 *South African Journal of International Affairs* (2008).

Jorgen Orstrom Moller, 'The advantages of a thin version', in Christopher May and Adam Winchester, eds, *Handbook of the Rule of Law* (Edward Elgar 2018) 32–33.

Andrew Moravcsik, 'The origins of human rights regimes: Democratic delegation in postwar Europe', 54 *International Organizations* (2000).

Wiktor Osiatyński, 'Paradoxes of constitutional borrowing', 2 *International Journal of Constitutional Law* (2003).

Gianluigi Palombella, 'Beyond legality – Before democracy: Rule of Law in the EU two level system', in Carlos Closa and Dimitry Kochenov, eds, *Reinforcing the Rule of Law oversight in the European Union* (Cambridge University Press 2016).

Laurent Pech and Dimitry Kochenov, 'Strengthening the Rule of Law within the European Union: Diagnoses, recommendations, and what to avoid', *Policy Brief* (June 2019), https://reconnect-europe.eu/news/policy-brief-june-2019/.

Marc Plattner, 'Populism, pluralism, and liberal democracy', 1(21) *Journal of Democracy* (2010).

Patricia Popelier, 'Consultation on draft regulation: Best practices and political objections', in Marta Tavares de Almeida and Luzius Mader, eds, *Proceedings of the 9th IAL congress quality of legislation – Principles and instruments* [Lisbon, 24–25 June 2010] (Nomos 2011).

Patricia Popelier, Armen Mazmanyan, and Werner Vandenbruwane, eds, *The role of constitutional courts in multilevel governance* (Intersentia 2013).

Lant Pritchett, Michael Woolcock, and Matt Andrews, 'Capability Traps? The Mechanisms of Persistent Implementation Failure', *CGD Working Article* 234 (Washington, DC, Center for Global Development 2010).

Arch Puddington, 'Breaking down democracy: Global strategies, and methods of modern authoritarians', 2017, https://freedomhouse.org/sites/default/files/June2017_FH_Report_Breaking_Down_Democracy.pdf (accessed June 2017).

Joseph Raz, 'The law's own virtue', 1 *Oxford Journal of Legal Studies* (2019).

Joseph Raz, 'The Rule of Law and its virtue', 93 *Law Quarterly Review* (1977).

Joseph Raz, 'The Rule of Law and its virtue', in J Raz, ed, *The Authority of law: Essays on law and morality* (Oxford University Press 1979).

Michel Rosenfeld, 'Legitimacy of constitutional democracy', 74 *Southern California Law Review* (2001).

Wojciech Sadurski, *Poland's constitutional breakdown* (Oxford University Press 2019) 243.

Kim Lane Scheppele, 'Autocratic legalism', 85 *The University of Chicago Law Review* (2018).

Mortimer Sellers, 'What is the rule of law and why it is important?', in James Silkenat, James Jr Hickey, and Peter Barenboim, eds, *The legal doctrines of the rule of law and the legal state (Rechtsstaat)* (Springer 2014).

Marco Antonio Simonelli, 'Thickening up judicial independence: The ECJ ruling in Commission v. Poland (C-619/18)', 2019, https://europeanlawblog.eu/2019/07/08/thickening-up-judicial-independence-the-ecj-ruling-in-commission-v-poland-c-619-18/ (accessed November 2019).

Jacek Sokołowski and Dariusz Stolicki, 'Przyczyny opóźnień w transpozycji dyrektyw europejskich do polskiego porządku prawnego w świetle analizy ilościowej krajowego procesu legislacyjnego [Reasons for delays in the transposition of European directives into the Polish legal order in the light of quantitative analysis of the national legislative process]', 2 *Przegląd Politologiczny* (2017).

Brian Tamanaha, 'The history and elements of the Rule of Law', *Singapore Journal of Legal Studies* (2012).

Gábor Attila Tóth, 'Authoritarianism', *Max Planck encyclopedia of comparative constitutional law*, February 2017.

Gábor Attila Tóth, 'Illiberal rule of law? Changing features of Hungarian constitutionalism', in Maurice Adams, et al., eds, *Constitutionalism and the Rule of Law* (Cambridge University Press 2017).

Janusz Trzciński and Michał Szwast, 'Social rights in Poland', in Krzysztof Wojtyczek, ed, *Social rights as fundamental rights: XIXth international congress of comparative law/le XIXe Congrès international de droit compare* (Eleven International Publishing 2016).

Mark Tushnet, 'Authoritarian constitutionalism', 100 *Cornell Law Review* (2015).

Mark Tushnet, 'The possibility of illiberal constitutionalism', 69 *Florida Law Review* (2017).

Márton Varju, 'A magyar jogrendszer és az Európai Unió joga: tíz év tapasztalata [The Hungarian legal system and the law of the European Union: Experiences of ten years]', in András Jakab and György Gajduschek, eds, *A magyar jogrendszer állapota* (MTA Társadalomtudományi Kutatóközpont, Jogtudományi Intézet, 2016).

Mila Versteeg and Tom Ginsburg, 'Measuring the rule of law: A comparison of indicators', 1 *Law and Social Inquiry* (2017).

Jeremy Waldron, 'Is the Rule of Law an essentially contested concept (in Florida)?', 21 *Law and Philosophy* (2002).

Jeremy Waldron, 'The concept of the rule of law', 1 *Georgia Law Review* (2008) 59–60.

Wojciech Włoch, '"Where the laws do not govern, there is no constitution": On the relationship between the Rule of Law and constitutionalism', Chapter 3 of this book.

Krzysztof Wojtyczek, ed, *Social rights as fundamental rights: XIXth international congress of comparative law/le XIXe Congrès international de droit compare* (Eleven International Publishing 2016).

Helen Xanthaki and Ulrich Karpen, eds, *Legislation and legisprudence in Europe. A comprehensive guide for scholars and legislative practitioners* (Oxford, Hart 2017).

Fareed Zakaria, 'The rise of illiberal democracy', 6 *Foreign Affairs* (1997) 22.

Aleardo Zanghellini, 'The foundations of the Rule of Law', 2 *Yale Journal of Law and the Humanities* (2016) 214.

Andreas Zimmermann, 'Understanding the Rule of Law: Conceptions and perspective', http://alrf.msk.ru/understanding_the_rule_of_law:conceptions_and_perspectives (accessed October 2019).

Part II

Rule of Law

A common value

2 European values and the Rule of Law

Andrzej Madeja

2.1. Introduction

For many, an issue of European values is obvious and causes no questions or doubts. Many people assume that they exist, some nearly feel their presence, many are attached to them, and the vast majority estimate them positively: after all, they are 'ours'. Those values seem constant, stable, and perpetual. They form a precise list, have solid meanings, and, of course, are significant for Europeans. Consequently, they serve as an objective criterion of judgements as well as a measure of dispelling doubts and solving problems in various spheres of collective existence. Moreover, they represent both theoretical and practical importance. However, the problem of European values is actually far more complicated or even ambiguous. This phenomenon is multidimensional and has many facets. Therefore, a common perception of European values, such as the one briefly sketched above, is very optimistic, yet oversimplified and even naïve.[1]

The purpose of this chapter is to explain a phenomenon of European values and judge the Rule of Law against such a background. The chapter consists of four main parts. It starts with a brief description of two axiological theories (idealism and materialism) and juxtaposes their assumptions (2.2.). It proceeds by presenting two perspectives on European culture and values (2.3). The first is a traditional vision of European cultural formation as based on three pillars (2.3.1); the second applies a sociological concept of super-culture coined by Pitirim A Sorokin (2.3.2). Section 2.4. and 2.5, respectively, investigate viable ways of how a list of European values could be formulated, describe their general characteristics, and ascertain the Rule of Law as one of the European values. Finally, in Section 2.6., this chapter refers to the importance of the European values and the Rule of Law in the process of European integration. It concludes in Section 2.7.

1 Nevertheless, that 'common perception' of European values must not be neglected in scientific analysis, because that's the way they (i.e. values) are perceived by people and exist in human consciousness. On the other hand, researchers shouldn't be reduced to reconstruction of this 'common perception'.

2.2. Theories of values[2]

Axiology, as an independent discipline, originated at the turn of 19th and 20th centuries. Its origin was one of the implications of the so-called 'anthropological revolution' which ultimately emancipated social sciences from a straightjacket of methodological naturalism. However, even before that thinkers and philosophers had tried to describe and explain matters we recognise pivotal for the modern axiology. Therefore, plenty of axiological concepts of diversified character and merit were coined over centuries.[3] One may have no doubts as to the richness of these views,[4] yet to reach the goals of the paper it seems reasonable to intentionally neglect nuances and simplify the perspective. Various axiological views contain similar and different (divergent or contradictive) assumptions. Both can serve as criteria of classification. Consequently, two approaches to a value problem will

2 RT Allen, *The Structure of Value* (Avebury 1993); R Attfield, *A Theory of Value and Obligation* (Croom Helm 1987); S Badir, MG Dondero and F Provenzano, eds, *Épistémologie et éthique de la valeur. Du sémiotique au rhétorique (et retour)* (Presses universitaires de Franche-Comté 2011); AJ Bahm, *Axiology. The Science of Values* (Rodopi 1993); H Borowski, *Wartość jako przeżycie. Wprowadzenie do aksjologii* (Wyd. UMCS 1992); R Boudon, *Le sens des valeurs* (Presses universitaires de France 1999); Ch Chakrabarti and R Vulich, eds, *Paradigms and Perspectives on Value and Reality* (Cambridge Scholars Publishing 2014); S Dziamski, *Aksjologia. Wstęp do filozofii wartości* (Wyd. Naukowe UAM 1997); S Dziamski, ed, *Z teorii i historii wartości* (Nakom 1990); RB Edwards, *The Essentials of Formal Axiology* (University Press of America 2010); KC Elliott, *A Tapestry of Values. An Introduction to Values in Science* (Oxford University Press 2017); EW Hall, *What is Value? An Essay in Philosophical Analysis* (Routledge 2000); SO Hansson, *The Structure of Values and Norms* (Cambridge University Press 2001); G Harman, *Explaining Value and other Essays in Moral Philosophy* (Clarendon 2000); I Hirose and J Olson, eds, *The Oxford Handbook of Value Theory* (Oxford University Press 2015); A Kocikowski, ed, *W kręgu aksjologii. Problematyka teoretyczna, historyczna i teoriopoznawcza* (Nakom 1990), vol. I–II; JJ Kupperman, *Value. and What Follows* (Oxford University Press 1999); RM Lemos, *The Nature of Value. Axiological Investigations* (University Press of Florida 1995); J Lipiec, ed, *Człowiek i świat wartości* (Krajowa Agencja Wydawnicza 1982); J Lipiec, ed, *Istnienie i poznanie wartości* (Eureka 1991); J Lipiec, *Świat wartości. Wprowadzenie do aksjologii* (AWA 2001); P Machamer and G Wolters, eds, *Science, Values, and Objectivity* (University of Pittsburgh Press 2004); W Mejbaum, *Człowiek w świecie wartości* (Uniwersytet Szczeciński 2000); F Orsi, *Value Theory* (Bloomsbury Academic 2015); L Ostasz, *Czym są wartości? Zarys aksjologii* (Wyd. UWM 2009); RW Perrett, eds, *Theory of Value* (Garland 2001); J Schindler and M Stabrowski, eds, *Spory o wartości. Od praktyki do teorii interpretacji aksjologicznych* (Chronicon 2016); W Stróżewski, ed, *Studia z teorii poznania i filozofii wartości* (Ossolineum 1978); W Stróżewski, *W kręgu wartości* (Znak 1992).

3 S Alexandre, *Évaluation et contre-pouvoir. Portée éthique et politique du jugement de valeur dans le stoïcisme romain* (Jérôme Millon 2014); J Gajda, *Gdy rozpadły się ściany świata. Teorie wartości w filozofii hellenistycznej* (Wyd. Uniwersytetu Wrocławskiego 1995); T Mazur, *Kapryśni bogowie Sokratesa. Człowiek i świat wartości w tradycji filozofii zachodniej*, (Wyd. Marek Derewiecki 2008); E Moutsopoulos, *L'univers des valeurs, univers de l'homme. Recherches axiologiques* (Académie d'Athènes, Centre de recherche sur la philosophie grecque 2005); A Niemczuk, *Filozofia dobra przed powstaniem aksjologii. Relacjonistyczne próby przezwyciężenia trudności obiektywizmu i subiektywizmu* (Wyd. UMCS 1994); T Chappell, ed, *Values and Virtues. Aristotelianism in Contemporary Ethics* (Clarendon Press 2006).

4 G Kloska, *Pojęcia, teorie i badanie wartości w naukach społecznych* (PWN 1982).

be presented and their ontological and epistemological assumptions juxtaposed. These are idealism (objectivism, cognitivism) and materialism (subjectivism, psychologism, sociologism).

2.2.1. Idealism (objectivism)[5]

The central assumption is that values objectively exist. Their source and origin vary as to a concept and author.[6] However, they form a constituent element of our reality. They are objective and form an independent class of beings. They are independent of us and external to us. They are perfect and universal. They possess determined merit. We cannot change, suspend, or eliminate values, as they are beyond our range. Supporters of axiological objectivism stress that in our life (as individuals and groups), we must follow them. We have to obey and realise them in practice, as they are sources of our obligations. From such a perspective, values serve the purpose of an objective criterion for our actions. Our judgments and estimations are derivative, as we formulate them on the basis of original (primary) values. Although we cannot experience them empirically, values could be perceived and learned. Every variation of axiological idealism ascribes a cognitive function to a specific element of a human psychic, such as a reason (Plato), conscience (Christianity), emotions (Max Scheller), or intuition (George Moore). From this axiological perspective, values are opposed to interests. The latter are individual, subjective, and egoistic. They express what an individual wants, demands or desires. They are associated with private gain and profit. They manifest my individual taste, views, opinions and thus they are coupled with my needs. It makes them inferior to values.

Objectivity and universality of values does not mean every person (regardless of age, epoch, generation, society) perceives values in the same way. Groups and

5 C Bermes, W Henckmann and H Leonardy, eds, *Person und Wert. Schelers ‚Formalismus'* (Alber 2000); G Fröhlich, *Form und Wert. Die komplementären Begründungen der Ethik bei Immanuel Kant, Max Scheler und Edmund Husserl* (Königshausen and Neumann 2011); P Grice, *The Conception of Value* (with an introduction by Judith Baker, Clarendon 1991); A Grzegorczyk, *Obecność wartości* (Wyd. Poznańskie 2010); PÆ Hutchings, *Kant on Absolute Value. A Critical Examination of Certain Key Notions in Kant's 'Groundwork of the Metaphysic of Morals' and of his Ontology of Personal Value* (Allen and Unwin 1972); EB Litwack, *Wittgenstein and Value. The Quest for Meaning* (Continuum 2009); B Österman, *Value and Requirements. An Enquiry Concerning the Origin of Value* (Avebury 1995); P Ramsey, *The Truth of Value. A Defense of Moral and Literary Judgment* (Humanities Press 1985); C Sharp, *The Origin and Evolution of Human Values* (2nd rev. ed, DP Press 2002), B Trochimska-Kubacka, *Absolutyzm aksjologiczny. Rekonstrukcja oparta na aksjologii Rickerta, Schelera i Hartmanna* (Wyd. Uniwersytetu Wrocławskiego 1999); AC Zijderveld, *Rickert's Relevance. The Ontological Nature and Epistemological Functions of Values* (Brill 2006).

6 J Bransen and M Slors, eds, *The Problematic Reality of Values* (Van Gorcum 1996); B Centi and W Huemer, eds, *Values and Ontology. Problems and Perspectives* (Ontos 2009); J Lipiec, ed, *Ontologia wartości* (UMCS 1990); J Lipiec, ed, *Rozdroża wartości. Prace z ontologii i epistemologii wartości* (Wyd. UJ 1992); P Orlik, ed, *Ku źródłom wartości* (Wyd. Naukowe Instytutu Filozofii UAM 2008).

individuals are different, and surely their will and intellect are not perfect. Thus, interpretations of objective values change over time and space. Nevertheless, it has no impact upon objectivity and universality of values. This assumption has a significance in practice, as different, divergent, even contradictory interpretations are underpinned with a sound claim of objectivity. Consequently, a question arises: who is right?

The last matter: to define European values against such a background. Values are objective or no-existent at all. In particular, they are universal and global. The conclusion we can derive is simple: there are no European values. At the uttermost, there is a regional variety (version) of universal values. Therefore, European values are the European perception of universal values and the European fashion of their implementation in social practice.

2.2.2. Materialism (sociological-psychological approach)[7]

This concept is far more complicated than the previous one. Values (just like notions and meanings) are crucial elements of human socio-cultural reality. The latter comprises two elements: patterns for behaviour (a culture with values, norms, and social roles)[8] and arranged, ordered social practice (a society, i.e., a network of interactions). These are two complementary hemispheres, two 'halves of the same apple'. None is more important, each has its significance, and none can exist without the other, either: there is no culture without society and no society without culture. They are closely interdependent and interconnected. Cultural patterns for behaviour have their origin in social practice (interaction, communication, and cooperation). Therefore, a culture is a product (creation), and it reflects human activity. On the other hand, culture is of normative and compulsory character. Thus, it is a matrix for our operations. In such a way, values have their source in a social practice. To explain this, several inborn dispositions and inclinations of humans must be invoked. The first is a natural predilection to judge, estimate, and evaluate, by which an

7 KJ Brozi, *Antropologia wartości. Ujęcie metodologiczne* (Wyd. UMCS 1989); D Graeber, *Toward an Anthropological Theory of Value. The False Coin of Our Own Dreams* (Palgrave 2001); S Marczuk, *Badanie wartości w socjologii: teoria i empiria* (Wyd. WSP Rzeszów 1988); C Matusewicz, *Psychologia wartości* (PWN 1975); M Misztal, *Problematyka wartości w socjologii* (PWN 1980); M Pagès, Nicole Ramognino and Fabienne Soldini, eds, *L'énigme de la valeur. Les paradoxes de son observation sociologique* (Publications de l'Université de Provence 2010); RA Podgórski, *Homo sociologicus w strukturze wartości* (Fosze 2008); L Pomeroy, *The New Science of Axiological Psychology* (Rem B Edwards ed, Rodopi 2005); S Stewart, *A Sociology of Culture, Taste and Value* (Palgrave Macmillan 2014); J Szymczyk, *Odkrywanie wartości. Z problematyki socjologiczno-aksjologiczne* (Polihymnia 2004); A Tyszka, *Kultura jest kultem wartości: aksjologia społeczna. Studia i szkice* (Wyd. Antyk-Marcin Dybowski 1999); K Zamiara, *ed*, *Wartości w świecie osobowym* (Wyd. Naukowe UAM 1999).

8 R Benedict, *Patterns of Culture* (Routledge 2019); K Żygulski, *Wartości i wzory kultury. Rozważania socjologa* (Instytut Wydawniczy CRZZ 1975).

individual presents his/her subjective attitude towards the world.[9] Performing this, each of us assumes a position towards elements of reality and simultaneously externalises his/her personality. Two processes are tightly coupled: the development and expression of an individual. Next, a person unconsciously starts treating his/her judgments as if they were objective, which means he/she absolutises them. Admittedly, not every estimation undergoes such a process, but only these that an individual finds principal (not relative), holistic (not partial), disengaged (not engaged), and disinterested (not self-interested). In effect, a subjective evaluation (judgment) is perceived as if it were objective. Moreover, it should be viewed as an origin of a value:[10] subjective judgments objectify into values.[11]

Humans are not self-sufficient, and as such, they need each other and one another. Thus, a collective existence has no alternative, as we are interdependent. What happens in a group is a natural process of conformity: a group brings pressure to bear upon its members and each of unconsciously subjects to it. As a result, they grow similar to each other. What becomes similar in such a way are also assessments (judgments, etc.) and, consequently, values. Every society possesses its collective consciousness. It comprises a lot, including values. They form a social axiology. Members of society find them objective and must respect them. But actually, values are intersubjective, as they seem objective only for the insiders.

Values belong to a psychological and cultural sphere, and as such, they are realised in social practice. Therefore, analyses of values require a double perspective to be adopted. First, values are cultural patterns for behaviour, and this is what is 'officially' declared as values. Secondly, values are manifested in social practice, i.e., values empirically respected at a behavioural level, even if it goes against the 'officially' declared values. To get to know which values are recognised in a given society, we must take into account both levels.[12]

9 J Czapiński, *Wartościowanie – zjawisko inklinacji pozytywnej* (Ossolineum 1985); M Karwatowska and A Siwiec, eds, *O wartościach i wartościowaniu: historia – literatura – edukacja* (Perfekta info 2012); S Kumar Mohanty, *Persons, Mind and Value* (D.K. Printworld 1999); K Najder-Stefaniak, *O działaniu i wartościowaniu* (Wyd. SGGW-AR 1986); G Nerlich, *Values and Valuing. Speculations on the Ethical Life of Persons* (Clarendon Press 1989).

10 H Joas, *Die Entstehung der Werte* (Suhrkamp 1997).

11 Z Najder, *Wartości i oceny* (Wyd. Naukowe PWN 2015); J Pieter, *Oceny i wartości*, (Śląsk 1973).

12 Together these levels form a social order. Concept of social order seems very useful to perceive values (or legal rules) not only as formal directives that form theoretical systems of regularity and coherence, but also as constituent elements of social reality. M Hechter and C Horne, eds, *Theories of Social Order* (Stanford Social Sciences 2009); T Nawrocki and W Świątkiewicz, eds, *Ład społeczny i jego prz, edstawienia* (Wyd. Uniwersytetu Śląskiego 2016); G Radnitzky and H Bouillon, eds, *Values and the Social Order* (Avebury 1995); H-P Widmaier, *Studia o ładzie społecznym* (Tadeusz Kowalak trans., Fundacja im. F Eberta 1995).

Additional matter makes a picture even more complicated. Today an individual enjoys a broad autonomy as to interpretation and application of values. Individuals formulate their list of values.[13] They do not create them (as humans, in general, cannot create *ex nihilo*) but formulate an individual scale of preferences. The latter, in turn, is determined by his/her life experiences, which means an individual axiological preference is inevitable.[14] That assumption does not contradict a general concept of a collective consciousness. Even an extensive 'axiological autonomy' has its limits. In the same way: even a very permissive society must maintain its coherence and protect its axiological core. It leads to the problem of conflict between the axiological perspective of group and individual.[15] In general, the individual's views and practices must stay in conformity with socially recognised values. If an individual breaches the rules of social game, his/her exploits meet with disapproval, and he/she suffers various forms of sanction.[16] However, social practice brings about a gradual transformation of social values. Therefore, axiological tensions are unavoidable because the socio-cultural reality is dynamic, its elements emerge spontaneously, and its binding character differs from the binding force of the law.

Relation of values to interests seems in the case of axiological materialism far different than in the case of axiological idealism. Individual interests are valuable, just as interests of society. Whoever possesses interests, may judge them positively. On the other hand, an individual may have the interest to protect and realise his/her values – the same in the case of society. Consequently, there is a slight difference between values and interests (if it is at all). They are the same matter (a need), but simply perceived in a different way. Values are needs seen from a macro-scale. They are widely recognised, positively assessed, uncontested, and uncontroversial. All members of a group agree to obey and follow them, and thus values seem 'objective'. Interests are individual and egoistic, but it does not always mean bad or immoral. Moreover, for a given person or group, these could be values, especially in the case of the so-called vital interests. Therefore, we recognise them as 'subjective', 'particular', or 'utilitarian' values.[17]

13 G Mathews, *Global Culture/Individual Identity. Searching for Home in the Cultural Supermarket* (Routledge 2005).

14 S Schwarz and F Wenisch, eds, *Values and Human Experience. Essays in Honor of the Memory of Balduin Schwarz* (Peter Lang 1999).

15 M Stocker, *Plural and Conflicting Values* (Clarendon Press 1992).

16 R Cohen-Almagor, ed, *Liberal Democracy and the Limits of Tolerance. Essays in Honor and Memory of Yitzhak Rabin* (University of Michigan Press 2000); P Dickey Young, H Shipley and TJ Trothen, eds, *Religion and Sexuality. Diversity and the Limits of Tolerance* (UBC Press 2015); A Siemaszko, *Granice tolerancji. O teoriach zachowań dewiacyjnych* (Wyd. Naukowe PWN 1993).

17 JM Halstead and MJ Taylor, *The Development of Values, Attitudes and Personal Qualities* (National Foundation for Educational Research 2000); L Hostyński, *Utilitarian Values* (Wyd. Adam Marszałek 2009); A Sayer, *Why Things Matter to People. Social Science, Values and Ethical Life* (Cambridge University Press 2011); T Rønnow-Rasmussen, *Personal Value* (Oxford University Press 2011).

A close relation and combination of four elements should be stressed here: needs[18] – emotions[19] – estimations – values. An individual experiences it in the following way: My needs (to possess, to experience) determine my position. I judge positively what I want to have or to stay in touch with. I want to save, to protect, to realise it. Therefore, 'good' means 'serving my needs'.[20] Consequently, literally everything can become a value: an item, a symbol, an idea, an institution, a person.

Assumptions of axiological materialism could be presented as it follows. Values are always subjective and relative, as they originate from judgments. Thus they are changeable over time and space. Nevertheless, for members of a given group, there are such values that are recognised as objective (social axiology as an element of collective consciousness), while an individual can possess their subjective (particular) values. In the case of both types of values (objective and individual), there are such that are recognised autotelic (do not serve any other value) and instrumental (serve to realise other values). Minimal conformity between individual and social axiology must be provided.

However, are we condemned to subjectivity? Is not there any hope for a universality?[21] After all, we are humans – we represent the same species. If we form mankind, perhaps there is a solid foundation at a biological level, as we have the same nature, instincts, predispositions, and needs. If values are coupled with needs, maybe then there is a hope to find axiological objectivity? Every person prefers different modes, fashions, and ways of satisfying these common needs.[22] Moreover, we are different, as we are formed by our experiences. A pure indeterminism and self-realisation are beyond human capacity. We are products of socialisation and enculturation that proceed within a specific socio-cultural sphere.[23]

18 H Borowski, *Potrzeby i wartości* (Wyd. Politechniki Lubelskiej 1999); K Trojan, *Potrzeby psychiczne i wartości oraz ich implikacje religijne* (WAM 2001); D Wiggins, *Ne, eds, Values, Truth. Essays in The Philosophy of Value* (3rd amended ed, Clarendon 2002).

19 G Hetman, *Uczucia i wartości według Jana Mazurkiewicza* (ZPH Motor 1995); M Strauss, *Volition and Valuation. A Phenomenology of Sensational, Emotional, and Conceptual Values* (University Press of America 1999).

20 This approach is widely accepted not only in social sciences, but also among philosophers, of course except for adherents of axiological objectivism and absolutism. J Deigh, *Emotions, Values, and the Law* (Oxford University Press 2011); S Roeser and C Todd, eds, *Emotion and Value* (Oxford University Press 2014); Ch Tappolet, *Emotions, Value, and Agency* (Oxford University Press 2016); P Unger, *Identity, Consciousness and Value* (Oxford University Press 1992).

21 R Audi, *Moral Value and Human Diversity* (Oxford University Press 2008), A-M Dillens, ed, *Le pluralisme des valeurs. Entre particulier et universel* (Publications des Facultés universitaires Saint-Louis 2003); A Tanrikulu, *Human Values, Moral Values and Social Value Judgements* (AuthorHouse 2016).

22 K Obuchowski, *Galaktyka potrzeb. Psychologia dążeń ludzkich* (Zysk i S-ka 2000).

23 J Cieluch, *Kształtowanie się systemu wartości: od dzieciństwa do wczesnej dorosłości* (Liberi-Libri 2013); T Frąckowiak and J Modrzewski, *eds, Socjalizacja a wartości* (ERUDITUS 1995), R Fischer, *Personality, Values, Culture. An Evolutionary Approach* (Cambridge University Press 2018); J Rich Harris, *The Nurture Assumption. Why Children Turn out the*

The highest level of Abraham Maslow's pyramid of needs reflects that. The apex is not self-realisation but self-actualisation: we can try to discover and experience our uniqueness.[24] Although society cannot eliminate our natural instincts and dispositions, it can affect or even distort their natural operation and functioning. Totalitarian regimes are excellent examples. In the case of the so-called open societies, this process assumes less intense form, but it still happens because the socio-cultural reality creates us. We grow similar to each other within its framework, and simultaneously we feel different from those living beyond our group.[25]

The question arises: how can we perceive European values as seen against this background? There are more than 40 independent socio-cultural groups on the continent, and they do not form any single, unitary, coherent body. Each of them possesses and cherishes its own values. Consequently, if a European society does not exist, there is no European culture neither European values, just as there are Polish or Hungarian. However, perhaps something that joins and connects us exists beneath or above European societies and their cultures? If it does, how to conceptualise it? This matter will be analysed in detail in Section 2.3.

The conclusion of this section is as follows. There are two different values concepts. They cannot be reconciled as theories. It is up to each of us to make a choice. An individual can perceive idealism as a description of the truth, while perceiving materialism as a fallacious concept, at best representing the views of scientists. On the other hand, materialism may seem a rational theory, while idealism represents a widespread but erroneous belief of the majority (a predominant perception of values). Nevertheless, they have something in common. Above all, values are good and deserve appreciation. They also have a normative character – individuals must obey, realise, and defend them.[26] Both axiological perspectives also leave no doubts that, in a social reality, we meet a vast array of interpretations regarding values. Axiological unity is never granted in practice.

2.3. European culture

2.3.1. Commonly recognised formula[27]

According to this view, the European culture's existence is beyond any doubt, as it is objective and perpetual. It is also estimated positively as good and moral.

Way They Do (Free Press 2009); K Ostrowska, *Wokół rozwoju osobowości i systemu wartości* (Centrum Metodyczne Pomocy Psychologiczno-Pedagogicznej MEN 1998); S Pinker, *The Blank Slate. The Modern Denial of Human Nature* (Penguin 2003); AE Szołtysek, *Filozofia człowieka: biologiczny rozwój a kulturowe kształtowanie* (Oficyna Wydawnicza Impuls 2015); A Uchoa Branco and J Valsiner, *Cultural Psychology of Human Values* (Information Age Pub. 2012).

24 A Maslow, *Motivation and Personality* (2nd ed, New Harper 1970).

25 S Ossowski, *Więź społeczna i dziedzictwo* (PWN 1966).

26 FJ Lis, *Wartości w kształtowaniu motywacji i organizacji życia społecznego* (Wydawnictwa Uczelniane 1996).

27 J Pilikowski, *Podróż w świat Europy* (WAM 2011); M Poradowski, *Dzieje cywilizacji europejskiej* (Nortom 2007); R Sobański, *Europa obojga prawa* (Księgarnia św. Jacka-Wydział Teologiczny Uniwersytetu Śląskiego 2006).

From this perspective, European values exist. They form a core of European culture. Just as the culture, they are objective and perpetual, since they are obvious and uncontroversial. As to its merit, the European culture is based on a triple foundation: the Roman law, Greek philosophy, and Christianity. These components are constant and unchangeable. Therefore, as to their merit, the European values correspond with 'the three pillars'. They bind us, and we are expected to obey and realise them in practice. 'The three pillars' are far more than just a source of inspiration, since the extent of allowed creative interpretation is narrow. Interpretation serves only to find a viable way (adequate to changing historical terms) in which objective values should be realised. Thus, there is only one general pattern of development. Whoever 'strays off the path' is wrong or misleading. Consequently, the identity of the continent and its inhabitants is fixed, while a latitude of self-determination is very severely limited. It could be noted that this perspective corresponds with an axiological idealism and universalism.[28] National European cultures are based on this triple foundation. An 'organic' terminology corresponds well with this perspective: national cultures stem or grow from it like branches from a tree trunk. They seem to be variations of the European culture's patterns, as they are all rooted in it. Thus, national cultures should be perceived as subcultures of European culture. It explains various similarities between national cultures. They are all descendants of the same ancestors. Consequently, national values (as core elements of national cultures) are local interpretations of European values. Once more: no contradiction allowed.

This widespread and often-invoked view has several shortcomings. They are presented and commented on below.

Firstly, adherents of such a vision of European culture completely reject other historical and socio-cultural factors that can be recognised as 'cornerstones' of Europe's cultural unity. 'The pillars' belong to the Ancient epoch, and everything that has happened after that seems secondary and derivative. They are, at best, the above-mentioned adaptive interpretations of original and objective patterns. They are accepted as such only if their conformity with 'the pillars' can be proved. Otherwise, they are malfunctions and deviations or even negations of the foundation. One could rhetorically ask here if the philosophy of the Renaissance and the

28 Axiological objectivism and absolutism (overtly represented by 'the three pillars') fully corresponds with crucial tenets of Christianity and the Catholic Church's teaching in Poland. Such a perspective is also very common among conservative and right-wing politicians. Moreover, this view is shared by various groups whose believes are different from the Church's or the government's official position. Therefore, we may treat it as a predominant view in Poland. I assume there is a linkage between this orientation and traditionalism which seems to be characteristic for a surprisingly big proportion of Poles, including social researchers (see n 27). M Giertych, *European Values* (Maciej Giertych 2007); M Giertych, *Quo vadis Europa* (Maciej Giertych 2009); S Kowalczyk, *Współczesny kryzys ideowo-aksjologiczny* (Wyd. KUL 2011); J Krucina, *Wznoszenie wartości podstawowych* (TUM Wyd. Wrocławskiej Księgarni Archidiecezjalnej 2007); S Kowalczyk, *Człowiek w poszukiwaniu wartości: elementy aksjologii personalistycznej* (Wyd. KUL 2016); K Mikulicki, *Wartości trwałe* (Alleluja 2004); J Zimny and R Król, eds, *Wartości drogą ku wzrastaniu* (KUL 2012).

Enlightenment or postmodernism – weren't they creative and original products, quite often irreconcilable with 'the pillars', and simultaneously Europe-wide factors that shaped the continent's character?

Secondly, in this vision supporters reckon among 'the pillars' only such phenomena that they find good and positive. Meanwhile, everything (our world, national cultures, or individual identities) is shaped by various factors, including the unpleasant and painful. In the case of Europe, it would be various calamitous conflicts, especially the bloody confession wars of the 16th–17th centuries, or the two world wars of the 20th century.[29]

Thirdly, 'the three pillars' are recognised as objective and perpetual. While, in fact, each of them is a cultural creation of a given social organisation that existed and functioned just as ours do. None of them 'descended from the sky'. Just the opposite: men of blood and flesh created them. Another question arises: why should we acknowledge them as being so special (as to their form or origin) and treat them in a privileged way? They should be judged just like any other historical phenomenon that originated in a social practice since time immemorial and affected our reality.

Fourth, for advocates of the view, each of 'the pillars' seems coherent and consistent, which cannot be proved. For example, what do its adherents mean by 'the Roman law'? *Lex duodecim tabularum* (5th century BC) or *Corpus iuris civilis* (6th century AD)? And, in the case of Greek philosophy – which period, current, or thinker? The same doubt arises due to an abundance of Christianity's interpretations. Actually, it seems that each of 'the pillars' is a joint name for a very complex phenomenon that originated a long time ago and evolved over centuries. They lack unitary and straightforward merit. Supporters of this view idealise them (they are concerned rather with a form: the law, a religion, a philosophy). Consequently, they profoundly simplify or completely neglect their complexity, richness, and internal contradictions.

Finally, these 'three pillars' can by no means be effectively combined into a coherent entirety. Is a Roman *damnatio ad bestiam* agreeable with a Christian precept of love and *hedone* of Epicureanism? What could be reconciled are the chosen elements derived from 'the pillars', which means indeed: an arbitrariness of choice and creative interpretation.

Quite often this vision of Europe and its culture is repeated and invoked without any reflection. It is useful, convenient, and serves important purposes. It seems coherent and convincing. It provides a sense of certainty and a strong foundation by stressing a historical continuity. Eventually, it became 'the truth' as a result of practical acceptance. Thus, no one has to prove it is right, for the majority have agreed it is so. While, in fact, it is a cliché, platitude, or stereotype: at least a misrepresentation, if not a mystification.[30] It is an ideologically motivated vision that serves various purposes. This picture is oversimplified, as

29 BG Martin, *The Nazi-Fascist New Order for European Culture* (Harvard University Press 2016); AP Roach and JR Simpson, eds, *Heresy and the Making of European Culture. Medieval and Modern Perspectives* (Ashgate 2013).

30 K Kowalski, *Europa: mity, modele, symbole* (Międzynarodowe Centrum Kultury 2002).

the reality is far too complex to be reflected in this simple formula. It, however, comprises certain right and apt elements. Notably, no one can reasonably deny that the cultural creations of Mediterranean Antiquity played a crucial role in shaping Europe's axiological dimension.[31] 'The three pillars' should be rather perceived as reservoirs from which a lot was derived. This process combined both: borrowing and creative interpretation. Very often, however, the results are surprisingly different from the substrates. Every cultural development assumes such a form as we make use of achievements of previous generations and modify them in our epoch. It is the meaning of 'heritage': we utilise the past in our way to satisfy contemporary needs.[32] We hold 'the yesterday' in the high esteem, yet we are not its blind followers. It explains why Europe is 'still in the making'.[33]

2.3.2. *European culture as a super-culture*

Any criticism should be constructive. Rejection of the above-described model of 'three pillars' means something ought to be offered instead. It is the notion of super-culture that seems to be a useful tool for explaining the vague matter of European culture. This concept was coined by Pitirim A Sorokin, an American of Russian origin, and one of the most brilliant sociologists of the 20th century.[34] A super-culture is a complex socio-cultural phenomenon. Its characteristics are briefly presented below.

A super-culture's existence depends upon several conditions.[35] Firstly, there must exist a group of societies that represent similarities or even have something in common (in some aspects, they have identical features). It can refer to various components of socio-cultural reality (e.g., values) and both levels: postulated

31 C Edwards, ed, *Roman Presences. Receptions of Rome in European Culture 1789–1945* (Cambridge University Press 1999); A Haltenhoff, A Heil and F-H Mutschler, eds, *Römische Werte als Gegenstand der Altertumswissenschaft* (KG Saur 2005); P Marciniak and DC Smythe, eds, *The Reception of Byzantium in European Culture since 1500* (Routledge 2016); P Mazurkiewicz, *Europeizacja Europy. Tożsamość kulturowa Europy w kontekście procesów integracji* (UKSW 2001); N Spencer, *The Evolution of the West. How Christianity Has Shaped Our Values* (Society for Promoting Christian Knowledge 2016); M Streeter, *The Mediterranean. Cradle of European Culture* (New Holland 2006); L Waelkens, *Amne adverso. Roman Legal Heritage in European Culture* (Leuven University Press 2015).

32 E Bieńkowska, *Spór o dziedzictwo europejskie: między świętym i świeckim* (W.A.B. 1999); G Delanty, *The European Heritage. A Critical Re-Interpretation* (Routledge 2017); HG Gadamer, *Dziedzictwo Europy* (Andrzej Przyłębski trans., SPACJA 1992); A Gieysztor, *O dziedzictwie kultury* (Towarzystwo Opieki nad Zabytkami 2000); K Kowalski, *O istocie dziedzictwa europejskiego: rozważania* (Międzynarodowe Centrum Kultury 2013); AG Lehmann, *The European Heritage. An Outline of Western Culture* (Phaidon 1984).

33 Z Bauman, *Europa: niedokończona przygoda* (Tomasz Kunz trans., Wyd. Literackie 2007).

34 Sorokin's works and views aren't well known neither appreciated in Poland. D Leonarska and K Wielecki, 'Pitirim Sorokin i jego absencja w polskiej socjologii' 13 *Roczniki Historii Socjologii* (2013) 47.

35 P Sorokin, *Social and Cultural Dynamics* (American Book Co. 1937) vol. IV 67–146; C Gryko, *Integralna teoria kultury Pitirima Sorokina* (Wyd. UMCS) 70–84.

(patterns for behaviour) and realised (social practice). Secondly, inhabitants of these societies must be aware of this fact and have to assess it positively. Thirdly, they must experience a sense of togetherness and belongingness to a grouping formed by their societies. It means their affiliation and loyalty exceeds a single society, while their identity is shaped by factors from beyond a society of their origin. Finally, they feel that they want to maintain this state of affairs and will defend it if it is imperilled. Necessary prerequisites for all these are intensive interactions between representatives of these societies, as otherwise, they would not be able to trace existing similarities. Further, contacts should generate for at least some positive implications, because a troublesome neighbourhood is never desired.

These terms can lead to the forming of a super-culture. It appears spontaneously in a long historical process. Super-culture can be perceived as a super-structure, while national cultures can be perceived as an infrastructure (foundation). The former develops on the latter. Super-culture never devours base cultures, as it would deprive itself of any basis. Thus, as to its features, it is derivative and secondary. Its existence and extent depend upon national cultures' similar and identical characteristics. Super-culture changes over time: it grows or diminishes according to a changing degree of similarities and identities between base cultures. It always consists of a core (formed by identities) and peripheries (comprising similarities). Nonetheless, a super-culture is not a simple 'passive' creation. It can affect base cultures. Thus, it is not a one-way relation (national cultures → super-culture), but an interplay (mutual influence or feedback) between the two. The main result of this interplay is in bringing about new similarities between base cultures. More precisely, a super-culture accelerates and intensifies an appearance of new identities and similarities. It should be stressed that a super-culture affects base cultures differently – it causes different (more profound or superficial) implications in each of them. Finally, a crucial element of a super-culture is its values[36] (both: the same and similar for base cultures). They manifest and reflect on what base (national) cultures have in common. And that is our Holy Grail – European values.

However, before the European super-culture occurred, there had existed certain similarities (especially in the case of values) between societies and their cultures. How to explain that phenomenon? Societies gained these similar features as they were exposed to the same phenomena.[37] They could be called 'European universalizing factors'. Among these, we can reckon (with reservations set out

36 M Wichrowski, 'Pitirim A Sorokin. Wartości w supersystemach społeczno-kulturowych' in ZJ Czarnecki and S Symotiuk, eds, *Historyczna dynamika wartości. Studia nad aksjologicznymi interpretacjami dziejów* (Wyd. UMCS 1990) 153. More on values in Sorokin's interpretation: F Cowell, *Values in Human Society. The Contribution of Pitirim A. Sorokin to Sociology* (Porter Sargent 1970); P Talbutt, Jr., *Rough Dialectics. Sorokin's Philosophy of Value* (with contributions by Lawrence T. Nichols, Pitirim A Sorokin, Rodopi 1998); EA Tiryakian, ed, *Sociological Theory, Values, and Sociocultural Change. Essays in Honor of Pitirim A. Sorokin* (Free Press of Glencoe 1963).

37 P Rietbergen, *Europa. Dzieje kultury* (Robert Bartołd trans., Książka i Wiedza 2001).

above) the Roman law, Greek philosophy, and Christianity. These three factors were elements (creations) of earlier and more advanced socio-cultural entities. They affected other societies in three general patterns. Winners and conquerors imposed them – that is, a process of a cultural clash and acculturation. They transferred – that is, a process of diffusion and inculturation. They were borrowed – that is, a process of reception, adaptation, and assimilation.

There were many other universalising factors of various characters, such as the Renaissance, the Age of Reason, the Enlightenment (all three as Europe-wide cultural currents), military conflicts, and world wars, political revolutions, economic crises, totalitarianisms, human rights concepts, postmodernism, industrial and technological revolutions, globalisation. They affected all societies, but every society experienced this influence in a specific way. For example, Christianity assumed a different form in various societies; the same is true of the Roman law: in various societies, it served different purposes. Moreover, universalising factors collided or even tended to cancel each other out. Therefore, the process of a super-culture's development is neither simple nor regular. Even though we can seek its beginnings, describe its origins, and trace its gradual progress,[38] its future effects are not as predictable in terms of their shape and merit, nor may they be perceived and treated as inviolable and sacrosanct.

2.4. European values

Presented above, the concept of the super-structure seems a useful measure to trace and find a list of European values. It is a sociological tool; thus, empirical data (and not politically motivated wishes) must be taken into consideration and processed in order to obtain conclusions. Therefore, what should be sought are similarities and common traits in European societies and their cultures. In general, a reconstruction of European values is a challenging endeavour. It is certainly not a perfect or infallible measure. Its weak points and limitations are mentioned below.

A crucial question arises: what data we should gather and how to process them to reach the goal? Theoretically, the procedure should look like this. There are two levels; each provides relevant information. The first is declaratory, comprises cultural patterns, and includes officially respected values. Technically, we must perform a public opinion survey. The second level is behavioural: here, we take into consideration social practice. We analyse both levels in a given European society and combine conclusions derived from each. Then, we repeat this operation in every European society. Eventually, we have to compare the effects of our efforts regarding all societies in order to trace identities and similarities. However, there is a fundamental problem with the scale. It is beyond sociologists' capacity

38 A Zamojski, *Tożsamość cywilizacji europejskiej: geneza, kompleks konstytuujący i kierunki transformacji* (Wyd. Uniwersytetu Jana Kochanowskiego 2015).

to gather and process such an amount of data. Thus no one has ever performed such a survey.

There is another, simpler, way. We can ask representatives of European societies what values they recognise as European (common and shared) and how they perceive (ontological status) and understand them (meanings). This approach is confined only to a declaratory level. It would reflect opinions and views on the phenomenon of European values borne by members of European societies. What we hoped to achieve is, at best, a list of values and a scale of preferences (determining inferiority and superiority of values). It would be useful to learn how given values are perceived and understood, i.e., to establish their meaning from the perspective of the groups that were interviewed. It would show us how meanings diverge across Europe. Nevertheless, we would not achieve clear-cut definitions but affectively underpinned associations and connotations.[39] Several questions arise here. Modern pluralistic societies are diversified, and consist of various groups. These groups participate in a culture differently.[40] It means they do not have equal access to its components and, by this, that they have a different perception of both national and European values. To solve the problem and gain credible data, we should interrogate members of separate groups that are representative of a given society's structure. The last phase of this research is to summarise the results of surveys performed in European societies and derive a conclusion.[41]

The third method is different. Identical and similar features of European societies and their cultures are reflected in their social institutions:[42] in their form, merit, and practice. Therefore, we analyse the structural elements of socio-cultural reality. Such a position is based on several assumptions. A social institution is a source of, and a base (foundation) for, social relations, and it determines a relation's form. To put it briefly, a social institution is a model of social relation. Every segment of society has its set of social institutions; for example, a family, an enterprise, a congregation, a university, the state. Social institutions are interconnected and form a society's institutional structure, i.e., its 'backbone' or 'skeleton'. Thus, they are the most solid and stable components of socio-cultural reality. Social institutions determine a social practice, but simultaneously a practice modifies institutions.[43] Once more, we observe an interplay of phenomena. What is to be stressed is that institutions are manifestations of tenacious practices. Naturally, divergences and tensions between institutions and practice are

39 Methodology of linguistics seems very useful in such analyses. J Bartmiński and M Grzeszczak, 'Jak rekonstruować kanon wartości narodowych i europejskich?' 26 *Etnolingwistyka* (2014) 21.

40 AM Molesztak, *Człowiek, kultura, uczestnictwo* (Wyd. UKW 2015); Andrzej Tyszka, *Uczestnictwo w kulturze. O różnorodności stylów życia* (PWN 1971).

41 KJ Brozi, *Antropologia wartości. Kategoria standardu kulturowego w badaniach nad wartościami* (Wyd. UMCS 1994).

42 J Turner, *The Institutional Order* (Longman 1997).

43 T Parsons, *On Institutions and Social Evolution* (University of Chicago Press 1982).

unavoidable. Their scale shows a gap between declared patterns for behaviour and social interactions. Further, every institution could be perceived as a bundle of cultural patterns for behaviour (values, norms, and social roles). Here we see a close interconnection between cultural and social elements.

Socio-cultural reality is not only very complicated but is also a *sui generis* world, which means in particular that social institutions are not material – instead, they are imagined or imaginary. Thus, we must localise them and describe their form and merit. Further, their deconstruction is not a simple process. Like always, we have to pay the costs of generalisation, as we can only find predominating features and tendencies at best. The conclusion cannot be unambiguous. At every stage of the research process, we can fall a victim to subjectivism and creative interpretations. Thus, the results of such efforts are always exposed to criticism.

Irrespective of the doubts, we may formulate a list of European values by invoking the results of the above-described methods.[44] These are: life and dignity; individualism and autonomy of man; privacy, family, childhood, maternity; liberty, property, and wealth; pleasure and satisfaction; beauty; equality, indiscrimination; justice; community and collective identity; solidarity and inclusiveness; trust, honesty, and loyalty; responsibility; empathy, sympathy, and love; good and goodness; tolerance and pluralism; humanitarianism; welfare and social justice; order, regularity, and predictability; sureness, stability, security; peace and coexistence; unity and cooperation; democracy: participation, debate, compromise, consent; the Rule/the state of Law, legality; decentralisation, self-government, subsidiarity; the state, patriotism, nationality, national identity and culture (a moderate ethnocentrism); progress, innovation, criticism, modernity, improvement; activism, entrepreneurship; efficiency; rationality and science; truth; tradition; religion, faith, piety; the natural environment.

European values have several features. Each has a meaning, but it changes over time, as it is dynamic. Every sphere of social activity has its specific value; for example, religion – piety. Sometimes the same values refer to various spheres; for example, love, rationality. Nevertheless, plenty of values refer to every single segment of society; for example, dignity, equality, humanitarianism. Although it is a very common view, European values do not represent any hierarchy, as no axiological system does. Just the opposite, quite often they are contrary to each

44 W Arts, J Hagenaars and L Halman, eds, *The Cultural Diversity of European Unity. Findings, Explanations and Reflections From the European Values Study* (Brill 2003); W Arts and L Halman, eds, *European Values at the Turn of the Millennium* (Brill 2004); W Arts and L Halman, eds, *Value Contrasts and Consensus in Present-Day Europe. Painting Europe's Moral Landscapes* (Brill 2013); P Bréchon and F Gonthic, eds, *Atlas des européens. Valeurs communes et différences nationalesed* (Colin 2013); MC Flamm, J Lachs and KP Skowroński, eds, *American and European Values. Contemporary Philosophical Perspectives* (Cambridge Scholars Publishing 2008); L Halman, I Sieben and M van Zundert, eds, *Atlas of European Values. Trends and Traditions at the Turn of The Century* (Koninklijke Brill 2012); J Koralewicz, ed, *The European Value System* (CCP IPS PAN 1999); A Kufer, *Europäische Wertegemeinschaft? Eine empirische Untersuchung gesellschaftlicher Werte in 27 EU-Staaten auf Basis sozialgeschichtlicher Analysen und aktueller Umfragedaten* (Lit 2013).

other; for example, tradition – innovation or liberty – and equality. They form a set (a pool), or rather a network (a cobweb), as they are interdependent and interconnected. Thus, when a given matter is decided in practice, several values must be balanced. The scale of preferences serves that purpose, but it also must be created. It implicates divergent or even contradictory interpretations (as to both: the scale of preferences and hierarchy of values) because they depend on national, political, or religious orientation.[45] It means Europeans enjoy a kind of autonomy in this operation, as we are not the same and have a right to differ. Paradoxically, this consequence of an individual's autonomy might be helpful: it is a moderate individualism that could serve as a common denominator or a point of reference,[46] as many European values refer to an individual's status. Finally, they have a dual character: on the one hand, these are our values – we want to have and protect them; on the other, we feel bound by them. It manifests our awareness we are similar and our eagerness to stay and act together. Therefore, European values, respect for them, and a sense of belongingness to this axiological community delimitate the extent of Europe as a cultural formation.[47]

2.5. The Rule of Law as a European value

Admittedly, the Rule of Law belongs to European values. It is an effect of various interconnected factors that had affected European societies over the centuries. These are political, legal, and philosophical concepts, including the law of nature, liberalism, positivism and analytical jurisprudence, democracy, and human rights. Other systems, utterly different in their characteristic, should also be mentioned here. These are absolutism and totalitarianism, which served as counter-examples, i.e., models that must be avoided at all costs.[48] On the other hand, these are

45 P Brzozowski, *Wzorcowa hierarchia wartości: polska, europejska czy uniwersalna? Psychologiczne badania empiryczne* (Wyd. UMCS 2007).

46 J Almqvist, *Human Rights, Culture and the Rule of Law* (Hart 2005); LS Bell, AJ Nathan, and I Peleg, eds, *Negotiating Culture and Human Rights* (Columbia University Press 2001); LM Friedman, *The Human Rights Culture. A Study in History and Context* (Quid Pro Books 2011); CT Szyjko, ed, *Prawa człowieka fundamentem Europy wartości* (Wyd. MM 2014); RA Wilson, ed, *Human Rights, Culture and Context. Anthropological Perspectives* (Pluto Press 1997); E Zamfir and F Maggino, eds, *The European Culture for Human Rights. The Right to Happiness* (Cambridge Scholars Publishing 2013).

47 P Dukes, ed, *Frontiers of European Culture* (with an introduction by Mike Hepworth, E Mellen 1996); TG Jordan, *The European Culture Area. A Systematic Geography* (3rd ed, HarperCollins College 1996); K Kujawińska Courtney, M Łukowska, and E Williams, eds, *European Culture in Diversity* (Cambridge Scholars Publishing 2011); J Wojtanowicz, *Europejska przestrzeń geograficzno-kulturowa* (Wyd. UMCS 2008).

48 H Albert, *Europa i okiełznanie władzy. Szczególna droga Europy do społeczeństwa otwartego* (Tadeusz Zatorski trans., Nomos 1998); A Bryk, *Konstytucjonalizm. Od starożytnego Izraela do liberalnego konstytucjonalizmu amerykańskiego* (Wyd. UJ 2013); H Izdebski, *Doktryny polityczno-prawne. Fundamenty współczesnych państw* (Wolters Kluwer 2017); J Malarczyk, ed, *Doktrynalne podstawy demokracji konstytucyjnej* (Wyd. UMCS 1996); H Rot, ed, *Demokratyczne państwo prawne (aksjologia, struktura, funkcje)* (Wyd. Uniwersytetu Wrocławskiego 1994).

historical events and processes: revolutions (e.g., Dutch, English, and French) and wars (especially wars of religion and World War II) initiated and waged in order to realise or fight down a given concept.[49] These are examples of universalising factors that affected and penetrated all European societies and their cultures. Yet, it happened on a distinct scale and at a different depth. It should also be remembered that every society has its own unique openess to external factors which is one of its inherent features. It might be called a criterion of receptiveness and absorptive capacity. Further, very important are national experiences and social practices, especially exploits of elites regarding political and legal matters. Moreover, universalising factors collide with each other. Finally, there is a matter of more or less favourable objective terms (of various character: economic, political, etc.) under which the process went. Therefore, reception and its effects could be different.

Consequently, we have several national variations and interpretations of the Rule of Law. It leads to a question about 'a genuine European model of the Rule of Law'. Due to the factors and terms described above, it seems very unlikely that there is such a pan-European model. What Europeans are left with is to arrive at compromise as to the core elements of the concept (present in the European super-culture) and recognise a latitude of its practical implementation at a national level.

As a value,[50] the Rule of Law has an allocentric (socio-centric) and political character, as it directly refers to a group (a society) and its political organisation (the state and the law). Indeed, it is not a value in itself (autotelic). It is an instrumental, procedural, or institutional value, which serves to realise other values, such as freedom, equality, and security. Here we see that, indirectly, it serves egocentric values. Today it has a post-positivist (substantive) form; thus, a law-maker does not enjoy unlimited latitude.[51] Therefore it is not a *Gesetzesstaat*, but a *Rechtsstaat*, as a legal system should be axiologically underpinned.[52] This matter leads to a question: does it serve to realise cultural or socially recognised values (i.e., social axiology)? It is a complex and delicate matter, but the answer seems to be essential.

Surely the Rule of Law (as an instrumental value) serves to realise legal values. We must keep in mind that socio-cultural values and legal values[53] are not the

49 C Tilly, *European Revolutions 1492–1992* (Blackwell 1996).

50 H Rot, 'Praworządność jako wartość' in H Groszyk, ed, *Problemy teorii i filozofii prawa* (UMCS 1985) 241.

51 E-W Böckenförde, *Państwo prawa w jednoczącej się Europie* (Paweł Kaczorowski trans., ISP-PAN 2000).

52 S Oliwniak and H Święczkowska, ed, *Axiology of the Modern State under The Rule of Law: Selected Issues* (University of Białystok 2009).

53 T van den Brink, M Luchtman, and M Scholten, eds, *Sovereignty in the Shared Legal Order of the EU. Core Values of Regulation And Enforcement* (Intersentia Publishing Ltd. 2015); TE Davitt, *The Basic Values in Law. A Study of the Ethico-Legal Implications of Psychology and Anthropology* (American Philosophical Society, 1968); A Górski, *Wspólne wartości w prawie karnym a konstytucyjne przeszkody w ich realizacji. Rozważania o metodach i celu europeizacji*

same. The latter exists in a unique sphere: only in the law. They have a different origin: they are intentionally created and inserted into the law. As such, they have a different character: they manifest the state of affairs appreciated and desired by a lawgiver. They are polymorphous, as they assume various forms in the law, for example, general principles, institutional and procedural rules, bans or individual rights and obligations. They serve different purposes: a legal system requires coherence, both formal and material (including axiological), and legal values provide the latter. Consequently, they are crucial for further creation and application of the law. They also serve as a cornerstone for a community of citizens and their political identity, which primarily refers to constitutional values.[54]

In general, legal values should be counterparts of cultural values as to their merit. Consequently, the axiology of the law should fit social axiology and the law should serve to realise cultural values. This conformity has positive implications, as it strengthens the legitimacy and increases the efficiency of the law. However, several problems regarding that could be witnessed. Firstly, which values should be realised: officially declared (postulated) or realised in social practice (empirically perceived at a behavioural level). Moreover, legal values express a preference of a lawgiver, i.e., winners of political rivalry. Thereby, legal values are at least a subjective interpretation of cultural values. Sometimes they belong to an utterly subjective political vision of the winner, and they quite often have a form of a compromise reached between political options. Concluding, there is always a gap between cultural values (social axiology) and legal values (the law's axiology). There is no doubt that even a post-positivist concept of the Rule of Law will not guarantee avoidance of collisions between legal and cultural values.[55]

---

prawa karnego (Centrum Europejskie Natolin 2005); D Kiełczewski, 'Wartości ekologiczne w systemie polskiego prawa' (1996) III *Studia Ekonomiczne* 141; M Kordela, 'Zasada prawa jako normatywna postać wartości' (2006) LXVIII (1) *Ruch prawniczy, Ekonomiczny i Socjologiczny* 39; K Michałowska, *Niemajątkowe wartości życia rodzinnego w polskim prawie cywilnym* (CH Beck 2017); P Stein, J Shand, *Legal Values in Western Society* (Edinburgh University Press 1974); A Szafrański, *Prawo energetyczne: wartości i instrumenty ich realizacji* (CH Beck 2014); J Zimmermann, ed, *Wartości w prawie administracyjnym* (Lex a Wolters Kluwer business 2015).

54 V Ferreres Comella, *Constitutional Courts and Democratic Values. A European Perspective* (Yale University Press 2009); SE Gottlieb, ed, *Public Values in Constitutional Law* (University of Michigan Press 1993); S Grundmann, *Constitutional Values and European Contract Law* (Kluwer Law International 2008); R Piotrowski and A Szmyt, eds, *Trybunał Konstytucyjny na straży wartości konstytucyjnych, 1986–2016* (Wolters Kluwer 2017); P Winczorek, 'Aksjologiczne podstawy nowej konstytucji' (1988) 12 *Państwo i Prawo* 4; P Winczorek, 'Konstytucja i wartości' in Janusz Trzciński, ed, *Charakter i struktura norm konstytucji* (Wyd. Sejmowe 1997) 35; M Zieliński, 'Zasady i wartości konstytucyjne' in Andrzej Bałaban and Przemysław Mijal, eds, *Zasady naczelne Konstytucji RP z 2 kwietnia 1997 roku*, (Wydawnictwo Naukowe Uniwersytetu Szczecińskiego 2011) 21; Z Ziembiński, *Wartości konstytucyjne* (Wyd. Sejmowe 1993).

55 J Tasioulas, ed, *Law, Values and Social Practices* (Dartmouth 1997).

2.6. European values and European integration

Values prove their significance when they are realised in social practice. Because of this, they play a crucial role within a group. European values refer to coexistence and cooperation on a European scale. However, there is no European society, nation, *demos*, or *populus*. The biggest social group in Europe is a society with its national tradition, culture, economics, and political system. What we are left with are relations between societies, i.e., international relations, as every society possesses its political organisation, i.e., the state. European values should carry their function in this dimension.

The perception of an individual is always affected by his/her socio-cultural reality, as every person is a product of socialisation. Moreover, European societies are pluralistic and diversified, and their inhabitants have various political and religious orientations. As a result, many groups (not only societies) have many interpretations. Politicians and public officials have their political views and preferences, too. It makes the axiological debate across Europe even more severe. Undoubtedly, the European Union and Europe are not the same. However, the EU provides a basis for efficient debate and cooperation between European societies. Further, the Union possesses a unique enforcement mechanism that refers to achieved compromises and taken commitments. Thus, European values and the EU acquire a unique significance for each other. The invocation of the European heritage in the Union Treaty's Preamble[56] confirms that assumption.

There is a close correlation between the European super-culture (and its values) and the integration process. The former serves as a factual basis for European integration.[57] European solidarity (*la solidarité du fait*)[58] is based on common and shared values and interests. EU institutions are embodiments of the solidarity (therein values) and realise it in their practice. Thereby, loyalty towards the institutions is a necessary manifestation of European solidarity. It is a form of compliance with common values and interests. Moreover, the institutions play

56 The Treaty on European Union [henceforth: TEU] and the Treaty on the Functioning of the European Union [henceforth: TFEU], signed December 13th 2007 in Lisbon. Consolidated versions: [2012] OJ C 326/0001 – 0390.

57 *Héros, valeurs et symboles de l'Europe* (Université catholique de Louvain 1998).

58 Notion of solidarity was a central issue of solidarism, a political concept coined in the second half of 19th century and based on assumption formulated mainly by Emile Durkheim and Leon Duguit. French lawyer, politician, and prime minister Léon Bourgeois (1851–1925) transferred tenets of solidarism to an international level. Perspective of integrational solidarism was adapted by socialists and social democrats and provided a base for their European unity concepts. Léon Bourgeois, *Solidarité* (Colin 1896). This notion was also and propagated by another French lawyer and politician Robert Schuman (1886–1963), one of the European Founding Fathers. It was a corner stone of his integration concept realised in practice in the post-war reality. His interpretation of solidarity was based on precepts of Christianity, as he was a pious roman catholic and a Christian democrat. Robert Schuman, 'L'Europe est une communauté spirituelle et culturelle' [1953] Annuaire Européen 17.

the role of guardians of what is common and shared. They have been equipped with the necessary measures to serve this purpose.[59]

Simultaneously, integration provides favourable terms for further development of the European super-culture. Within the EU, members learn how to stay close and cooperate. It stimulates the gradual growth of mutual trust and solidarity, especially in the Council of the EU,[60] and reinforces a sense of togetherness. The number of common values will not increase, but their perceptions converge, and this is enough to make participants more prone to reach consent. The EU possesses its own values (Art. 2 TEU) that it should realise in its operations (Art. 3 TEU).[61] It must be stressed that these are not European values, as they are legal values set out in the Treaty. It cannot be different. The whole EU is a legal creation – the law is its substratum and the main measure it applies in practice. The Treaty values list has extended over time, adequately to the development of European institutionalised cooperation (within the Communities and the Union). Yet, the EU values are only a proportion of European values, as they refer to spheres in which the Union is operational (for example, there is no goodness, piety, or beauty). The EU values are at best legal counterparts of European values, or rather they are legal counterparts of a performed conceptualisation of European values. The EU values have a form of a compromise. This bargain was nailed among politicians and officials representing member states; thus, it is an elite and political vision. It could be presented in the following sequence: European values – their conceptualisation (compromise reached among national governments) – legal values of the EU – EU law and the national law.

The EU values have a practical meaning in a decision-making process, even though they do not represent any permanent hierarchy, just as they undergo divergent interpretations. Member State representatives have their own perception of values (ideologically or nationally motivated), scales of preferences, and interests (particular values). Therefore, discrepancies and controversies cannot be avoided in the future, so one can say that the Union's values are a smokescreen hiding dirty schemes, or that they are a fancy ornament without any meaning. However, the EU values form a framework or a point of reference for debates. They delimitate an area within which a compromise should be sought and found. Such a list of values facilitates negotiations, as it represents what all member states (i.e., politically organised societies) appreciate and hold in high esteem

59 A Jakab and D Kochenov, *The Enforcement of EU Law and Values. Ensuring Member States' Compliance* (Oxford University Press 2017).

60 P Ludlow, 'Diplomacy with Different Rules: Learning to Negotiate in the EEC' in M-T Bitsch, W Loth, R Poidevin, eds, *Institutions européennes et identités européennes* (Bruylant 1998) 241.

61 P Boniface, ed, *Quelles valeurs pour l'Union européenne?* (Presses universitaires de France 2004); L Potvin-Solis, ed, *Les valeurs communes dans l'Union européenne* (Bruylant 2014); J Sozański, *Ogólne zasady prawa a wartości Unii Europejskiej (po traktacie lizbońskim) – studium prawnoporównawcze* (Wyd. Adam Marszałek 2012); J Wilk and B Walczak, *Elementy aksjologii Unii Europejskiej* (Ignatianum-WAM 2009).

(Art. 2 TEU). It is an important ideological and psychological factor that shapes a sense of belongingness and a common identity. Finally, respect for EU values (as counterparts of European values) supports the legitimacy of the Union and its operations. Certainly, the EU values will not relieve politicians of arduous and laborious efforts to find a solution, as they do not substitute for talks and debates. They seem to be a measure that can make negotiations more efficient if only governments were willing to use it.

The EU values play an essential role in the interpretation of the law at both the European and national levels. A national law-maker should obey the Union's values and provide conformity of national legal values with the EU values. It is an example of the above-mentioned matter of axiological coherence of a legal system.

Last but not least, the Rule of Law is among fundamental EU values, which has a dual reason. On the one hand, this value is one of the European values. If the Union is based on the European heritage (TEU Preamble), the Rule of Law must be taken into consideration. On the other hand, the Union is a 'legal community' (*die Rechtsgemeinschaft*):[62] a legal creation acting by the law. The inefficiency of EU law reduces the Union to a theoretical structure. Thus, the Rule of Law is a *condition sine qua non* of its survival. It leaves no doubt why this value represents a unique practical significance within the EU and explains the origin of the above-mentioned mechanism of enforcement.

The crucial finding of this part is that a Member State is obliged to respect the EU values, including the Rule of Law. The reason is not their status as 'European', but its legal character. Naturally, a margin of interpretation is quite broad. Therefore, Member States should try to reach through debates a compromising formula of the EU values and obey it, while the institutions are entitled to protect and realise that shared view. Thus, the EU values have a significant role within the Union, which has even increased during turbulent periods of crises, as they are cornerstones of common identity.[63]

2.7. Conclusion

It seems that, in a public sphere, no one enjoys any unique right or privilege to speak of European values in the last resort, nor should anyone be deprived of such a right. There is no 'oracle' speaking the truth. Scientific approaches are not entirely reliable; they are susceptible to subjective interpretations and criticism. Even if science provided fully viable measures, a social practice still would not be determined by rational theories. Contrarily, it would still be ruled by myths and

62 This notion was applied by the first President of the European Commission Walter Hallstein to describe the EEC. W Hallstein, 'Die EWG – Eine Rechtsgemeinschaft (12 III 1962)' in Walter Hallstein, *Europäische Reden* (Deutsche Verlags-Anstalt 1979) 342.

63 M Cichocki, 'Od funkcjonalnej do substancjalnej europejskiej tożsamości – zmiana podejścia do roli europejskiej wartości' 71 (2) *Sprawy Międzynarodowe* (2018) 41.

stereotypes, just as it has been for centuries.[64] Scientific theories are too complicated, and do not provide simple answers to difficult questions. People prefer myths and stereotypes, as the latter offers a clear and sharp picture of the socio-cultural world. The reality is, in fact, far more complicated, but people do not want to become aware of that. The complexity of the world is intimately connected with scientific theories. On the other hand, when people believe in something, they bring it into being, and submit themselves to its representation. It is a predilection of human beings and, consequently, an unavoidable feature of our socio-cultural world, that makes it (i.e. our world) a *sui generis* reality. This is crucial when we estimate the potential and practical significance of scientific theories.

Therefore, European culture and values neither exist nor are binding, unless one assumes so, i.e., humans recognise their existence and form. Consequently, European values appear when we conceptualise them. Every conceptualisation is creative and aprioristic, as every person and group has particular preferences that cannot be rationally proved or disproved. Everyone is free to follow precepts of axiological idealism or to choose a model of European super-culture. Therefore, when the process of conceptualisation has ended, European values assume a particular shape and merit. Everyone is allowed to perform such an operation. Consequently, everyone can have their vision of European values, which comprises their array, meanings, form, and essence (nature). Finally, every society and every social group has its own interpretation.

European societies and cultures have similarities, but still, there are numerous dissimilarities[65] that should not be disregarded. European societies and their cultures are still ethnocentric, even though it is a modern and moderate form of ethnocentrism.[66] Europeans cherish their national traditions with pleasure and pride. Yet, they are forbidden to treat others with hatred and disdain. Controversies and arguments between societies are allowed, but they must be solved without the use of force.

Therefore, European culture and European values do not exist in a form that national cultures and national values do. What exists and operates is the European

64 I Błocian and E Kwiatkowska, eds, *Współczesna obecność mitu* (Studia mitoznawcze. vol. 2, Wyd. Adam Marszałek 2012); R Parton Howells, *The Interpretation of Popular Culture as Modern Myth* (University of Cambridge 1994); L Kołakowski, *Obecność mitu* (Prószyński i S-ka 2005); M Demetri, *Modern Myths and the Realities behind Them* (Quiller 1997); R Marszałek, *Mythos redivivus* (Scholar 2010); M Midgley, *Science as Salvation. A Modern Myth and its Meaning* (Routledge 1994); A Wickham, *The Black Book of Modern Myths* (e-book, Cornerstone Digital 2011).

65 M Koźmiński, ed, *Cywilizacja europejska. Różnorodność i podziały* (Towarzystwo Autorów i Wydawców Prac Naukowych Universitas 2014).

66 G Baumann, *The Multicultural Riddle. Rethinking National, Ethnic, and Religious Identities* (Routledge 1999); M Buchowski, ed, *Oblicza zmiany: etnologia a współczesne transformacje społeczno-kulturowe* (Wyd. ECO-PSO 1996); T Hylland Eriksen, *Ethnicity and Nationalism. Anthropological Perspectives* (3rd ed, Pluto Press 2010); M Szmeja, ed, *Etniczność. O przemianach społeczeństw narodowych*, (Nomos 2008); Maykel Verkuyten, *The Social Psychology of Ethnic Identity* (Psychology Press 2005).

super-culture with European values. It is a scientific model providing a tool for conceptualisation and analyses. It takes into consideration the rationally perceived *status quo*, instead of pious wishes and political or religious motivations. The super-culture and its values express our European sense of unity, readiness and will to cooperate. It also provides a cultural basis for common actions. However, it changes and is susceptible to creative interpretations. Unarguably, the Rule of Law is one of the European values, and thus, it has different interpretations and modes of implementations. European values and EU values are not the same. The Union does not possess a monopoly on the formulation and interpretation of European values. However, the latter gains a unique significance in European integration. What plays a crucial role here is size, the scale of operation, the practical implications of the process, and its contemporary institutional structure, i.e., the EU. Nonetheless, a hiatus separating the merit of European values and the EU's values is unavoidable, as every conceptualisation is creative. The Rule of Law is one of the legal values of the Union. Consequently, EU members must obey what was collectively decided among them. It includes the EU's interpretation of European values and various attempts of their implementation. In practice, it means obedience towards EU law and institutions.

The last and crucial matter that requires a clear answer is as follows: is the Rule of Law a common European value? Are we allowed to reckon it among what we feel is our common continental heritage? Admittedly and beyond any doubt, yes, it is. Nevertheless, such a clear-cut answer, although satisfying and tempting due to its unequivocalness, requires a reservation.

As presented above, all elements of socio-cultural reality (including values) must be conceptualised (as to their essence and merit) – otherwise, they neither assume their existence nor affect individuals. Moreover, by this procedure, values acquire (or rather, they are granted by groups and individuals acting unconsciously) various forms and merit. To put it briefly: incontestable existence does not eliminate divergent or even contradictory interpretations. Values even undergo permanent reinterpretations and therefore are always 'in the making' – never complete.

When estimating the Rule of Law as one of the European values, this peculiar feature of values should be linked with a phenomenon of 'universalising factors'. We must not forget that various European communities (societies, nations, etc.) had a different past. Thus, the perception of the 'true' Rule of Law concept varies across Europe, and no one rejects or even questions it. It merely means differences in meaning, significance, and ways of realisation. This diversity of perceptions is unavoidable and somehow natural. We cannot declare that a given interpretation of the Rule of Law is worse or better unless we exchange a scientific approach for a political one.

Divergences and contradictions are one aspect of the matter. The other, which corresponds with the essence of super-culture, is similarity. Universalising factors make various socio-cultural realities grow similar features. Furthermore, divergent perceptions and interpretations do not eliminate a process of gradual convergence of some elements. Contrarily: it occurs spontaneously, especially under favourable terms. Interactions and transactions between societies are crucial stimulating factors. However, it all depends upon the intentions and mutual attitudes of members of groups (especially their elites), as not every interaction implicates positive effects or is desired. The European status quo overtly shows that national perceptions may surprisingly converge with the passing of time. Nevertheless, they will never become identical.

Peaceful coexistence and fruitful cooperation may intensify this process. Participants may try to reach compromise as to essential matters of common concern, such as values, the Rule of Law, its meaning, elements, and forms of implementation, and they can formalise and protect it – just as it has been done in the case of the EU. Neither societies nor their governments are, however, compelled to partake in such a 'common-semantics-forming' endeavour. Participation is a matter of both idealism and realism, combining a sense of shared heritage and current interests. Outsiders are not interested in a close cooperation (and its profits), but they will leave their options open, and may cherish and realise in practice their own interpretation of the Rule of Law (as both a value and a political concept). Insiders, regardless of why they have joined the cooperation, will gain benefits and shall obey the compromise and change their practices accordingly (both in external relations and at home).

Therefore, the above-mentioned coexistence of national (socio-cultural) and international (super-cultural) versions of the Rule of Law is possible, but it requires conscious decisions regarding a given country's politics. It ensures that a national perception and practice of the Rule of Law will not infringe on the compromising formula, which means the following: we agreed to keep talking and seeking common interpretations that are acceptable for all of us; national governments must not neglect to react and cooperate whenever it is needed.

It shall be noted that the eagerness to arrive at a 'value-and-semantics-compromise' implies that a given society is ready to change its cultural patterns and practices. Such readiness might be understood as a precondition for seeking a compromise. Undoubtedly, a government's decision to participate in talks tending to a compromise is political in character, but it must be underpinned by an awareness of moods in a country. Otherwise, it may implicate many difficulties in the future.

Although for a scientist, national culture and super-culture are both cultural formations, a statistically minded person would perceive the former as more valuable. Super-culture and its elements might seem inferior or even dangerous. We may take it for granted that ultimate axiological absolutism and the stereotyped 'three pillars approach' make it far more difficult to agree to any change, as existing cultural formations are perceived as 'natural', 'decreed', or 'sacrosanct', and should not be shaped by deliberately undertaken human actions. Consequently, an 'artificial' compromise must seem less significant than national patterns and practices. Moreover, a compromise could be even understood as a disgraceful betrayal of absolutely good values. Therefore, not only political or economic views play a role in the origin of a universal formula of the Rule of Law. What seems even more important are the elements of human psychology shaped by collective ways of thinking and a collective perception of the world. Consequently, a sheer acceptance of the Rule of Law (as a value) in a given society is not enough. An attitude towards other societies' visions of the world, as well as an openness for novelty, are equally important to formulate and respect a common version of the Rule of Law.

Whoever is a partaker in cooperation must play the game. If they disregard the compromise (similarly to when they do not comply with formal decisions implementing it), they show disloyalty towards neighbours and partners. A positive attitude to the compromise and its active acceptance seems a necessary condition of participation; it follows that those for whom such a compromise has become unbearable (or never has been entirely acceptable) should leave a community.

The final conclusion is that the Rule of Law is a European value. Nevertheless, it will not have a precise and accurate pan-European meaning unless we have reached compromise on its essence, elements, and forms of implementation. It is undoubtedly difficult and shall be followed by an ongoing process of further negotiations, which will most probably never guarantee the elimination of national differences.

Bibliography

Primary sources

Konstytucja Rzeczpospolitej Polskiej (Constitution of the Republic of Poland). *Official Journal* (1997), No. 78, pos. 483.

The Treaty on European Union and the Treaty on the functioning of the European Union. *Consolidated Versions* (2012) OJ C 326/0001 – 0390.

Secondary sources

Hans Albert, *Europa i okiełznanie władzy. Szczególna droga Europy do społeczeństwa otwartego* (Tadeusz Zatorski trans., Nomos 1998).

Sandrine Alexandre, *Évaluation et contre-pouvoir. Portée éthique et politique du jugement de valeur dans le stoïcisme romain* (Jérôme Millon 2014).

Richard T Allen, *The structure of value* (Avebury 1993).

Jessica Almqvist, *Human rights, culture and the Rule of Law* (Hart 2005).

Robin Attfield, *A theory of value and obligation* (Croom Helm 1987).

W Arts, Jacques Hagenaars, and Loek Halman, eds, *The cultural diversity of European Unity. Findings, explanations and reflections from the European values study* (Brill 2003).

W Arts and Loek Halman, eds, *European values at the turn of the millennium* (Brill 2004).

W Arts and Loek Halman, eds, *Value contrasts and consensus in present-day Europe. Painting Europe's moral landscapes* (Brill 2013).

Robert Audi, *Moral value and human diversity* (Oxford University Press 2008).

Sémir Badir, Dondero Maria Giulia, and Provenzano François, eds, *Épistémologie et éthique de la valeur. Du sémiotique au rhétorique (et retour)* (Presses universitaires de Franche-Comté 2011).

Archie J Bahm, *Axiology. The science of values* (Rodopi 1993).

Jerzy Bartmiński and Monika Grzeszczak, 'Jak rekonstruować kanon wartości narodowych i europejskich?', 26 *Etnolingwistyka* (2014).

Zygmunt Bauman, *Europa: niedokończona przygoda* (Tomasz Kunz trans., Wyd. Literackie 2007).

Gerd Baumann, *The multicultural riddle. Rethinking national, ethnic, and religious identities* (Routledge 1999).

Lynda S Bell, Andrew J Nathan, and Ilan Peleg, eds, *Negotiating culture and human rights* (Columbia University Press 2001).

Ruth Benedict, *Patterns of culture* (Routledge 2019).

Christian Bermes, Wolfhart Henckmann, and Heinz Leonardy, eds, *Person und Wert. Schelers ‚Formalismus'* (Alber 2000).

Ewa Bieńkowska, *Spór o dziedzictwo europejskie: między świętym i świeckim* (W.A.B. 1999).

Ilona Błocian and Ewa Kwiatkowska, eds, *Współczesna obecność mitu* (Studia mitoznawcze. vol. 2, Wyd. Adam Marszałek 2012).

Ernst-Wolfgang Böckenförde, *Państwo prawa w jednoczącej się Europie* (Paweł Kaczorowski trans., ISP-PAN 2000).

Pascal Boniface, ed, *Quelles valeurs pour l'Union européenne?* (Presses universitaires de France 2004).

Henryk Borowski, *Potrzeby i wartości* (Wyd. Politechniki Lubelskiej 1999).

Henryk Borowski, *Wartość jako przeżycie. Wprowadzenie do aksjologii* (Wyd. UMCS 1992).

Leon Bourgeois, *Solidarité* (Colin 1896).

Jan Bransen and Marc Slors, eds, *The problematic reality of values* (Van Gorcum 1996).

Pierre Bréchon and Frédéric Gonthie, eds, *Atlas des européens. Valeurs communes et différences nationalesed* (Colin 2013).

Ton van den Brink, Michiel Luchtman, and Miroslava Scholten, eds, *Sovereignty in the shared legal order of the EU. Core values of regulation and enforcement* (Intersentia Publishing Ltd. 2015).

Krzysztof Jarosław Brozi, *Antropologia wartości. Ujęcie metodologiczne* (Wyd. UMCS 1989).

Krzysztof Jarosław Brozi, *Antropologia wartości. Kategoria standardu kulturowego w badaniach nad wartościami* (Wyd. UMCS 1994).

Andrzej Bryk, *Konstytucjonalizm. Od starożytnego Izraela do liberalnego konstytucjonalizmu amerykańskiego* (Wyd. UJ 2013).

Piotr Brzozowski, *Wzorcowa hierarchia wartości: polska, europejska czy uniwersalna? Psychologiczne badania empiryczne* (Wyd. UMCS 2007).

Michał Buchowski, ed, *Oblicza zmiany: etnologia a współczesne transformacje społeczno-kulturowe* (Wyd. ECO-PSO 1996).

Beatrice Centi and Wolfgang Huemer, eds, *Values and ontology. Problems and perspectives* (Ontos 2009).

Chandana Chakrabarti and Richard Vulich, eds, *Paradigms and perspectives on value and reality* (Cambridge Scholars Publishing 2014).

Timothy Chappell, ed, *Values and virtues. Aristotelianism in contemporary ethics* (Clarendon Press 2006).

Marek Cichocki, 'Od funkcjonalnej do substancjalnej europejskiej tożsamości – zmiana podejścia do roli europejskiej wartości', 71 (2) *Sprawy Międzynarodowe* (2018).

Jan Cieluch, *Kształtowanie się systemu wartości: od dzieciństwa do wczesnej dorosłości* (LiberiLibri 2013).

Raphael Cohen-Almagor, ed, *Liberal democracy and the limits of tolerance. Essays in honor and memory of Yitzhak Rabin* (University of Michigan Press 2000).

Frank Cowell, *Values in human society. The contribution of Pitirim A. Sorokin to sociology* (Porter Sargent 1970).

Janusz Czapiński, *Wartościowanie – zjawisko inklinacji pozytywnej* (Ossolineum 1985).

Thomas E Davitt, *The basic values in law. A study of the ethico-legal implications of psychology and anthropology* (American Philosophical Society 1968).

John Deigh, *Emotions, values, and the law* (Oxford University Press 2011).

Young Pamela Dickey, Heather Shipley, and Tracy J Trothen, eds, *Religion and sexuality. Diversity and the limits of tolerance* (UBC Press 2015).

Anne-Marie Dillens, ed, *Le pluralisme des valeurs. Entre particulier et universel* (Publications des Facultés universitaires Saint-Louis 2003).

Paul Dukes, ed, *Frontiers of European culture* (with an introduction by Mike Hepworth, E Mellen 1996).

Seweryn Dziamski, *Aksjologia. Wstęp do filozofii wartości* (Wyd. Naukowe UAM 1997).

Seweryn Dziamski, ed, *Z teorii i historii wartości* (Nakom 1990).

Rem B Edwards, *The essentials of formal axiology* (University Press of America 2010).

Kevin C Elliott, *A tapestry of values. An introduction to values in science* (Oxford University Press 2017).

Thomas Hylland Eriksen, *Ethnicity and nationalism. Anthropological perspectives* (3rd ed, Pluto Press 2010).

Comella Victor Ferreres, *Constitutional courts and democratic values. A European perspective* (Yale University Press 2009).

Ronald Fischer, *Personality, values, culture. An evolutionary approach* (Cambridge University Press 2018).

Matthew Caleb Flamm, Lachs John, and Skowroński Krzysztof Piotr, eds, *American and European values. Contemporary philosophical perspectives* (Cambridge Scholars Publishing 2008).

Tadeusz Frąckowiak and Modrzewski Jerzy, eds, *Socjalizacja a wartości* (ERUDITUS 1995).

Lawrence M Friedman, *The human rights culture. A study in history and context* (Quid Pro Books 2011).

Günter Fröhlich, *Form und Wert. Die komplementären Begründungen der Ethik bei Immanuel Kant, Max Scheler und Edmund Husserl* (Königshausen and Neumann 2011).

Hans-Georg Gadamer, *Dziedzictwo Europy* (Andrzej Przyłębski trans., SPACJA 1992).

Janina Gajda, *Gdy rozpadły się ściany świata. Teorie wartości w filozofii hellenistycznej* (Wyd. Uniwersytetu Wrocławskiego 1995).

Maciej Giertych, *European values* (Maciej Giertych 2007).

Maciej Giertych, *Quo vadis Europa* (Maciej Giertych 2009).

Aleksander Gieysztor, *O dziedzictwie kultury* (Towarzystwo Opieki nad Zabytkami 2000).

Adam Górski, *Wspólne wartości w prawie karnym a konstytucyjne przeszkody w ich realizacji. Rozważania o metodach i celu europeizacji prawa karnego* (Centrum Europejskie Natolin 2005).

Stephen E Gottlieb, ed, *Public values in constitutional law* (University of Michigan Press 1993).
David Graeber, *Toward an anthropological theory of value. The false coin of our own dreams* (Palgrave 2001).
Paul Grice, *The conception of value* (with an introduction by Judith Baker, Clarendon 1991).
Stefan Grundmann, *Constitutional values and European contract law* (Kluwer Law International 2008).
Czesław Gryko, *Integralna teoria kultury Pitirima Sorokina* (Wyd. UMCS 2000).
Anna Grzegorczyk, *Obecność wartości* (Wyd. Poznańskie 2010).
Everett W Hall, *What is value? An essay in philosophical analysis* (Routledge 2000).
Walter Hallstein, 'Die EWG – Eine Rechtsgemeinschaft (12 III 1962)', in Walter Hallstein, ed, *Europäische Reden* (Deutsche Verlags-Anstalt 1979).
Loek Halman, Inge Sieben, and Marga van Zundert, eds, *Atlas of European values. Trends and traditions at the turn of the century* (Koninklijke Brill 2012).
J Mark Halstead and Monica J Taylor, *The development of values, attitudes and personal qualities* (National Foundation for Educational Research 2000).
Sven Ove Hansson, *The structure of values and norms* (Cambridge University Press 2001).
Gilbert Harman, *Explaining value and other essays in moral philosophy* (Clarendon 2000).
Judith Rich Harris, *The nurture assumption. Why children turn out the way they do* (Free Press 2009).
Michael Hechter and Christine Horne, eds, *Theories of social order* (Stanford Social Sciences 2009).
Grzegorz Hetman, *Uczucia i wartości według Jana Mazurkiewicza* (ZPH Motor 1995).
Iwao Hirose and Jonas Olson, eds, *The Oxford handbook of value theory* (Oxford University Press 2015).
Lesław Hostyński, *Utilitarian values* (Wyd. Adam Marszałek 2009).
Richard Parton Howells, *The Interpretation of Popular Culture as Modern Myth* (University of Cambridge 1994).
Patrick Æ Hutchings, *Kant on absolute value. A critical examination of certain key notions in Kant's 'groundwork of the metaphysic of morals' and of his ontology of personal value* (Allen and Unwin 1972).
Hubert Izdebski, *Doktryny polityczno-prawne. Fundamenty współczesnych państw* (Wolters Kluwer 2017).
András Jakab and Dimitry Kochenov, *The enforcement of EU law and values. Ensuring member states' compliance* (Oxford University Press 2017).
Hans Joas, *Die Entstehung der Werte* (Suhrkamp 1997).
Terry G Jordan, *The European culture area. A systematic geography* (3rd ed, HarperCollins College 1996).
Małgorzata Karwatowska and Adam Siwiec, eds, *O wartościach i wartościowaniu: historia – literatura – edukacja* (Perfekta info 2012).
Dariusz Kiełczewski, 'Wartości ekologiczne w systemie polskiego prawa', 41 III *Studia Ekonomiczne* (1996).
Gerhard Kloska, *Pojęcia, teorie i badanie wartości w naukach społecznych* (PWN 1982).
Andrzej Kocikowski, ed, *W kręgu aksjologii. Problematyka teoretyczna, historyczna i teoriopoznawcza* (Nakom 1990), vol. I–II.

Leszek Kołakowski, *Obecność mitu* (Prószyński i S-ka 2005).

Jadwiga Koralewicz, ed, *The European value system* (CCP IPS PAN 1999).

Marzena Kordela, 'Zasada prawa jako normatywna postać wartości', LXVIII (1) *Ruch prawniczy, Ekonomiczny i Socjologiczny* (2006).

Stanisław Kowalczyk, *Człowiek w poszukiwaniu wartości: elementy aksjologii personalistycznej* (Wyd. KUL 2016).

Stanisław Kowalczyk, *Współczesny kryzys ideowo-aksjologiczny* (Wyd. KUL 2011).

Krzysztof Kowalski, *Europa: mity, modele, symbole* (Międzynarodowe Centrum Kultury 2002).

Krzysztof Kowalski, *O istocie dziedzictwa europejskiego: rozważania* (Międzynarodowe Centrum Kultury 2013).

Maciej Koźmiński, ed, *Cywilizacja europejska. Różnorodność i podziały* (Towarzystwo Autorów i Wydawców Prac Naukowych Universitas 2014).

Jan Krucina, *Wznoszenie wartości podstawowych* (TUM Wyd. Wrocławskiej Księgarni Archidiecezjalnej 2007).

Courtney Krystyna Kujawińska, Łukowska Maria, and Williams Evan, eds, *European culture in diversity* (Cambridge Scholars Publishing 2011).

Joel J Kupperman, *Value ... and what follows* (Oxford University Press 1999).

Ramon M Lemos, *The nature of value. Axiological investigations* (University Press of Florida 1995).

Dorota Leonarska and Krzysztof Wielecki, 'Pitirim Sorokin i jego absencja w polskiej socjologii', 13 *Roczniki Historii Socjologii* (2013) 47.

Józef Lipiec, ed, *Człowiek i świat wartości* (Krajowa Agencja Wydawnicza 1982).

Józef Lipiec, ed, *Istnienie i poznanie wartości* (Eureka 1991).

Józef Lipiec, ed, *Ontologia wartości* (UMCS 1990).

Józef Lipiec, ed, *Rozdroża wartości. Prace z ontologii i epistemologii wartości* (Wyd. UJ 1992).

Józef Lipiec, *Świat wartości. Wprowadzenie do aksjologii* (AWA 2001).

Franciszek Jan Lis, *Wartości w kształtowaniu motywacji i organizacji życia społecznego* (Wydawnictwa Uczelniane 1996).

Eric B Litwack, *Wittgenstein and value. The quest for meaning* (Continuum 2009).

Piers Ludlow, 'Diplomacy with different rules: Learning to negotiate in the EEC', in Marie-Thérèse Bitsch, Wilfried Loth, and Raymond Poidevin, eds, *Institutions européennes et identités européennes* (Bruylant 1998).

Peter Machamer and Gereon Wolters, eds, *Science, values, and objectivity* (University of Pittsburgh Press 2004).

JanMalarczyk, ed, *Doktrynalne podstawy demokracji konstytucyjnej* (Wyd. UMCS 1996).

Demetri Marchessini, *Modern myths and the realities behind them* (Quiller 1997).

Stanisław Marczuk, *Badanie wartości w socjologii: teoria i empiria* (Wyd. WSP Rzeszów 1988).

Robert Marszałek, *Mythos redivivus* (Scholar 2010).

Abraham Maslow, *Motivation and personality* (2nd ed, New Harper 1970).

Gordon Mathews, *Global culture/individual identity. Searching for home in the cultural supermarket* (Routledge 2005).

Czesław Matusewicz, *Psychologia wartości* (PWN 1975).

Tomasz Mazur, *Kapryśni bogowie Sokratesa. Człowiek i świat wartości w tradycji filozofii zachodnie* (Wyd. Marek Derewiecki 2008).

Piotr Mazurkiewicz, *Europeizacja Europy. Tożsamość kulturowa Europy w kontekście procesów integracji* (UKSW 2001).

Wacław Mejbaum, *Człowiek w świecie wartości* (Uniwersytet Szczeciński 2000).
Kinga Michałowska, *Niemajątkowe wartości życia rodzinnego w polskim prawie cywilnym* (CH Beck 2017).
Mary Midgley, *Science as salvation. A modern myth and its meaning* (Routledge 1994).
Kazimierz Mikulicki, *Wartości trwałe* (Alleluja 2004).
Maria Misztal, *Problematyka wartości w socjologii* (PWN 1980).
Aldona Małgorzata Molesztak, *Człowiek, kultura, uczestnictwo* (Wyd. UKW 2015).
Evanghélos Moutsopoulos, *L'univers des valeurs, univers de l'homme. Recherches axiologiques* (Académie d'Athènes, Centre de recherche sur la philosophie grecque 2005).
Zdzisław Najder, *Wartości i oceny* (Wyd. Naukowe PWN 2015).
Krystyna Najder-Stefaniak, *O działaniu i wartościowaniu* (Wyd. SGGW-AR 1986).
Tomasz Nawrocki and Wojciech Świątkiewicz, eds, *Ład społeczny i jego przedstawienia* (Wyd. Uniwersytetu Śląskiego 2016).
Graham Nerlich, *Values and valuing. Speculations on the ethical life of persons* (Clarendon Press 1989).
Andrzej Niemczuk, *Filozofia dobra przed powstaniem aksjologii. Relacjonistyczne próby przezwyciężenia trudności obiektywizmu i subiektywizmu* (Wyd. UMCS 1994).
Kazimierz Obuchowski, *Galaktyka potrzeb. Psychologia dążeń ludzkich* (Zysk i S-ka 2000).
Sławomir Oliwniak and Halina Święczkowska, eds, *Axiology of the modern state under the Rule of Law: Selected issues* (University of Białystok 2009).
Piotr Orlik, ed, *Ku źródłom wartości* (Wyd. Naukowe Instytutu Filozofii UAM 2008).
Francesco Orsi, *Value theory* (Bloomsbury Academic 2015).
Stanisław Ossowski, *Więź społeczna i dziedzictwo* (PWN 1966).
Lech Ostasz, *Czym są wartości? Zarys aksjologii* (Wyd. UWM 2009).
Bernt Österman, *Value and requirements. An enquiry concerning the origin of value* (Avebury 1995).
Krystyna Ostrowska, *Wokół rozwoju osobowości i systemu wartości* (Centrum Metodyczne Pomocy Psychologiczno-Pedagogicznej MEN 1998).
Michèle Pagès, Ramognino Nicole, and Soldini Fabienne, eds, *L'énigme de la valeur. Les paradoxes de son observation sociologique* (Publications de l'Université de Provence 2010).
Talcott Parsons, *On institutions and social evolution* (University of Chicago Press 1982).
Talcott Parsons, *The social system* (Taylor & Francis 2005).
Roy W Perrett, ed, *Theory of value* (Garland 2001).
Józef Pieter, *Oceny i wartości* (Śląsk 1973).
Jerzy Pilikowski, *Podróż w świat Europy* (WAM 2011).
Steven Pinker, *The blank slate. The modern denial of human nature* (Penguin 2003).
Ryszard Piotrowski and Andrzej Szmyt, eds, *Trybunał Konstytucyjny na straży wartości konstytucyjnych, 1986–2016* (Wolters Kluwer 2017).
Ryszard Adam Podgórski, *Homo sociologicus w strukturze wartości* (Fosze 2008).
Leon Pomeroy, *The new science of axiological psychology* (Rem B. Edwards, ed, Rodopi 2005).
Michał Poradowski, *Dzieje cywilizacji europejskiej* (Nortom 2007).
Laurence Potvin-Solis, ed, *Les valeurs communes dans l'Union européenne* (Bruylant 2014).
Gerard Radnitzky and Hardy Bouillon, eds, *Values and the social order* (Avebury 1995).

Paul Ramsey, *The truth of value. A defense of moral and literary judgment* (Humanities Press 1985).
Boudon Raymond, *Le sens des valeurs* (Presses universitaires de France 1999).
Peter Rietbergen, *Europa. Dzieje kultury* (Robert Bartołd trans., Książka i Wiedza 2001).
Sabine Roeser and Cain Todd, eds, *Emotion and value* (Oxford University Press 2014).
Toni Rønnow-Rasmussen, *Personal value* (Oxford University Press 2011).
Henryk Rot, ed, *Demokratyczne państwo prawne (aksjologia, struktura, funkcje)* (Wyd. Uniwersytetu Wrocławskiego 1994).
Henryk Rot, 'Praworządność jako wartość', in Henryk Groszyk, ed, *Problemy teorii i filozofii prawa* (UMCS 1985).
Andrew Sayer, *Why things matter to people. Social science, values and ethical life* (Cambridge University Press 2011).
Jacek Schindler and Marcin Stabrowski, eds, *Spory o wartości. Od praktyki do teorii interpretacji aksjologicznych* (Chronicon 2016).
Robert Schuman, 'L'Europe est une communauté spirituelle et culturelle', 17 *Annuaire Européen* (1953).
Stephen Schwarz and Fritz Wenisch, eds, *Values and human experience. Essays in honor of the memory of Balduin Schwarz* (Peter Lang 1999).
Clifford Sharp, *The origin and evolution of human values* (2nd rev. ed, DP Press 2002).
Andrzej Siemaszko, *Granice tolerancji. O teoriach zachowań dewiacyjnych* (Wyd. Naukowe PWN 1993).
Remigiusz Sobański, *Europa obojga prawa* (Księgarnia św. Jacka-Wydział Teologiczny Uniwersytetu Śląskiego 2006).
Pitirim A Sorokin, *Social and cultural dynamics* (American Book Co. 1937) vol. IV.
Jarosław Sozański, *Ogólne zasady prawa a wartości Unii Europejskiej (po traktacie lizbońskim) – studium prawnoporównawcze* (Wyd. Adam Marszałek 2012).
Peter Stein and John Shand, *Legal values in western society* (Edinburgh University Press 1974).
Simon Stewart, *A sociology of culture, taste and value* (Palgrave Macmillan 2014).
Michael Stocker, *Plural and conflicting values* (Clarendon Press 1992).
Michael Strauss, *Volition and valuation. A phenomenology of sensational, emotional, and conceptual values* (University Press of America 1999).
Władysław Stróżewski, ed, *Studia z teorii poznania i filozofii wartości* (Ossolineum 1978).
Władysław Stróżewski, *W kręgu wartości* (Znak 1992).
Adam Szafrański, *Prawo energetyczne: wartości i instrumenty ich realizacji* (CH Beck 2014).
MariaSzmeja, ed, *Etniczność. O przemianach społeczeństw narodowych* (Nomos 2008).
Adolf E Szołtysek, *Filozofia człowieka: biologiczny rozwój a kulturowe kształtowanie* (Oficyna Wydawnicza Impuls 2015).
Cezary T Szyjko, ed, *Prawa człowieka fundamentem Europy wartości* (Wyd. MM 2014).
Jan Szymczyk, *Odkrywanie wartości. Z problematyki socjologiczno-aksjologiczne* (Polihymnia 2004).
Abdulkadir Tanrikulu, *Human values, moral values and social value judgements* (AuthorHouse 2016).
Christine Tappolet, *Emotions, value, and agency* (Oxford University Press 2016).
John Tasioulas, ed, *Law, values and social practices* (Dartmouth 1997).

Charles Tilly, *European revolutions 1492–1992* (Blackwell 1996).

Beata Trochimska-Kubacka, *Absolutyzm aksjologiczny. Rekonstrukcja oparta na aksjologii Rickerta, Schelera i Hartmanna* (Wyd. Uniwersytetu Wrocławskiego 1999).

Kazimierz Trojan, *Potrzeby psychiczne i wartości oraz ich implikacje religijne* (WAM 2001).

Jonathan Turner, *The institutional order* (Longman 1997).

Andrzej Tyszka, *Kultura jest kultem wartości: aksjologia społeczna. Studia i szkice* (Wyd. Antyk-Marcin Dybowski 1999).

Andrzej Tyszka, *Uczestnictwo w kulturze. O różnorodności stylów życia* (PWN 1971).

Branco Angela Uchoa and Jaan Valsiner, *Cultural psychology of human values* (Information Age Pub. 2012).

Peter Unger, *Identity, consciousness and value* (Oxford University Press 1992).

Maykel Verkuyten, *The social psychology of ethnic identity* (Psychology Press 2005).

Marek Wichrowski, 'Pitirim A Sorokin. Wartości w supersystemach społeczno-kulturowych', in Zdzisław Jerzy Czarnecki and Stefan Symotiuk, eds, *Historyczna dynamika wartości. Studia nad aksjologicznymi interpretacjami dziejów* (Wyd. UMCS 1990).

Alasdair Wickham, *The black book of modern myths* (e-book, Cornerstone Digital 2011).

Hans-Peter Widmaier, *Studia o ładzie społecznym* (Tadeusz Kowalak trans., Fundacja im. F Eberta 1995).

David Wiggins, *Needs, values, truth. Essays in the philosophy of value* (3rd amended ed, Clarendon 2002).

Richard A Wilson, ed, *Human rights, culture and context. Anthropological perspectives* (Pluto Press 1997).

Janina Wilk and Barbara Walczak, *Elementy aksjologii Unii Europejskiej* (Ignatianum-WAM 2009).

Piotr Winczorek, 'Aksjologiczne podstawy nowej konstytucji', 12 *Państwo i Prawo* (1988) 4.

Piotr Winczorek, 'Konstytucja i wartości', in Janusz Trzciński, ed, *Charakter i struktura norm konstytucji* (Wyd. Sejmowe 1997).

Józef Wojtanowicz, *Europejska przestrzeń geograficzno-kulturowa* (Wyd. UMCS 2008).

Elena Zamfir and Filomena Maggino, eds, *The European culture for human rights. The right to happiness* (Cambridge Scholars Publishing 2013).

Krystyna Zamiara, ed, *Wartości w świecie osobowym* (Wyd. Naukowe UAM 1999).

Adam Zamojski, *Tożsamość cywilizacji europejskiej: geneza, kompleks konstytuujący i kierunki transformacji* (Wyd. Uniwersytetu Jana Kochanowskiego 2015).

Maciej Zieliński, 'Zasady i wartości konstytucyjne', in Andrzej Bałaban and Przemysław Mijal, eds, *Zasady naczelne Konstytucji RP z 2 kwietnia 1997 roku* (Wydawnictwo Naukowe Uniwersytetu Szczecińskiego 2011).

Zygmunt Ziembiński, *Wartości konstytucyjne* (Wyd. Sejmowe 1993).

Anton C Zijderveld, *Rickert's relevance. The ontological nature and epistemological functions of values* (Brill 2006).

Jan Zimmermann, ed, *Wartości w prawie administracyjnym* (Lex a Wolters Kluwer business 2015).

Jan Zimny and Roman Król, eds, *Wartości drogą ku wzrastaniu* (KUL 2012).

Kazimierz Żygulski, *Wartości i wzory kultury. Rozważania socjologa* (Instytut Wydawniczy CRZZ 1975).

3 'Where the laws do not govern, there is no constitution' – On the relationship between the Rule of Law and constitutionalism

Wojciech Włoch

3.1. Introduction

It seems almost hopeless to attempt to write about the principle of the Rule of Law. The long history of analysing and presenting this idea, clarifying the concepts, and building up the principle makes it possible for us to validly assume that everything has already been said since the stances were taken and the arguments formulated. In this essay, I do not wish to state anything new on the subject. On the contrary, I would like to suggest that one should go back to Aristotle and look at the principle of the Rule of Law from the perspective of his 'Politics'. The return to Aristotle's work was inspired in two different ways. Firstly, the work is undoubtedly the foundation for reflection on the Rule of Law and research on political systems; and secondly, the work is so time-distant from all the contemporary debates and so general in its meaning that it may serve as a point of reference for concepts coming from times closer to our time. The main thesis of this chapter is reflected in the quote from Aristotle, cited in the title: 'where the laws do not govern, there is no constitution'.[1] The implementation of the Rule of Law requires having a certain concept of what the law should be like, and hence one needs to formulate a conception of justice. Modern constitutionalism is a certain implementation of the principle of the Rule of Law if we assume that it is an expression of a specific concept of a just system.

In the first part of the essay, I shall make an abstract (that is, the one not referring to a specific type of a constitutional system) reconstruction of the Rule of Law included in Aristotle's 'Politics'. In the second part, I wish to compare Aristotle's concept and its relation to a formal understanding of the Rule of Law. In the third part, I shall consider the relationship between the Rule of Law and modern constitutionalism. In the fourth part, I am going to highlight that the implementation of both the principle of the Rule of Law and the principles of constitutionalism call for the fulfilment of the practice defined by the requirements of civic virtues.

1 Aristotle, *Politics* (H Rackham trans., Harvard University Press 1993) 1292a (the edition contains the original text and translation).

3.2. The principle of the Rule of Law – *Nómos* and *eunomía* as one

In 'Politics', Aristotle[2] asks the question of 'whether it is more advantageous to be ruled by the best men or by the best laws'.[3] While good and fair governance by the best people seems to be a desirable goal, regardless of the system in which it would be fulfilled, the demand of the rule of the best law may seem unclear. Can it be possible for the laws themselves to 'govern'? Is it not people who make laws? Or maybe it is about transcendent laws, evident and revealed to people, and therefore independent of their will. If the matter concerned a simple division, that is 'the worst people versus the best law' or 'the best people versus the worst law', despite the indecisiveness about the meaning of the terms used, the first intuitive answer would be to point at what the best option would be. In a situation when people rule, regardless of whether they are the best of people or not, governance can be easily imagined as some people being subject to the power of 'other people' (or 'another person'). As in Thomas Hobbes' work,

> THE POWER *of a man* (to take it universally), is his present means, to obtain some future apparent good', while the highest power of a man is the power of the state 'that has the use of all their [people] powers depending on his [commonwealth or state] will.[4]

If it is the people who form a political body of the state and its specialised organs, then governance will always be the power of people over people. Aristotle does not think otherwise when stating: 'but inasmuch as "constitution" means the same as "government", and the government is the supreme power in the state, and this must be either a single ruler or a few or the mass of the citizens'.[5] The notion of the Rule of Law does not mean 'non-human' governance, as long as the Rule of Law refers to the field of politics[6] which may temporarily be described as an institutionalised form of exercising power.[7] The Rule of Law is the rule of

2 The following analysis of Aristotle's 'Politics' is not a historical analysis, because it is neither about reconstructing Aristotle's views to be placed within a historical context, nor is it about showing their historical meaning; it is, rather, a reconstruction of a certain way of thinking about the Rule of Law. Therefore, we treat 'Politics' (and the works of other quoted authors likewise) as a theoretical proposal, and we analyse it from the point of view of the issue that we are interested in. Regarding historical interpretations, see literature (prepared by Wolfgang Kullmann) in Aristoteles, *Politik* (F Susemihl trans., Rowohlt Taschenbuch Verlag 2014) 28–37.

3 Aristotle, n 1, 1286a.

4 T Hobbes, *Leviathan* (Oxford University Press 1998) 58.

5 Aristotle, n 1, 1279a.

6 'Politics' in a very general understanding of the concept, referring to the understanding of a political community given by Max Weber, see M Weber, *Economy and Society. An Outline of Interpretive Sociology* (G Roth and C Wittich, eds, University of California Press 1978) 901 et seq.

7 See JM Maravall and A Przeworski, 'Introduction', in JM Maravall and A Przeworski, eds, *Democracy and the Rule of Law* (Cambridge University Press 2003) 3–4.

the people but, at the same time, the rule with a specific characteristic constituting its own specificity.

According to the aforementioned notion, 'the rule of the people' is associated with the possession of means which enable the achievement of certain goals, the 'future apparent good', as Hobbes names it. The choice of goals and means that help to achieve them may be determined by various factors: from one's own self-perceived interest to the ideologically established public interest. At the same time, a decision-making entity does not always have the knowledge or know the criteria to fully determine what is right for him/her in a given situation: does one always have to strive to derive personal gain, or maybe because of this kind of attitude, will one be deprived of the possibility to make use of other goods in a further period?[8] In other words, the person who acts is not always able to assess the relationship between a personal good and a common good. The question, therefore, is what could constitute such a common good. The existence and the sustainable functioning of the state are undoubtedly examples of such a good: 'while it comes into existence for the sake of life, it exists for the good life'.[9] A state can be perceived by individuals as an institutional structure whose functioning is beneficial to everyone.[10] The representatives of political power may be tempted to care only for their own 'future apparent good', either explicitly valuing it more than other goods, or making a mistake in identifying goods and equating a personal good with the common good of all citizens.[11] Political particularism threatens the state itself when acting to derive personal gain leads to malfunctioning of state institutions, and as a result, it is at the expense of the common good. Assuming that the state is a common good, its system should be defined in such a way as to motivate political power to achieve this common good. Therefore, the arbitrariness of political power should be limited.[12] Therefore, what is needed here is the factor limiting its voluntarism and particularism. Aristotle points out that law may be such a factor indeed.[13] Hence, the first temporary definition of the Rule of Law would be that it means governments of people limited by law.

8 The free-rider problem, analysed in rational choice theory, illustrates that striving for cost-free consumption of public goods; that is, the consumption of the public good without bearing the costs of its production, may lead to their total disappearance. Assuming that the possibility of consuming public goods is desirable due to each person's individual strategies, it is in the interest of these individuals to show solidarity and to cooperate in the production process of these goods. Therefore, it is necessary to have an institutional structure that would ensure both the use of public goods and the incurring of costs related to their production. See JH Turner, *The Structure of Sociological Theory* (Wadsworth Publishing Company 1998) chapter 24.

9 Aristotle, n 1, 1252 b.

10 According to John Rawls, we can define them as an element of the basic structure of society seen as a system of cooperation that benefits everyone. See J Rawls, *A Theory of Justice* (The Belknap Press of Harvard University Press 1999) 4–5.

11 See Aristotle, n 1, book III, chapter 6.

12 See M Krygier, 'The Rule of Law: Pasts, Presents, and Two Possible Futures', 12 ***Annual Review of Law and Social Science*** (2016) 199–229.

13 Aristotle, n 1, book III, chapter 11.

However, the question is, is it enough to set a number of norms limiting power to realize the idea of the Rule of Law. After all, political authorities may then apply norms in such a way as to pursue their own goals, and, in consequence, use these norms as a means to achieve goals and not as a limitation of their own will. It would be interesting to know why, then, Aristotle perceives law as the very factor of limiting the arbitrariness of power.

A properly established norm cannot by itself constitute a limitation of power, just as it does not itself regulate the behaviour of its addressees. Depending on the goals and circumstances, both the internal motivations as well as the external stimuli forcing the addressees to comply with the norms are necessary here.[14] The effectiveness of a law is, first of all, determined by the legitimacy of the norms which make the addressees think that law is right and that is why they will act accordingly.[15] Second of all, the establishment of state institutions must make it possible to create a system of incentives leading to compliance with all legal norms.[16] Regarding the first condition, it may be said that when it is met, the law is not only a properly established system of norms but also a justified one, expressing a specific concept of justice.[17] 'For justice exists only between men whose mutual relations are governed by law'.[18] As far as politics is concerned, justice 'is found among men who share their life with a view to self-sufficiency, men who are free and either proportionately or arithmetically equal'.[19] From this perspective,

14 It reflects Kant's distinction between moral and legal philosophy, where the first is an attitude of action according to the fundamental principle of morality, and the second is an attitude of compliance with legal norms. The first can refer to moral legitimacy, and the latter to the effectiveness of influencing behaviours, see I Kant, *The Metaphysics of Morals* (M Gregor trans., Cambridge University Press 1991) 45–47. Regarding the law within a democratic system, it may be claimed that it fulfils the condition of morality when the addressees consider this law as the one they would establish for themselves, see J Habermas, *Between Facts and Norms. Contributions to a Discourse Theory of Law and Democracy* (W Rehg trans., The MIT Press 1996) 89–90 et seq., whereas the condition of effectiveness is fulfilled when all the state institutions react to behaviours in contradiction with this law, see H Kelsen, *Pure Theory of Law* (M Knight trans., The Lawbook Exchange 2005) 208–211. The important thing is that the law must meet both conditions to be called democratically legitimised law.

15 See Habermas, n 14, 120–121.

16 See S Holmes, 'Lineages of the Rule of Law', in Maravall and Przeworski, n 7, 28 et seq. Reference can be made here to Montesquieu's well-known words: 'So that one cannot abuse power, power must check power by the arrangement of things. A constitution can be such that no one will be constrained to do the things the law does not oblige him to do or be kept from doing the things the law permits him to do', Montesquieu, *The Spirit of the Laws* (AM Cohler, BC Miller, HS Stone trans., Cambridge University Press 1998) 155–156.

17 Referring to J Rawls' distinction between a concept and a conception (a one-to-many relation), we may state that the concept of justice is defined by the role it is supposed to fulfil, whereas the conception is a specific interpretation of this role. See Rawls, n 10, 9. Various types of systems differ, among others, in the underlying conceptions of justice. See Aristotle, n 1, book IV.

18 Aristotle, *The Nicomachean Ethics* (D Ross trans., Oxford University Press 2019) 1134a.

19 Ibid.

the law should give every citizen equal treatment:[20] 'it is just for no one person to govern or be governed more than another, and therefore for everybody to govern and be governed alike in turn. And this constitutes law; for regulation is law'.[21] Now the meaning of the Rule of Law may be extended. Laws govern when the actions of both political authorities and citizens are determined by general and impartial legal norms arising from a specific conception of justice.[22] Such a conception excludes arbitrary governments which, in general, are about

> assigning too much to oneself of things good in themselves and too little of things evil in themselves. This is why we do not allow a *man* to rule, but *rational principle*,[23] because a man behaves thus in his own interests and becomes a tyrant.[24]

The law, if it is an expression of a certain conception of justice, restrains human aspirations and gives them a reasonable form in the sense that laws, being general and not individual, must be justified as these which fulfil the principle of 'equal treatment of what is equal'. Justice requires intersubjectively acceptable reasons, and it is not an indication of mandatory compliance with norms. The Rule of Law is the rule of the people, yet subject to a reasonable form and all the related requirements resulting from the adopted conception of justice.

Regarding the second condition, namely the incentives for taking actions that are in accordance with the law, Aristotle does not suggest an a priori and universal institutional solution, but formulates some general terms of the 'well-ordered government' (*eunomía*).[25] The well-established law (in compliance with

20 In this article we do not discuss the criteria of being a citizen, which are determined in various ways within various regimes. It is about a general rule. The difference between the classical concept and the post-revolutionary concept is well shown in Hannah Arendt: 'Isonomy guaranteed *istotes*, equality, but not because all men were born or created equal, but, on the contrary, because men were by nature (*physei*) not equal, and needed an artificial institution, the *polis*, which by virtue of its nomos would make them equal. Equality existed only in this specifically political realm, where men met one another as citizens and not as private persons. The difference between this ancient concept of equality and our notion that men are born or created equal and become unequal by virtue of social and political, which is to say man-made, institutions can hardly be over-emphasized. The equality of the Greek *polis*, its isonomy, was an attribute of the *polis* and not of men, who received their equality by virtue of citizenship, not by virtue of birth', H Arendt, *On Revolution* (Penguin Books 1990) 30–31.

21 Aristotle, n 1, 1287a.

22 The Rule of Law does not mean binding the law with the transcendent laws of nature, see J Frank, *A Democracy of Distinction, Aristotle and the Work of Politics* (The University of Chicago Press 2005) 117, but with the conception of justice of a given political community.

23 In the original work it is *lógos*. In 'Politics', we may read: 'He therefore that recommends that the law shall govern seems to recommend that God and reason alone shall govern', Aristotle, n 1, 1287a.

24 Aristotle, n 18, 1134a.

25 'Wohlgesetzlichkeit' in German, see Aristotele, n 2, 1294a.

the substantive and formal requirements) is certainly a matter of importance and the one giving significance to the Rule of Law,

> but to have good laws enacted but not obey them does not constitute well-ordered government. Hence one form of good government must be understood to consist in the laws enacted being obeyed, and another form in the laws which the citizens keep being well enacted (for it is possible to obey badly enacted laws).[26]

Eunomía is a necessary condition for the establishment of the Rule of Law; however, it is not sufficient. The institutional guarantee of the compliance with the law and the pragmatic rules of its creation are not synonymous with the Rule of Law itself, but just a condition for establishing law in practice. In addition, compliance with the law is not only based on external stimuli, since it depends on the attitudes of citizens as well. A technically correct process of law-making that will allow the law to be perceived as 'understandable, purposeful and consistent', increases the likelihood of lawful conduct,[27] but does not mean that this law will automatically be in line with the conception of justice adopted in a given system. Thus, the Rule of Law is grounded both on the conception of justice and on the requirements contained in the concept of *eunomía*. The Rule of Law is the government in which the actions of both political and state authorities, as well as the citizens themselves, are determined by a general and impartial law arising from a specific conception of justice, the law which was established in a proper manner, and which is usually respected by the addressees. The institutional environment should encourage both the creation and compliance with the applicable law (in accordance with the substantive and formal requirements). The concept of the Rule of Law thus consists of both a moral and political element; that is, a system that implements a specific conception of justice, as well as an institutional and pragmatic element, namely, the necessity for laws to influence social and political practices.[28]

3.3. Formalist reduction of the Rule of Law – The Rule of Law as *eunomía*

If the aforementioned reconstruction of the principle of the Rule of Law is correct, then Hobbes's allegation is not valid:

26 Aristotle, n 1, 1294a.

27 Weber's rational legitimisation, see Weber, n 6, 205, can truly make the law 'capable of guiding the behaviour', as stated by Joseph Raz, see J Raz, 'The Rule of Law and its Virtue', in J Raz, *Authority of Law. Essays on Law and Morality* (The Clarendon Press 1979) 214.

28 In this approach, the Rule of Law is to a large extent a certain telos one should strive to achieve, and not a ready-made and context-independent set of requirements which should be met or a series of institutions that should be established. See M Krygier, 'The Rule of Law: Legality, Teleology, Sociology', in G Palombella and N Walker, eds, *Relocating the Rule of Law* (Hart Publishing 2009) 57 et seq.

> error of Aristotle's politics, that in a well ordered commonwealth, not men should govern, but the laws. What man, that has his natural senses, though he can neither write nor read, does not find himself governed by them he fears, and believes can kill or hurt him when he obeyeth not? Or that believes the law can hurt him; that is, words, and paper, without the hands and swords of men?[29]

The principle of the Rule of Law does not include a strong separation of the Rule of Law from the rule of the people. On the other hand, it is true the rule states that not only fear of the consequences of non-compliance with the norm is a factor that influences the behaviour of addressees. The essence of Hobbes' criticism in his 'Leviathan' can be found in the statement that Aristotle's position underestimates the importance of the institutional system of coercion and overestimates the importance of the conception of justice (the legitimisation of law) in ensuring the effectiveness of the law. The application of the law is not related to its conformity with the conception of justice but consists only in the fact that it comes from an authorised source.[30] 'For the legislator, is he that maketh the law. And the commonwealth only prescribes, and commandeth the observation of those rules, which we call law: therefore the commonwealth is the legislator'.[31] Only the lawful legislator (a sovereign) has the power to establish the law, whereas the task of the state is to implement it effectively. The legislator is not bound by any civil laws, since they who make laws are not subject to them.[32] In this vision, the law becomes a separate and autonomous normative system, not related to non-legislative concepts and criteria. The formal legitimacy; that is, the establishment of law by a proper body, and social effectiveness of the law, meaning its influence on human behaviour, are the very basic and sufficient criteria of legitimacy.[33] The Rule of Law is replaced with 'the rule by law'. In this paradigm, thinking about law is almost devoid of a normative element expressed in the conception of justice, and is focused on the instrumental aspect of the law, namely its effectiveness in achieving one's goals. These goals are defined entirely and autonomously by the legislator, but it must be done in the form of law, to be exact by the legal norms established by proper authority and available for its addressees; in addition, its application and compliance is institutionally guaranteed by the state's coercion.[34] In this way, *eunomía* has been reduced to formal *Reschtsstaat.*[35]

29 Hobbes, n 4, 454.

30 See R Dworkin, *Taking Rights Seriously* (Harvard University Press 1978) 17.

31 Hobbes, n 4, 176.

32 Ibid., 215.

33 See Kelsen, n 14, 208–211.

34 As Habermas points out, the sovereign power is not limited in the sense that it should be effective and provide a stable political system, see Habermas, n 14, 90–92.

35 BZ Tamanaha, *On the Rule of Law. History, Politics, Theory* (Cambridge University Press 2004) 92 et seq., M Rosenfeld, 'The Rule of Law and the Legitimacy of Constitutional Democracy', 74 *Southern California Law Review* (2001) 318 et seq.

The idea of the Rule of Law limited to the 'form of law' (*ius* without *iustum*) in an extreme way expresses the Pure Theory of Law of Hans Kelsen, who completely ignores moral and political issues.[36] 'A state not governed by law is unthinkable; for the state only exists in acts of state, and these are actions performed by individuals and attributed to the state as a juristic person'.[37] In the most general sense, each state is a legal state, because the interpretation of certain laws and regulations as 'state laws and regulations' is possible only on the basis of legal norms. 'That the state creates the law merely means that individuals, whose acts, on the basis of law, are attributed to the state, create the law'.[38] Every law of a state authority requires legal legitimacy. This type of legitimacy has nothing to do with non-legal (moral or political) justification. In this sense, a law of a given authority has a legal meaning when it is based on a legal norm. Every rule-making law is legally regulated by state authorities, and therefore, this is an application of superior norms. Every legal norm established in the form prescribed by law is a valid law and applies as long as it is not abrogated. The normativist and purely legal principle of legitimacy means that 'a norm of a legal order is valid until its validity is terminated in a way determined by this legal order or replaced by the validity of another norm of this order'.[39] The goals that are to be achieved due to legislation are of no importance from this perspective. 'Any kind of content might be law'[40] and the fact that certain legal norms do not meet our standards of justice (or other non-legislative criteria) does not affect their validity in any way.

The legislator may 'rule by law' in the sense that they have relative freedom to establish the law. The legislator is, however, subject to the rules of law-making, and thus limited by them. In this way, the law-maker is 'governed' by the laws. One may say that the normativist view of the Rule of Law gives an extreme expression of the procedural rationality concept, according to which 'the procedures should be maximally reliable methods for arriving at the decisions that we are mandating in our substantive standards'.[41] This is particularly evident in Kelsen's concept of the essence of the constitution, which reduces its essential function to the establishment of a procedure authorising rule-making laws.[42] From this point of view, a constitution establishes procedures (substantive standards) that guarantee objective validity to legislative acts (normativist legitimacy). Kelsen completely got rid of the moral and political elements from the essence of a constitution and reduced them to be a formal and legal basis of given legislation. In this approach, every constitution provides every legal order with [legal]

36 Kelsen distinguishes the legal and political meaning of the *Rechtsstaat* concept, see Kelsen, n 14, 312. Above, we limit ourselves to legal significance.

37 Ibid., 312.

38 Ibid.

39 Ibid., 209.

40 Ibid., 198.

41 D Lyons, *Ethics and the Rule of Law* (Cambridge University Press 1984) 198.

42 See R Alexy, 'Hans Kelsens Begriff der Verfassung', in SL Paulson and M Stolleis, eds, *Hans Kelsen. Staatsrechtslehrer und Rechtstheoretiker des 20. Jahrhunderts* (Mohr Siebeck 2005) 334–336, 340.

validation, because every order has its 'rulemaking method', but it is an extremely formal lawfulness.[43]

The formal concept of the Rule of Law[44] is found in the words of Joseph Raz, who states that

> the Rule of Law is just one of the virtues which a legal system may possess and by which it is to be judged. It is not to be confused with democracy, justice, equality (before the law or otherwise), human rights of any kind or respect for persons or for the dignity of a man. A non-democratic legal system based on the denial of human rights, on extensive poverty, on racial segregation, sexual inequalities, and religious persecution may, in principle, conform to the requirements of the Rule of Law better than any of the legal systems of the more enlightened Western democracies. This does not mean that it will be better than those Western democracies. It will be an immeasurably worse legal system, but it will excel in one respect: in its conformity to the Rule of Law.[45]

An undemocratic legal system, based on the denial of human rights, immense poverty, racial segregation, inequalities between the sexes, and religious persecution, so that it can be regarded as lawful, would have to be as 'such that they [i.e., addressees of law] *can* find out what it is and act on it. [...] *it must be capable of guiding the behaviour of its subjects*'.[46] *Can* people, deprived of human rights, living in extreme poverty, subjected to racial segregation, experiencing inequalities between the sexes and religious persecution, really do something? Without granting them any legal empowerment, they not so much *can* but *must*. In such a specific situation, in which individuals have no causative power, the law appears as a *necessity* and not a *possibility*.[47] Adopting the view of addressees, the law of this undemocratic legal system is not law but violence, it does not express obligations, but political force dressed in legal robes. The law may, therefore, be used to achieve personal goals of political power, and yet still comply with the formal criteria of the Rule of Law; for instance, that all the laws should be prospective, open, clear, relatively stable, and there should be institutions that ensure their effectiveness.[48]

43 Obviously, Kelsen notes that a constitution includes a lot of content that goes beyond the legislative procedure, but it is the content that is somewhat incidental and contingent in terms of politics. See Kelsen, n 14, 221–224.

44 Tamanaha, n 35, 91 et seq.

45 Raz, n 27, 211. He once states his opinion differently in J Raz, 'The Law's Own Virtue', 39 (1) *Oxford Journal of Legal Studies* (2019) 1–15.

46 Raz, n 27, 214 [emphasis by WW].

47 Regarding the law as an opportunity, see HLA Hart, *The Concept of Law* (Clarendon Press 1994) chapter III.

48 Raz, n 27, 214–218. See critique of Raz's concept JA Sempill, 'Ruler's Sword, Citizen's Shield: The Rule of Law and the Constitution of Power', XXXI *Journal of Law & Politics* (2016) 333–417.

The formal meaning of the Rule of Law is limited to the effectiveness of affecting the behaviour of its addressees, reducing law to the role of an instrument of governance. It means moving away from Aristotle's idea which describes the law as a measure of limiting arbitrariness. Making law general and non-particularistic was to prevent it from becoming just an instrument of political power.[49] It comes to the situation that, on the one hand, formal theories avoid describing a complicated relation between legal concepts and morality and politics, but then again they, on the other hand, make legal concepts subordinated to the political will by reducing the role of law to a political instrument. From the point of view of Aristotle, the value of the Rule of Law is that it expresses the necessity to introduce institutional norms and mechanisms that restrain particularism and arbitrariness of political power. The formal concept of the Rule of Law, in contrast, instructs us how to effectively use the law as a means, but not for what purposes it should be used.[50] According to Aristotle's interpretation of the idea that we have adopted, the law is not only a tool, but it also has a certain value, because it serves the objectives set by a specific conception of justice. The fact that the formal conception rejects the relation between law and other normative systems condemns law to political instrumentalism. It might be assumed that an important viewpoint for this conception is the point of view of public authorities[51] that are interested in the most effective ways of influencing human behaviours. The addressees of legal norms are treated as an object to be governed, not an autonomous entity, and, to paraphrase Kant, they are only *a means*, not *an end* at the same time.[52] The formal notion of the Rule of Law becomes problematic when we take the view of a citizen who is entitled 'to govern and be governed'.[53] If therefore, the citizens, i.e., individuals who cannot be of the passive status,[54] are the addressees of legal regulations, then not every content may become a law (contrary to Kelsen), because the law should provide the citizens with real possibilities of action (as opposed to Raz).[55] For this reason, as Aristotle puts it, where citizens are treated only as objects and tools, the laws do not govern there.

49 On the subject of non-instrumental dimension Rule of Law, see Sempill, n 48, 359–366.

50 See bureaucratic point of view, Ibid., 395–397; see also Krygier, n 12.

51 See J Raz, 'Kelsen's Theory of the Basic Norm', in SL Paulson and B Litschewski-Paulson, eds, *Normativity and Norms. Critical Perspectives on Kelsenian Themes* (Clarendon Press 1998) 47–68.

52 See I Kant, *Groundwork of the Metaphysics of Morals* (M Gregor trans., Cambridge University Press 1997) 37.

53 Aristotle, n 1, 1287a.

54 Georg Jellinek distinguishes four statuses; that is, a relation to the state which qualifies the individual; the passive status (status subjectionis) is the sphere of individual duty ('benefits to the state'); the negative status (status libertatis) is a sphere free from the state power; the positive status (status civitatis) is the legal capacity granted to the individual to make claims regarding specific state activities (benefits); the active status (or the status of 'active citizenship') is granting the individual the ability to take actions on behalf of the state. See G Jellinek, *System der Subjektiven Öffentlichen Rechte* (Verlag von JCB Mohr 1905). The full legal empowerment of the individual would include all of these statuses.

55 Therefore, the criteria for citizenship are crucial in the initial assessment of the Rule of Law; for instance, if citizenship is an exclusive right, the legislator could treat non-citizens only as

3.4. Constitutionalism as the institutionalisation of the Rule of Law – *Nómos* and *eunomía* reintegrated

From a point of view of a citizen, and from a broader perspective of addressees of legal norms, submitting to legislation without any safety measures may seem as dangerous as being in the proverbial *state of nature*.[56] Regarding this kind of approach, the legal system and state institutions are to provide something more than just a stable system in which all the behaviours of political power are predictable and/or take a certain form of legal authorisation. Regardless of the extent to which legislation meets the criteria of formal correctness, it may appear to the addressees as 'brute power'[57] if they do not have any possibility of articulating their preferences and defending their basic interests or rights. According to the Aristotelian idea of the Rule of Law, political power would differ from the naked force in the way that it would not be particularistic and arbitrary. This difference is emphasised by John Locke who points out that 'public good' is the ultimate goal of the process of law-making and law application.[58] This 'public good' plays a similar role as the concept of justice in Aristotle's works being the criterion for distinguishing any order based on the threat of coercion, regardless of whether it is given by a bandit or an absolutist body, from the common norms established by a legally legitimised obligation.[59] The teleological and non-particularistic dimension of law helps to distinguish it from naked power since the legislator is obliged to achieve a specific goal and cannot just change the content of law arbitrarily. From the point of view of the author of the 'Two Treatises on Government', the institutional means used to achieve it are as follows: the guarantees for individual rights, the participation of citizens in the legislative process, and the separation of powers. In other words, legislation should be bound by law (in compliance

a means, while citizens would have to be considered as subjects. By adopting the conception of justice, which states that every human being is also an end in itself, it is impossible for us to say that laws govern in such a state.

56 'If government is to be the remedy of those evils, which necessarily follow from men's being judges in their own cases, and the state of nature is therefore not to be endured; I desire to know what kind of government that is, and how much better it is than the state of nature, where one man, commanding a multitude, has the liberty to be judge in his own case, and may do to all his subjects whatever he pleases, without the least liberty to anyone to question or control those who execute his pleasure? And in whatsoever he doth, whether led by reason, mistake, or passion, must be submitted to? Much better it is in the state of nature, wherein men are not bound to submit to the unjust will of another: and if he that judges, judges amiss in his own, or any other case, he is answerable for it to the rest of mankind', J Locke, *Two Treatises of Government and A Letter Concerning Toleration* (Yale University Press 2003) §13.

57 See I Sánches-Cuenca, 'Power, Rules, and Compliance', in Maravall and Przeworski, n 7, 65–66.

58 Locke, n 56, § 3.

59 It is to answer St. Augustine's question: 'Justice being taken away, then, what are kingdoms but great robberies? For what are robberies themselves, but little kingdoms? The band itself is made up of men; it is ruled by the authority of a prince, it is knit together by the pact of the confederacy; the booty is divided by the law agreed on', Augustine, *The City of God* (M Dods trans., Modern Library 2000) book IV, chapter 4.

with the substantive and formal requirements), and it must be consistent with the intended purpose of the existence of a given system.

> But though men, when they enter into society, give up the equality, liberty, and executive power they had in the state of nature, into the hands of the society, to be so far disposed of by the legislative as the good of the society shall require; yet it being only with an intention in every one the better to preserve himself, his liberty and property [...]; the power of the society, or legislative constituted by them, can never be supposed to extend farther than the common good [...]. And so whoever has the legislative or supreme power of any commonwealth, is bound to govern by established standing laws, promulgated and known to the people, and not by extemporary decrees.[60]

Locke thus formulates a general idea of modern constitutionalism[61] which combines the principle of binding political power with higher law along with the conception of justice based on the rights of an individual, and the political legitimacy of the legislation process.[62]

The doctrine of Immanuel Kant in the form of the 'constitution of a pure republic' idea as a model for all state systems features a philosophical approach to the idea Rule of Law. 'Pure republic' is a system

> that makes *freedom* the principle and indeed the condition for any exercise of *coercion*, as is required by a rightful constitution of a state in the strict sense of the word. [...] This is the only constitution of a state that lasts, the constitution in which *law* itself rules and depends on no particular person.[63]

'The constitution of a pure republic' is, in other words, 'the Idea of a constitution in harmony with the natural right of man, one namely in which the citizens obedient to the law, besides being united, ought also to be legislative'.[64] The concept of the Rule of Law expressed in the Kantian idea of a pure republic is intended by the author to be universal.

> The republican constitution is a constitution that is established, first, according to principles of the *freedom* of the members of a society (as human beings), second, according to principles of the *dependence* of all on a single, common legislation (as subjects), and third, according to the law of the *equality* of the

60 Locke, n 56, §131.

61 'The notion of constitutional government is of course by no means revolutionary in content or origin; it means nothing more or less than government limited by law, and the safeguard of civil liberties through constitutional guarantees', Arendt, n 20, 143.

62 He refers to Aristotle who states that there is no Rule of Law 'when the decrees of the assembly over-ride the law', Aristotle, n 1, 1292a.

63 I Kant, n 14, 148.

64 I Kant, *The Conflict of the Faculties* (M Gregor trans., Abaris Books 1979) 163–165.

> latter (as *citizens of the state*). The *republican* constitution is the only kind of constitution that follows from the idea of an original contract, upon which all laws legislated by a people must be based, and is, therefore, as concerns right, itself the one on which all the civil constitutions are originally based.[65]

The law in a republican system is closely related to human and political rights. The function of law is to establish conditions enabling the use of freedom by all people.[66]

> The rights of humankind must be held sacred, whatever it may cost those in power. One cannot pursue a half measure here and devise a hybrid, pragmatically conditioned right (between right and utility). Instead, all politics must bend its knee before right but can hope to arrive at the point, however gradually, where it can shine perpetually.[67]

Freedom gives law sense and law allows realising freedom. In this approach, the Rule of Law expresses the primacy of law which subordinates the idea of freedom over a particular political will.[68]

Modern constitutionalism – says Dieter Grimm – consists of two elements: the sovereignty of the people (democracy), and the hierarchy of the norms of common and constitutional law (the Rule of Law).[69] The legal organisation of a state ensures that the activities of its bodies can be perceived as based on the norms of 'superior law',[70] thus having legal legitimacy. However, the fact that this 'superior law' is an expression of citizens' will, it provides political power with democratic legitimacy. Constitutionalism institutionalises democracy because

> from the perspective of democratic constitutional theory, the constitution is the foundation of the state's exercise of power, not merely its organizing and

65 I Kant, *Toward Perpetual Peace and Other Writings on Politics, Peace, and History* (DL Colclasure trans., Yale University Press 2006) 74–75.

66 'We may define a republic to be, or at least may bestow that name on, a government which derives all its powers directly or indirectly from the great body of the people; and is administered by persons holding their offices during pleasure, for a limited period, or during good behaviour', A Hamilton, J Madison, J Jay, *The Federalist with The Letters of "Brutus"* (T Ball, ed, Cambridge University Press 2003) 182. 'The genius of Republican liberty, seems to demand on one side, not only that all power should be derived from the people; but, that those entrusted with it should be kept in dependence on the people', Ibid., 170.

67 I Kant, n 65, 104.

68 In such a universalistic approach, the idea of the Rule of Law can be the foundation for the peaceful coexistence of republics, but also for the establishment of a community of law-abiding states, see Ibid.

69 D Grimm, 'The Achievement of Constitutionalism and its Prospects in a Changed World', in M Loughlin, JP McCormick and N Walker, eds, *The Twilight of Constitutionalism?* (Oxford University Press 2012) 8–11.

70 E W Böckenförde, 'The Concept and Problems of Constitutional State', in E-W Böckenförde, *Constitutional and Political Theory. Selected Writings* (M Künkler and T Stein, eds, T Dunlap trans., Oxford University Press 2017) 141.

> limiting element. [...] it is the constitutive and limiting normative basis of every state decision-making authority. [...] There are no legal titles "before" and "outside" of the constitution that could authorize the lawful action by state organs. [...] By contrast, in a democracy, all state action requires a legal grounding *in* the constitution, because that is the only way it acquires its foundation and legitimacy.[71]

According to Giovanni Sartori, the concept of constitutionalism is closely related to the Rule of Law.

> In order for us to be governed by laws, or by means of laws, the lawmakers themselves must be subject to law. [...] The problem has been tackled, within the constitutional state, by arranging the legislative procedure in such a way that the "form of law" also implies control of its content. A large number of constitutional devices are, in effect, intended to create the conditions of a lawmaking process in which *ius* will remain tied to *iustum*, in which law will remain the right law.[72]

In this approach, constitutionalism combines the formal concept of the Rule of Law with a material (substantial) concept;[73] that is, it combines legalism with democracy and human rights.[74] The purely formal concept of the Rule of Law completely bypasses the *iustum* dimension claiming that everything that has a 'form of law' (legally authorised standards) is a law regardless of content. The situation is different from the perspective of the material concept because it involves certain standards that would allow perceiving legal norms as fulfilling certain requirements: it would provide individuals with basic laws and political empowerment so that they could be considered as respecting the principle of

71 E-W Böckenförde, 'The Historical Evolution and Changes in the Meaning of the Constitution', in Böckenförde, n 70, 162.

72 G Sartori, *Theory of Democracy Revisited* (Chatham House Publishers 1987) 322–323.

73 Fallon argues that the concept of the Rule of Law cannot simply be reduced to a simple and narrow definition. Indicating the way the Rule of Law functions in the tradition of American constitutionalism, Fallon states that 'perfectly realized, the Rule of Law would be rule (i) in accordance with the originally intended and understood meaning of the directives of legitimate, democratically accountable law-making authorities, cast in the form of intelligible rules binding on citizens, governmental officials, and judges alike, (iii) as identified and elucidated in an interpretive process guided by publicly accessible norms and characterized reason-giving, and (iv) consistent with legitimate public purposes sound, shared principles of political morality. When law, in the positivist sense, fails to satisfy any of these elements, the Rule of Law is less than completely realized, but still may (or may not) be more nearly approximated than it is scorned or abandoned', RH Fallon, Jr., 'The Rule of Law as a Concept in Constitutional Discourse', 1 97 *Columbia Law Review* (1997) 38.

74 See J Habermas, 'Über den inneren Zusammenhang von Rechtsstaat und Demokratie', in UK Preuß, ed, *Zum Begriff der Verfassung. Die Ordnung des Politischen* (Fischer Taschenbuch Verlag 1994) 83–94.

democracy.[75] In other words, constitutionalism is a form of institutionalisation[76] of the Rule of Law by means of a positive higher law that implements the concept of justice based on the rights of an individual and the political legitimacy of legislation by citizens.

Constitutionalism contains a certain limitation of what can be considered *nomós*, and of what *eunomía* is to be for. If the idea of the Rule of Law involves granting *persons* legal possibilities of action, and not just making addressees the *subjects* of imperious decisions, it must be connected with the idea of humanity:[77]

> the human being and in general every rational being *exists* as an end in itself, *not merely as a means* to be used by this or that will at its discretion; instead he must in all his actions, whether directed to himself or also to other rational beings, always be regarded *at the same time as an end*.[78]

In other words, the Rule of Law concept must also include a material element (*iustum*, mentioned by Sartori), if it is to be something more than an empty legitimation formula. Lon Fuller argues that the Rule of Law can be presented as a certain legal utopia, namely the situation

> in which all rules are perfectly clear, consistent with one another, known to every citizen, and never retroactive. In this utopia the rules remain constant through time, demand only what is possible, and are scrupulously observed by courts, police, and everyone else charged with their administration.[79]

The formation of such a utopian idea of lawfulness sets out the criteria according to which we can assess the state of the lawfulness of a given country. Having evaluation criteria is pointless if the evaluators cannot use them, and for that, a certain scope of freedom (for example, freedom of thought and speech) is needed. Accordingly, if Fuller's criteria are to matter to us as citizens of a given state, then we the citizens must be able to use these criteria, therefore we cannot be treated

75 See the dissimilar position of Brian Tamanaha, which links democracy with the formal concept, Tamanaha, n 35, 99 et seq.

76 'One of the main characteristics of institutions is that they are impersonal, in the sense that their functioning does not depend on the idiosyncrasy of individuals. An institution is well designed when it is not affected by the replacement of the individuals who have to act in accord with its rules. Whatever the preferences of individuals who have to act institutionally, the institution survives when the incentives it creates induce individuals to comply with the rules. In this sense, there is Rule of Law when politics is fully institutional, that is, when every political act is done according to the institutional rules', Sánchez-Cuenca, n 57, 63. In contrast to Ignacio Sánchez-Cuenca, we shall assume that full institutionalisation is a certain goal, not an observable fact. The difference between these two comes from the fact that we refer not only to the formal but also to the material aspect of the Rule of Law.

77 Sempill, n 48, 365.

78 I Kant, n 52, 37.

79 LL Fuller, *The Morality of Law* (Yale University Press 1969) 41.

only as *a means*, but also as *an end*. Therefore, it can be assumed that the requirements related to formal law-making gain particular relevance only when one is looking from the point of view of the adopted conception of justice, because these requirements are intended to make law implementation easier.

John Rawls argues that in the fundamental sense, the Rule of Law expresses the concept of formal justice, i.e., 'the regular and impartial administration of public rules',[80] included in the formal concept. However, even in such a basic understanding, the Rule of Law concept cannot be interpreted as morally indifferent, because the legal system operating in accordance with it becomes valued only when it relates to the concept of freedom.

> A legal system is a coercive order of public rules addressed to rational persons for the purpose of regulating their conduct and providing the framework for social cooperation. When these rules are just, they establish a basis for legitimate expectations. They constitute grounds upon which persons can rely on one another and rightly object when their expectations are not fulfilled. If the bases of these claims are unsure, so are the boundaries of men's liberties.[81]

If a legal system realises the idea of freedom, then it should guarantee political freedom in a special way. 'This guarantee means that the worth of the political liberties to all citizens, whatever their social or economic position, must be approximately equal, or at least sufficiently equal, in the sense that everyone has a fair opportunity to hold public office and to influence the outcome of political decisions'.[82] In Rawls' interpretation, the guarantee of political rights and freedoms is an indispensable *iustum* condition of a constitutional system. It is only when a legislative procedure guarantees a certain scope of fundamental freedoms that it can be considered as lawful. They represent *constitution the essentials* and are the basis of democratic and 'liberal principle of legitimacy', which means that

> our exercise of political power is fully proper only when it is exercised in accordance with a constitution the essentials of which all citizens as free and equal may reasonably be expected to endorse in the light of principles and ideals acceptable to their common human reason.[83]

It expresses the concept of justice and modern constitutionalism that combines the rights of an individual and a democratic procedure into one political system.[84]

80 Rawls, n 10, 206.
81 Ibid., 207.
82 J Rawls, *Political Liberalism* (Columbia University Press 1993) 327.
83 Ibid., 137.
84 Jürgen Habermas indicates that the inclusion of civic rights of participation in the form of human rights is a necessary condition for democratic practice – the democratic idea of self-determination must be ensured through the medium of law. See Habermas, n 74, 89–90.

The Rule of Law concept in the above approach emphasises the condition that legislative procedures should implement the idea of democratic empowerment of citizens. Jürgen Habermas highlights that

> the law receives its full normative sense neither through its legal form per se, nor through an a priori moral content, but through a procedure of law-making that begets legitimacy. [...] The idea behind government by law requires that the collectively binding decisions of an authority that must make use of the law to fulfil its own functions are not only cast in the form of law but are for their part legitimated by statutes enacted in accordance with that procedure.[85]

From this perspective, the idea of the Rule of Law combines the condition of the existence of procedures regulating the legislation with the condition to pursue the idea of democracy by such procedures: 'the organization of the constitutional state is ultimately supposed to serve the politically autonomous self-organization of a community that has constituted itself with the system of rights as an association of free and equal consociates under law'.[86] The material and democratic concept of the Rule of Law expresses the idea of political autonomy, perceiving the citizen as the subject of supreme power and the source of legitimisation of political decisions. Ronald Dworkin writes that

> the constitution sets out a general political scheme that is sufficiently just to be taken as settled for reasons of fairness. Citizens take the benefit of living in a society whose institutions are arranged and governed in accordance with that scheme, and they must take the burdens as well, at least until a new scheme is put into force either by discrete amendment or general revolution.[87]

When the 'form of law' (*ius*) serves the implementation of democratic principles (*iustum*), then the law, established in accordance with the constitution, has both legal and moral or political legitimacy. So, there is a situation of specific balance between legality and democracy: legality serves democracy as a form of its institutionalisation, and that is why a democratic will is, on the one hand, bound by the norms of the constitution, and on the other hand, thanks to the norms it can exist and function.[88] Constitutionalism cannot mean the domination of one of the above elements over the other, but their 'cooperation': 'as the law ought to govern all things while the magistrates control particulars, and we ought to judge this to be constitutional government'.[89]

85 Habermas, n 14, 135.
86 Ibid., 176.
87 Dworkin, n 30, 106.
88 S Holmes, 'Precommitment and the paradox of democracy', in J Elster and R Slagstad, eds, *Constitutionalism and Democracy* (Cambridge University Press 1993) 226–228.
89 Aristotle, n 1, 1292a.

3.5. The Rule of Law as a civic virtue – *Praxis* of the Rule of Law

In Aristotle's dilemma, from the first part of this essay, the rule of the best laws governing the people is an alternative to the rule of the best people. Modern constitutionalism, in the form presented by us, constitutes a certain concept of what conditions should be met to make it possible for 'the best laws' to govern. According to such a concept, 'the best laws' are the laws laid down through the legislative process in the form provided for in the constitution implementing two principles, namely, the sovereignty of the people and the guarantee of human rights. Ultimately, the constitution is based on the principle of humanity, meaning an individual cannot be reduced to being an object of law, which is ensured by the two aforementioned principles.[90] Laws that do not meet material and formal constitutional requirements would be unjust.

> The laws are good or bad, just or unjust, simultaneously with and similarly to the constitutions of states (though of course it is obvious that the laws are bound to be adapted to the constitution); yet if so, it is clear that the laws in conformity with the correct constitutions must necessarily be just and those in conformity with the divergent forms of constitution unjust.[91]

Modern constitutionalism contains a certain concept of 'just laws', which is intended to limit the arbitrariness and particularism of political power. This concept is the expression of the prescriptive concept of the constitution, i.e., the concept which provides the answer for the question of what qualities a state system should have. In other words, modern constitutionalism 'formulates a challenging program',[92] which must be implemented in order for a given state to be considered a 'constitutional state'. According to Horst Dreier, the 'milestone' of constitutional theory is a claim that a man is free not by virtue of privileges, but by virtue of a human right,[93] which is defined by Kant as an 'innate right'.[94] Within this concept, the Rule of Law takes place when political power is not allowed to deprive individuals of their 'innate rights'. And political power cannot deny citizens their rights when these individuals have political rights, which enables them to participate in the procedure of law-making. One can, therefore, interpret democratic constitutionalism as a kind of answer to the old question of political philosophy of which system can be considered the best.[95] The best system would

90 'A rational being belongs as a *member* to the kingdom of ends when he gives universal laws in it but is also himself subject to these laws. He belongs to it *as sovereign* when, as lawgiving, he is not subject to the will of any other', I Kant, n 52, 41.

91 Aristotle, n 1, 1282b.

92 H Dreier, *Gilt das Grundgesetz ewig? Fünf Kapitel zum modernen Verfassungsstaat* (Carl Friedrich von Simens Stiftung 2009) 16.

93 See Ibid., 9.

94 I Kant, n 14, 63.

95 See L Strauss, *The City and the Man* (The University of Chicago Press 1978) 17 et seq.

be the system that implements the principles of people's sovereignty and the inalienable rights of the individual. In this sense, constitutionalism is something more than just the implementation of the Aristotelian idea of the Rule of Law,[96] because it combines the principle of the primacy of law over a particular political will not so much with a *certain* conception of justice, as with the one *defined* by these two aforementioned principles.[97]

For Aristotle 'the best constitution is the system under which anybody whatsoever would be best off and would live in felicity'.[98] For that reason, there 'is the supreme elementary principle that has been often stated, that of taking precautions that the section desirous of the constitution shall be stronger in number than the section not desirous of it'.[99] According to Rawls, a constitution will only establish a stable political system when it is based on socially accepted principles that constitute the criteria of legitimacy.[100] In the broad sense of Georg WF Hegel,

> the guarantee of a constitution (i.e. the necessity that the laws be reasonable, and their actualisation secured) lies in the collective spirit of the nation, – especially in the specific way in which it is itself conscious of its reason. […] the guarantee lies also at the same time in the actual organisation or development of that principle in suitable institutions.[101]

The special significance of a constitution is based on its rooting in the beliefs of citizens, which are reflected in political and legal institutions. Acceptance for a constitution creates a 'collective spirit' manifesting itself in the functioning of institutions. A legitimised democratic constitution may constitute the real basis of a legal system, and thus constitute the primacy of the Rule of Law over a particularistic political will. There must be a specific kind of connection between citizens as well as their associations and institutions of the state, which prevents these institutions from being perceived as something unfamiliar and different from the citizens' associations. A 'political attitude' must develop within the society:

> The political disposition, i.e. patriotism in general, is certainty based on *truth* […] and a volition which has become habitual. As such, it is merely

96 Tamanaha emphasises that 'the relationship between the Rule of Law and democracy is asymmetrical: the Rule of Law can exist without democracy, but democracy needs the Rule of Law, for otherwise democratically established laws may be eviscerated at the stage of application by not being followed', Tamanaha, n 35, 37.

97 Aristotle himself also expresses his preferences regarding 'the best system' in his 'Politics'. Speaking of the 'Aristotelian idea', I mean the abstract view of the Rule of Law from the first part of this essay.

98 Aristotle, n 1, 1324a.

99 Ibid., 1309b.

100 See Rawls, n 82, 38–39.

101 GWF Hegel, *Hegel's Philosophy of Mind. Translated from the Encyclopaedia of the Philosophical Sciences* (W Wallace trans., Oxford, Clarendon Press 1894) § 540.

> a consequence of the institutions within the state [...] – This disposition is in general one of *trust* (which may pass over into more or less educated insight), or the consciousness that my substantial and particular interest is preserved and contained in the interest and end of an other (in this case, the state), and in the latter's relation to me as an individual [als Einzelnem]. As a result, this other immediately ceases to be an other for me, and in my consciousness of this, I am free.[102]

Thus, we are dealing with the Rule of Law when the political system and legislation complying with this system become for the citizens their deeply held values, while as 'common values', they are integrated with an individual value system of every individual citizen. Trust perceived as a political attitude is a necessary condition for the state to mean something more than a formal *Rechtsstaat*, which still may be of some value for citizens, but constitutes an external and separate 'being' governed only by its own logic and guided by its own goals.[103]

The development of the aforementioned political attitude is at the heart of a democratic system only if the citizens are to be the highest subject of authority, which is to say not only a subject formally recognised as such by the constitutional declarations, but also the one making a real contribution to legislation through a specific political practice.[104] A democratic identity of those who govern and those who are governed remains a fiction when those who are governed are passive and do not identify themselves with the political system. A democratic system, as a form of implementing the idea of the Rule of Law, requires the formation of the virtue of being a citizen.[105] According to Aristotle, virtue means taking a particular act or function to a higher degree. Virtue is a permanent disposition 'which makes a man good and which makes him do his own work well'.[106] It refers to such properties of human activity that allow the goal to be fully achieved. Referring to Aristotle's virtue ethics, Alasdair MacIntyre defines virtue as 'an acquired human quality the possession and exercise of which tends to enable us to achieve those goods which are internal to practices and the lack of which effectively prevents us from achieving any such goods'.[107] At the same time, the practice is not any

102 GWF Hegel, *Elements of the Philosophy of Right* (HB Nisbet trans., Cambridge University Press 2003) § 268.

103 It can be said that, from the point of view of an individual, the formal *Rechtsstaat* may manifest itself as the autopoietic one, which is functional but unfamiliar and closed, see Habermas, n 14, 48 et seq.

104 J Habermas, 'Three Normative Models of Democracy' in S Benhabib, ed, *Democracy and Difference. Contesting the Boundaries of the Political* (Princeton University Press 1996) 21–30.

105 Below we shall discuss the virtue of a citizen in general without giving any specific set of virtues. To read more on this topic in WA Galston, *Liberal Purposes. Goods, Virtues, and Diversity in the Liberal State* (Cambridge University Press 1991).

106 Aristotle, n 18, 1106a.

107 A MacIntyre, *After Virtue. A Study in Moral Theory* (University of Notre Dame Press 2007) 191.

activity, but a coherent and complex form of 'socially established cooperative human activity through which goods internal to that form of activity are realised in the course of trying to achieve those standards of excellence which are appropriate to, and partially definitive of, that form of activity'.[108] The internal goods of a given practice are the goods of the whole community in which it takes place. The community in which the virtue of a citizen is realised is the state understood as 'a partnership of citizens in a government'.[109] As an active citizen, the individual influences the shape of this community, and as its members, they identify their own good with the good of the community, which is connected with the necessity of restraining their own intentions and aspirations. Aristotle claims that 'the good citizen must have the knowledge and the ability both to be ruled and to rule, and the merit [*arête*] of the good citizen consists of having a knowledge of the government of free men on both sides'.[110] Referring to Kant, we may claim that a citizen should to be both a legislator and a member of the state.[111] A civic practice requires the involvement in political processes as well as the compliance with the law resulting from these processes. And referring directly to the democratic system, it is necessary for political rights of civic participation to ensure both the legitimacy of legislation and the compliance with the law. The individual may play the roles of both those who govern and are governed by adopting certain approaches; that is, they can perceive certain issues from an individual as well as a general perspective, accepting both individual or collective good as a criterion. The integration of these two perspectives may happen literally, because everyone who holds public functions is also a citizen, and every citizen has access (more or less formalised) to the public service. In general, the citizen's perspective requires activity that takes into account the good of the entire political community and restraining individual aspirations and goals. Therefore, it is related to refraining from actions to only give a priority to the citizen's own privileged position and their own good.[112] Therefore, if Aristotle binds the Rule of Law with the subject of general and non-particularistic law, then the state being close to such an ideal could be described as the one where the citizens strive for their political practice to be as much compliant with the requirements of civic virtue as possible. On the other hand, abandoning the ideal of the Rule of Law may indicate that the virtue of civic practice is not well-developed in a given country at the civic and/or public level, and thus does not define the 'attitudes' of those who govern and/or those who are governed.

108 Ibid., 187.

109 Org. *koinonía politôn politeías*, Aristotle (n1) 1276b. In Aristotle, *Politics* (E Barker trans., Oxford University Press 1995) 1276b: 'an association of citizens in a constitution'.

110 Aristotle, n 1, 1277b.

111 I Kant, n 52, 41.

112 While Kant points out that it is not in accordance with the moral law that one considers oneself an exception, see I Kant, n 52, Sieyès shows that privileges and particularism cannot be combined with the universality of law, see E-J Sieyès, 'What Is the Third Estate?' in E-J Sieyès, *Political Writings: Including the Debate between Sieyès and Tom Paine in 1791* (M Sonenscher trans., Hackett Publishing Company 2003).

The Rule of Law can be realised in the state in which citizens act publicly in accordance with the requirements of civic virtue. 'Then the virtue of the state is of course caused by the citizens who share in its government being virtuous; and in our state all the citizens share in the government'.[113] On the whole, the Rule of Law is not so much a set of ready-made institutional solutions[114] but a civic practice of acting for the benefit of a given political community. Without civic virtue, even the best legally established institutions and procedures will not work in accordance with the principle of the 'Rule of Law, not the rule of people'. If the rulers and the governed do not restrain their desires and they only pursue their personal goals, then the law will be only a means to achieve these goals. It cannot, therefore, be concluded that, in this case, the political attitude has developed properly, namely, there is no trust and identification of individual interests with the common good. Such a case is basically similar to Hobbes' state of nature, in which every individual or actor will use all possible means to increase their power.[115] The principle of the Rule of Law, however, introduces a limitation in the structure of social practice which requires taking into account the good of the political community as a whole. If this good is at least to some extent implemented in practice, then we can say that we are beginning to come out of the state of nature and enter the path of the Rule of Law.

> For the laws should be laid down, and all people lay them down, to suit the constitutions – the constitutions must not be made to suit the laws; for a constitution is the regulation of the offices of the state in regard to the mode of their distribution and to the question what is the sovereign power in the state and what is the object of each community, but laws are distinct from the principles of the constitution and regulate how the magistrates are to govern and to guard against those who transgress them.[116]

A democratic constitution must be based on the virtues of citizens acting both as 'rulers' ('legislators') and 'the governed' ('subjects') if it is to be not only a political declaration but, above all, a systemic practice. Laws do not govern where only a particular will matters and where there are no universal norms. 'Where the laws do not govern there is no constitution'[117] because, in such a case, it is impossible to speak of any regulation of political power: political power decides sovereignly, and it is limited only by its power and ability to achieve its own goals.

3.6. Conclusion

The idea of the Rule of Law outlined in this essay should be treated as a regulative idea rather than a criterion for qualifying particular political systems whether they

113 Aristotle, n 1, 1332a.
114 See Krygier, n 28, 47–52.
115 Hobbes, n 4, chapter XIII.
116 Aristotle, n 1, 1289a.
117 Ibid., 1292a.

are or are not fully in the spirit of the idea. One may only wish to make this idea a reality, not replicate it. It can also be an instrument to assess a specific systemic reality and to postulate reforms based on the guidelines which this idea gives. Modern constitutionalism can be seen as an attempt to implement the idea of the Rule of Law adopted at a specific stage of historical and political development. It does not mean that this is the 'end of history', i.e., a conceptually optimal form of the political system of the state. It may be assumed that the implementation of this idea will take various forms in the future. If these various forms limit the arbitrariness and particularism of political power and the law will be something more than an instrument of governance, then the laws will govern. Of course, such a general idea does not just inspire to make some simple rules on how to put it into practice. This idea requires invention and imagination to enable state institutions to function effectively, and to make everyone see sense and value in the compliance with legal norms. In other words, it is to answer the question of what conditions would have to be met to make it possible that the action in accordance with the law resulted not only from external coercion but also from the free will of the person acting. The difficulty in finding the answer to this very question means that the history of political ideas will continue.

Bibliography

Robert Alexy, 'Hans Kelsens Begriff der Verfassung', in Stanley L Paulson and Michael Stolleis, eds, *Hans Kelsen. Staatsrechtslehrer und Rechtstheoretiker des 20. Jahrhunderts* (Mohr Siebeck 2005) 333–352.

Hannah Arendt, *On Revolution* (Penguin Books 1990).

Aristoteles, *Politik* (Franz Susemihl trans., Rowohlt Taschenbuch Verlag 2014).

Aristotle, *Politics* (Ernest Barker trans., Oxford University Press 1995).

Aristotle, *Politics* (Harris Rackham trans., Harvard University Press 1993).

Aristotle, *The Nicomachean Ethics* (David Ross trans., Oxford University Press 2019).

Augustine, *The City of God* (Marcus Dods trans., Modern Library 2000).

Ernst-Wolfgang Böckenförde, 'The concept and problems of constitutional state', in Ernst-Wolfgang Böckenförde, ed, *Constitutional and political theory. Selected writings* (Mirjam Künkler and Tine Stein, eds, Thomas Dunlap trans., Oxford University Press 2017) 141–151.

Ernst-Wolfgang Böckenförde, 'The historical evolution and changes in the meaning of the constitution', in Ernest-Wolfgang Böckenförde, ed, *Constitutional and political theory. Selected writings* (Mirjam Künkler and Tine Stein, eds, Thomas Dunlap trans., Oxford University Press 2017) 152–168.

Horst Dreier, *Gilt das Grundgesetz ewig? Fünf Kapitel zum modernen Verfassungsstaat* (Carl Friedrich von Simens Stiftung 2009).

Ronald Dworkin, *Taking Rights Seriously* (Harvard University Press 1978).

Richard H, Jr Fallon, 'The Rule of Law as a Concept in Constitutional Discourse', 1(97) *Columbia Law Review* (1997) 1–56.

Jill Frank, *A Democracy of Distinction. Aristotle and the Work of Politics* (The University of Chicago Press 2005).

Lon L Fuller, *The Morality of Law* (Yale University Press 1969).

William A Galston, *Liberal Purposes: Goods, Virtues, and Diversity in the Liberal State* (Cambridge University Press 1991).

Dieter Grimm, 'The achievement of constitutionalism and its prospects in a changed world', in Petra Dobner and Martin Loughlin, eds, *The twilight of constitutionalism?* (Oxford University Press 2012) 3–22.

Jürgen Habermas, *Between Facts and Norms. Contributions to a Discourse Theory of Law and Democracy* (William Rehg trans., The MIT Press 1996).

Jürgen Habermas, 'Three Normative Models of Democracy', in Seyla Benhabib, ed, *Democracy and difference. Contesting the boundaries of the political* (Princeton University Press 1996) 21–30.

Jürgen Habermas, 'Über den inneren Zusammenhang von Rechtsstaat und Demokratie', in Urlich K Preuß, ed, *Zum Begriff der Verfassung. Die Ordnung des Politischen* (Fischer Taschenbuch Verlag 1994) 83–94.

Alexander Hamilton, Madison James, and Jay John, *The federalist with the letters of 'Brutus'* (Terence Ball, ed, Cambridge University Press 2003).

Herbert LA Hart, *The Concept of Law* (Clarendon Press 1994).

Georg WF Hegel, *Elements of the Philosophy of Right* (Hugh B. Nisbet trans., Cambridge University Press 2003).

Georg WF Hegel, *Hegel's Philosophy of Mind. Translated from the Encyclopaedia of the Philosophical Sciences* (William Wallace trans., Oxford, Clarendon Press 1894).

Thomas Hobbes, *Leviathan* (Oxford University Press 1998).

Stephen Holmes, 'Lineages of the Rule of Law', in José M. Maravall and Adam Przeworski, eds, *Democracy and the Rule of Law* (Cambridge University Press 2003) 19–61.

Stephen Holmes, 'Precommitment and the paradox of democracy', in Jon Elster and Rune Slagstad, eds, *Constitutionalism and democracy* (Cambridge University Press 1993) 195–240.

Georg Jellinek, *System der Subjektiven Öffentlichen Rechte* (Verlag von JCB Mohr 1905).

Immanuel Kant, *Groundwork of the metaphysics of morals* (Mary Gregor trans., Cambridge University Press 1997).

Immanuel Kant, *The Conflict of the Faculties* (Mary Gregor trans., Abaris Books 1979).

Immanuel Kant, *The metaphysics of morals* (Mary Gregor trans., Cambridge University Press 1991).

Immanuel Kant, *Toward Perpetual Peace and Other Writings on Politics, Peace, and History* (David L Colclasure trans., Yale University Press 2006).

Hans Kelsen, *Pure Theory of Law* (Max Knight trans., The Lawbook Exchange 2005).

Martin Krygier, 'The Rule of Law: Legality, Teleology, Sociology', in Gianluggi Palombella and Neil Walker, eds, *Relocating the Rule of Law* (Hart Publishing 2009) 45–70.

Martin Krygier, 'The Rule of Law: Pasts, Presents, and Two Possible Futures', 12 *Annual Review of Law and Social Science* (2016) 199–229.

John Locke, *Two Treatises of Government and A Letter Concerning Toleration* (Yale University Press 2003).

David Lyons, *Ethics and the Rule of Law* (Cambridge University Press 1984).

Alasdair MacIntyre, *After Virtue. A Study in Moral Theory* (University of Notre Dame Press 2007).

José M Maravall and Przeworski Adam, 'Introduction', in José M. Maravall and Adam Przeworski, eds, *Democracy and the Rule of Law* (Cambridge University Press 2003) 1–18.

Montesquieu, *The Spirit of the Laws* (Anne M Cohler, Basia C Miller, Harold S Stone trans., Cambridge University Press 1998).
John Rawls, *A Theory of Justice* (The Belknap Press of Harvard University Press 1999).
John Rawls, *Political Liberalism* (Columbia University Press 1993).
Joseph Joseph Raz, 'Kelsen's theory of the basic norm', in Stanley L Paulson and Bonnie Litschewski-Paulson, eds, *Normativity and norms. Critical perspectives on Kelsenian themes* (Clarendon Press 1998) 47–68.
Joseph Joseph Raz, 'The law's own virtue', 39(1) *Oxford Journal of Legal Studies* (2019) 1–15.
Joseph Joseph Raz, 'The Rule of Law and its Virtue', in J Raz, ed, *Authority of law. Essays on law and morality* (The Clarendon Press 1979) 210–229.
Michael Rosenfeld, 'The Rule of Law and the Legitimacy of Constitutional Democracy', 74 *Southern California Law Review* (2001) 1307–1351.
Ignacio Sánches-Cuenca, 'Power, Rules, and Compliance', in José M Maravall and Adam Przeworski, eds, *Democracy and the Rule of Law* (Cambridge University Press 2003) 62–93.
Julian A Sempill, 'Ruler's Sword, Citizen's Shield: The Rule of Law & the Constitution of Power', XXXI *Journal of Law and Politics* (2016) 333–417.
Emmanuel-Joseph Sieyès, 'What Is the Third Estate?', in Emmanuel-Joseph Sieyès, ed, *Political writings. Including the debatte between Sieyès and Tom Paine in 1791* (Michael Sonenscher tr, Hackett Publishing Company 2003) 92–162.
Leo Strauss, *The City and the Man* (The University of Chicago Press 1978).
Brian Z Tamanaha, *On the Rule of Law. History, Politics, Theory* (Cambridge University Press 2004).
Jonathan H Turner, *The Structure of Sociological Theory* (Wadsworth Publishing Company 1998).
Max Weber, *Economy and Society. An Outline of Interpretive Sociology* (Guenther Roth and Claus Wittich, eds, University of California Press 1978).

Part III

Rule of Law in national practice

Is it a common value?

4 The Rule of Law, democracy, and human rights in Hungary

Tendencies from 1989 until 2019

András Jakab and Eszter Bodnár

4.1. Introduction

This chapter provides an overview of the constitutional developments that have taken place in Hungary over the last 30 years. To understand the background, it starts with a short history of Hungarian constitutional law, including the democratic transition in 1989–1990, and then describes the transition of 2010–2012. The chapter primarily focuses on the current state of the Hungarian constitutional system, which is analysed in the light of the essential constitutional values that represent the basis of Western constitutional states (the Rule of Law, democracy, and fundamental rights). Finally, the last part of the chapter concentrates on the social and cultural context and sets out the actual practices and narratives behind the formal rules of the constitutional system.

4.2. A short history of Hungarian constitutional law

Until the mid-20th century, Hungary did not have a constitutional charter but instead had a so-called historical constitution which, similarly to the traditional English constitution, consisted of doctrines and several important (substantively important but formally ordinary) statutes. The first attempt to create a written constitution was made during the short period of the Hungarian Soviet Republic after World War I, but it did not influence subsequent constitution-making processes. After World War II, the foundations of a new democratic and republican regime were regulated in Act I of 1946 on the Form of the State of Hungary, the provisions of which also reappeared in later constitutional texts. However, this was not a proper constitutional charter, but only the settlement of a few state-related matters at the level of an ordinary statute, and the constitutional system was soon changed by a Soviet-type socialist dictatorship.

Paradoxically, Hungary's first written constitution was adopted during the socialist era. Act XX of 1949 on the Constitution of the Hungarian People's Republic was, for the most part, a translation of the 1936 Soviet ('Stalin') Constitution. The system was based on the collectivisation of the means of production, the centralisation of state power, the instrumentalisation of law, the dictatorship of the proletariat (in practice: of the leadership of the communist party), the exclusivity of socialism as the political ideology, and the binding of the applicability of rights to the fulfilment of duties. The 1949 Constitution explicitly referred to these in several places.

The political transition in 1989 was paired with constitutional changes. As a result of the so-called 'National Roundtable' talks (a negotiation between new democratic movements and the state party as well as organisations such as trade unions), Act XXXI of 1989 on the Amendment of the Constitution was adopted and promulgated on 23 October 1989, along with the proclamation of the Republic.[1] It was formally a constitutional amendment and not a new constitution but, in substance, together with the statutes that were adopted shortly after, it fundamentally changed the constitutional system. Accordingly, one often spoke of the 1989–1990 Constitution, although the official constitution was still from 1949.

The content of the 1989–1990 Constitution came mainly from Western European constitutions (especially from the German Basic Law), some state-organisational solutions from Act I of 1946 on the [Republican] Form of Government of Hungary. The constitutional foundations were those of liberal democracy, and a constitutional court was established as the main institution of constitutional review. Its jurisprudence has interpreted the often-brief constitutional provisions, thus making an enormous contribution to the development of the Hungarian constitutional system and constitutional culture.[2]

Two key moments in the period between 1989–1990 and 2010 had the most influence on the constitutional system: the ratification of the European Convention on Human Rights in 1993, and accession to the European Union in 2004. Accession to the European Convention on Human Rights (ECHR) meant, on the one hand, complementing the national legal protection system through an international mechanism. On the other hand, accession to the ECHR also supported the domestic legal system, both as a benchmark for constitutional review and as an aid to the interpretation of any domestic legal norm. As a prerequisite for EU accession, numerous laws and regulations were re-enacted or amended in order to make them EU compliant. This was necessary for Hungary's acceptance into the common European constitutional area (pre-accession conditionality).[3]

The 1989–1990 Constitution was by no means perfect. It was based on a fragile compromise and was accordingly unstable. The constitutional reform was prepared in a short time, which resulted in a text with gaps and contradictions.

1 About the history of the National Roundtable and the constitutional changes in 1989–1990, see I Kukorelli, 'Alkotmánytörténeti áttekintés' in E Bodnár and Z Pozsár-Szentmiklósy, eds, *Alkotmányos tanok* (Budapest, I. HVG-Orac 2018) 214–229. October 23 1989 was symbolic: it was the 33rd anniversary of the 1956 anti-Soviet revolution.

2 A special feature of Hungarian constitutional doctrine, the 'invisible constitution' (developed by László Sólyom, the first president of the Constitutional Court) is defined as the texture of decisions of the Constitutional Court. In a concurring opinion by Sólyom, see 23/1990 (X.31) CC decision.

3 See P Sonnevend, 'Alapvető jogaink a csatlakozás után', 2 *Fundamentum* (2003).

The Constitutional Court could hardly rely on national constitutional traditions, which is why it often transplanted Western European solutions. The constitution failed to symbolise the democratic transition and lacked political legitimacy: politicians regarded it as a necessary evil, but it was hardly known to the general population. In addition, the high level of flexibility resulted in a number of amendments.[4]

There were several attempts in the 1990s and 2000s to adopt a new constitution, but all failed due to a lack of compromise: the adoption of a new constitution would have required a two-thirds majority of the Members of Parliament. From 1994 to 1998, the left-liberal coalition had such a majority and even tried to involve the opposition parties in a constitutional process. However, because of coalition-internal conflicts, this attempt also failed.

4.3. The constitutional changes between 2010 and 2012

After winning the election with more than two-thirds of the mandates in 2010, the governing coalition of Fidesz and KDNP announced that they would use their majority to adopt a new constitution. The draft of a new Hungarian constitution was prepared behind closed doors, in a non-transparent way, and neither the members of the opposition parties nor civil society organisations were involved. The bill was submitted by members of the governing coalition on 14 March 2011 and adopted by the Parliament barely a month later, on 18 April 2011. None of the opposition parties voted in favour of the new constitution: some of them did not participate in the parliamentary debate, which was already partisan anyway, while the others voted 'no'. The new constitution, called the 'Fundamental Law' (FL), was promulgated by the President of the Republic on 25 April 2011 and entered into force on 1 January 2012.

The constitution-making process was followed with great interest by the European institutions. The Venice Commission of the Council of Europe issued two opinions during the process,[5] the European Parliament adopted a resolution on the Hungarian Fundamental Law, and a few months later held a debate on Hungary. None of these actions had any real impact on the constitutional-making process and (except for a few technical details) the text of the Constitution.

The name 'Fundamental Law' (*Alaptörvény*) represents a certain historicising attitude that avoids the word 'constitution', which would refer to a single document.[6] It implies respect for the historical constitution mentioned above.

4 See in detail P Sonnevend, A Jakab, L Csink, 'The constitution as an instrument of everyday party politics: the Basic Law of Hungary' in A von Bogdandy and P Sonnevend, eds, *Constitutional Crisis in the European Constitutional Area* (Oxford, Hart 2015) 33–109.

5 Opinion on three legal questions arising in the process of drafting the new constitution of Hungary (No 614/2011, 28 March 2011); Opinion on the new Constitution of Hungary, (No. 618/2011, Venice, 17–18 June 2011) (Venice Commission Op 618/2011).

6 H Küpper, *Einführung in das ungarische Recht* (München, Beck 2011) 295; A Vincze and M Varju, 'Hungary the New Fundamental Law' in 3 *European Public Law* (2012) 437.

Contrary to the political rhetoric that suggested a break in continuity, about 80% of the text came from the democratic constitution of 1989–1990. Decision-makers most likely realised that it would have been too risky for them to experiment with completely new solutions. Therefore, they rejected ideas for introducing a semi-presidential system or a bicameral system. Hungary continues to be a parliamentary system with a one-chamber Parliament.

There have been some codification improvements, as well as some positive content changes, such as the introduction of a debt brake. The new parts of the text include, in part, symbolic or ideological elements, such as a liberal catalogue of fundamental rights with ad hoc exceptions, a conservative preamble, and anti-Marxist rhetoric. But they are rather contradictory and eclectic. For example, on the one hand, there is parliamentary sovereignty justifying the curtailment of the powers of the Constitutional Court; on the other hand, the budgetary authority of the Parliament is limited by a veto power of the Budget Council. The process and the text seem to be motivated by ad hoc decisions: pragmatism was probably stronger than any ideological component.[7]

The original text of the Fundamental Law of March 2011 contained no transitional provisions at all. Point 3 of the Final Provisions of the Fundamental Law referred to the Transitional Provisions which had to be adopted in the same procedure as the amendments to the Fundamental Law itself. On this basis, on 30 December 2011, the Parliament acting *as constituent power* adopted a kind of appendix to the Fundamental Law, the Transitional Provisions. However, in addition to regulating the transitional period between the old and the new constitution, the Transitional Provisions contained several substantive provisions. Some of them included specific restrictions on fundamental rights or were apparently designed to undermine the jurisprudence of the Constitutional Court. However, in a dramatic decision of 45/2012. (XII. 29.), the Constitutional Court stated that Parliament had exceeded its constitutional power by adding rules to the Transitional Provisions which did not have the character of transitional provisions. As a result, the Constitutional Court overturned these overriding regulations.

The tendency to constitutional voluntarism was also reflected in the changes that followed the adoption of the Fundamental Law because sometimes the desired political result was not achieved on the first attempt. The Fundamental Law has been changed seven times to this day.

The most important of the amendments was the Fourth Amendment.[8] The main part of this amendment tried to reverse the above-mentioned decision of the Constitutional Court in that it annulled the non-transitional parts of the Transitional Provisions. The Parliament decided to unify the two parts of the text of the Constitution and added the provisions of the Transitional Provisions

7 Sonnevend, et al., n 4, 108.

8 For a plausibly worrying analysis of the Fourth Amendment, see Pierre-Alain Collott, 'Difficulté contre-majoritaire et usage impérieux du pouvoir constitutant dérivé au regard de la quatrième révision de la Loi fondamentale de Hongrie' 96 *Revue française de Droit constitutionnel* (2013) 789–812.

into the text of the Fundamental Law. These reinstated rules included substantive provisions, such as the competence of the President of the National Judicial Office to reallocate court cases [Article 27 paragraph (4) of the Fundamental Law of Hungary], and the suspension of the statute of limitations of criminal offences not prosecuted in the communist regime for political reasons [Article U paragraph (6) of the Fundamental Law of Hungary]. Apart from that, the Fourth Amendment reversed virtually all politically sensitive decisions the Constitutional Court had handed down after the 2010 elections. It was achieved by incorporating the content of the laws repealed by the Constitutional Court into the constitutional text itself and thus making it constitutional law.[9] This amendment resulted in a Fundamental Law with many specific exceptions to fundamental rights and numerous rules normally regulated at the level of an ordinary statute. It reduced not only the level of protection of fundamental rights but also the possibility of constitutional review, which was further reinforced by stricter initiating requirements and new deadlines. Finally, the Fourth Amendment also 'overruled' the Constitutional Court rulings given before the entry into force of the Fundamental Law.[10] Whether this means the prohibition of citation of previous cases, the invalidation of the content of former case-law, or is merely a rhetorical exercise, remains controversial in the literature. The Amendment also included in the text that the Constitutional Court can review constitutional amendments only on formal grounds but not on substance, thereby eliminating any activist efforts of the Court.[11] The Venice Commission criticised the Fourth Amendment in its opinion,[12] and the Fifth Amendment took into account a few of the critical remarks (unrealistically tight deadlines for some procedures at the Constitutional Court, reallocation of cases by the President of the Regional Court).

The Seventh Amendment, adopted in June 2018, must be viewed in light of the government's anti-migration propaganda campaign. Its main topic was migration, but in connection with it, it also obliged all state institutions to protect the constitutional self-identity and Christian culture of Hungary,[13] and set limits to the participation of the European Union: it 'shall be consistent with the fundamental rights and freedoms laid down in the Fundamental Law, and shall not limit Hungary's inalienable right of disposal related to its territorial integrity, population, form of government and governmental organisation'.[14]

9 See e.g., Art L(1) about the definition of family, Art VII(2) and (3) about the recognition of churches.

10 Point 4 of the Closing and Miscellaneous Provisions.

11 Based on this new provision, the Constitutional Court rejected the initiatives to review the Fourth Amendment [12/2013. (V. 24.) CC decision]. See an analysis in A Vincze, 'Az Alkotmánybíróság határozata az Alaptörvény negyedik módosításáról. Az alkotmánymódosítás alkotmánybírósági kontrollja', 3 *Jogesetek Magyarázata* (2013) 3–12.

12 European Commission for Democracy through Law (Venice Commission), *Opinion on the Fourth Amendment of the Fundamental Law of Hungary* (No 720/2013, 14 June 2013) (Venice Commission Op 720/2013).

13 Art R(4).

14 Art E(2).

The Fundamental Law maintained the system of the cardinal acts (other translations: two-thirds laws, priority laws): statutes whose adoption, amendment, and repeal require a two-thirds majority, and in the hierarchy stand between ordinary statutes and the constitution. The number of topics that must be regulated by a cardinal act is still high, but the two-thirds requirement now primarily concerns state organisation rather than fundamental rights. Cardinal acts create the risk of blockading future governments which, in the case of everyday political decisions, e.g., about economic and financial issues, is problematic.[15] From 2011 to 2013, new cardinal acts were enacted in almost all areas of constitutional law, with the result that the entire constitutional system was changed.

4.4. Overview of the current constitutional system in light of the most important constitutional principles

Since the entry into force of the Fundamental Law, there have been many other changes to the constitutional system. We cannot provide a complete overview of all these changes in this brief chapter, but instead we aim to provide a snapshot of the central issues of the current state of the Hungarian constitutional system.

4.4.1. The Rule of Law and separation of powers: Lacking stability and political instrumentalisation

Although amendment of the Fundamental Law requires an increased majority of two-thirds of the MPs, it is, in fact, quite flexible, because since the adoption of the Fundamental Law, the Hungarian Government has had such a majority for most of that time. The constitution, therefore, became a tool of politics. The amendments served everyday party-political needs, either by responding to the decisions of the Constitutional Court or by neutralising possible constitutional concerns about certain legislative projects.

Additionally, following 2010, the actual operation of the legal order was marked by an increasing instrumentalisation of legislation – that is, the use of law-making as a power politics tool – as well as unpredictability, undermining legal certainty.[16] Since then, the number of laws enacted has been continuously growing, with increasingly shorter time frames dedicated to their adoption.

15 The scope of cardinal acts has also been criticised by the Venice Commission in its Opinion 621/2011 on the New Constitution of Hungary, Adopted by the Venice Commission at its 87th Plenary Session (Venice, 17–18 June 2011).

16 On the lack of legal certainty, see P Tölgyessy, 'Politika mindenekelőtt: Jog és hatalom Magyarországon', in A Jakab and Gy Gajduschek, eds, *A magyar jogrendszer állapota* (Budapest, Magyar Tudományos Akadémia Társadalomtudományi Kutatóközpont Jogtudományi Intézet 2016) 17; Á Szalai and A Jakab, 'Jog mint a gazdasági fejlődés infrastruktúrája' in A Jakab and Gy Gajduschek, eds, *A magyar jogrendszer állapota* (Budapest, Magyar Tudományos Akadémia Társadalomtudományi Kutatóközpont Jogtudományi Intézet 2016) 116.

On the one hand, this is unfavourable from the point of view of legal certainty, and on the other hand, it has a negative impact on the quality of legislation, making frequent amendments necessary.[17]

While the new Fundamental Law maintained the most important institutions of the constitutional system, it took several steps aimed at weakening the checks and balances placed on the government. The Constitutional Court, which had played a crucial role in ensuring the separation of powers over the previous decades, was the first target of these measures. Even before the adoption of the Fundamental Law, the number of members of the Constitutional Court was raised from 11 to 15, enabling the government to elect 5 new justices at once.[18]

The Fundamental Law narrowed the competences of the Constitutional Court in various ways. First, the Fourth Amendment explicitly prohibited the review of the constitutional amendments, except in formal matters.[19] As already mentioned, it also overturned the Constitutional Court rulings given before the entry into force of the Fundamental Law.[20] The Fundamental Law also excluded a wide range of issues from the jurisdiction of the Constitutional Court; for example, in all cases relating to the state budget, taxes, duties, contributions, and tariffs.[21] It created a serious loophole in the Fundamental Law; a broad field in which the Constitution cannot be applied through judicial review.

Before the Fundamental Law came into force, anyone could apply to the Constitutional Court with a norm-control initiative. The Fundamental Law abolished the *actio popularis* and instituted constitutional complaint following German patterns.[22] This change, which had long been demanded by constitutional lawyers, was intended to reduce the workload of the Constitutional Court. De facto, however, this led to a balance that made the Constitutional Court more of a counterweight to the ordinary courts, but not to legislative and executive power. In the last couple of years, the Constitutional Court has delivered judgments in considerably fewer cases than previously and has often taken a minimalist, non-activist attitude in politically sensitive cases, using rather weaker means

17 For the statistics of the modifications of freshly adopted statutes, see M Sebők, B Kubik, and Cs Molnár, 'A törvények formális minősége – egy empirikus vázlat' in Zs Boda and A Szabó, eds, *Trendek a Magyar politikában 2. a Fidesz és a többiek: pártok, mozgalmak* (Budapest, Magyar Tudományos Akadémia Társadalomtudományi Kutatóközpont Politikatudományi Intézet, Napvilág 2017) 300, 304.

18 Act LXI of 2011 'A Magyar Köztársaság Alkotmányáról szóló 1949. évi XX. törvénynek az Alaptörvénnyel összefüggő egyes átmeneti rendelkezések megalkotása érdekében szükséges módosításáról'.

19 Art 24(5) of the FL.

20 However, the intent of the Parliament was not entirely fulfilled. The Constitutional Court in the 13/2013. (VI. 17.) CC decision stated that it is entitled to use the statements of its decisions taken prior to the entry into force of the Fundamental Law, if the language and the context of interpreted provision of the Fundamental Law is essentially the same as that of the 1989 Constitution.

21 Art 37(4) FL.

22 Art 24 FL.

(e.g., it does not annul unconstitutional rules, but only warns the legislature that there has been a failure to enact certain rules) or by just not deciding at all.[23]

While in the case of the Constitutional Court, the raising of the number of the members helped to change the composition, the renaming of other institutions provided an opportunity for the presiding leaders to be exchanged. The six-year mandate of the incumbent Data Protection Commissioner was prematurely brought to an end by the creation of a new National Agency for Data Protection. This step was challenged by the European Commission before the European Court of Justice, and, finally, the Hungarian government paid the former Data Protection Commissioner compensation to avoid diverse supranational judicial proceedings.[24] Article 25 paragraph (1) of the Fundamental Law stipulated that the highest judicial body would be the *Kúria* (historical Hungarian name for the Supreme Court), and, as a consequence, the President of the Supreme Court would have his term of office terminated upon the entry into force of the Fundamental Law. The former President of the Supreme Court turned to the European Court of Human Rights and won the case; however, his successor remained in office. As most of the officials of constitutional institutions are to be elected by a two-thirds majority of the Parliament, the governing coalition had the power to select them without the consent of the opposition parties (e.g., the Civil Rights Commissioner, the President of the *Kúria*, the President of the National Electoral Office, the Attorney General, the members of the National Electoral Commission, the President of the National Audit Office, or the President of the National Bank).

Another target of the political takeover was the judiciary. The Fundamental Law established a new institution for the administrative issues of the judicial branch, the National Judicial Office. Its president, also elected by two-thirds of MPs, has the most important competencies, namely the appointment of judges and presidents of courts. Although this power has been limited partly due to the criticism of the Venice Commission, the President of the National Judicial Office continues to have a significant influence in these areas. There are many credible reports, some of them publicised by the media, that on the level of actual practices a personal relationship with the head of the National Judicial Office was considered to be more important than the official criteria of merit. It painfully corrodes the informal elements of judicial independence.[25]

As a result of the introduction of a new age limit even before the entry into force of the Fundamental Law in 2011, approximately 10% of all judges, including

23 E Bodnár, F Gárdos-Orosz, Z Pozsár-Szentmiklósy: Hungary: 'Hungary: The State of Liberal Democracy', in R Albert, D Landau, P Faraguna, Š Drugda, eds, *Global Review of Constitutional Law* (Boston College/Clough Center for the Study of Constitutional Democracy 2018) 130–133.

24 Case C-288/12 *European Commission v Hungary* [2012] OJ C 227.

25 M Bencze and A Bodó, 'A magyar bírósági rendszer hatékonyságát és az ítélkezés színvonalát befolyásoló strukturális és személyi feltételek' in A Jakab and Gy Gajduschek, eds, *A magyar jogrendszer állapota* (Budapest, Magyar Tudományos Akadémia Társadalomtudományi Kutatóközpont Jogtudományi Intézet 2016) 441.

many in leadership positions, were dismissed within a year. Since the ruling was declared unconstitutional by the Constitutional Court and by the European Court of Justice, many have returned to their judicial roles (but not in leadership positions). The latest step in the reform of the judicial system is the introduction of a separate administrative court system through the Seventh Amendment of the Fundamental Law. These courts will decide on remedies against administrative law decisions, including in politically sensitive areas such as elections or freedom of assembly. According to the critics, including the Commissioner for Human Rights of the Council of Europe,[26] the new administrative court system, and in particular the strong powers of the Minister of Justice in its administration, may pose a risk to judicial independence. With reference to relevant international criticisms, the introduction of independent administrative jurisdiction following the European elections in June 2019 was suspended indefinitely.

4.4.2. Representative and direct democracy: Manipulation and decreasing opportunities

The Fundamental Law changed the scope of the electorate by removing the limitation on the right to vote that required a voter to be a resident in Hungary. It had a significant impact on the results of the last elections,[27] as it added thousands of new voters living around the world to the voters' lists, who mainly supported the governing coalition.[28]

The parliamentary electoral system was also been redesigned to include elements that favour the larger parties. As a result, the electoral system became less proportional: in the last election (2018), the governing coalition received 66.8% of the seats in Parliament with 48% of the votes. In its report about the 2018 parliamentary elections, the OSCE ODIHR Limited Election Observation Mission found that the elections

> were characterized by a pervasive overlap between state and ruling party resources, undermining contestants' ability to compete on an equal basis. Voters had a wide range of political options, but intimidating and xenophobic rhetoric, media bias and opaque campaign financing constricted the space for genuine political debate, hindering voters' ability to make a fully-informed choice.[29]

26 www.coe.int/en/web/commissioner/-/commissioner-calls-on-hungary-s-president-to-return to the-parliament-the-legislative-package-on-administrative-courts.

27 Due to Act CXIII of 2018, adopted in December 2019, these voters will also be able to vote at the European Parliamentary elections.

28 See the detailed numbers at www.valasztas.hu and an analysis in E Bodnár and B Varsányi, 'Decision of the Hungarian Constitutional Court on the Exercise of the Right to Vote of Hungarian Citizens Living Abroad' in M Szabo, PL Láncos and R Varga, eds, *Hungarian Yearbook of International Law and European Law* (The Hague, Eleven International Publishing 2017).

29 ODIHR Limited Election Observation Mission Final Report, Hungary Parliamentary Elections 8 April 2018 (Warsaw, 27 June 2018).

In the last few decades, the procedures of direct democracy played an important role in Hungary's constitutional system. The new Fundamental Law annulled the citizens' initiative (an agenda-setting tool where voters could influence the agenda of the Parliament by collecting enough signatures) but maintained the national and local referenda. In practice, initiatives that originate from the voters or political parties face almost insurmountable hurdles: the Electoral Commission and the *Kúria*, which are responsible for examining the clarity and constitutionality of the referendum questions, systematically reject the politically more critical issues. The only national referendum held since 2010 was initiated by the government about the migration quota of the European Union – a question that should not have been accepted, given that the Fundamental Law stipulates that a national referendum can only be held about issues that fall under the competence of the Parliament. However, the referendum was invalid in the end because of the low voter turnout.

4.4.3. *Human rights: Liberal catalogue of fundamental rights with exceptions and diminishing effectiveness*

The Fundamental Law included a Western-type catalogue of fundamental rights that was even wider than that of the 1989–1990 Constitution and included some new rights stemming from the EU Charter of Fundamental Rights, e.g., the prohibition of cloning,[30] or the right to a good administration.[31]

However, the Fourth and Seventh Amendments to the Fundamental Law introduced some specific exceptions to various fundamental rights, which sought to 'correct' the case-law of the Constitutional Court. For example, Article IV paragraph (2) of the Fundamental Law contains the possibility of a life sentence without parole for 'intentional violent crimes'. The European Court of Human Rights held that the Hungarian regulation is incompatible with the Convention because it constitutes inhuman or degrading treatment,[32] but the regulation remained unchanged.

Overruling the decision of the Constitutional Court, which had held that the concept of a family limited to the marriage of a man and a woman was too narrow, since the State should also protect the long-term emotional and economic partnerships of persons living together,[33] the Fourth Amendment amended Article L paragraph (1) of the Fundamental Law, according to the new text, 'family ties are based on marriage or the relationship between parents'. Thus, the Fundamental Law today excludes some different forms of families in the sociological sense from the legal definition of family.

30 Art III (3).
31 Art XXIV.
32 T.P. and A.T. v. Hungary, no. 37871/14 and 73986/14, Judgment of 4 October 2016.
33 43/2012 (XII. 20.) CC decision.

The overruling of a decision of the Constitutional Court[34] concerning churches was also the aim of the Fourth Amendment. It inserted a requirement into the constitutional text that the Parliament shall be responsible in the future for deciding whether to approve a particular religious community as a 'church'.[35] Moreover, against these decisions of the Parliament there was no effective remedy.

Taking into account also the legal rules below the constitution (in ordinary or in cardinal statutes) and especially the everyday practice, the analysis shows that the level of protection of fundamental rights has been significantly reduced; for example, in the case of the freedom of information or the freedom of assembly. Procedures in serious cases are pending before national and international fundamental rights forums; e.g., concerning academic freedom in the case of the so-called lex CEU,[36] the freedom of association regarding the labelling of NGOs as 'supported from abroad',[37] or the human dignity of people penalised because of their homelessness.[38]

4.5. The constitutional system in the context of the legal culture and international, social, and cultural background

Just looking at the Fundamental Law alone is not enough to understand the Hungarian constitutional system. Many of the problems can be found in ordinary or cardinal statutes or the actual practice of authorities, and can only be understood in light of their political, social, and cultural background.[39] Selective personal continuity in independent institutions, the election and appointment of public officials without consensus or debate, and finally the informal influence exerted on the institutions' activities by these new leaders impede the independence of these institutions, thereby posing a risk to the separation of powers.[40]

Although the text of the Fundamental Law, with some exceptions, could provide the basis of a more-or-less well-functioning constitutional state, factors

34 6/2013 (III. 1.) CC decision.

35 Art VII (2).

36 European Commission v. Hungary, Case no. C-66/18. The Constitutional Court suspended its decision until the decision of the CJEU. 3199/2018. (VI. 21.) CC decision and 3200/2018. (VI. 21.) CC decision.

37 European Commission v. Hungary, Case no. C-78/18. The Constitutional Court suspended its decision until the decision of the CJEU. 3198/2018. (VI. 21.) CC decision.

38 Four judges turned to the Constitutional Court and asked for review of the statutory provision. Cases no. III/01727/2018, III/01829/2018, III/01704/2018, and III/01628/2018.

39 A Jakab, 'What Is Wrong with the Hungarian Legal System and How to Fix it', *MPIL Research Paper* No. 2018-13, <https://ssrn.com/abstract=3213378> (accessed 13 July 2018).

40 For an empirical analysis of government influence on the Hungarian Constitutional Court, see Z Szente, 'The Political Orientation of the Members of the Hungarian Constitutional Court between 2010 and 2014', 123 *Const.Stud.1.1* (2016) 123–149.

outside the constitution have the opposite effect. Institutionalised corruption, the lack of (and further decreasing of) media pluralism,[41] politically biased application of laws, and illiberal political rhetoric all contribute to the gradual weakening of the rule of law institutions. The various Rule of Law indices (*Freedom in the World, World Justice Project Rule of Law Index, Worldwide Governance Indicators Rule of Law Index*) show similar results: a slow, step-by-step erosion, starting from a quite good starting point.[42] This is shown in Figure 4.1 using the values in the Bertelsmann Transformation Index.

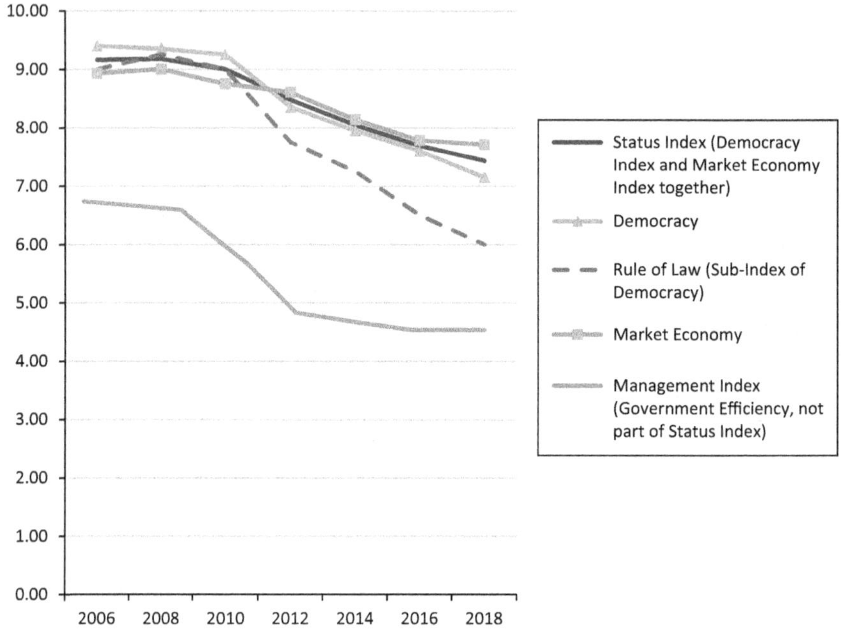

Figure 4.1 The Bertelsmann Transformation Index depicted on a diagram, data on Hungary from the period 2006–2018. Source: Jakab, n 39, 14.

It can be seen from the figure that Hungary was initially just below the maximum value of 10 with a value of about 9 points. The index values show that no sudden crash took place, and instead, there was slow but steady erosion, which got worse each year. Since February 2019, Freedom House no longer classifies Hungary as 'free' in its rating, but only as 'partially free', making Hungary the *only* EU member state which does not qualify anymore as 'free'.

41 The media pluralism is under attack since 2010. See a detailed analysis in A Brouillette, A Bátorfy, M Dragomir, É Bognár, D Holdis, 'Media pluralism monitor 2016 – Hungary', https://cmpf.eui.eu/media-pluralism-monitor/mpm-2016-results/hungary/.

42 Jakab, n 39, 14.

While the constitution-making process in 2011 and the following changes of the constitutional system were followed with a high level of interest by the European institutions (both in the Council of Europe and the European Union), their recommendations and inquiries remained mostly unheard. Even some of the obligatory decisions of the European Court of Human Rights and the Court of Justice of the European Union did not result in action being taken by the relevant Hungarian institutions. The EU postponed the adoption of stricter actions in order to protect the Rule of Law until recently. On 12 September 2018, the European Parliament recommended that the Council should declare that there is a clear risk of a serious breach by Hungary of the values referred to in Article 2 TEU.[43] It may lead to the application of the Article 7 TEU mechanism. However, a unanimous vote is required to suspend Hungary's voting rights and impose sanctions – a move that can be blocked by any other single Member State.

4.6. Conclusion

In the last three decades, the Hungarian legal system has undergone two fundamental transformations: the first was the dismantling of socialism and the construction of liberal democracy, the second was the dismantling of liberal democracy and the establishment of a hybrid regime. The first meant a conscious approximation to the Western European values of modern constitutionalism (in general: protection of fundamental rights and the separation of powers; more specifically, human dignity as a key concept and strong constitutional court in the state organisation), while the second signified a gradual, yet deliberate departure from it. This erosion of the Rule of Law since 2010 can also be demonstrated quantitatively with the Rule of Law indices.

So far, the steps taken by the EU have proved insufficient to halt or reverse this downward trend. However, without serious external pressure, there is little chance that this process will change in the near future. Moreover, even if the constitutional system is restored someday, the rebuilding of the legal culture that surrounds the constitutional system will be a prolonged and challenging process.

Bibliography

Mátyás Bencze and Attila Badó, 'A magyar bírósági rendszer hatékonyságát és az ítélkezés színvonalát befolyásoló strukturális és személyi feltételek', in Jakab András and Gajduschek György, eds, *A magyar jogrendszer állapota* (Budapest, Magyar Tudományos Akadémia Társadalomtudományi Kutatóközpont Jogtudományi Intézet 2016) 415–441.

Eszter Bodnár, Fruzsina Gárdos-Orosz, and Zoltán Pozsár-Szentmiklósy, 'Hungary: The state of liberal democracy', in Richard Albert, David Landau, Pietro Faraguna,

43 European Parliament resolution of 12 September 2018 on a proposal calling on the Council to determine, pursuant to Article 7(1) of the Treaty on European Union, the existence of a clear risk of a serious breach by Hungary of the values on which the Union is founded (2017/2131(INL)).

and Šimon Drugda, eds, *Global Review of Constitutional Law* (Boston College/ Clough Center for the Study of Constitutional Democracy 2018) 138–142.

Eszter Bodnár and Benedek Varsányi, 'Decision of the Hungarian Constitutional Court on the exercise of the right to vote of Hungarian citizens living abroad', in Marcel Szabo, Petra Lea Láncos, and Réka Varga, eds, *Hungarian yearbook of international law and European law* (The Hague, Eleven International Publishing 2017) 427–458.

Amy Brouillette, Marius Dragomir, Éva Bognár, and Dumitrita Holdis, 'Media pluralism monitor 2016 – Hungary', October 2016, https://cmpf.eui.eu/media-pluralism-monitor/mpm-2016-results/hungary (accessed May 2020).

Pierre-Alain Collot, 'Difficulté contre-majoritaire et usage impérieux du pouvoir constitutant dérivé au regard de la quatrième révision de la Loi fondamentale de Hongrie', 96 *Revue française de Droit constitutionnel* (2013) 789–812.

András Jakab, 'What Is Wrong with the Hungarian Legal System and How to Fix it', *MPIL Research Paper No. 2018/13* (2018), https://ssrn.com/abstract=3213378 (accessed 13 July 2018).

István Kukorelli, 'Alkotmánytörténeti áttekintés', in E Bodnár and Z Pozsár-Szentmiklósy, eds, Alkotmányos tanok I (Budapest, HVG-Orac 2018) 214–228.

Herbert Küpper, *Einführung in das ungarische Recht* (München, Beck 2011).

ODIHR, 'ODIHR limited election observation mission final report', *Hungary Parliamentary Elections 8 April 2018* (Warsaw, 27 June 2018).

Miklós Sebők, Bálint Kubik, and Csaba Molnár, 'A törvények formális minősége – egy empirikus vázlat', in Boda Zsolt and Szabó Andrea, eds, *Trendek a Magyar politikában 2. a Fidesz és a többiek: pártok, mozgalmak* (Budapest, Magyar Tudományos Akadémia Társadalomtudományi Kutatóközpont Politikatudományi Intézet, Napvilág 2017) 285–310.

Pál Sonnevend, 'Alapvető jogaink a csatlakozás után', 2 *Fundamentum* (2003) 27–37.

Pál Sonnevend, András Jakab, and Lóránt Csink, 'The constitution as an instrument of everyday party politics: The basic law of Hungary', in Armin von Bogdandy and Sonnevend Pál, eds, *Constitutional crisis in the European constitutional area* (Oxford, Hart 2015) 33–110.

Ákos Szalai and András Jakab, 'Jog mint a gazdasági fejlődés infrastruktúrája', in Jakab András and Gajduschek György, eds, *A magyar jogrendszer állapota* (Budapest, Magyar Tudományos Akadémia Társadalomtudományi Kutatóközpont Jogtudományi Intézet 2016) 116.

Zoltán Szente, 'The political orientation of the members of the Hungarian Constitutional Court between 2010 and 2014', 123 *Const.Stud.1.1* (2016) 123–149.

Péter Tölgyessy, 'Politika mindenekelőtt: Jog és hatalom Magyarországon', in Jakab András and Gajduschek György, eds, *A magyar jogrendszer állapota* (Budapest, Magyar Tudományos Akadémia Társadalomtudományi Kutatóközpont Jogtudományi Intézet 2016) 17–42.

Venice Commission, 'Opinion 621/2011 on the new constitution of Hungary, adopted by the Venice Commission at its 87th Plenary Session (Venice, 17–18 June 2011).

Attila Vincze, 'Az Alkotmánybíróság határozata az Alaptörvény negyedik módosításáról. Az alkotmánymódosítás alkotmánybírósági kontrollja', 3 *Jogesetek Magyarázata* (2013) 3–12.

Attila Vincze and Márton Varju, 'Hungary the New Fundamental Law', 3*European Public Law* (2012) 437–453.

5 The Rule of Law

The Hungarian perspective

Tímea Drinóczi

5.1. Introduction

This chapter summarises the value-level non-compliance with the European Rule of Law, which also implies the disagreement of the political idea this concept represents according to the Rule of Law Checklist of the Venice Commission.[1] It follows from the concept of the European Rule of Law that this Checklist could be used as a benchmark when assessing the Hungarian approaches to the European Rule of Law as a value. The Rule of law Checklist mentions the criteria of equality, non-discrimination, and an independent judiciary, which maintains the constitutional supremacy and legality, legal certainty, prevention against the abuse (misuse) of power, and access to justice. The Rule of Law concept of the Checklist seems to embrace a more substantive understanding of the Rule of Law,[2] as it fits the European or Western type of (liberal) constitutionalism the EU and the European states have nurtured.[3]

The acquis-compliance is outlined by recalling the jurisprudence of the Hungarian Constitutional Court (CC) on the domestic Rule of Law interpretation, and the application of EU law by the legislative and judicial powers in

1 Rule of Law Checklist (Adopted by the Venice Commission at its 106th Plenary Session (Venice, 11–12 March 2016). Undoubtedly, the role and mission of the Venice Commission and that of the EU are different; but, as they profess the same values, including the rule of law, they do cooperate. See e.g., the new EU Framework to strengthen the Rule of Law, n 7; W Hoffmann-Riem, 'The Venice Commission of the Council of Europe – Standards and Impact', 2 *EJIL* (2014) 595. It thus makes sense to use the already available Checklist.

2 For a summary on the thin and thick concepts, see e.g., J Moller, 'The advantages of a thin version', in C May and A Winchester, eds, *Handbook of the Rule of Law* (Edward Elgar 2018); A Bedner, 'The promise of a thick view', in C May and A Winchester, eds, *Handbook of the Rule of Law* (Edward Elgar 2018).

3 See e.g., D Kochenov, 'The EU and the Rule of Law – Naïveté or a grand design?', 5 *University of Groningen Faculty of Law Research Paper Series* (2018) 10. Even the ECJ seems to have thickened up judicial independence by the decision on the Polish judicial independence. MA Simonelli, 'Thickening up judicial independence: The ECJ ruling in Commission v. Poland (C-619/18)', https://europeanlawblog.eu/2019/07/08/thickening-up-judicial-independence-the-ecj-ruling-in-commission-v-poland-c-619-18/. This indirectly supports the view on the thick (European) understanding of the Rule of Law.

Hungary. This chapter will elaborate only on the former. Regarding the latter, it only refers to what has been covered in Chapter 1, which can be briefly summarised as follows: as a Member State, Hungary's compliance rate positions it as an average performer among the EU27. EU law, as a matter of fact, 'imposes particular political, albeit rather weak, legal constraints on the Hungarian […] political leaderships'.[4]

5.2. Value level and political ideal – hollowing out the European Rule of Law

In Hungary, having always been influenced by Prussian and German legal traditions, the German understanding of the Rule of Law has always informed the constitutional jurisprudence and the scholarly literature. Even the Hungarian equivalent of the rule of law [*jogállam*] is a literal translation of the German expression of *Rechtsstaat*. In the first 20 years after the transition, no severe Rule of Law issues occurred, and there were no suspicions regarding a systematic threat to the realisation of this principle in Hungary. The transition was a peaceful and smooth process,[5] assisted by the Constitutional Court. In 2004, Hungary joined the European Union. It meant that Hungary had fulfilled the Copenhagen criteria, which, among others, include the adherence to the Rule of Law. As is well known, difficulties emerged after the 2010 parliamentary election.

5.2.1. Legality and legal certainty – manipulating the constitution and upholding the law regardless of its content and spirit

When the constitution can be changed according to the daily political interest of the leading political party (seven times in seven years), and when the Constitutional Court is packed, the supremacy of the constitution, as well as legality, is neither a political nor a legal reality. The Fundamental Law (FL), to a certain extent, has illiberal[6] content. It is divisive and more ideological than neutral. It provides a lower level of protection of some liberties than the previous constitution. It is neither participatory nor popular in terms of its creation but embraces a strong and

4 See T Drinóczi and A Bień-Kacała, 'Illiberal constitutionalism and the European Rule of Law', Chapter 1 of this book, 36.

5 See e.g., M Bánkuti, G Halmai, and KL Scheppele, 'From Separation of Powers to a Government without Checks: Hungary's Old and New Constitutions' in GA Tóth, ed, *Constitution for a Disunited Nation. On Hungary's 2011 Fundamental Law* (CEU Press 2012) 241–242.

6 This content is not consistent with that of the teleological constitutions of post-liberal constitutionalism. JM Farinucci-Fernós, 'Post-liberal constitutionalism', 1 *Tulsa L Review* (2018) 35–47. More on Hungary, see e.g., T Drinóczi and A Bień-Kacała, 'Illiberal Constitutionalism: The Case of Hungary and Poland', 20 *German Law Journal* (2019) 1140–1145; AL Pap, *Democratic Decay in Hungary* (Routledge 2017); P Sonnevend, A Jakab, L Csink, 'The Constitution as an Instrument of Everyday Party Politics: The Basic Law of Hungary', in A von Bogdandy and P Sonnevend, eds, *Constitutional Crisis in the European Constitutional Area* (Beck – Hart – Nomos 2015) 33–109.

exclusive majoritarianism. It provides for a weak constitutional protection due to the packed nature of the CC and the threats the independence of the prosecution and ordinary judiciary meet. These imply that both the content of the law and decisions of the courts and the CC that are in conformity with the FL might as well be 'illiberal', too.

The Hungarian law-making process is not inclusive but accelerated, poorly prepared, in terms of consultation and impact assessment, and ad hoc in nature.[7] These phenomena, as Jakab and Bodnár mentioned it,[8] affect legal certainty as well. Legitimate expectations are also frustrated, not to mention the disrespect of the prohibition on detrimental retroactive legislation in 2010 when the possibility of detrimental retroactive legislation became a constitutional rule. In this respect, during 2010–2011, not even one of the most crucial, and never contested, components of the thinnest concept of the Rule of Law[9] was observed in Hungary.

It also follows from the concept of illiberal constitutionalism that public authorities do comply with illiberal laws. They do so, eventually, even if the compliance with the particular piece of legislation, which might be a remnant of the previous constitutionalism[10] or has not been profoundly transformed due to the existing constraints on public power, is not in the interest of the regime. For that, they would need a court decision. However, even the right to access to court is used as an instrument to either widen the political playground or delay the enforcement of lawful interests and rights. Therefore, it does not matter if a court would instruct the state to comply with the law, e.g., in freedom of information cases. This compliance would not entail political harm, but it can proudly be said that the law was upheld, the courts rendered justice, the particular fundamental right could be, eventually, enforced.

The separation of power, in terms of personnel, seems to be missing in Hungary. Key positions are occupied by personal friends of the prime minister (or by their relatives), such as the Prosecutor General, who is supposed to be a *sui generis* independent actor, the President of the Republic, who is *ex lege* supposed to be a neutral head of state and who appoints judges, the President of the National Judicial Office, the Chairperson of the Parliament, who determines and influences parliamentary procedures and how the opposition can exercise its oversight function and rights to participate in the debates.[11]

7 T Drinóczi, 'Legislation in Hungary', in H Xanthaki and U Karpen, eds, *Legislation in Europe: A Country to Country Guide* (Hart Publishing, forthcoming).

8 See A Jakab and E Bodnár, ' The Rule of Law, Democracy and Human Rights in Hungary: Tendencies from 1989 until 2019' Chapter 4 of this volume 110.

9 See e.g., J Raz, 'The rule of law and its virtue' in J Raz, ed, *The authority of law: Essays on law and morality* (Oxford University Press 1979) or for a summary, Moller, n 2, Bedneer, n 2.

10 For a concept of this see, GA Tóth, 'Illiberal rule of law? Changing features of Hungarian constitutionalism', in M Adams et al., eds, *Constitutionalism and the Rule of Law* (Cambridge University Press 2017).

11 See e.g., the case of Karácsony and Others v. Hungary, Application Nos. 42461/13 and 44357/13. The case originated in the imposition of fines on several members of the

Exceptions in emergencies are not adequately regulated in Hungary[12] – which is another failure if we think about the Rule of Law Checklist. The scholarly literature has not been concerned about the introduction of the 'crisis situation caused by mass migration' in 2015; nonetheless, it raises serious questions. The first is that the 'crisis situation' pretends not to be an emergency, because it is not stipulated in the FL under the chapter on Special Legal Order, but it acts like one. It does give extra, and de facto unlimited, power to the government, unnecessarily and disproportionally limiting the liberties and violating the constitutional principles of criminal law. Second, it has been continuously extended since it expired for the first time. However, the extension has never had justifiable grounds as the statutory conditions of extension have never been met.[13]

5.2.2. Access to justice and judicial independence – compromised and centralised

The remodelling of constitutionalism and the Rule of Law in the field of judicial power have two distinct characteristics.

The first is that the remodelling is being made under the guise of reforms which appear to be necessary, and which sometimes meet the expectations of the wider public and professional community. The government addresses constitutional changes (the introduction of the *Kúria* to replace the Supreme Court),[14] real structural matters (nomination of Constitutional Court judges[15] and the

Hungarian parliament who had chosen to show their opposition to various new laws by ways other than through the traditional parliamentary speeches and submissions.

12 T Drinóczi, 'Special Legal Orders: Challenges and Solutions', 4 *OsteuropaRecht* (2016) 420–437; T Drinóczi, 'Central and Eastern European constitutional formulas: The abuse and observance of constitutions in times of emergency', The 10th IACL-AIDC World Congress, Seoul, 2018 Workshop – Abuse of the Constitution in Times of Emergency, www.researchgate.net/publication/335762469_Central_and_Eastern_European_constitutional_formulas_the_abuse_and_observance_of_constitutions_in_times_of_emergency/stats.

13 The de facto situation of migration gives reason for far less concern than is communicated in the biased media and by political communication campaigns. Moreover, even though the reasons based on which the Government extends this situation are supposed to be publicly available as per the Freedom of Information Act, those who want to access them, i.e., media or different NGOs, need to bring the case before the court. The court proceedings, however, cannot restore the time wasted which gravely affects the efficiency of civil control mechanisms. For more on this, see T Drinóczi and Á Mohai, 'Has the migration crisis challenged the concept of the protection of the human rights of migrants? The case of Ilias and Ahmed v. Hungary1, in E Kużelewska; A Weatherburn, and D Kloza, eds, *Irregular migrations as a challenge for democracy* (Intersentia Cambridge 2018) 97–112.

14 The FL changed the name of the Supreme Court to *Kúria*. It eventuated the premature termination of the mandate of its president. Case Baka v. Hungary (application n 20261/12) indicated that Mr. Baka was removed because he, in his capacity as the President of the Supreme Court, publicly expressed professional opinion about the constitutional changes in Hungary.

15 The new nomination rules for Constitutional Court judges, already introduced in 2011, also addressed an existing challenge. Judges had been nominated by a parliamentary committee

workload of ordinary courts),[16] and social issues (retirement age of judges).[17] It might even come up with an idea of an otherwise supportable institutional change, such as the reform of the administration of justice in Hungary.[18] Nevertheless, the introduction of the criticised[19] administrative judiciary was, probably as a result of political pressure around the time of the European Parliament elections in the spring of 2019,[20] postponed.

The second feature is that by these reforms, on which the political power stubbornly insists until it is not in its interest anymore, the government compromises the primary constituent elements of judicial independence.

The threat of removal (the Baka and retirement case) could lead to chilling effects and self-censorship, which can not only affect the freedom of expression but the freedom of the judge to decide on cases without any undue influence. Transfer of cases can frustrate the right to access to court and the right to the assigned judge. Its temporary existence in the legal system, as it appeared in the

composed of an equal number of MPs from each parliamentary fraction (parity system) and elected by the two-thirds majority of the Parliament. Indeed, this mechanism made nominations impossible or degraded them to simple political bargaining, which is why this phenomenon needed to be addressed: the representation in the nominating committee was modified by shifting from the parity system to proportional representation; that is, the bigger fraction in the Parliament has more MPs in this committee.

16 The President of the National Judicial Office (NJO) could assign cases on her own discretion. This type of transfer of cases was part of the FL between spring and autumn of 2013 (Fourth and Fifth Amendments). It was apparently used for political purposes under the pretence of structural reforms, i.e., easing the workload of the judiciary. See e.g., the Opinion 663/2012 of the Venice Commission, and T Drinóczi, 'Constitutional politics in contemporary Hungary', 1 *ICL Journal* (2016) 63–98.

17 It led to the change in senior positions at courts, which is assumed to have been in the interest of the leading political power. This situation has substantially changed after neither the decision of the CJEU nor the subsequent legislation of the Hungarian government managed to make the laws compatible with EU law. See Decision 33/2012 (VII. 17.) CC and Case C-286/12 in which it was established that Hungary has failed to fulfil its obligations of Council Directive 2000/78/EC of 27 November 2000 establishing a general framework for equal treatment in employment and occupation. To put it in a comparative perspective, it is curious that the Court in 2018 held that a similar Polish reform (targeting the lowering of the retirement age of judges of the Supreme Court) breaches the principles of the irremovability of judges and judicial independence. Commission v. Poland C-619/18.

18 This reform was truly welcomed and affected the administration of judiciary by the NJO and its supervisory body, the National Judicial Commission (NJC). However, the reform led to the arbitrary exercise and monopolisation of power in the hand of the President of the NJO. The NJC repeatedly warned in its report of February 2019 [11/2019. (II.06.) decision of the Commission] that many of the actions of the President of the NJO, such as decision on appointments, management positions, non-cooperation with the NJC, had been unlawful.

19 Hungarian Helsinki Committee, 9 December 2018, https://jogaszvilag.hu/napi/az-alkotmanybirosaghoz-fordul-a-kozigazgatasi-birosagok-miatt-az-ellenzek/.

20 The Fidesz party's membership in the European People's Party (EPP) was suspended. www.epp.eu/press-releases/fidesz-membership-suspended-after-epp-political-assembly/.

FL in 2013 and previously in the Transitory Provisions to the FL (2012) is an example of opportunistic legislation. The reform on the administration of judiciary created a system in which all administrative decision concerning the court system is in one loyal hand, without effective oversight. It undoubtedly makes the administration easier and thus more efficient.

In the meantime, however, the judges are helpless and, while some of them stay, others leave the bench. Some judges have chosen to speak out. They had submitted applications to senior management positions and have gone to court when the President of the NJO refused their application without any legal ground. Others have been elected to the NJC and, as members, try to make the President of the NJO accountable. Some of them have been initiating preliminary ruling producers asking the CJEU if a particular piece of Hungarian legislation, including the one jeopardising judicial independence, is compatible with EU law.

As a result of these actions, it has become clear that the President of the NJO, apparently, cannot be held accountable for her unlawful appointment decisions in courts,[21] or removed by the Parliament.[22] There are other domestic actions as well which intend to support her total impunity. In the summer of 2019 a judge, Csaba Vasvári, suspended a criminal proceeding and asked the CJEU if laws concerning, amongst other things, the position and actions of the President of the NJO who has been already criticised by many fora,[23] are consistent with EU law, and, most importantly, if the judiciary is independent or not.[24] The Prosecutor General rapidly requested the *Kúria* to review the request, which ruled that the suspension of the particular case and the initiation of the preliminary ruling procedure are illegal if the subject matter of the request is not the interpretation or validity of EU law, but concerns questions irrelevant from the viewpoint of the outcome of the pending case. In the meantime, due to the infringement of judicial duties, a disciplinary procedure was initiated against the judge and got withdrawn. The disciplinary tribunal did not provide justification, claiming that the disciplinary procedure was a confidential one, but emphasised that its legal base was not the fact that the judge had asked the preliminary question.

21 Even though the lower court held that the decision on a particular appointment to senior managerial position was unlawful, the upper court decided that the President of the NJO cannot be sued.

22 In June 2019, the NJC initiated the removal of the President of the NJO at the Parliament due to the continuous abuse of power. The Parliament voted against the notion. https://birosag.hu/hirek/kategoria/birosagokrol/az-orszaggyules-megerositette-hivatalaban-az-obh-elnoket?_ga=2.265817423.1326036992.1568874584-167214665.1568874584

23 See e.g., European Association of Judges (Report on the fact-finding mission of the EAJ to Hungary, www.iaj-uim.org/iuw/wp-content/uploads/2019/05/Report-on-the-fact-finding-mission-of-a-delegation-of-the-EAJ-to-Hungary.pdf) and the European Council (Recommendation on the 2019 National Reform Programme of Hungary and delivering a Council opinion on the 2019 Convergence Programme of Hungary.

24 DG Szabó, 'A Hungarian Judge Seeks Protection from the CJEU – Part I', https://verfassungsblog.de/a-hungarian-judge-seeks-protection-from-the-cjeu-part-i/.

Neither the possible chilling effect that has intentionally been created by these bodies[25] nor the fact that the question on the judicial independence[26] has arrived at Luxemburg[27] can be denied.[28]

5.2.3. *Equality is questionable and the abused (misused) power*

There is always a justification for the government's, or the public administration's, action. It is either the abused language of human rights, with the claim that they interpret the law differently when they argue that something is just the opposite (e.g., freedom of information cases), or the continuous populist invocation of the popular will which has made the Fidesz party win the past three elections with an overwhelming majority. When it is needed to speak louder about fundamental rights, in the interest of the regime, i.e., political leaders, the Fundamental Law is amended.

The Seventh Amendment is a great example of a pure abuse of the language of human rights. It introduced a new restriction concerning how the right to peaceful assembly can be exercised. The new rules on limitation go way beyond the commonly accepted necessary and proportionality test and the 'peaceful nature' of a protest or any other public event. As a result, 'exercising the right to freedom of expression and assembly shall not impair the private and family life and home of others'. The political goal was obvious: preventing demonstrations at the house of the prime minister, and claiming that the privacy of others enjoys prevalence over a political right that is exercised occasionally and has to be peaceful anyhow, under any circumstances.[29]

25 Similarly see, e.g., Ibid., and P Bárd, 'Luxemburg as the Last Resort. The Kúria's Judgment on the Illegality of a Preliminary Reference to the ECJ', https://verfassungsblog.de/luxemburg-as-the-last-resort/

26 The concern behind this request is very similar to the request of the Polish courts in the AK and Others case. See, Judgment of the Court of Justice of the European Union of 19 November 2019 in Joined cases C-585/18,C-624/18 and C-625/18, AK and Others versus the Supreme Court (the independence of the judiciary is not ensured but it is up to the Polish courts to decide on this matter in a particular case), and the implementation of this ruling by different chambers of the Supreme Court (disregard the decision made by the non-independent judicial body), https://ruleoflaw.pl/translation-of-supreme-court-rulings-applying-ecj-judgment-of-19-november-2019/.

27 Case C-564/19.

28 It still remains to be seen how the CJEU will decide and what kind of political, legislative, and judicial reaction it will generate in Hungary if these responses will be similar to the Polish ones, which mainly try to prevent any criticism against the office of judges, including the implementation of the Supreme Court's decision.

29 Article VI(1) FL reads as follows: 'Everyone shall have the right to have his or her private and family life, home, communications and good reputation respected. Exercising the right to freedom of expression and assembly shall not impair the private and family life and home of others'.

5.3. Enforceable legal measure compliance

5.3.1. Jurisprudence of the CC in the first 20 years

During the first two decades, the CC continued to develop its doctrine on the Rule of Law, mainly when exercising the constitutional interpretation and the ex-post norm control[30] competence, which later was an *actio popularis* procedure. The CC, based on Article 2 of the Constitution ('independent and democratic state of the rule of law' [*független és demokratikus jogállam*]), made the following conceptualisation and considered the elements collected below as either the 'constituent parts of the Rule of Law' or the 'requirements that follow from the Rule of Law'.

In 1990, the Court said that the Rule of Law in the Constitution is to be interpreted in a formal sense, i.e., a thin understanding of the term; if there is a substantive issue at hand, other constitutional provisions apply, except when there is none. Article 2 can be directly applicable only in the absence of other applicable constitutional provisions.[31] In 1991 it added that the principle of the Rule of Law is not a secondary rule but an independent constitutional norm, the violation of which, in itself, can amount to the unconstitutionality of laws.[32]

Legal certainty, which was identified as the most crucial component of the Rule of Law,[33] also requires that no arbitrary decision be made during any exercise of power by the state and its organs or representatives.[34] Legal certainty also demands that the whole body of the law, its specific parts and provisions be clear, unambiguous, their impact predictable, and their consequences foreseeable by those to whom the laws are addressed. The prohibition of detrimental retroactive legislation is also a component of legal certainty.[35] Legal certainty embodies the protection of already acquired rights too, which includes some entitlements of the social security system and already granted fixed-termed tax allowances, etc.[36] The provision of an 'appropriate *vacatio legis*' is also connected to the Rule of Law and legal certainty. If it is not observed and its lack is ostensive, heavily jeopardised, or violates the Rule of Law, the particular piece of legislation is deemed

30 The *actio popularis* character of ex-post norm control guaranteed that the legislative organs did not merely have to fear annulment in case of unconstitutionality but also had to consider the fact that virtually anybody might control their activity and set in motion the abstract ex-post constitutional review mechanism.

31 Decision 31/1990 (XII. 18.) CC.

32 Decision 11/1992 (III. 5.) CC.

33 E.g., decisions 25/1992 (IV. 30.), 35/1994 (VI. 24.), 43/1995 (VI. 30.) CC.

34 E.g., decision 35/1994 (VI. 24.) CC. An administrative reform is to be deemed unconstitutional if it intends to accomplish the reforms by hollowing-out or deliberately setting aside the guarantee-rules of the Constitution. E.g., decision 131/2008 (XI. 3.) CC.

35 E.g., decisions 25/1992 (IV. 30.), 35/1994 (VI. 24.), 43/1995 (VI. 30.) CC.

36 E.g., decision 43/1995 (VI. 30.) CC. T Drinóczi and G Juhász, 'Social Rights in Hungary', in Krzysztof Wojtyczek, ed, *Social Rights as Fundamental Rights: XIXth International Congress of Comparative Law/le XIXe Congrès International de Droit Compare* (Eleven International Publishing 2016) 171–206.

to be unconstitutional.[37] The law is also unconstitutional if it violates the legal hierarchy, which is also viewed as one of the guarantees of legal certainty.[38]

The Court also attributed a value-content to the Rule of Law when it defined it as a fundamental value of Hungary,[39] which aims at the restriction of state intervention into the private lives of individuals and legal persons.[40] In other cases, the CC was ready to apply a thicker Rule of Law concept and justify its violation by referring to some value contents or neighbouring notions, such as democratic legitimacy,[41] the effective exercise of constitutional powers and good faith,[42] and the separation of powers.[43]

The Court interpreted Article 2 of the Constitution widely and took the opportunity to deduce other principles and rights from the constitutional principle of the Rule of Law. It could easily do it as, firstly, it viewed itself as a guarantor of the constitutional and Rule of Law revolution. Secondly, based on the competences under the Constitution, it could straightforwardly come up with interpretation and enforcement of the Rule of Law. Even if the term remained the same in Article B of the FL, circumstances have been changed since 2012.

5.3.2. Narrowed applicability of the Rule of law by the CC since 2010

Balázs Szalbot[44] gives an overview of how the application of the Rule of Law principle has been changed under the FL and after the considerable restriction of the ex-post norm control power of the CC and the introduction of the new constitutional complaint procedure. Pursuant to these new rules, the Court can, for

37 E.g., decisions 34/1991. (VI. 15.), 25/1992. (IV. 30.), 10/2001. (IV. 12.) CC. In certain cases, the Court was satisfied with a 'minimum *vacatio legis*' but it did annul Acts because 'appropriate *vacatio legis*' as explained above was not ensured. E.g., decisions 43/1995. (VI. 30.), 44/1995. (VI. 30.) CC. Pap I, 'A jogbiztonság formai eleme: a kellő felkészülési idő követelménye' [Formal component of the rule of law: The requirement of an appropriate *vacatio legis*], 1 *Kodifikáció* (2013) 14.

38 Decision 142/2010. (VII. 14.) CC.

39 Ibid.

40 Decision 32/1991 (VI. 6.) CC.

41 The violation of procedural rules of decision-making, i.e., the disrespect of different majority rules or legally prescribed consultation, may amount to its unconstitutionality. E.g., decisions 16/1998 (V. 8.) and 30/2000. (X. 11.) CC. The Court, however, has rarely annulled an Act based on the failure of consultation. Drinóczi, n 7.

42 The requirement of exercising powers of constitutional importance effectively and in a good faith, and the cooperation between state organs also stem from the principle of the rule of law. E.g., decisions 8/1992 (I. 30.), 12/2006 (IV. 24) CC.

43 The Constitution did not have any explicit provision on the separation of powers, therefore the CC, already in 1993, declared it as a constituent part of the Rule of Law, and one of the most significant criteria of substantive constitutionalism. E.g., decision 38/1993 (VI. 11.) CC.

44 B Szalbot, 'Jogállamiság mint Alaptörvényben biztosított jog [The rule of law as a right guaranteed by the Fundamental Law]', 4 *Arsboni* (2015) 17–25. This below discussion is based on his findings.

the first time, review the constitutionality of judicial decisions, and does not have a freedom to consider ex-post norm control initiative from anybody except those who are entitled to do so, i.e., the Government, by one-quarter of the Members of Parliament, by the ombudsman, by the President of the *Kúria* (supreme court), and by the Prosecutor General.[45] The workload of the CC changed; the vast majority of its cases are now based on a constitutional complaint against a judicial decision.[46] These types of constitutional complaints are admissible if an infringement of 'a right ensured by the Fundamental Law' can successfully be claimed.

Thus, the CC, under the new regime, has to decide whether petitioners can invoke an infringement of the Rule of Law principle in the constitutional complaint procedure. In other words, the question becomes: whether the constitutional principle of the Rule of Law is enforceable at all in the Hungarian legal system. The possibility for the Court to continue its earlier fertile practice, under which the enforceable 'rights ensured by the Constitution' was deducible from the principle of the Rule of Law and appeared in a non-taxative manner,[47] has been narrowed down. In the new jurisprudence, the principle of the Rule of Law [Article B of the FL] is enforceable only if the legislative power does not observe two criteria. The first is the prohibition of the detrimental retroactive legislation, and the second is the 'appropriate *vacatio legis*'. Consequently, in a procedure that alleges infringement of 'a right ensured by the FL' by a judicial decision, which constitutes the majority of the cases of the CC, the violation of these requirements cannot even be claimed.

5.3.3. Instrumental use of the Rule of Law by the CC since 2010

The Constitutional Court in 2012 and 2013 managed to use the Rule of Law in the widest sense imaginable when it decided on the unconstitutionality of the Transitory Provisions,[48] and then completely forget about it when it declined to review the constitutionality of the Fourth Amendment. Both show a tendency of instrumental use of the concept but with contrary purposes.

Referring to the substantive concept of the Rule of Law, which also binds the constitution-making power, was a heroic but quite arguable attempt to set aside the Transitory Provisions (adopted 31 December 2011; TP) from the legal system. In the decision 45/2012 (XII. 29), the CC annulled certain provisions of the TP, which later become the subjects of the infamous Fourth Amendment.

45 Arts 27 and 24 and 24/A of the Act CLI of 2011 on the CC. It seems to be highly unlikely that the Government or the Prosecutor General, who is seen as a loyal public servant of the Fidesz Party, most particularly the Prime Minister (https://hungarianspectrum.org/2016/05/16/viktor-orban-and-his-protector-peter-polt-the-prosecutor-general/), would initiate the process.

46 As a rough estimation, it can be reported that the ex-post norm control cases form around 5–6%. Procedures in which the constitutionality of a piece of legislation is examined form around 25% of the number of the constitutional complaint procedures initiated against a judicial decision. See more about statistics at https://hunconcourt.hu/statistics/.

47 Decision 1140/D/2006 CC.

48 Circumstances of the case see in Drinóczi, n 16, 63–98.

The Court stressed the uncertain nature of the TP in terms of legal hierarchy. Despite its texts and adoption process, the Court refused to view the TP as an expression of the will of the constituent power. If the CC had done so it would not have been able to review and partially annul it.[49] In its effort to annul the TP, the Court defined some constitutional requirements which even the constituent power has to respect. It deduced these requirements from Article B of the FL, which defines Hungary as an 'independent and democratic state of the rule of law' [*független és demokratikus jogállam*]. In this decision, the Rule of Law possesses all its previously deduced components and even much more: it binds the constitution-making power as well as involves the following new requirements. First, a state must have only one constitution so that the constitutional content can easily be detected (rejecting the de facto reality of the idea that the TP is a constitution, too). Second, all modifications to a constitution shall be incorporated into its text. Third, provisions to be adopted as a part of the text shall be of constitutional importance and a coherent fit. The new provisions should also not be contradictory to one another. Fourth, extraconstitutional rules that appear at the supranational and international level shall be present in the constitutional texts as it is required by the concept of constitutional legality. The Court warned that in certain situations it would review the realisation of the substantive elements of the 'democratic state of the rule of law'. It also noted that the level of the realisation of the Rule of Law could not be reduced. All these implied a possibility of a future substantive review of constitutional amendments, even in the absence of the power to do so.

To avoid such a review, the Fourth Amendment explicitly allowed the Court to conduct a formal review, which means that its substantive version is constitutionally excluded. Thus, when it was called for examining the Fourth Amendment and applying the understanding of the Rule of Law it developed in its decision from 2012, it declined. The CC claimed that a de facto substantial review on the Fourth Amendment was requested and it did not have the power to conduct this type of review on constitutional amendments.[50]

The ideological changes towards constitutionalism and the Rule of Law, as well as the consolidation of illiberal constitutionalism, could not leave alone the jurisprudence of the CC, either. As opposed to the first 20 years, which show the application of a thicker/less thin approach to the Rule of Law, in the last decade, the CC turned to a thinner and instrumental use of the Rule of Law.

5.4. Conclusion

Against this background, and in the context of the theory of the European Rule of Law depicted in Chapter 1, it can be concluded that neither the equality

49 At that time, the CC did not have any competence to review the act of the constituent power in any way. T Drinóczi, F Gárdos-Orosz, and Z Pozsár-Szentmiklósy, 'Formal and informal constitutional amendment in Hungary', MTA Law Working Papers 2019/18, https://jog.tk.mta.hu/uploads/files/2019_18_Drinoczi_GardosOrosz_PozsarSzentmiklosy.pdf).

50 Ibid.

(non-discrimination), the prevention of the abuse (misuse) of power, nor the other elements of the benchmark of the Checklist of the Venice Commission are realised in Hungary to a satisfactory extent. Each segment of the Rule of Law is compromised. The failure to adhere to the European Rule of Law requirements, in terms of value and political ideal, is systematic, politically induced and supported, and widespread in the legal system. It seems that the new Hungarian approach towards the Rule of Law, as a value and a principle, retains only the so-called formal legality. Formal legality is part of each thin concept of the Rule of Law and extends to the application and enforcement of the enforceable EU law.

In this sense, the European Rule of Law is a universal value of the EU only if we take Hungary, where it is not present in the same sense as in the other members of the value community that the EU represents, out of the picture.

The changes introduced after 2010 affecting the CC and its powers have three implications: first, the Court can reject applications that invoke a thicker understanding of the Rule of Law already melted from Article 2 of the Constitution. Second, in the constitutional complaint procedure, no invocation of the violation of the Rule of Law principle can be admissible. Third, the infringement of Article B of the FL can be claimed only in procedures that allege the unconstitutionality of pieces of legislation, which is only a small fragment of the entire workload of the CC. The Court nowadays takes a thinner approach towards the Rule of Law, as compared to the first 20 years, which is mainly due to the changes in powers, procedures, and admissibility criteria, and thus can be viewed as one of the legitimate readings of Article B of the FL. Nevertheless, the inconsistency of the role the Rule of Law possesses in the current constitutional system indicates and instrumental use of the law and an authoritarian attitude of the majority of CC judges.

In terms of the legal concept of the Rule of Law, its thinnest version is implemented in Hungary along with the everyday application of the EU law which, as explained in Chapter 1, represents an aspect of the European Rule of Law. In this sense, the Rule of Law that would be viewed as common sense or general theory[51] is a common European value. As such, however, it does not say anything about the community it features, as this understanding of the Rule of Law is, purposefully, too general and thin. It seems that, unless we want to lose focus, we have to thus insist on the fact that the understanding of the Rule of Law that is evolved and nurtured in Europe, regardless of the enforcement struggles,[52] is not implemented in Hungary. This concept is not a common value anymore, if the community, i.e., the European Union, still has renegade Members States, such as Hungary (and Poland).

51 C May and A Winchester, 'Introduction to the Handbook of the Rule of Law, in C May and A Winchester, eds, *Handbook of the Rule of Law* (Edward Elgar 2018) 1, RM Fallon Jr, '"The rule of law" as a concept in constitutional discourse', 1 *Columbia Law Review* (1997) 7.

52 See e.g., D Kochenov and A Jakab, eds, *The Enforcement of EU Law and Values* (Oxford University Press 2017); L Pech and D Kochenov, 'Strengthening the Rule of Law Within the European Union: Diagnoses, Recommendations, and What to Avoid', *Policy Brief* (June 2019), https://reconnect-europe.eu/news/policy-brief-june-2019/.

Bibliography

Miklós Bánkuti, Gábor Halmai, and Kim Lane Scheppele, 'From separation of powers to a government without checks: Hungary's old and new constitutions', in Gábor Attila Tóth, ed, *Constitution for a disunited nation. On Hungary's 2011 fundamental law* (CEU Press 2012) 237–268.

Petra Bárd, 'Luxemburg as the Last Resort. The Kúria's Judgment on the Illegality of a Preliminary Reference to the ECJ', https://verfassungsblog.de/luxemburg-as-the-last-resort/ *VerfBlog*, 2019/9/23 (accessed October 2019).

Adriaan Bedner, 'The promise of a thick view', in Christopher May and Adam Winchester, eds, *Handbook of the Rule of Law* (Edward Elgar 2018) 37–47.

Tímea Drinóczi, 'Central and Eastern European constitutional formulas: The abuse and observance of constitutions in times of emergency', The 10th IACL-AIDC World Congress, Seoul, 2018, Workshop – Abuse of the constitution in times of emergency, www.researchgate.net/publication/335762469_Central_and_Eastern_European_constitutional_formulas_the_abuse_and_observance_of_constitutions_in_times_of_emergency/stats (accessed August 2019).

Tímea Drinóczi, 'Constitutional politics in contemporary Hungary', 1 *ICL Journal* (2016) 63–98.

Tímea Drinóczi, 'Legislation in Hungary', in Helen Xanthaki and Ulrich Karpen, eds, *Legislation in Europe: A Country to Country Guide* (Bloomsburry 2020).

Tímea Drinóczi, 'Special Legal Orders: Challenges and Solutions', 4 *OsteuropaRecht* (2016) 420–437.

Tímea Drinóczi, and Agnieszka Bień-Kacała, 'Illiberal constitutionalism and the European Rule of Law', Chapter 1 of this book.

Tímea Drinóczi and Agnieszka Bień-Kacała, 'Illiberal Constitutionalism: The Case of Hungary and Poland', 20 *German Law Journal* (2019) 1140–1166.

Tímea Drinóczi, Fruzsina Gárdos-Orosz, and Pozsár-Szentmiklósy Zoltán, Formal and informal constitutional amendment in Hungary. MTA Law Working Papers 2019/18, https://jog.tk.mta.hu/uploads/files/2019_18_Drinoczi_GardosOrosz_PozsarSzentmiklosy.pdf(accessed October 2019).

Tímea Drinóczi and Ágoston Mohai, 'Has the migration crisis challenged the concept of the protection of the human rights of migrants? The case of Ilias and Ahmed v. Hungary1', in Elżbieta Kużelewska, Amy Weatherburn, and Dariusz Kloza, eds, *Irregular migrations as a challenge for democracy* (Cambridge, Intersentia 2018) 97–112.

Richard M, Jr, Fallon, '"The rule of law" as a concept in constitutional discourse', 1 *Columbia Law Review* (1997) 1–56.

Jorge M Farinucci-Fernós, 'Post-liberal constitutionalism', 1 *Tulsa L Review* (2018) 35–47.

Wolfgang Hoffmann-Riem, 'The Venice Commission of the Council of Europe – standards and impact', 2 *EJIL* (2014) 579–597.

Dimitry Kochenov, 'The EU and the Rule of Law – Naïveté or a grand design?', 5 *University of Groningen Faculty of Law Research Paper Series* (2018) 1–21.

Dimitry Kochenov and András Jakab, eds, *The enforcement of EU law and values* (Oxford University Press 2017).

Christopher May and Adam Winchester, 'Introduction to the handbook of the Rule of Law', in Christopher May and Adam Winchester, eds, *Handbook of the Rule of Law* (Edward Elgar 2018) 1–20.

Jorgen Orstrom Moller, 'The advantages of a thin version', in Christopher May and Adam Winchester, eds, *Handbook of the Rule of Law* (Edward Elgar 2018) 21–33.

András László Pap, *Democratic Decay in Hungary* (Routledge 2017).

Laurent Pech and Dimitry Kochenov, 'Strengthening the Rule of Law within the European Union: Diagnoses, recommendations, and what to avoid', *Policy Brief* (June 2019), https://reconnect-europe.eu/news/policy-brief-june-2019/.

Joseph Raz, 'The Rule of Law and its virtue', in Raz, Joseph, ed, *The authority of law: Essays on law and morality* (Oxford University Press 1979) 211–230.

Marco Antonio Simonelli, 'Thickening up judicial independence: The ECJ ruling in Commission v. Poland (C-619/18)', 2019, European Law Blog, https://europeanlawblog.eu/2019/07/08/thickening-up-judicial-independence-the-ecj-ruling-in-commission-v-poland-c-619-18/.

Pál Sonnevend, András Jakab, and Lóránt Csink, 'The Constitution as an Instrument of Everyday Party Politics: The Basic law of Hungary', in Armin von Bogdandy and Pál Sonnevend, eds, *Constitutional crisis in the European constitutional area* (Beck – Hart – Nomos 2015) 46–123.

Dániel G Szabó, 'A Hungarian judge seeks protection from the CJEU – part I', *VerfBlog*, 2019/7/28, https://verfassungsblog.de/a-hungarian-judge-seeks-protection-from-the-cjeu-part-i/ (accessed September 2019).

Balázs Szalbot, 'Jogállamiság mint Alaptörvényben biztosított jog [The rule of law as a right guaranteed by the Fundamental Law]', 4 *Arsboni* (2015) 17–25.

Gábor Attila Tóth, 'Illiberal rule of law? Changing features of Hungarian constitutionalism', in Maurice Adams, et al., eds, *Constitutionalism and the Rule of Law* (Cambridge University Press 2017) 386–415.

6 The Rule of Law

The Polish perspective

Iwona Wróblewska

6.1. Introduction

This chapter discusses the issue of the reduction in the importance of the Rule of Law in Poland after the general elections in 2015. It reveals the specific character of the discourse on the Rule of Law in Poland after 1989, and the ways of understanding the principle in both legal doctrine and the rulings of the Constitutional Tribunal (CT). Domestic and European legal circles are of the opinion that the actions taken by the current Government of Poland violate the most crucial elements of the Rule of Law. Above all, the chapter focuses on the following issues: the contradistinction between democracy and the Rule of Law, the weakening of the authority of law, marginalisation of the significance of the Constitution by non constitutional changes in the constitutional order, the lowering of law-making standards, and a redefinition of the principle of the separation of powers. This is accompanied by an examination of the assertions emphasising the idea of the good of the nation as a value standing above the law, and defining democracy as the rule of the majority not being bound by law, which are typical of a populist agenda. This chapter puts forward the opinion that these actions not only lead to a violation of substantial elements of the Rule of Law, but that they are also contrary to the fundamental requirement of this concept, according to which state authorities act on the basis and within the limits of the law.

6.2. The origins of the Rule of Law in Poland and the specific character of the Polish discussion of the Rule of Law

The principle of the Rule of Law is set out in Article 2 of the Polish Constitution: 'The Republic of Poland shall be a democratic state ruled by law and implementing the principles of social justice'.[1] Polish legal doctrine nevertheless lacks a

1 In the following text, the terms 'state ruled by law', 'state of law', and 'legal state' will be used synonymously.

comprehensive analysis of the concept of the Rule of Law.[2] Constitutionalisation of the principle of the democratic state of law, which took place in 1989 in the so-called December Amendment to the communist Constitution of 1952, referred to the German concept of the Rule of Law (*Rechtsstaat*). Before 1989, in Poland, the Rule of Law was defined by the term '*praworządność*', which could be translated as 'lawfulness', and was close in meaning to the principle of legality, i.e., to the directive to obey the law addressed to organs of public authority.[3] For many decades 'lawfulness' had been used to legitimise real socialism,[4] which is why during the political transformation it has been rejected by many legal scholars as a concept with a 'bad tradition'.[5] However, the contemporary discussion of the concept of the legal state should be treated as a continuation of former disputes between the procedural and substantive views of 'lawfulness',[6] keeping in mind that 'lawfulness' as 'the basic rule of the democratic state of law'[7] is a narrower concept. Due to the fact that the term has no equivalent in other languages, in translations from Polish, it is used as an alternative to the term 'Rule of Law'.[8]

From a political aspect, the introduction of the concept of 'state of law' to the Constitution was intended to emphasise the departure from the totalitarian state and the reference to the achievements of the legal sciences and judicatures of Western European countries. The assimilation of the *Rechtsstaat* concept resulted primarily from the fact that Polish legal science derived its most thorough knowledge of the 'state of law' from the country that is Poland's closest neighbour, but that does not mean that the Polish and German concepts are identical.[9]

2 E Morawska, *Klauzula państwa prawnego w Konstytucji RP na tle orzecznictwa Trybunału Konstytucyjnego* [The Rule of Law Clause in the Constitution of the Republic of Poland in the background of judicial decisions of the Constitutional Tribunal] (Dom Organizatora TNOiK 2003) 111.

3 The principle of legality is expressed in Article 7 of the Constitution: 'The organs of public authority shall function on the basis of, and within the limits of, the law.'

4 In the communist legal doctrine of the period of the Polish People's Republic, the Rule of Law was identified with the concept of observing the law, and thus the authorities were able to legitimise their own actions and subordinate those of political opponents under the guise of their violating the legally established law. See S Wronkowska, 'Zarys koncepcji państwa prawnego w Polskiej literaturze politycznej i prawnej' [Outline of the concept of the state of law in Polish political and legal literature], in *Polskie dyskusje o państwie prawa* [Polish discussions on the state of law], S Wronkowska, ed, (Wydawnictwo Sejmowe 1995) 63.

5 A Pułło, 'Państwo prawne (uwagi w zw. z art. 1 Konstytucji RP)' [State of law (comments regarding Article 1 of the Polish Constitution)], 28 *Studia Iuridica* (1995) 127.

6 See A Kubiak, 'Państwo prawne – idea, postulaty, dylematy' [State of law – idea, postulates, dilemmas], 8 *Państwo i Prawo* (1993) 18.

7 See the judgment of the Constitutional Tribunal of 16 November 2003 (SK 34/03).

8 S Biernat, 'Zasada the Rule of Law a definiowanie pojęcia państwa prawa'[The Rule of Law and defining the concept of the state of law], in M Aleksandrowicz, A Jamróz, and L Jamróz, eds, *Demokratyczne państwo prawa. Zagadnienia wybrane* [The democratic state of law. Selected issues] (Temida 2 2014) 28.

9 E Morawska, n 2, 52, 54.

The unique character of the discussions about the Rule of Law in Poland (as well as in other post-communist Central and Eastern European countries) lies in the fact that this principle was formed principally by the rulings of the constitutional courts. It means that the elements included in the concept, called 'derivative principles', specific or detailed rules, were expressed under the influence of practical needs and depended on the *ratio decidendi* of the cases considered by the Constitutional Tribunal.[10] Polish constitutionalists have not formulated set definitions of the term 'Rule of Law' but indicated certain elements that, according to them, define the concept.

6.3. The understanding of the Rule of Law in constitutional case-law and legal doctrine

In my opinion, the perception of the principle of the Rule of Law in Poland, when it comes to some of its core components, does not differ from those in other European countries. The essence and fundamental premise of every concept of the 'state of law' is an acknowledgement that law is the supreme means of regulating social relations within the state, and the requirement for state authorities to act on the basis and within the limits of the law, which is equivalent to the principle of legality.

A set of procedural and structural guarantees is supposed to safeguard observance of the law by public authorities.[11] Procedural guarantees are expressed by institutional rules, such as free common elections, separation of powers, the independence of the judiciary, and liability of public officers for violations of the law. Structural guarantees comprise those by which legal institutions protect the rights of citizens, such as the rights to an impartial court, to a constitutional judiciary, and an ombudsman. Another set of conditions refers to the necessity of respecting by the law certain formal and substantive requirements.[12] As mentioned before, the most significant role in forming the content of the principle being analysed has been played in Poland by the Constitutional Tribunal.[13] A distinctive

10 Ibid. 111.

11 K Działocha, 'Państwo prawne w warunkach zasadniczych zmian systemu prawa RP' [The state of law in the situation of fundamental changes in the Polish legal system], 1 *Państwo i Prawo* (1992) 18.

12 The differentiation between formal and substantive content, although common in the Polish legal literature, is not supported by any separately elaborated theoretical concept, and the CT does not pay any special attention to this distinction. It can be assumed, in a simplified manner, that what concerns dignity, rights, and freedoms or justice is in the form of material values, while what is related to the manner of action of public authorities takes on a formal dimension. The difficulty with explicit qualification particularly concerns the principle of proportionality or the right to a court. For more on this topic, see I Wróblewska, *Zasada państwa prawnego w orzecznictwie Trybunału Konstytucyjnego RP* [The Principle of the Rule of Law in Judicial Decisions of the Constitutional Tribunal] (Dom Organizatora TNOiK 2010) 69.

13 Established in 1982; started adjudicating in 1986.

feature of CT rulings is their emphasis on the formal (procedural) elements of the Rule of Law, related to the quality of law, the so-called principles of correct legislation, such as: the principle of legal certainty, *lex retro non agit*, the protection of rights previously acquired, the requirement for appropriate *vacatio legis*, the principle of determinacy of legal provisions, protection of the so-called 'interests in progress', the prohibition on changes in tax law during the tax year, and others.[14] The most characteristic feature of the period after 1997, with regard to the Rule of Law, was that, apart from the formal elements, some of the so-called substantive elements of the principle previously mentioned only in the case-law have been explicitly included in the text of the Constitution of the Republic of Poland (e.g., the right to life, the principle of the protection of human dignity, the right of access to a court, the right to privacy). However, the Tribunal has firmly stated that the inclusion of Rule of Law in the Constitution does not mean depriving the principle of its substantive content as formerly elaborated by the Tribunal's case-law, as it would lead to an 'axiological deformation' of the principle and would 'give it a crippled form unknown to other political systems'.[15] It is worth noting that the broad interpretation of the Rule of Law clause in the early period of the transformation has resulted in allegations of excessive judicial activism,[16] which was a problem known to many other countries,[17] including Hungary.[18]

The final, extremely important assumption regarding the concept of a legal state concerns the political system. Analysis of the statements of most representatives of the legal doctrine in the period of political transformation leads to the conclusion that the existence of a democratic system of government was treated as a *sine qua non* for the Rule of Law.[19] It seems that, under Polish conditions, the democratic legitimation of power and the democratic way of law-making, as well as the perception of the terms 'democracy' and 'the Rule of Law' as almost synonymous, formed the most significant evidence of rejection of the totalitarian period.[20]

Summarising these introductory remarks, it should be noted that the Polish perspective (taking into account the constitutional tradition, the doctrinal positions and constitutional case-law) assumes the combining of certain formal and material requirements with the values contained in the democratic system in the

14 For more, see Wróblewska, n 12, 67–187.

15 See the judgment of 25 November 1997 (K 26/97). Nevertheless, in the event of questioning whether a normative act complies with the standards of the Rule of Law, which are specified in other provisions of the Constitution, the control should be based on detailed constitutional provisions.

16 For an overview of the arguments put forward in the Polish legal doctrine and the reconstruction of the position of the CT: Wróblewska, n 12, 201–242.

17 See, inter alia, KM Holland, *Judicial Activism in Comparative Perspective* (Palgrave Macmillan UK 1991).

18 A Sajó, 'Reading the Invisible Constitution: Judicial Review in Hungary', 15(2) *Oxford Journal of Legal Studies* (1995) 253–267.

19 Authors cited by Morawska, n 2, 145.

20 Pułło, n 5, 122.

formula of the state of law. This relationship is visible in the complementary formulation used in Article 2 of the Constitution, which establishes 'the superior overall structure of a democratic, legal and just state'.[21] This article seems to have a unifying function, determining the relationship between the state and the law, the way it is created and its social function. The CT rulings utilise a formulation according to which 'the implementation of justice [...] is an essential complement to [...] (...the democratic legal state'.[22] Therefore the Constitution apparently rejects the formalist concept of the Rule of Law and binds the law with its content (values) and the manner of enactment. At the same time, at the time of forming the paradigm of the Rule of Law, one could observe a tendency to understand the requirements imposed on the legislator in the state of law in a formal way, i.e., by emphasising the importance of particular principles of law-making, and not their actual auxiliary role in realising the principles of individual freedom and dignity.[23]

6.4. Current actions dismantling the Rule of Law in Poland

After winning the general elections in 2015, the right-wing Law and Justice Party began to implement a programme of reforms called 'The Good Change'. In legal circles, actions taken by the Government and Parliament, both bodies being supported by the President, are seen to violate most of the above-mentioned principles in the standard formulation of the Rule of Law. The majority of the actions described below relate to the functioning of the judiciary and the targeting of its independence.

6.4.1. The rule of the majority versus the Rule of Law

From the beginning of its rule, the Law and Justice Party has ignored the 'ruled by law' component in the definition of the political system of the Republic ('a democratic state ruled by law'). Democracy understood as *the rule of the majority not being bound by the law* has started to be brought to the fore. In their populist statements, politicians have emphasised the idea of the welfare of the nation as a value standing above the law, even above the Constitution.

It seems that such a concept of democracy, omitting a number of essential components such as the protection of minorities or the separation of powers, reducing it basically to the hegemony of the majority, is key to understanding the course of actions presented in the following paragraphs. These actions confirm

21 P Tuleja, 'Komentarz do art. 2 Konstytucji' [Commentary on Article 2 of the Constitution] in M Safjan and L Bosek, eds, *Konstytucja RP Komentarz*, [Polish Constitution. Commentaries] vol. 1, (CH Beck 2016) 217.

22 The judgment of the Constitutional Tribunal of 24 June 1998 (K 3/98).

23 Wronkowska, n 4, 75, 76.

the departure from the liberal-democratic system, which posits the pivotal role of law in the field of politics. At the beginning of the transformation in the 1990s, it was strongly emphasised that a prerequisite of the Rule of Law was the existence of a system of legal norms 'largely autonomous from the state, as a political organization implementing specific political objectives'.[24]

Currently, the authorities see this relationship differently: the law plays the role of an instrument in relation to politics. The justification for this is allegedly the need to restore the balance between law and politics. Intellectual support for this attitude is provided by the so-called theory of 'political constitutionalism', which, unlike legal constitutionalism, does not allow excessive formalisation and separation of legal norms from real life, and which means that the sovereign, not lawyers, has a decisive influence on the legislation.[25] However, as is argued in the literature, the systemic changes starting from 2015 cannot be perceived as bringing about political constitutionalism.[26] This concept is simply used to justify the disabling and capture of the constitutional courts.[27] In practice, law has been reduced to an instrument for pursuing the ad hoc, current goals of those in power, while 'the will of the nation' is a slogan used to justify passing laws in a manner distant from the standards of proper legislation (see Section 6.4.4.). This leads to the unprecedented degeneration of the role of Parliament, which effectively becomes a 'machine for passing laws' drafted by the Government.

As far as the relationship between the notion of democracy and the Rule of Law is concerned, one might think that the current Polish rulers use the value of democracy (in the sense of the will of the people) against the Rule of Law. Such an argument can be found, for example, in the Polish response to the Venice Commission's opinion[28] on 'The Good Change' in the Constitutional Tribunal.[29] Government experts there argued that the Commission's experts did not understand the Polish Constitution, which establishes the primacy of the people's will, expressed in the elections, over the law, including the Constitution itself. Questioning the role of the Constitution as superior law is clearly contrary to its

24 Działocha, n 11, 14.

25 See A Czarnota, 'The Constitutional Tribunal', *VerfBlog*, 2017/6/03 <https://verfassungsblog.de/the-constitutional-tribunal> (accessed 25 May 2019).

26 T Drinóczi and A Bień-Kacała, 'Illiberal constitutionalism in Hungary and Poland: The case of judicialization of politics' in in A Bień-Kacała, L Csink, T Milej, and M Serowaniec, eds, *Liberal constitutionalism – Between individual and collective interests* (The Nicolaus Copernicus University Press 2017) 94, 106.

27 Ibid. 88.

28 Opinion on amendments to the Act of 25 June 2015 on the Constitutional Tribunal of Poland, adopted by the Venice Commission at its 106th Plenary Session (Venice, 11–12 March 2016) <www.venice.coe.int/webforms/documents/?pdf=CDL-AD(2016)001-e> (accessed 26 January 2019).

29 The Report of the Team of Experts on the Issues of the Constitutional Tribunal of 15 July 2016 <www.sejm.gov.pl/media8.nsf/files/ASEA-ADRKBW/$File/Raport%20Zespo%C5%82u%20Ekspert%C3%B3w%20do%20spraw%20Problematyki%20Trybuna%C5%82u%20Konstytucyjnego.pdf> (accessed 26 January 2019).

Article 8, according to which it is the supreme law of the Republic of Poland. As the Constitutional Tribunal noted, 'even a democratically elected Parliament has no competence to make decisions that would be contrary to the basic law, also when their justification is the abstractly understood welfare of the nation'.[30]

In Polish legal doctrine, there is a certain tension between the values of democracy and law expressed in Article 2 of the Constitution. It does not, however, constitute a reason for separating them; rather, it results in both values mutually limiting each other,[31] which gives the desired effect of balancing them. Arguments that confront the above values in the sense of *a priori* recognising the superiority of one over the other essentially constitute a departure from the above-mentioned (see Section 6.3) position of the doctrine, the tradition of Polish constitutionalism and the previous case-law of the Constitutional Tribunal.

6.4.2. *The weakening of the authority and role of law*

Emphasising the idea of the good of the nation as a value standing above the law, even above the Constitution, leads to the weakening of the authority of law as a regulator of all activities of the state, its organs in particular, and thus undermines the most fundamental assumption of the Rule of Law constituting its *sine qua non*. Calling this function of law into question is contrary to the most basic (that is formal, narrow) understanding of the Rule of Law, which assumes that the law is respected and meets particular formal requirements. It is extremely dangerous, as it weakens the authority of law and greatly diminishes the significance of the Constitution as the basis of the legal system and the most important normative act in the state. It is also a starting point for the performance of the actions described below, which would not have been possible without questioning the existing legal order.

Unfortunately, it should be noted that respect for the law and legal awareness has never been high in Poland. This has resulted partly from the historical background, especially the long periods of lack of sovereignty of the Polish state, when legal regulations were imposed by the partitioning powers and occupiers, or the era of Soviet influence, when the law was often oppressive towards the citizens. All these factors contributed to a tendency in Polish society to distance itself from the law and its observance. On the other hand, since the beginning of the political transformation, no effort has been made to raise the legal awareness of the Polish people. There has been a common belief that the law is created by lawyers for lawyers and that it is incomprehensible to ordinary citizens. The Constitution has been neither well known nor appreciated by the citizens. The Constitution has also been presented by its critics as the effect of the 'rotten compromise' and the legacy of 'the round table' negotiations, during which the communist state

30 The judgment of the CT of 9 December 2015 (K 35/15).

31 M Granat, *Prawo konstytucyjne. Pytania i odpowiedzi*, [Constitutional law. Questions and answers] (Wolters Kluwer 2016) 63.

and its officials have not been held accountable. As a result the watchwords of those in power nowadays, inter alia, about how the nation, as the sovereign, will dictate the direction of the law, are well received. This does not mean, however, that the laws currently adopted have been the subject of wide consultation in interested social or professional groups. On the contrary, the authorities claim that only they themselves are able to read 'the will of the nation', relying not on consultation but on the results of surveys, choosing solutions that will allow the survey support to increase.

Another vivid manifestation of an attitude disregarding the authority not only of law but also of Parliament, is creating laws that are not supposed to work. A glaring example of this was the case of the adoption on 6 February 2018 of a controversial amendment to the Act on the Institute of National Remembrance, which became the subject of worldwide commentary. It was published[32] and came into force, but the *Marshal of the Senat* declared that until the matter had been settled by the Constitutional Tribunal, the law would not be applied.[33] The provision in question was Article 55a[34] of the Act, which imposed a jail term on anyone who claimed that Polish citizens were responsible for or complicit in the Holocaust. This type of action leads to a paradox whereby the authorities do not intend to apply the law they have enacted. That in turn means questioning of the principles of legality and legal certainty.

6.4.3. *Dismantling of the Constitution*

Actions targeted at the Polish Constitution in the period 2015–2018 have been elaborated upon in some detail in the Polish legal literature and by journalists. The range of expressions that have been used to describe this phenomenon is quite interesting, as it seems to convey a concern about a serious threat to the constitutional order, e.g., 'hostile takeover of constitutional order'[35] or 'constitutional violence'.[36] The Constitution is treated not as a framework to restrict politics but as a political tool.

32 Dz.U. 2018 poz. 369.

33 <www.tvn24.pl/wiadomosci-z-kraju,3/karczewski-w-jeden-na-jeden-ustawa-o-ipn-nie-bedzie-dzialac,816548.html> (accessed 26 January 2019).

34 On 27 June 2018, as a result of international pressure, the *Sejm* introduced another amendment and this provision was repealed, Dz.U. 2018 poz. 1277.

35 M Wyrzykowski, 'Wrogie przejęcie' porządku konstytucyjnego' ['Hostile takeover' of the constitutional order] <http://konstytucyjny.pl/wrogie-przejecie-porzadku-konstytucyjnego-miroslaw-wyrzykowski> (accessed 26 January 2019). *Idem*, 'Bypassing the Constitution or changing the constitutional order outside the constitution', in A Szmyt and B Banaszak, eds, *Transformation of Law Systems in Central, Eastern and South-Eastern Europe in 1989–2015, Liber Amicorum in Honorem Prof. Dr. Dres. HC Rainer Arnold*, (Gdańsk University Press 2016).

36 M Matczak, 'Powstrzymać przestępstwo konstytucyjne' [To stop constitutional crime] <https://wiadomo.co/prof-marcin-matczak-powstrzymac-przestepstwo-konstytucyjne> (accessed 26 January 2019).

The mechanisms used by the Government to dismantle the constitutional order established in 1997 are described below. These changes had been possible primarily due to selective and arbitrary application of constitutional norms.

Above all, what we are dealing with here are non-constitutional changes to the constitutional order[37] performed by use of three methods: passing ordinary laws; actions of the executive; and activities at the level of political declarations.

In the first case the ruling party, not having the necessary majority in Parliament to carry out the procedure of formal constitutional amendment, changes the norms governing the operation of key state organs by means of ordinary laws, in a manner that bypasses the Constitution, leading to the weakening of some state organs or to the 'deprivation of their competence'.[38] This kind of amendment occurred in the case of the shortening of the four-year term of office of judges, who are, along with MPs and senators, chosen members of the National Council of the Judiciary, as specified in Article 187.3 of the Constitution.[39] The second case concerned the shortening of the term of office of the First President of the Supreme Court (SC), specified in Article 183.3 of the Constitution.[40] This change resulted in wide resistance within legal circles and also led to social protests. On the day the new law came into force[41] the First President of the Supreme Court, supported by the General Assembly of the SC judges, announced that acting directly on the basis of the provisions of the Constitution, she will remain in her post until 2020.

Another attempt to change the Constitution by means of an ordinary law[42] (from which the authorities have eventually withdrawn) was through the introduction of qualified majority voting (of two-thirds) in the CT, although Article 190.5 of the Constitution provides for majority voting (meaning an ordinary majority).

Another drastic example of violation of the Rule of Law principle by exercise of executive power is the failure to publish in the *Journal of Laws* three rulings of the CT that, in the Prime Minister's opinion, were issued in violation of provisions of law. The refusal to publish the rulings of the CT was in breach of the obligation arising from Article 190.2 of the Constitution.[43] In practice, it meant that Article 190.3 of the Constitution, which provides that the decisions of the CT shall enter into force on the day of publication, could not be implemented. The rulings were finally published as a result of pressure from the European Commission, but with simultaneous annotation in a special Act to the effect that they were issued

37 Wyrzykowski, n 35.

38 J Trzciński and M Szwast, 'Formalne i nieformalne zmiany konstytucji', [*Formal and informal constitutional changes*] <www.rp.pl/Opinie/308079978-Formalne-i-nieformalne-zmiany-konstytucji---pisza-Janusz-Trzcinski-i-Michal-Szwast.html> (accessed 26 January 2019).

39 The Act of 8 December 2017, Dz.U. 2018 poz. 3.

40 The Act of 8 December 2017, Dz.U. 2018 poz. 5.

41 4 July 2018.

42 The Act of 22 December 2015, Dz.U. 2015 poz. 2217.

43 The judgment of 9 March 2016 (K 47/15); the judgment of 11 August 2016 (K 39/16); the judgment of 7 November 2016 (K 44/16). These judgments confirmed, inter alia, the partial unconstitutionality of the changes introduced by Law and Justice Party to the Constitutional Tribunal Act.

in violation of the law and refer to Acts that no longer apply.[44] It is worth noting that the publication of judgments does not require an additional Act because such an obligation stems directly from the Constitution.

The last of the mechanisms mentioned above consists of introducing into the public domain expressions obviously contrary to the wording of the Constitution but in line with particular political goals. In one of his international interviews, Prime Minister M. Morawiecki, describing Poland, used the term 'democratic nation state'[45] instead of 'democratic state ruled by law', thereby changing the meaning of the fundamental rules of the Polish political system. This type of statement should be seen in the broader context of nation-building activity, which is one of the most important political goals of those currently in power. Consistent, purposeful, and systematic endeavours to create a community bond between Polish citizens based on the national criterion[46] are visible in all spheres of activity of the Government and institutions subordinated to it, as well as government-related organisations, both in domestic and foreign policy.[47]

Clearly, all the changes mentioned above were possible through the selective, arbitrary, instrumental application of the Constitution, consisting of interpretation of select provisions in isolation from the rest. An example of such a *contra legem* interpretation is the appointment of members of the National Council of the Judiciary (NCJ) by MPs instead of their election by the judges, which was the previous practice. It was argued that the Constitution does not directly express an obligation to form the Council in this way. In line with this interpretation, the system of creation of the Council, which had been in operation since 1989, has been altered.[48] In fact, the Constitution does only indicate that the NCJ will include 15 judges along with representatives of other authorities.[49] However, when interpreting its provisions, account should be taken of the clearly defined political position of the Council as a body appointed to safeguard the independence of courts and judges, as well as of the clear separation of three groups of subjects representing each of the authorities in the NCJ, each of them appointed differently. Filling the NCJ almost entirely with the Sejm's nominees makes it completely dependent on politicians.

6.4.4. *'Anti-principle of improper law-making'*

The quality of law created in Poland has been criticised since the beginning of the transformation period. The current rules on legislative technique[50] are not formally binding on the legislator, but they should not be avoided 'without

44 The Act of 12 April 2018, Dz.U. 2018 poz. 849.

45 An interview for the German magazine 8 *Der Spiegel* (2018).

46 M Migalski, *Budowanie narodu. Przypadek Polski w latach 2015–2017* [Building a nation. The case of Poland in 2015–2017] (Fundacja Liberte 2018) 7.

47 Ibid. 229–317. The author indicates examples of nation-building activities in such areas as: history, museology, nomenclature, monetary policy, army, diplomacy, education or media.

48 See Article 9a of Law amending the Law of 12 May 2011 on NCJ, Dz.U. 2018 poz. 3.

49 Article 187.1 of the Constitution of 1997.

50 Ordinance of the Prime Minister of 20 July 2002, consolidated text: Dz.U. 2016, poz. 283.

important reason'.[51] The normative significance of these principles is primarily due to the fact that they are functionally linked to Article 2 of the Constitution, and more precisely to the rule of legal security resulting from the 'state of law' clause. Against the background of the CT case-law so far, there is no doubt that the creation of law in a clear, correct, and comprehensible manner is a fundamental standard of the Rule of Law. Treating law as a tool for realising current political goals has a direct impact on its quality. In the opinion of the legal community, the manner of implementing the legislative process in the VIIIth parliamentary term dramatically departs from the principles and norms set out in the Constitution and all subconstitutional Acts.[52]

Activities implementing the 'anti-principle of improper law-making'[53] would above all include: legislative haste; abuse of special modes of law-making (separate and urgent); lack of social consultation or illusory consultation; and failure to keep proper *vacatio legis*. The separate mode of law-making enables renunciation of negotiations, opinion-making, and public consultation processes. Within the urgent mode, controversial methods were used, such as: shortening the time allowed for deputies' speeches as far down as to one minute; block voting on amendments (not by subject but depending on which parliamentary faction submitted them); not reading the content of amendments; working during the night or ignoring warnings about errors in the drafts reported by parliamentarians and employees of legislative offices.[54] These violations of the principles of correct legislation not only violate the Rule of Law, but also in fact show the weakness of democracy in Poland.[55]

6.4.5. *Redefinition of the principle of the separation of powers*

The principle of the separation of powers is a long-standing tradition in Polish constitutionalism; after 1989 it was interpreted by reference to the Rule of Law principle, and the 1997 Constitution lists it alongside the checks and balances principle.[56] Violations of the principle of the separation and balance of powers may be seen in activities aimed at subordinating the power of the judiciary to the power of the executive. Laws adopted over the last two years have affected the entire structure of the administration of justice in Poland, influencing the CT, the

51 See the judgment of the CT of 24 May 1994 (K 1/94).

52 Wyrzykowski, n 35.

53 Expression used by Wyrzykowski, n 35.

54 Specific examples of legislative pathologies are described in detail in the Citizens' Communications of the Legislation Forum on the quality of the legislative process, <www.batory.org.pl/upload/files/Programy%20operacyjne/Odpowiedzialne%20Panstwo/%20Komunikat_OFL.pdf oraz http://obserwatoriumdemokracji.pl/wp-content/uploads/2016/03/XI_Komunikat_OFL.pdf> (accessed 29 January 2019).

55 On the necessary relationship between the quality of states' legislation, democracy, and the Rule of Law, see T Drinóczi, 'Concept of quality in legislation – revisited: matter of perspective and a general overview', 36 *Statute Law Review* 2015.

56 Article 10.1: 'The system of government of the Republic of Poland shall be based on the separation of and balance between the legislative, executive and judicial powers'.

NCJ, the SC, ordinary courts, the prosecution service, and the National School of Judiciary. These activities have already been extensively discussed in Polish and foreign literature.[57] Instead of introducing necessary reforms of the judiciary consisting of real improvements to court procedures and strengthening the legal protection of citizens, a large-scale turnaround of staff was performed. The chronology of the alterations conducted within the judiciary proves that what we are dealing with here is systemic abolition of the principle of the separation of powers.

After the changes to the staffing of the CT, another important step was subordinating the NJC, the body that nominates candidates as future judges, including as judges of the Supreme Court to the Minister of Justice. In the cases of both the CT and the NJC, the phenomenon of 'hollowing out', known to authoritarian systems, is particularly visible. The process consists of draining the institutions of their competences and thus retaining them as 'empty shells', not able to perform their real functions.[58] Many legal authorities have stated explicitly that the current NCJ, elected by the *Sejm* and not, as previously, by the judges themselves, does not have the competence conferred upon the Council by the Constitution of the Republic of Poland, and that its resolutions are thus, by their very nature, null and void.[59] Amendments to the judiciary regulations are not only being strongly opposed in legal circles in Poland, they have also evoked clearly negative reactions from international institutions, such as the Venice Commission, the European Judges Association and the UN Human Rights Council. The reforms in question were the basis for the initiation, on 20 December 2017, of the procedure under Article 7.1 of the Treaty on European Union by the European Commission, due to the existence of 'a clear risk of serious breach' of the Rule of Law.[60]

Additionally, in response to the changes to the functioning of the Supreme Court introduced by the new Act of 8 December 2017,[61] on 2 July 2018 the European Commission decided to refer the case to the Court of Justice of the EU (CJEU).[62] The changes in question reduced the retirement age of judges, and therefore prematurely shortened the term of office of the First President and forced some of

57 See, e.g., A Bień-Kacała, 'Poland within the EU – Dealing with the Populist Agenda', 4 *Osteuropa Recht* (2017) 439–442.

58 M Matczak, 'Poland's Constitutional Crisis: Facts and Interpretation' <http://monitorkonstytucyjny.eu/wp-content/uploads/2018/07/Matczak_Polands-Constitutional-Crisis-Facts-and-interpretations_0.pdf> (accessed 29 January 2019).

59 So claims, inter alia, the former President of the SC (1990–1998) Adam Strzembosz, the former President of the CT (1993–1997), and the former Ombudsman (2000–2006) Andrzej Zoll, <http://konstytucyjny.pl/1600-2/> (accessed 29.01.2019). The Polish Judges Association, Iustitia, describing the current NCJ, talks about the 'body that claims to be the National Council of the Judiciary' <www.iustitia.pl/2435-komunikat-prasowy-po-spotkaniu-zarzadu-ssp-iustitia-z-oddzialami-z-dnia-14-07-2018-r> (accessed 29 January 2019).

60 <https://eur-lex.europa.eu/legal-content/EN/TXT/?uri=CELEX%3A52017PC0835> (accessed 29 January 2019).

61 Dz.U. 2018 poz. 5.

62 Case C-619/18 *European Commission v Poland*.

the judges to retire. Further, the regulations did not specify the criteria to be followed by the President on deciding to extend the judicial term of office and did not provide for the possibility of judicial review of such a decision. The European Commission decided that the amendments violated the principle of the independence of the judiciary, including the principle of the irremovability of judges, and that Poland thus was not meeting its obligations under Article 19.1 of the Treaty on European Union in connection with Article 47 of the Charter of Fundamental Rights of the European Union. Seeking to obtain an ad hoc effect in negotiations with the EU, the Polish authorities implemented the decision of the CJEU on the immediate suspension of the provisions in question[63] and adopted another law on the SC in urgent mode,[64] partially reversing the effects of the reform. Its adoption does not entail, however, the restoration of the Rule of Law, because judges are still being nominated by the politicised NCJ. The sole procedure of passing the Act, which took just a few hours, the lack of social and institutional consultations, or any substantive discussion of the project, provides another clear example of violation of the basic principles of law-making in a law-abiding state. In the event the European Commission decided not to withdraw the complaint, probably bearing in mind previous government activities violating the Rule of Law in the judicial sphere.[65]

According to the principle of separation of powers, introduced in Poland after the transformation of the political system and confirmed on the basis of the currently binding Constitution of the Republic of Poland and CT case-law, each of the powers of the state should possess competencies substantially corresponding with their essence, and what is more, each of them should retain a certain minimum of exclusive competence enabling them to retain that essence.[66] As far as the power of the judiciary is concerned, 'division' means also 'autonomy', because the essence of the administration of justice is that it should be exercised only by the courts, and the other authorities cannot interfere in the acts of the judiciary.[67] The manner of interpreting the principle of the separation of powers, enforced by the currently governing bodies, radically differs from the conclusions laid down above. In the populist rhetoric of the Government, the Polish Parliament, as a representative of the will of the nation, is confronted with undemocratic, uncontrolled courts supporting the interests of oligarchic minorities.[68] The constitutional judiciary is, according to that view, a particular threat to democracy. In order to obtain the legitimacy of the sovereign, it should be

63 Decision of the Vice-President of the CJEU of 19 October 2018.

64 Dz.U. 2018 poz. 2507.

65 M. Mendelski argues that the adoption of the Western liberal perspective results in problems with objective evaluation of possible infringements of the Rule of Law. He states that, despite similar abuses, the alarm bells from EU institutions only ring in the case of conservative, nationalist governments. See idem. 'Europeanization and the Rule of Law: Towards a Pathological Turn', 40 *Southeastern Europe* (2016) 371.

66 See, e.g., the judgment of the CT of 21 November 1994 (K 6/94).

67 Ibid.

68 See the Report, n 29, 25.

subject to various constraints imposed by Parliament.[69] It is worth noting that the above-mentioned view is supported by the reference to the principle of the democratic state of law,[70] against which it actually stands in complete opposition. For it is the courts and the tribunals that fulfil the role of 'guardian of the Rule of Law' according to the principle of the separation of powers. This role cannot be performed if the independence of the courts and of the judges is not guaranteed.[71]

It is difficult not to form the impression that all of the activities aimed at interpreting the principle of the division of powers in a manner taking Parliament's leading role into account actually lead to complete erosion of this principle and to the return to the principle of uniformity of state power known in the previous communist political system.[72]

6.4.6. *Rule of Law in constitutional review after 2015*

The most important step in the process of dismantling the Constitution was undeniably the paralysis of the CT. From November 2015 until December 2016, six laws prepared by the Law and Justice Party concerning the CT were passed, and many controversial changes of personnel were made consisting, inter alia, of allowing so-called quasi-judges to adjudicate (these quasi-judges have taken the place of the judges elected by the previous Parliament, although the latter have not completed their terms of office).[73] It has already been mentioned that three judgments of the CT unfavourable to the authorities were suspended from publication for about two years. In two opinions of the Venice Commission regarding the crisis concerning the CT and related to particular amendments, it was stated that they pose a threat to the Rule of Law, democracy, and human rights, and the solutions adopted in them are aimed at slowing down and paralysing the

69 Ibid., 8.

70 Ibid.

71 Some authors supporting the reforms of the judiciary are of the opinion that, in the countries of Central and Eastern Europe at the time of the transformation in the sense of the Rule of Law, the importance of the independence of the judiciary and the competence of the constitutional courts to carry out inspections was unduly stressed. See M Mendelski, 'The Rule of Law', in A Fagan, P Kopecky, eds, *The Routledge Handbook of East European Politics* (Routledge 2017) 117. In his opinion, the concept of the Rule of Law was even reduced to a postulate to strengthen the judiciary, which led to the judicialisation of politics and juristocracy. In a similar manner, L Morawski commented that the Polish Constitution of 1997 gave the CT 'enormous and uncontrolled power which led before 2015 to excessive judicial activism and political engagement of judges'. See idem 'Critical Response', *VerfBlog*, 2017/6/03 <https://verfassungsblog.de/a-critical-response/> (accessed 29 January 2019).

72 The Constitution of 22 July 1952.

73 For more on this topic see, inter alia, A Bień-Kacała, 'Polish Constitutional Tribunal: A systemic reform or a hasty political change', 1 *DPCE Online* (2016). A supporter of the current changes, A Czarnota, is of a different opinion. Although he admits that the PiS party, 'creatively interprets law and sometimes bends it', it nevertheless rightly appointed judges who represent its legal worldview. It is to be based on 'principle of supremacy of the Parliament in relation to constitutional review and acceptance of a rule of judicial restraint not judicial activism which was earlier the norm'. A Czarnota, n 26.

Tribunal. The majority in Polish legal circles believe that the CT is now a completely politicised body, subordinate to the Government.[74]

The situation described above is not without impact on the way the CT performs its judicial function. An analysis of the CT judicature from the last three years does not yet lead to conclusions about the shape of the case-law, but certain characteristic features may be noted. Hence, on the one hand, the principle of the Rule of Law, composed of other detailed rules, was formally present in the judgments of the CT as the basis for reviewing the constitutionality of law, which would indicate the continuation of the interpretation technique previously applied. On the other hand, a drastic departure from the previous arrangements regarding the meaning of freedom and rights in the state of law could be observed. For example, in the judgment of 16 March 2017 on the Law on Assemblies, which confirmed that the Law is constitutional, the CT stated that freedom of assembly is an element of the Rule of Law, but interpreted it in a manner that contradicts its essence, completely ignoring previous abundant case-law on that freedom.[75] The Law on Assemblies introduces the concept of 'cyclical assemblies' devoted to patriotic and historic events, and gives them priority over all other assemblies.[76] A provincial governor (appointed by the Prime Minister) shall decide whether an assembly is considered 'cyclical'. In the justification for the ruling, a new vision of the relationship between an individual and the state is presented, different from that which was used to reconstruct on the basis of the current Constitution of the Republic of Poland of 1997. This vision assumes the subordination of the individual to the state, and radical limitation of his/her freedom in order to protect the rights of the majority and privilege the forms of using this freedom preferred by the state.[77] The decision of the CT fits very well with the vision of a state in which the will of its political leaders stands above the law, self-government, and the spontaneous initiative of citizens.

It is common in legal circles to question the independence of the CT and its ability to fulfil its functions. Common and administrative courts show considerable restraint in directing requests for the interpretation of the Constitution to the CT. This phenomenon is accompanied by the emergence of an idea in Polish legal science, proposing the need for deconcentrated control of constitutionality

74 This was openly admitted by one of the quasi-judges of the current CT, L Morawski (see his speech from 9 May 2017 at a scientific conference at the University of Oxford), who, while answering a question about whether he represents the Tribunal or the current Government, explained that he represents both institutions. For the conference record, see <www.law.ox.ac.uk/news/2017-05-11-oxford-symposium-polish-constitutional-crisis-sparks-public-debate> (accessed 29.01.2019).

75 See, e.g., the judgments of the CT of 18 January 2006 (K 21/05), 10 July 2008 (P 15/08), 18 September 2014 (K 44/12).

76 The Act of 13 December 2016 (Dz.U. 2017 poz. 579). This law was used to celebrate the anniversary of the catastrophe in Smoleńsk, where the twin brother of Jarosław Kaczyński died. It eventually became a regular political rally.

77 M Florczak-Wątor, 'Commentary on the Polish Constitutional Tribunal's Judgment of 16th March 2017, Case No. Kp 1/17', 2 *Przegląd Konstytucyjny* (2018) 120–128.

performed by the courts.[78] This view is supported by the reference to Article 8 of the Constitution, which expresses the principle of direct application of its provisions.[79] It states that, when deciding on an individual case, the court may refuse to apply the provision if it finds that it cannot be reconciled with the Constitution.

6.5. Conclusion

The term 'state of law' has political significance in the sense that both advocates and opponents of specific legal solutions are willing to refer to the state of law in their arguments. The reconstruction of this concept in Polish constitutionalism leads to the conclusion that – as in other European countries – it is connected with the basic principles of the liberal-democratic political system.[80] The turn towards illiberal constitutionalism, which has been observed in Poland since 2015, mainly consists of departing from the institutions of the state of law, such as the separation of powers, an independent judiciary, or a constitutional judiciary.

Forcing the paradigm of unrestrained sovereign power of the nation is incompatible with the essence of the Rule of Law, which consists of legal restriction of any authority (even the most democratically legitimised one). The chronology of actions taken by the ruling party, despite their seemingly chaotic character, indicates that we are dealing with the systematic dismantling of the Rule of Law. In this context, attempts to link the present government actions with the republican tradition,[81] as allegedly being closer to the Polish identity, are not convincing. Republicanism is after all about concern for individual freedom and preventing excessive concentration of power by appealing to the Rule of Law, legality and the separation of powers.[82] As liberalism, it is incompatible with the concept of the priority of politics in relation to law.

Finally, it is worth noting the unintended effects of the actions of the ruling majority described above, which paradoxically strengthen the Rule of Law at the

78 T Koncewicz, 'Unconstitutional capture and constitutional recapture. Of the Rule of Law, separation of powers and judicial promises', 3 *Jean Monnet Working Paper* (2017) 30 and following. For some arguments against this concept presented from the point of view of the Rule of Law, see T Drinóczi, A Bień-Kacała, 'Constitutions and constitutionalism captured: Shaping illiberal democracies in Hungary and Poland', 20 *German Law Journal* (2019).

79 R Balicki, 'Bezpośrednie stosowanie konstytucji'[Direct application of the constitution] 4 *Krajowa Rada Sądownictwa* (2016) 13–19.

80 This state of affairs is criticised by scholars in favour of those currently in power. M Mendelski believes that, while in Western Europe the liberal Rule of Law has served political unity, in Central and Eastern Europe it has functioned as an abstract concept, detached from society, unable to bind the elites to the ordinary citizens or have the law rooted in them. Similarly, it attributes negative influence to the process of European integration as a continuation of the liberal movement. In this context, he writes about the so-called 'pathological effects of Europeisation'. M Mendelski, 'The EU's pathological power: The failure of external Rule of Law promotion in South Eastern Europe', 39(3) *Southeastern Europe* (2015) 318–346.

81 This is what, e.g., the already mentioned quasi-judge L Morawski did when he stated that the present government defends Republican values as being closer to the Polish constitutional identity than the 'orthodox liberalism' represented by the opposition. Morawski, n 72.

82 W Ciszewski, 'Republikańskie odczytanie Konstytucji Rzeczypospolitej Polskiej [A Republican Interpretation of the Polish Constitution]', 4 *Przegląd Konstytucyjny* (2017) 21.

social level. Numerous protests against the government reforms have indicated the activation of civil society, accompanied by an increase in legal awareness, visible primarily in a growing interest in the text of the Constitution, which for some communities has become a symbol of the struggle for observance of the law.

Bibliography

Ryszard Balicki, 'Bezpośrednie stosowanie konstytucji' [Direct application of the constitution], 4 *Krajowa Rada Sądownictwa* (2016) 13–19.

Agnieszka Bień-Kacała, 'Poland within the EU – Dealing with the Populist Agenda', 4 *Osteuropa Recht* (2017) 428–443.

Agnieszka Bień-Kacała, 'Polish Constitutional Tribunal: A systemic reform or a hasty political change', 1 *DPCE Online* (2016) 1–14.

Stanisław Biernat, 'Zasada the Rule of Law a definiowanie pojęcia państwa prawa' [The Rule of Law and defining the concept of the state of law], in M Aleksandrowicz, A Jamróz, and L Jamróz, eds, *Demokratyczne państwo prawa. Zagadnienia wybrane* [The democratic state of law. Selected issues] (Temida 2014) 25–45.

Wojciech Ciszewski, 'Republikańskie odczytanie Konstytucji Rzeczypospolitej Polskiej [A republican interpretation of the Polish Constitution]', 4 *Przegląd Konstytucyjny* (2017) 5–32.

Adam Czarnota, 'The Constitutional Tribunal', *VerfBlog*, 2017/6/03, https://verfassungsblog.de/the-constitutional-tribunal (accessed 25 May 2019).

Timea Drinóczi, 'Concept of quality in legislation – Revisited: Matter of perspective and a general overview', 36 *Statute Law Review* (2015) 211–227.

Timea Drinóczi and Agnieszka Bień-Kacała, 'Constitutions and constitutionalism captured: Shaping illiberal democracies in Hungary and Poland', 20 *German Law Journal* (2019) 1140–1166.

Timea Drinóczi and Agnieszka Bień-Kacała, 'Illiberal constitutionalism in Hungary and Poland: The case of judicialization of politics', in A Bień-Kacała, L Csink, T Milej, and M Serowaniec, eds, Liberal constitutionalism – Between individual and collective interests (The Nicolaus Copernicus University Press 2017) 73–108.

Kazimierz Działocha, 'Państwo prawne w warunkach zasadniczych zmian systemu prawa RP', [The state of law in the situation of fundamental changes in the Polish legal system], 1 *Państwo i Prawo* (1992) 13–27.

Monika Florczak-Wątor, 'Commentary on the Polish Constitutional Tribunal's judgment of 16th March 2017, case no. Kp 1/17', 2 *Przegląd Konstytucyjny* (2018) 120–147.

Mirosław Granat, *Prawo konstytucyjne. Pytania i odpowiedzi [Constitutional law. Questions and answers]* (Wolters Kluwer 2016) 1–436.

Kenneth M Holland, *Judicial activism in comparative perspective* (Palgrave Macmillan UK 1991) 1–220.

Tomasz Koncewicz, 'Unconstitutional capture and constitutional recapture. Of the Rule of Law, separation of powers and judicial promises', 3 Jean Monnet Working Paper (2017) 1–56.

Andrzej Kubiak, 'Państwo prawne – idea, postulaty, dylematy' [State of law – idea, postulates, dilemmas], 8 *Państwo i Prawo* (1993) 15–26.

Marcin Matczak, 'Poland's Constitutional Crisis: Facts and Interpretation', 6 July 2018, http://monitorkonstytucyjny.eu/wp-content/uploads/2018/07/Matczak_Polands Constitutional-Crisis-Facts-and-interpretations_0.pdf (accessed 29 January 2019).

Marcin Matczak, 'Powstrzymać przestępstwo konstytucyjne' [To stop constitutional crime], 12 June 2018, https://wiadomo.co/prof-marcin-matczak-powstrzymac-przestepstwo-konstytucyjne (accessed 26 January 2019).

Martin Mendelski, 'Europeanization and the Rule of Law: Towards a pathological turn', 40 *Southeastern Europe* (2016) 346–384.

Martin Mendelski, 'The EU's pathological power: The failure of external Rule of Law promotion in South Eastern Europe', 39(3) *Southeastern Europe* (2015) 318–346.

Martin Mendelski, 'The Rule of Law', in A Fagan and P Kopecky, eds, *The Routledge Handbook of East European politics* (Routledge 2017) 1–378.

Marek Migalski, *Budowanie narodu. Przypadek Polski w latach 2015–2017* [Building a nation. The case of Poland in 2015–2017] (Fundacja Liberte 2018) 1–344.

Elżbieta Morawska, *Klauzula państwa prawnego w Konstytucji RP na tle orzecznictwa Trybunału Konstytucyjnego* [The Rule of Law clause in the constitution of the Republic of Poland in the background of judicial decisions of the Constitutional Tribunal] (Dom Organizatora TNOiK 2003) 1–415.

Lech Morawski, 'Critical response', *VerfBlog*, 2017/6/03, https://verfassungsblog.de/a-critical-response/ (accessed 29 January 2019).

Andrzej Pułło, 'Państwo prawne (uwagi w zw. z art. 1 Konstytucji RP)' [State of law (comments regarding article 1 of the Polish Constitution)], 28 *Studia Iuridica* (1995) 121–130.

András Sajó, 'Reading the invisible constitution: Judicial review in Hungary', 15(2) *Oxford Journal of Legal Studies* (1995) 253–267.

Janusz Trzciński and Michał Szwast, 'Formalne i nieformalne zmiany konstytucji', [*Formal and informal constitutional changes*], 7 August 2012, www.rp.pl/Opinie/308079978-Formalne-i-nieformalne-zmiany-konstytucji---pisza-Janusz-Trzcinski-i-Michal-Szwast.html (accessed 26 January 2019).

Piotr Tuleja, 'Komentarz do art. 2 Konstytucji' [Commentary on Article 2 of the Constitution] in M Safjan and L Bosek, eds, Konstytucja RP Komentarz, [Polish Constitution. Commentaries] vol. 1, (CH Beck 2016) 1–86.

Sławomira Wronkowska, 'Zarys koncepcji państwa prawnego w Polskiej literaturze politycznej i prawnej' [Outline of the Concept of the state of law in Polish political and legal literature], in S Wronkowska, ed, *Polskie dyskusje o państwie prawa* [Polish discussions on the state of law], (Wydawnictwo Sejmowe 1995) 63–80.

Mirosław Wyrzykowski, 'Bypassing the constitution or changing the constitutional order outside the constitution', in A Szmyt and B Banaszak, eds, *Transformation of law systems in Central, Eastern and South-Eastern Europe in* 1989–2015, *Liber Amicorum in Honorem Prof. Dr. Dres. HC Rainer Arnold* (Gdańsk University Press 2016) 159–178.

Mirosław Wyrzykowski, 'Wrogie przejęcie' porządku konstytucyjnego' ['Hostile takeover' of the constitutional order], 25 March 2019, http://konstytucyjny.pl/wrogie-przejecie-porzadku-konstytucyjnego-miroslaw-wyrzykowski (accessed 26 January 2019).

Part IV

Rule of Law and supranational struggles

Is it a common value?

7 Rule of Law in Hungary

What can law and politics do?

Lóránt Csink

7.1. To begin with

In recent years, the decade-long issue of the Hungarian 'Rule of Law' has become a popular topic, not only inside the borders of Hungary but also internationally. The question is about much more than an element of constitutional law.[1] For the European Union, it is not just about the protection of the Rule of Law. It is much more about the protection of common values, the protection of European identity. Unsurprisingly, the Hungarian Rule of Law is a trendy topic for many politicians and lawyers.

This chapter does not attempt to determine whether Hungary is under the Rule of Law. Instead, it intends to analyse what law and politics can do in order for Hungary to be (or remain) under the Rule of Law.

Therefore, the paper first examines the link between the so-called 'illiberal' governance and Rule of Law. Secondly, it summarises the European criticisms towards the condition of the Hungarian Rule of Law, both legal and political. Among others, the chapter calls special attention to the Article 7 procedure as a newer element in this Rule of Law debate. Thirdly, the paper analyses what lies beyond the debate; i.e., what law and politics are and how they influence the Article 7 procedure. Lastly, the paper sums up the possible ways for protecting the Rule of Law in Hungary.

7.2. Rule of Law and illiberalism

7.2.1. Rule of Law in the European Union

The most important, unanimously accepted achievement of European history is dismantling absolutistic regimes and placing all actions of states and individuals

1 Former versions of the paper were presented at conferences in Prague (International Conference 'Traditional Concepts: New Perspectives, New Challenges'. ICON-S CEE, 29 March 2019), in Toruń (Polish – Hungarian Seminar. Nicolaus Copernicus University, 9 May 2019), and in Budapest (Constitutional Court of Hungary, 15 May 2019). The resulting discussions and comments helped me a lot in finalising the paper; I'm especially grateful to Matej Avbelj, Agnieszka Bień-Kacała, Tímea Drinóczi, Andrzej Madeja, Anna Młynarska-Sobaczewska, Gusztáv Nagy, Lénárd Sándor, and Tamás Tóth.

under the Rule of Law. In our long history, both the experience of 17–18th-century absolutism and the dictatorships of the 20th century show that absolute power must be restricted and, on a social level, the law has proved to be the most accurate tool to achieve this purpose. In European legal culture, the necessity of the Rule of Law can hardly be debated.

While the Rule of Law is a common European *value*, on *constitutional law* terms it is interpreted differently in national legal systems. There are (at least) three different considerations to set the limits of law and state power: the French constitutionalism (*l'État de droit*), the English Rule of Law, and the German *Rechtsstaat*. This is not simply an issue of linguistic diversity; they are also different in content. The French constitutionalism is rooted in the work of Montesquieu. It examines the institutional boundaries of state power and lays a strong emphasis on the separation of administration and judiciary. On the other hand, the English Rule of Law ensures procedural guarantees against arbitrary decision-making to keep everyone (including the state) under the Rule of Law. The German *Rechtsstaat* implements material requirements (protection of human rights, democracy, etc.) into the legal system.[2]

The situation is even more complex when it comes to evaluating the Rule of Law by quantitative measures. For instance, the World Justice Project,[3] the World Bank,[4] and the United Nations[5] point out different factors upon which they evaluate and score the countries, and they establish a rank amongst them. Such a ranking can be very useful in many aspects, but the outcome of the evaluation also varies along different factors. Furthermore, they consider the Rule of Law more to be like a norm (a command) than a value.

As a consequence, if the Rule of Law is considered not in a political but in a theoretical way, one finds that the value is everything but 'common'. Being sarcastic: the Rule of Law is a common value as long as one does not define what it exactly is.

Despite the differences, the European Union makes a concerted effort to universalise the Rule of Law and to give common standards. Still, EU legislation fails to define what Rule of Law really is.[6] Instead of making a separate definition, the Union strongly relies on the statements of the Venice Commission that analysed Rule of Law with a comparative approach. Relying on Bingham's definition, the Venice Commission declares that Rule of Law is a state in which 'all persons and authorities within the state, whether public or private, should be bound by and entitled to the benefit of laws publicly made, taking effect (generally) in the

2 AZs Varga, *From Ideal to Idol. The Concept of the Rule of Law* (Dialóg Campus, Budapest 2019), https://akfi-dl.uni-nke.hu/pdf_kiadvanyok/web_PDF_From_Ideal_to_Idol.pdf, 19–20.

3 https://worldjusticeproject.org/sites/default/files/documents/WJP-ROLI-2019-Single%20Page%20View-Reduced_0.pdf.

4 https://data.worldbank.org/indicator/IC.LGL.CRED.XQ.

5 www.un.org/en/events/peacekeepersday/2011/publications/un_rule_of_law_indicators.pdf.

6 Á Mohay and Á Lukonits, 'Protecting the Rule of Law as a Fundamental Value of the EU – The Article 7 Procedure and Beyond' 4 *Osteuropa Recht* (2017) 402.

future and publicly administered in the courts'.[7] However, on a European level, there is no unanimous understanding or any normative description of Rule of Law, which leaves room for interpretations.

On the level of the treaties of the European Union, Article 2 of the Treaty on the European Union (TEU) prescribes the basic values of the Union. Everyday communication refers to the Article as the 'Rule of Law clause' of the European Union, whereas it is not just about Rule of Law. The wording of the article is as follows:

> The Union is founded on the values of respect for human dignity, freedom, democracy, equality, the Rule of Law and respect for human rights, including the rights of persons belonging to minorities. These values are common to the Member States in a society in which pluralism, non-discrimination, tolerance, justice, solidarity and equality between women and men prevail.

Before analysing Rule of Law, it is worth starting with the second sentence saying that 'these values are common to the Member States'. The sentence claims that Article 2 does not normatively prescribe democracy, Rule of Law, and other values to the Member States. Instead, it says that the values are common ones; consequently, they are in the national constitutional systems, and they had been there before stating them by the TEU. Article 2 of the TEU is a declaration that influences the operation of the Union and the Member States. In other words: Article 2 influences legislation and polities in a way that they respect these values both on a national and on a European level.

7.2.2. Illiberalism in Hungary

In a political context, illiberalism is a sobriquet. Most liberal politicians and scholars blame the Hungarian governance as illiberal which, in this context, means that the country deviates from the liberal democratic policy. In fact, illiberalism is not an allegation but the self-proclaimed ideology of Hungarian governance.

The word illiberalism came from Fareed Zakaria in 1997, who referred to illiberalism as a system that grants free elections but has limited access to human rights. It is noteworthy that Zakaria was rather sceptical about illiberalism:

> Illiberal democracies gain legitimacy, and thus strength, from the fact that they are reasonably democratic. Conversely, the greatest danger that illiberal democracy poses – other than to its own people – is that it will discredit liberal democracy itself, casting a shadow on democratic governance.[8]

7 Venice Commission, Report on the Rule of Law, Adopted by the Venice Commission at its 86th plenary session (Venice, 25–26 March 2011) CDL-AD(2011)003rev.

8 F Zakaria, 'The Rise of Illiberal Democracies' 6 *Foreign Affairs* (1997) 42.

Almost 20 years thereafter, in 2014, Hungarian PM Viktor Orbán used illiberalism in a very different context. He blamed liberalism for not protecting national values and for risking the incurrence of huge debts. He reckoned that Hungary is not a group of individuals but a community to be built and strengthened. He referred to

> an illiberal state, a non-liberal state [that] does not reject the fundamental principles of liberalism such as freedom, and I could list a few more, but it does not make this ideology the central element of state organisation, but instead includes a different, special, national approach.

He concluded that, according to the liberal doctrine, 'everything is permitted that is not forbidden', while the illiberal doctrine says that 'don't do what you don't want to be done to you'.[9]

This approach is close to Immanuel Kant's categorical imperative in the Critique of Pure Reason, which is a real and legitimate philosophical standpoint. However, neither in Hungary nor internationally is illiberalism understood in this sense; instead, they consider illiberalism to also cover populism, corruption, the restriction of human rights, and the lack of political culture. Such phenomena are also frequent criticisms towards Hungary, but they are not features of illiberalism as it was described above. In political communication, illiberalism is not the ideological base of the Hungarian governance *but the Hungarian governance itself.* This distinction is of central importance.

7.2.3. Is there an illiberal Rule of Law?

No one denies, not even in Hungary, that Rule of Law must be maintained. Both scholars and politicians are unanimous in this question. According to the government's position, illiberalism is not the refusal of Rule of Law but the refusal of a political view, namely liberalism. It adds that the Rule of Law grants free choice among views. The government likes to refer to the protection of national identity, which, in their view, also covers the protection of illiberalism.

The standpoint of the European Union is utterly different. In the European Union, Rule of Law is not just a norm but a conviction, a principle that defines the identity of the entire Union. Therefore, the definition of Rule of Law is a very slippery issue, and this is the reason why the Union takes precautions to preserve Rule of Law. The European Union considers the violation of the Rule of Law in one Member State as an issue indirectly affecting other Member States too, which calls for definite steps to be taken.[10]

9 Viktor Orbán's speech at Tusnádfürdő (Transsylvania) on 25 July 2014.

10 See Sylwia Majkowska-Szulc's conclusions in this book. S Majkowska-Szulc, 'Safeguarding the European Union's core values: The EU Rule of Law mission in Poland', Chapter 8 of this book, 190–191.

The mainstream ideological view finds it impossible that a state under the Rule of Law, or a democracy could be based on anything other than the liberty of the individuals.[11] According to this view, illiberalism falls beyond the scope of Rule of Law, and since preserving Rule of Law is part of the identity of the Union, they take steps against illiberalism in order to protect Rule of Law. Yet the Hungarian perspective is that the Union is not about to defend but to defeat something, namely the (the illiberal) national identity.

Ironically, both the European Union and Hungary refer to the protection of identity when making steps against one another.

Is it possible for an illiberal state to be under the Rule of Law? The professional advocate's answer is: it depends. It depends if one relies on the academic definition of illiberalism or on its practice in Hungary. And it also depends if one considers Rule of Law as a normative rule that can be interpreted freely or as a political value.

As for the first option: it is entirely possible for a society under the Rule of Law to be built on principles like 'do love your neighbour!' and 'don't do what you don't want to be done to you!', whilst also preserving fundamental rights. Yet if governance misuses power, disrupts checks and balances, or segregates groups of society, these measures are against Rule of Law, ***irrespective of the ideology the governance is based on.***

As for the second option: if Rule of Law is not just a legal framework but an ideology, a cornerstone of the 'ever-perfect Union', then the system is less tolerant of those whose ideology differs; those who challenge the mainstream ideology of the 1970s–1980s West and of the 1990s East: liberalism.

The European Union reckons that illiberalism endangers its own political philosophy. Therefore, it is essential to clarify if one considers Rule of Law in a legal or in a political perspective: do we want to protect a value choice, or do we want to apply a legal norm? Yet the distinction between them is not entirely clear.

7.3. International criticisms towards the Hungarian Rule of Law

7.3.1. The Hungarian Rule of Law and the Venice Commission

Since the Fidesz takeover in 2010, the Venice Commission of the Council of Europe has considered issues 17 times that either directly or indirectly pertain to the Hungarian Rule of Law. They are as follows:

1. 943/2018 – Hungary – Law on the entry into force of the Law on Administrative Courts and certain transitional Rules;

11 'Illiberal democracy – there's no such a thing' – CJEU president Koen Lenaert's statement at the Hungarian Academy of Science in the conference on 'Constitutional EU-identity' (Budapest, 8 March 2019).

2. 941/2018 – Hungary – Joint Opinion on Section 253 on the special immigration tax of Act XLI of 20 July amending certain tax laws and other related laws and on the immigration tax;
3. 919/2018 – Hungary – Opinion on the compatibility of the Hungarian Government's 'Stop Soros' draft legislative package with international human rights standards;
4. 891/2017 – Hungary – Opinion on Act XXV of 4 April 2017 on the Amendments of Act CCIV of 2011 on National Education;
5. 889/2017 – Hungary – Opinion on the Draft Law on the Transparency of Organisations receiving support from abroad;
6. 798/2015 – Opinion on the Act CLXXV of 2010 on Media Services and Mass Media; Act CIV of 2010 on the Freedom of Press and the Fundamental Rules of Media and Content, and on the Hungarian tax Laws on progressive Tax on Advertising revenue of media;
7. 720/2013 – Opinion on the Fourth Amendment to the Fundamental Law of Hungary;
8. 683/2012 – Opinion on the Cardinal Acts on the Judiciary that were amended following the adoption of CDL-AD(2012)001 of Hungary;
9. 672/2012 – Opinion on Act CXII of 2011 on informational Self-determination and Freedom of Information of Hungary;
10. 671/2012 – Opinion on the Act on the Rights of Nationalities of Hungary;
11. 668/2012 – Opinion on Act CLXIII of 2011 on the Prosecution Service and Act CLXIV of 2011 on the Status of the Prosecutor General, Prosecutors and other Prosecution Employees and the Prosecution Career of Hungary;
12. 665/2012 – Opinion on Act CLI of 2011 on the Constitutional Court of Hungary;
13. 664/2012 – Opinion on Act CCVI of 2011 on the right to freedom of conscience and religion and the legal status of churches, denominations and religious communities of Hungary;
14. 663/2012 – Opinion on Act CLXII of 2011 on the Legal Status and Remuneration of Judges and Act CLXI of 2011 on the Organisation and Administration of Courts of Hungary;
15. 662/2012 – Joint Opinion on the Act on the Elections of Members of Parliament of Hungary;
16. 621/2011 – Opinion on the new Constitution of Hungary;
17. 614/2011 – Opinion on three legal questions arising in the process of drafting the New Constitution of Hungary.

Among them, this paper analyses only those that pertain to the Article 7 procedure.

1) Concerning the constitution-making process:

> the Venice Commission notes that the constitutional legal order continues to be based, in Hungary, on a Constitution which, although amended several times since 1989, dates back to 1949.
>
> Against this background, the adoption of a new Constitution, in line with the current legal standards and reflecting the most recent evolutions

within society, is a legitimate aim. The Commission nevertheless finds that the current process of preparing the draft new Constitution in view of its rapid adoption (foreseen for April 2011) raises a number of concerns which would deserve careful consideration by the Hungarian Authorities.

These include the lack of transparency of the process and, several weeks before its adoption, the absence of a public draft for the new Constitution, the absence of dialogue between the majority and the opposition, the insufficient opportunities provided to enable an adequate public debate on such a fundamental process, and its very limited timeframe.

Increased flexibility, openness and spirit of compromise are key elements for all stakeholders concerned, and should enable them, beyond their political background and orientations, to adopt a legitimate and sustainable Constitution, in line with the democratic standards and widely accepted by the Hungarian society.[12]

2) As for the migration tax (that involved NGOs to a great extent), the Venice Commission reckoned:

> The Venice Commission and ODIHR consider that in some instances, taxation may constitute not only a restriction on the right to property, but also as an interference with individuals' and entities' freedom of expression and freedom of association. First, according to Principle 4 of the Joint Guidelines on Freedom of Association, founders and members shall be free in the determination of the objectives and activities of their associations, including the scope of operations. Legislation pertaining to associations should not dictate nor disproportionately restrict the objectives and activities that associations wish to pursue and undertake, including by providing a restrictive list of permissible objectives or activities or through a narrow interpretation of the legislation relating to the objectives and activities of associations. Legal provisions restricting associational activities should not jeopardise the effective operation of NGOs.
>
> This applies regardless of whether or not the position being advocated is popular. Therefore, the imposition of the special tax on associations for a number of lawful objectives and activities indicated in the legislation qualifies as an interference with the right to freedom of association of non-governmental organisations.
>
> Secondly, NGOs should be free to undertake research, education and advocacy on issues of public debate, regardless of whether the position taken is in accord with government policy or requires a change in the law. The Joint Guidelines on Freedom of Association state that »[a]

12 Venice Commission, Draft Opinion on three legal questions arising in the process of drafting the new constitution of Hungary, Adopted by the Venice Commission at its 86th Plenary Session (Venice, 25–26 March 2011) CDL(2011)016.

ssociations shall have the right to freedom of expression and opinion through their objectives and activities. This is in addition to the individual right of the members of associations to freedom of expression and opinion. Associations shall have the right to participate in matters of political and public debate, regardless of whether the position taken is in accord with government policy or advocates a change in the law«.

Given the fact that some lawful activities of NGOs indicated in Section 253(2) such as media campaigns, educative activities, building and operating networks and propaganda activities are relevant to determine whether an activity should be qualified an »immigration-supporting activity« which will lead to the imposition of a significant tax, Section 253 on the special immigration tax has a chilling effect on and constitute an interference with the freedom of expression of those organisations when engaging in lawful activities.[13]

It is noteworthy that the migration tax is still an existing tax (1 of the 58 taxes that are valid in Hungary), but up until now, there has not been a single Forint transferred to the central budget from this tax.[14] Moreover, the central budget for 2019 did not even plan any income from this tax.[15] Presumably, neither the potential taxpayers nor the tax agencies focus on this tax too much.

3) Another issue concerning NGOs was the Hungarian Act on their support; NGOs now have to pay an extra tax after any income they receive from abroad. The Venice Commission noted:

> The rationale behind the exclusion of a number of associations and organisations from the scope of application of the Draft Law is not entirely clear, as the requirement of transparency should certainly apply to all civil society organisations.

The Commission also commented

> that the period of three years during which a civil society organisation may not receive any foreign funding in order to be entitled to initiate a deregistration procedure is quite long and appears to be arbitrary. It is recommended to replace it with a one-year period. This would not, in any way, hamper the objective of the Draft Law and would also make the registration and deregistration procedures more coherent.[16]

13 Venice Commission and OSCE ODIHR, Joint Opinion on Section 253 on the special immigration tax of Act XLI of 20 July amending certain tax laws and other related laws and on the immigration tax, Adopted by the Venice Commission at its 117th Plenary Session (Venice, 14–15 December 2018), CDL-AD(2018)035.

14 https://hvg.hu/gazdasag/20190719_bevandorlasi_kulonado_soros_ado.

15 www.allamkincstar.gov.hu/hu/koltsegvetesi-informaciok/koltsegvetes_merleg_1/222/.

16 Venice Commission, Opinion on the Draft Law on the Transparency of Organisations receiving support from abroad, Adopted by the Venice Commission at its 111th Plenary Session (Venice, 16–17 June 2017, CDL-AD(2017)015, 889/2017.

4) The Venice Commission has also examined the new system of administrative courts chosen by Hungary in light of existing principles and standards for the independence of justice and separation of powers, which are key requirements of the Rule of Law. The Commission's analysis has placed special emphasis, beyond the individual provisions of the two laws, on the accumulated effect of the above-mentioned provisions adopted in the current legal framework of the last decade, associated with large-scale constitutional and legislative measures.[17] Finally, the administrative courts have never been established in Hungary; the Fundamental Law mentioned them as existing institutions for a while, then the Seventh Amendment repealed the reference to administrative courts and jurisdiction.

5) The situation of the media is one of the most important topics concerning Rule of Law. The Venice Commission found it problematic that the Media Council can impose severe fines. They missed the regulation that would define

> whether a sanction should be applied, and, if so, the level of sanction, in order to reduce any chilling effect caused by uncertainty in the application of the two Acts. Similarly, the Media Act should specify that heavy sanctions seriously affecting normal functioning of a media outlet should be used as a measure of last resort (for example, for repeated calls for unlawful mass violence) and should not be immediately enforceable. In addition, the rules governing election of the members of the Media Council should be changed to ensure fair representation of socially significant political and other groups and of the media community in this body. The method of appointment and the position of the Chairperson of the Media Council/the President of the Media Authority should be revisited in order to reduce concentration of powers and secure political neutrality of that figure.[18]

6) Among constitutional amendments, the Fourth Amendment proved to be the most problematic. The Venice Commission concluded:

> In constitutional law, perhaps even more than in other legal fields, it is necessary to take into account not only the face value of a provision, but also to examine its constitutional context. The mere fact that a provision also exists in the constitution of another country does not mean that it

17 Venice Commission, Opinion on the Law on Administrative Courts and the Law on the entry into force of the Law on Administrative Courts and certain transitional Rules, Adopted by the Venice Commission at its 118th Plenary Session (Venice, 15–16 March 2019), CDL-AD(2019)004, 943/2018.

18 Venice Commission, Opinion on the Act CLXXV of 2010 on Media Services and Mass Media; Act CIV of 2010 on the Freedom of Press and the Fundamental Rules of Media and Content, and on the Hungarian tax Laws on progressive Tax on Advertising revenue of media, adopted by the Venice Commission at its 103rd Plenary Session(Venice, 19–20 June 2015), CDL-AD(2015)015, 98/2015.

also 'fits' into any other constitution. Each constitution is the result of balancing various powers. If a power is given to one state body, other powers need to be able to effectively control the exercise of this power. The more power an institution has, the tighter control mechanisms need to be constructed. Comparative constitutional law cannot be reduced to identifying the existence of a provision the constitution of another country to justify its democratic credentials in the constitution of one's own country. Each constitution is a complex array of checks and balances and each provision needs to be examined in view of its merits for the balance of powers as a whole.

However, the Fourth Amendment itself brings about or perpetuates shortcomings in the constitutional system of Hungary. The main concerns relate to the role of the Constitutional Court and to a lesser extent the ordinary judiciary. In the field of human rights in general, several issues are regulated in a manner disregarding earlier decisions by the Constitutional Court.

Mainly due to international pressure, the Fifth Amendment withdrew the most-criticised elements of the Fourth Amendment. Jurisprudence also intended to 'soften' the wording of the Fundamental Law. Although the Fourth Amendment repealed the previous decisions of the Constitutional Court, nevertheless, the Constitutional Court stated that there was no obstacle to refer to previous judgments in case the rational basis of the constitutional provisions are the same.[19]

7.3.2. The Hungarian Rule of Law in the European Parliament

7.3.2.1. The Tavares report and its effects

Legal committees of the European Parliament had raised their concerns on the Hungarian Rule of Law well before the Article 7 procedure started. MEP Rui Tavares was the rapporteur at the Committee on Civil Liberties, Justice and Home Affairs that submitted a report to the European Parliament on 25 June 2013.

The report examined the changes in Hungary in general. It stated that the key element is the protection of Article 2 of TEU:

> whereas the common values enshrined in Article 2 TEU constitute the core of the rights enjoyed by persons living within the EU and especially by EU citizens, irrespective of their nationality and no matter where they might consider themselves to belong in cultural or religious terms, and whereas such persons can fully enjoy those rights only if the EU's fundamental values and principles are upheld'. It also stated: „whereas the values set out in Article 2 TEU have to be addressed politically and legally, this being an indispensable foundation of our democratic society, and whereas, therefore,

19 13/2013. (VI. 17.) decision of the CC.

> Member States, as well as all the EU institutions, must commit themselves to them, clearly and unambiguously.

The report covers several topics. It analysed the situation of the Fundamental Law and cardinal statutes and raised a concern that the Fundamental Law was adopted by the votes of the governing supermajority, and the opposition had no real chance to express their standpoint. It also noted that even though the Constitutional Court, upon the initiative of the ombudsman, annulled the Transitional Provisions to the Fundamental Law, the Fourth Amendment inserted many criticised elements into the constitutional text. In Hungarian academic life, this phenomenon was called 'overconstitutionalisation'. The report stated that cardinal statutes cement issues into the power of the legal order that should have been left to simple majority (family law, taxation).

The report evaluated as the weakness of checks and balances that the competences of the Constitutional Court had changed and *actio popularis* terminated. It also criticised that the office of the commissioner for data protection had been terminated and that the central budget was supervised by the Budget Council, missing full democratic legitimacy.

The independence of the judiciary also proved to be an important part of the report. It reckoned that the legal framework did not provide the independence of the Constitutional Court and the administration of the judiciary. It did not ensure the irremovability of the judges either. It raised special attention to the retirement age of the justices[20] and the competence of the National Judicial Office (an organ for the administration of judiciary) to transfer cases from one court to another.[21]

Concerning the electoral system, the report reckoned that the system had been changed with no real consult with parties in the opposition.

The report 'expresses concern at the effects of the provision of the Fourth Amendment banning political advertising in the commercial media since, although the stated aim of this provision is to reduce political campaign costs and create equal opportunities for the parties, it jeopardises the provision of balanced information'. It also 'deplores the fact that the creation of the state-owned Hungarian News Agency (MTI) as the single news provider for public service broadcasters, while all major private broadcasters are expected to have their own news service, has meant it has a virtual monopoly on the market, as most of its news items are freely available'. To conclude, the report found that Hungarian media pluralism was jeopardised.

As for the protection of minorities, the report acknowledged the legal framework protecting the Roma community, adding that its real enforcement was lacking. It also found it problematic that the notion of family in the Fundamental Law is based on the conventional family model and excludes same-sex couples.

20 An Act reducing the retirement age of judges from 70 to 62 that resulted in the termination of many judges, especially in higher courts.

21 Critics say that the transfer potentially affected the right to a fair trial and the right of a lawful judge.

Concerning freedom of religion, the report raises concerns that the Fourth Amendment delegated the Parliament the exclusive competence to decide which communities are acknowledged as churches, without proper legal reasoning.

In conclusion, the report found the situation inapplicable to the principles stipulated in Articles 2, 3, (1), and 4 of TEU.

The report declares an important value choice. It reaffirms that its present resolution is not only about Hungary, but inseparably about the European Union as a whole, and its democratic reconstruction and development after the fall of the 20th-century totalitarianisms. It is about the European family, its common values and standards, its inclusiveness, and its capacity to engage in dialogue. It is about the need to implement Treaties, which all Member States have voluntarily acceded to. It is about the mutual help and mutual trust that the Union, its citizens and its Member States need to have if these Treaties are to be not just words on paper, but the legal basis for a true, just and open Europe respecting fundamental rights.

Subsequently, the document detailed recommendations to the organs of the European Union and to Hungary.

The European Parliament voted on the report with 370 in favour, 249 against, and 82 restrained from voting. This indicates that not only left-wing parties but most of the EPP deputies also voted in favour. Although the report resulted in no direct legal consequence, it had a serious political effect. It showed that the position of Fidesz was less strong in its own fraction (the EPP) than it was previously believed, as some of its members also seem to have voted for the report.

As a result, infringement procedures against Hungary were put in place, which brought the Hungarian government to surrender. The Parliament adopted the Fifth Amendment to the Fundamental Law that withdrew most of the criticised elements of the Fourth Amendment.

7.3.2.2. The Sargentini report

A new element of the Rule of Law debate is that on 12 September 2018, the European Parliament launched the procedure called Article 7 of the Treaty of the European Union (TEU) against Hungary. The procedure relied on MEP Judith Sargentini's report,[22]

The European Parliament pointed out 12 issues in which they had concerns against Hungary:

- the functioning of the constitutional and electoral system;
- the independence of the judiciary and of other institutions and the rights of judges;

22 www.europarl.europa.eu/sides/getDoc.do?pubRef=-//EP//TEXT+REPORT+A8-2018-0250+0+DOC+XML+V0//EN.

- corruption and conflicts of interest;
- privacy and data protection;
- freedom of expression;
- academic freedom;
- freedom of religion;
- freedom of association;
- the right to equal treatment;
- the rights of persons belonging to minorities, including Roma and Jews, and protection against hateful statements against such minorities;
- the fundamental rights of migrants, asylum seekers, and refugees;
- economic and social rights.

The annex to the report was to verify that Hungary infringed the values stipulated in Article 2 of the TEU. The present paper does not intend to argue whether the statements of the report are correct or false, yet it is interesting to consider the context of the report to have an overall picture of Article 7. The report is heterogeneous in several aspects. There are

- conceptual, systematic problems (competences of the Constitutional Court, risk of corruption) and particular issues (measures against the Norwegian Fund, gender stereotypes in school books);
- legal and political issues; the report does not only criticise the Hungarian legislation and jurisprudence but also political statements (like the 'Stop-Soros' campaign, patriarchal stereotypes);
- government policies (migration, legislation) and issues delegated to authorities independent to the government (Constitutional Court, judiciary, Media Council).

The report is more like a 'To-Do List'; it mentions topics in three or four paragraphs. This way, it cannot even introduce the problems in detail, and it is impossible to give a legally founded verification. On the contrary, opposing the report, the Hungarian government has conducted a study that analyses the problems raised in detail. Interestingly, the answer is more than three times longer than the report itself (ca 109 pages while the report is only 30 without attachments). It is of a rather different nature; its structure links to the report but does not evaluate the problems, instead, it focuses on the verification of the Hungarian standpoint.

Two monologues do not make a dialogue. The European Parliament and the Hungarian government speak of different things; the Sargentini report and the government's answer put together do not result in a constructive dialogue. Does one conclude from the Sargentini report that Hungary is not under the Rule of Law, or could the government 'defend' the Hungarian standpoint and prove that it is still under the Rule of Law? In order to attempt an answer, the nature of Article 7 must be analysed.

7.3.2.3. The Article 7 procedure

Article 7 of the TEU is often referred to as a 'nuclear bomb' in the hands of the European Union; not only because of its effect, but also because it was understood that the Article is merely a threat never to be applied. After Article 7 was initiated against Hungary, scholars of constitutional law started to focus more on the procedure.

According to the wording of Article 7 of the TEU:

1. On a reasoned proposal by one third of the Member States, by the European Parliament or by the European Commission, the Council, acting by a majority of four fifths of its members after obtaining the consent of the European Parliament, may determine that there is a clear risk of a serious breach by a Member State of the values referred to in Article 2. Before making such a determination, the Council shall hear the Member State in question and may address recommendations to it, acting in accordance with the same procedure.

   The Council shall regularly verify that the grounds on which such a determination was made continue to apply.
2. The European Council, acting by unanimity on a proposal by one third of the Member States or by the Commission and after obtaining the consent of the European Parliament, may determine the existence of a serious and persistent breach by a Member State of the values referred to in Article 2, after inviting the Member State in question to submit its observations.
3. Where a determination under paragraph 2 has been made, the Council, acting by a qualified majority, may decide to suspend certain of the rights deriving from the application of the Treaties to the Member State in question, including the voting rights of the representative of the government of that Member State in the Council. In doing so, the Council shall take into account the possible consequences of such a suspension on the rights and obligations of natural and legal persons.

   The obligations of the Member State in question under the Treaties shall in any case continue to be binding on that State.

The origin of Article 7 stems back to 2000 when Austria established a coalition government after the parliamentary elections, and the far-right Freedom Party of Austria (Freiheitliche Partei Österreichs) became a member of the government. A total of 14 Member States considered the Rule of Law to be endangered in Austria, at which point they, rather than the Union, took steps against Austria. The measures taken did not appear in any official document of the European Union, yet it is symbolic that the Portuguese Prime Minister, who was the president of the European Council at that time, announced the measures on 4 February 2000, and the French president holding the presidency of the Council at the time ceased them on 12 September 2000.[23] Interestingly, Article 7 had existed prior to

23 A Osztovits, *Az Európai Unióról és az Európai Unió működéséről szóló szerződések magyarázata.* [*Commentary to the Treaty on the European Union and to the Treaty on the Functioning of the European Union*] (Wolters Kluwer, Budapest 2011) 80.

these events; it was introduced by the Treaty of Amsterdam in 1997. However, the procedure was even more complicated than it is today, which may also have resulted in the Member States opting for taking bilateral, diplomatic steps instead of using the measures of the Union. Presumably, the Treaty of Lisbon (2007) simplified the procedure with regard to the events of 2000.

There is very little practical experience concerning the Article 7 procedure; the procedures against Poland and Hungary are in very early stages. With regard to the wording of the Article, the procedure seems overcomplicated, and it leaves too much room for different interests of the Member States and those of the Union. Furthermore, it is unclear what it really protects, and it is problematic to prove the infringement of the requirements of the Rule of Law.[24]

It is also questionable if the procedure mentioned in Section 1 (risk of serious breach) is a precondition of the procedure of Section 2 (serious and persistent breach). Neither is it clear how 'risk' and 'breach' relate to one another.

The procedure against Hungary has given rise to another issue: the requested majority to launch Article 7. According to Article 354 of the Treaty on the Functioning of the European Union (TFEU):

> For the purposes of Article 7 of the Treaty on European Union on the suspension of certain rights resulting from Union membership, the member of the European Council or of the Council representing the Member State in question shall not take part in the vote and the Member State in question shall not be counted in the calculation of the one third or four fifths of Member States referred to in paragraphs 1 and 2 of that Article. Abstentions by members present in person or represented shall not prevent the adoption of decisions referred to in paragraph 2 of that Article.
>
> For the adoption of the decisions referred to in paragraphs 3 and 4 of Article 7 of the Treaty on European Union, a qualified majority shall be defined in accordance with Article 238(3)(b) of this Treaty.
>
> Where, following a decision to suspend voting rights adopted pursuant to paragraph 3 of Article 7 of the Treaty on European Union, the Council acts by a qualified majority on the basis of a provision of the Treaties, that qualified majority shall be defined in accordance with Article 238(3)(b) of this Treaty, or, where the Council acts on a proposal from the Commission or from the High Representative of the Union for Foreign Affairs and Security Policy, in accordance with Article 238(3)(a).
>
> For the purposes of Article 7 of the Treaty on European Union, the European Parliament shall act by a two-thirds majority of the votes cast, representing the majority of its component Members.

The TFEU stipulates two requirements: a two-thirds majority of the valid votes cast on the one hand, and the absolute majority on the other, i.e., the votes for

24 Balázs F, 'Alternatív kommentár az EUSZ 7. cikkéhez [Alternative commentary to Article 7 TEU]', 2 *Közjogi Szemle* (2016) 9.

initiating the procedure should be more than half of all members of the European Parliament.

When the European Parliament voted in relation to Hungary, 448 deputies voted in favour and 197 against the report, while 48 deputies abstained. According to the position of the European Parliament, such a result is sufficient to initiate the procedure. Yet literally, there were 693 votes cast, and 448 is less than the two-thirds of 693 (according to this interpretation, 462 votes would have been necessary). The European Parliament did not accept such an interpretation and it did not consider the abstain votes as 'votes cast'. What about the abstain votes?

Unfortunately, European parliaments have different standpoints and customs in the question. The Hungarian constitution requires a qualified majority in several issues in which the two-thirds majority is required. In the praxis of the Hungarian Parliament, abstain votes are also validly cast votes, and they have to be counted. Had the Hungarian parliament voted on the Sargentini report with such a ratio, it would have certainly been invalid. Many other parliaments in Europe have different views, and they do not add abstain votes to the result. In Westminster, it is not possible to abstain, for instance. The European Parliament had the same standpoint. Yet it resulted in distrust both in Hungary and in the European Parliament: the Hungarian position is that the European Parliament is politically motivated, and it is against the wording of the TFEU, while the European Parliament suggests that the Hungarian government refers to manifestly ill-founded legal terms.

7.4. Rule of Law between law and politics

7.4.1. The nature of law and politics

In legal studies, there is a belief: the law is important, politics is not. If a lawyer labels a procedure (the Article 7 procedure, for instance) as political, then he/she does not take it seriously enough, but rather, tries to marginalise its importance, which is in favour of the government's position. To defeat this stereotype, it is essential to differentiate law and politics in an academic way.

According to the classic differentiation of legal and political decision-making, legal decisions are based on legal authority; political decisions are based on a value choice. Legal decisions (at least in Civil Law countries) are always based on law; particular decisions are made in one specific way because they are the ones deduced from the abstract law. On the contrary, political decision-makers, according to their own value choice, intend to shape society. To set an everyday example: the decision to reduce personal income tax is a political decision that is made by evaluating the resulting economic and social benefits and disadvantages. On the other hand, collecting personal income tax is a legal decision. Tax authorities do not evaluate whether collecting the tax is fair or economical, but they consider whether it derives from the law.

However, the separation of political and legal decisions in practice is not always clear. Political decisions also have a legal background. It is not only the case that there is a *legal procedure* for making political decisions (like the standing orders of parliaments that stipulate the procedure of law-making). More significantly, human rights and principles limit the possible content of political decisions. Constitutional rights, democracy, and the Rule of Law have more and more influence on political decision-making, especially since the second half of the 20th century, the Rule of Law has become a normative principle that all decisions have to adhere to.[25] In other words, if a political decision is against the Rule of Law, then it is unconstitutional, and it cannot be made. This results in political decisions becoming legal decisions; the Rule of Law (as a legal authority) restricts the content of the decision.

A good example of this is the suspension of the British parliament during the Brexit debate: the political decision whether the parliament has sittings or not became a subject of judicial review, and the courts examined on the basis of the law whether the decision of the suspension (more precisely: the initiative for suspension) was legal.[26]

American jurisprudence uses the political question doctrine according to which courts are not involved in the affairs of political branches.[27] The doctrine is unknown in Europe, where all decisions can be measured by law; law provides a framework for political decision-making.

I conclude that there is no clear distinction between political and legal decisions. The two are not entirely separate, but political decisions can be made in the framework of the law. One may observe that the framework is getting narrower, limiting political (value choice based) decision-making.

7.4.2. Legal and political decision-making

It comes from the Rule of Law that actions must be determined based on the law (the decision has a legal basis) and in a procedure that is prescribed by law. Consequently, decisions are under the Rule of Law if they meet the following three criteria:

1) the procedure is launched due to a legal cause (i.e., stipulated by law);
2) the procedure is prescribed by law and
3) there is a judicial organ that makes the decision.

To set a simple example: a state under the Rule of Law can only punish someone for stealing because the Criminal Code prescribes what stealing is and considers it a crime (No 1.). Furthermore, the Criminal Procedure Code regulates the procedure of the trial, stipulates the rights of the defendant (No 2.), and the court

25 Varga, n. 2, 27.

26 R (on the application of Miller) (Appellant) v The Prime Minister (Respondent) [2019] UKSC 41. www.supremecourt.uk/cases/docs/uksc-2019-0192-judgment.pdf.

27 I Marosi and L Csink, 'Political Questions in the United States and in France', 4 *Studia Iuridica Caroliensia* (2009) 113–124.

concludes whether the defendant is guilty or not (No 3.). In case any of the above criteria is not fulfilled, the procedure is not under the Rule of Law. If the court establishes the definition of crime post-hoc, or there are no clear rules for the trial, or if it is not the court that makes the decision, the process is not under the Rule of Law in legal terms. All criteria must be fulfilled simultaneously.

7.4.3. The nature of Article 7

Let us examine whether the criteria mentioned above for legal decisions are fulfilled with regard to the Article 7 procedure, which helps determine the extent to which it is legal or political.

In Article 7 of the TEU, legal and political elements are combined/intermingled. As for the legal elements, the purpose of Article 7 is to protect the well-known values of constitutional law. The precondition of initiating the procedure is a substantial risk to these values (as it is mentioned in Sections 1) and a serious breach thereof (Section 2).[28] On the other hand, the procedure also contains political elements; moreover, the political elements dominate the procedure. Political organs (European Parliament, Council, Commission, governments of the Member States) are entitled to make decisions, and it is a decision based on a value judgment whether they establish the presence of a substantial risk or breach. Notably, the CJEU safeguards only the procedural guarantees; the court has no competence to review the Rule of Law or its possible breach. Remarkably, the stages of Article 7 are gradual; measures can be taken step by step. Such a method leaves room for (political) dialogue among the parties involved.

Applying the criteria of the test, the Article 7 procedure

1) is launched because of legal reasons ('breach' or 'risk' of fundamental values);
2) TEU describes the procedure (legal procedure);
3) the European Parliament makes the decision, not courts (political decision-making).

Here there is a significant difference between the infringement procedure and the Article 7 procedure. At first sight, the procedures are very much alike; in both cases, a Member State is challenged because of infringing on the regulation of EU law. Yet, in the case of the infringement procedure, the Commission first sends a letter of formal notice requesting information from the country concerned. If the country provides no information or if this is not satisfactory, the Commission sends a reasoned opinion to the country, and, finally, it can challenge the country at the CJEU. Unlike the infringement procedure, the Article 7 procedure does not provide a legal forum to dispute it.

Consequently, the question if a Member State is under the Rule of Law, i.e., it respects the values of Article 2, is a political decision in a legal procedure. Neither

28 Osztovits, n. 23, 80.

initiating Article 7, nor the evaluation of the outcome of the procedure is a judicial (legal) decision. As a matter of fact, the rules of the procedure and the organs participating in the decision cannot even make it possible for Article 7 to decide if a country is under the Rule of Law. It does not mean that the decision is made arbitrarily but that the subject of the decision is something other than the law.

Analysing the nature of Article 7, I conclude that the procedure aims to highlight if the organs of the European Union (European Parliament, Council, and Commission) and the Member States of the European Union *consider another Member State as a Rule of Law state.* In other words: *Article 7 is not able to prove that Hungary is not under the Rule of Law but it is able to show: the Union does not believe that Hungary is under the Rule of Law.*

The question of whether Hungary is under the Rule of Law does connect to the Article 7 procedure, but neither the success nor the failure of the procedure answers this question. There can be Rule of Law states against which the Article 7 procedure was successful, while it is also possible that the state is not under the Rule of Law, but the Article 7 procedure still failed.

7.5. Possibilities to strengthen the mechanisms of the Rule of Law

In Chapter 9, Agnieszka Grzelak reckons that 'the situation in Poland and Hungary has confirmed that the measures provided in the Treaties are not sufficient to effectively counteract certain risks or infringements of the Rule of Law that may occur in the Member States'.[29] Indeed, it is unlikely that the Article 7 procedures result in a direct legal consequence in either of the countries.

The first question to clarify is an obvious one: do we want to strengthen the mechanisms of the Rule of Law on a European level at all? It would benefit the preservation of 'common values' and strengthen the political community. Without proper Rule of Law mechanisms, the Union would step back to the economic community. However, it is noteworthy that any change in the mechanisms protecting the Rule of Law would limit the competences of the Member States. Consequently, it also changes the relationship between the Union and the Member States. I venture to say, the unified and obligatory interpretation of the common principles and the establishment of its protection would transform the European Union into a federal state.[30]

If we answer the question positively and we are committed to strengthening the mechanisms of the Rule of Law, we need to decide whether to do that in the

29 A Grzelak, 'Are the EU Member States still masters of the Treaties? The EU Rule of Law concept as a means of limiting national authorities', Chapter 9 of this book, 213.

30 It is noteworthy that, during the establishment of the German State, Bismarck was against the incorporation of fundamental rights to the imperial constitution because he found it contrary to the autonomy of the states (Länder). K Stern, *Das Staatsrecht der Bundesrepublik Deutschland. Vol. 5* (München, CH Beck, 2000). 362.

field of law or in the field of politics. It is noteworthy that European constitutional actors usually prefer to engage in a dialogue about the Rule of Law with the offending member states;[31] i.e., they prefer political solutions to legal ones.

Present debates on the Article 7 procedure show that the political solution for strengthening the Rule of Law is more likely. It is a frequently discussed option that the budget of the European Union should provide less money for states infringing on the Rule of Law. Another option is that the Union puts political pressure on the government in question: this is what we see now between the Fidesz and the European People's Party (EPP). Interestingly, the Fidesz – EPP link is strongly related to the Rule of Law, and it bears a huge impact on the outcome of the Article 7 procedure.

In addition, there are suggestions to strengthen the mechanisms underlying the Rule of Law (including Article 7 procedure) in the field of law, which seems less likely to be implemented. As described above, there are three criteria to transform the Article 7 procedure into a purely legal process: legal ground, legal procedure, and judicial decision-making. The procedure already meets the second criteria. It also meets the first one, yet it would be more appropriate if either the TEU or the adjudication of the CJEU were to determine what the Rule of Law really is. By now, the process does not meet the third criterion: the decision is not a judicial one.

It has been suggested that 'the most potent tool to defend the Rule of Law in the EU is an infringement action by the Commission',[32] however, the Commission does not seem to base an infringement procedure solely on Article 2 the TEU.

One solution might be that the CJEU is involved in the procedure as having the *last word* if a Member State is under the Rule of Law or not. Such a change would undoubtedly ensure that the procedure is a legal one, but it could easily lead to the centralisation (perhaps federalisation) of the EU, as this would strengthen the importance of CJEU in issues that are mostly domestic. Based on this approach, courts would review the common principles.

As for this option, Bogdandy suggests that first, the national judiciaries should protect the principles stipulated in Article 2 of the TEU, as long as the Member State generally ensures them. This general level of protection is presumed. If this assumption is violated, supranational fora (EU organs) have to apply the fundamental rights.[33] However, it not only gave the CJEU a new competence (reviewing Rule of Law) but 'raising of the principle of Rule of Law to normative rank opens a gate that would probably never be closed: a tool for the EU bodies that can be used without restriction'.[34]

31 R Uitz, 'The Perils of Defending the Rule of Law Through Dialogue', 15 *European Constitutional Law Review* (2019) 2.

32 Ibid., 15.

33 A von Bogdandy, M Kottmann, C Antpöhler, J Dickschen, S Hentrei, and M Smrkolj, 'Reverse Solange – Protecting the Essence of Fundamental Rights against EU Member States', 2 *Common Market Law Review* (2012) 491.

34 AZs Varga, 'The Basic Law of Hungary and the Rule of Law' 4 *Osteuropa Recht* (2017) 393.

Instead of the possibilities mentioned above, I propose the following option. I suggest that political organs should define the core of the Rule of Law, the most basic normative elements that are binding to all Member States. CJEU should have supervision on the fulfilment of the core, but they should interpret the core in a narrow sense only to avoid the inflation of the Rule of Law and allow enough space for the particular countries.

What are the implications of the above considerations on the procedure against Hungary? The Sargentini report and its adoption by the European Parliament does not verify that Hungary is not under the Rule of Law. The government's reaction to the report does not verify that Hungary is under the Rule of Law, despite its efforts to do so. The procedure initiated against Hungary on 12 September 2018 indicates that the European Parliament has no confidence that Hungary is under the Rule of Law. All forthcoming events are in the distant future.

Bibliography

Armin von Bogdandy, Matthias Kottmann, Carlino Antpöhler, Johanna Dickschen, Simon Hentrei, and Maja Smrkolj, 'Reverse solange – Protecting the essence of fundamental rights against EU Member States', 2 *Common Market Law Review* (2012) 489–519.

Balázs Fekete, 'Alternatív kommentár az EUSZ 7. Cikkéhez' [Alternative commentary to Article 7 TEU]', 2 *Közjogi Szemle* (2016) 1–11.

Sylwia Majkowska-Szulc, 'Safeguarding the European Union's core values: The EU Rule of Law mission in Poland', Chapter 8 of this book.

Ildikó Marosi and Lóránt Csink, 'Political Questions in the United States and in France', 4 *Studia Iuridica Caroliensia* (2009) 113–124.

Ágoston Mohay and Ádám Lukonits, 'Protecting the Rule of Law as a fundamental value of the EU – The article 7 procedure and beyond', 4 *Osteuropa Recht* (2017) 530–533.

András Osztovits, *Az Európai Unióról és az Európai Unió működéséről szóló szerződések magyarázata. [Commentary to the Treaty on the European Union and to the Treaty on the Functioning of the European Union]* (Budapest, Wolters Kluwer, 2011) 3355.

Klaus Stern, *Das Staatsrecht der Bundesrepublik Deutschland. Vol. 5* (München, CH Beck, 2000).

Renáta Uitz, 'The Perils of Defending the Rule of Law Through Dialogue', 15 *European Constitutional Law Review* (2019) 1–16.

Zs András Varga, 'The Basic Law of Hungary and the Rule of Law', 4 *Osteuropa Recht* (2017) 530–533.

Zs András Varga, *From ideal to idol. The concept of the Rule of Law* (Dialóg Campus, Budapest, 2019), https://akfi-dl.uni-nke.hu/pdf_kiadvanyok/web_PDF_From_Ideal_to_Idol.pdf.

Fareed Zakaria, 'The Rise of Illiberal Democracies' 6 *Foreign Affairs* (1997) 22–43.

8 Safeguarding the European Union's core values

The EU Rule of Law mission in Poland

Sylwia Majkowska-Szulc

8.1. Introduction

The topic of this chapter deals with safeguarding the values the European Union is based on. To this end, the role of the Court of Justice of the European Union in controlling the respect for EU values has been analysed. The value of the Rule of Law has served as a model since that is the value most frequently referred to in recent times. The respect for the Rule of Law is not only a prerequisite for the protection of all fundamental values listed in Article 2 [TEU] but 'it is also a pre-requisite for upholding all rights and obligations derived from the Treaties and for establishing mutual trust of citizens, businesses and national authorities in respective legal systems of all other Member States'.[1] In fact, Poland is one of those Member States which are accused of undermining the European Rule of Law at present. Hungary is another Member State that has been regularly challenging the values of the European Union since 2010. Some legislative solutions similar to those ended with the judgment of the Court of Justice convicting Hungary for failure to fulfil its obligations were then introduced in Poland after 2015. For instance, in 2012, the Court of Justice stated that, by adopting a national scheme requiring the compulsory retirement of judges, prosecutors, and notaries when they reach the age of 62, Hungary has failed to fulfil its obligations.[2] A few years later, in 2019, the Court of Justice stated that, by providing that the measure consisting in lowering the retirement age of the judges of the Supreme Court (Poland) was to apply to judges in post who were appointed to that court before 3 April 2018, and, secondly, by granting the President of the Republic the discretion to extend the period of judicial activity of judges of that court beyond the newly fixed retirement age, the Republic of Poland had

1 Commission Statement by First Vice President Timmermans, European Parliament Plenary debate of 28 February 2018 on the Commission decision to activate Article 7(1) TEU as regards the situation in Poland.

2 Judgment of the Court (First Chamber) of 6 November 2012 in case C-286/12 European Commission v Hungary, ECLI:EU:C:2012:687. For the description of the national circumstances and its implications, see T Drinóczi, 'Temporal effects of decisions of the Hungarian Constitutional Court', in P Popelier, S Verstraelen, D Vanheule, B Vanlerberghe, eds, *The Effects of Judicial Decisions in* Time (Intersentia 2014) 87–106.

failed to fulfil its obligations.[3] What is more, in the above-mentioned case against Poland, Hungary intervened in support of the Republic of Poland. It was not the only situation where Hungary supported Poland within a proceeding concerning Polish legislative solutions modelled on Hungarian law recognised as contrary to European Union law.[4]

In general, the Court of Justice permanently ensures that Member States comply with obligations under the Treaties and has ensured, since 1952, that law is observed in the interpretation and application of the EU Treaties.[5] It means that the Court of Justice had gained tremendous experience over the decades, but in recent years there was a real challenge in that respect, inter alia, due to the changes introduced in Poland, starting from 2015. The diagnosis that Hungary and Poland pose a worse threat to the European Union than Brexit has even been given.[6] For this reason, the latest case-law issued in Polish cases is best suited to examining the issue referred to in the title of this chapter. Firstly, its initial aim is to determine the functions of Treaty provisions defining the values the European Union is founded on. Secondly, the procedural measures devoted to enforcing provisions defining the EU values have been determined and examined herein. Finally, the overall goal of the analysis is to determine whether the CJEU has sufficient procedural means at its disposal for the efficient safeguarding of the EU values in case of their breach by the Member States.

8.2. Functions of Treaty provisions defining the values of the European Union

First of all, it is crucial to determine whether the provisions establishing the EU values are binding, and then to ascertain the functions they perform. The values

3 Judgment of the Court (Grand Chamber) of 24 June 2019 in case C-619/18 European Commission v Republic of Poland, ECLI:EU:C:2019:531.

4 For instance: Judgment of the General Court (Ninth Chamber, Extended Composition) of 16 May 2019 in joined cases T-836/16 and T-624/17 Republic of Poland v European Commission, ECLI:EU:T:2019:338, concerning State aid and Polish tax on the retail sector, progressive tax levied on turnover, final decision classifying the measure as State aid incompatible with the internal market. A few years earlier, Hungarian tax legislation establishing an exceptional tax on the turnover of store retail trade and retail store chains was stated to be incompatible with EU law; this was because of the existence of a discriminatory effect and due to the indirect discrimination of foreign capital (Judgment of the Court (Grand Chamber), 5 February 2014 in in case C-385/12 Hervis Sport- és Divatkereskedelmi Kft. v Nemzeti Adó- és Vámhivatal Közép-dunántúli Regionális Adó Főigazgatósága, ECLI:EU:C:2014:47).

5 Article 19 TEU.

6 R McCrea, 'Hungary and Poland pose worse threat to EU than Brexit. Mutual recognition and trust among member states around legal systems vital to EU', Nov 4 *The Irish Times* (2019). See chapters on Hungary in this book: András Jakab and Eszter Bodnár, 'The Rule of Law, democracy and human rights in Hungary: Tendencies from 1989 until 2019', Chapter 4 of this book; Tímea Drinóczi, 'The Rule of Law: The Hungarian perspective', Chapter 5 of this book; Lóránt Csink, Rule of Law in Hungary. What can law and politics do?, Chapter 7 of this book.

on which the European Union is founded can be found in primary EU law, in particular, in the Treaty on the European Union. When adopting the Treaty on the European Union, the leaders of the Member States acted under the influence of the cultural, religious, and humanistic heritage of Europe, which resulted in universal values constituting inviolable and inalienable human rights, as well as freedom, democracy, equality, and the Rule of Law.[7] In addition, the Union is founded on the values of respect for human dignity, freedom, democracy, equality, and the Rule of Law, as well as the respect for human rights, including the rights of persons belonging to minorities. At the same time, it was emphasised that these values were common to the Member States in a society based on pluralism, non-discrimination, tolerance, justice, solidarity, and equality between women and men.[8] The fact that the values on which the European Union is based have been included in the Treaty on the European Union means that they have been signed by the heads of states or governments of all Member States and that they have been subject to ratification in all Member States.

The provisions of primary EU law defining the values on which the European Union is based perform specific functions, including systematising (structuring or organizational), stabilising, interpretative, repressive, and dynamising ones.[9] The systematising function means that the Treaty provisions defining the EU values constitute a link to other rules of EU law; hence, they construct a legal system. The provisions defining the values of the Union are characterised by a certain specificity because they concern not only the areas of law falling within the competence of the Union but also the areas falling within the competence of Member States. In addition, the systematising function is manifested in shaping the structure of substantial and political regulations in the EU legal area. For example, the system of national justice, in principle, rests upon the Member States' competence, but the EU values form the legal basis for the EU regulations in the field of judicial cooperation in civil and commercial matters and criminal matters. *A contrario*, a breach of one of the Union's core values by a Member State, can undermine the entire judicial cooperation system in the European Union. On the other hand, the stabilising function of the provisions defining the EU values is manifested in the justification of the solution adopted by seeking assessments consistent with the values on which the European Union is founded. In that sense, the legal provisions defining the EU values can serve as a criterion for assessing the admissibility of a particular national regulation. The above function of the EU values has justified, for example, the need to examine the legal changes which have been proposed in Poland since 2015 in terms of their compliance with the EU values, and in particular, the Rule of Law.

7 Recital 2 of Preamble to Treaty on European Union.

8 Article 2 TEU, Consolidated versions of the Treaty on European Union and the Treaty on the Functioning of the European Union, OJ C 202, 7.6.2016, 1–388.

9 J Harrison Watts and C Roberson, *Law and Society: An Introduction* (CRC Press 2013) 8. Moreover: Z Ziembiński, *Wstęp do aksjologii dla prawników* (Wydawnictwo Prawnicze 1990) 79–80.

The interpretative function of the provisions defining the EU values is mainly associated with a teleological method of interpretation. In the EU legal order, a teleological interpretation is expressed by means of *effet utile* of EU law. In fact, the teleological interpretation applies to the interpretation of both primary and secondary EU law, although that kind of interpretation is based on EU Treaties constituting the constitutional basis of the European Union. Consequently, the spirit and the purpose of the EU Treaties are the essences of their interpretation. According to the CJEU case-law, every provision of EU law must be placed in its context and interpreted in the light of the provisions of EU law as a whole, regard being made to the objectives thereof and to the state of its evolution at the date on which the provision in question is to be applied.[10] The preambles and initial articles of the EU Treaties which set out, *inter alia*, the values that the European Union is founded on, can be the legal basis for a teleological interpretation. In the case of the Court of Justice, the impetus for interpretation is the need to resolve a particular case brought by direct action or by a preliminary question. The CJEU decisions, together with their grounds, are formulated in such a way that the interpretation contained therein can be used not only to resolve the respective case, which was the impulse to issue a given ruling, but also in all similar cases.[11]

The repressive function of the Treaty norms determining the values of the European Union raises the issue of the European Union's values as an obligation. The relationship between the Union's values and the Member States' obligations can be reflected in two aspects. Firstly, the values of the Union can be considered as a starting point, and a paradigm of an action that complies with the obligation can be reached from that perspective. Secondly, if the Treaty obligations of the Member States are considered as a starting point, conduct complying with the Union's values will be covered by them. In the theory of law, the former solution can be predominantly found.[12] The notion of an obligation, in itself, implies a certain constraint that the law exerts in relation to the arbitrary will. However, as it has been shown at the outset, the values of the Union are subject to the will of the Member States. Simultaneously, the primary law of the European Union constitutes a formal basis for determining the will of Member States so that each Member State is obliged to act in compliance with the common will of all Member States. As a consequence, the Union values defined in such a way become an obligation under the law. In the context of the Rule of Law as an obligation, the actions by national authorities violating the values on which the Union is founded are qualified as breaches of the Treaty obligations.

The failure of a Member State to fulfil its Treaty obligations may be subject to two types of proceedings. On the one hand, in areas not covered by the Union's

10 Judgment of the Court of 6 October 1982 in case 283/81 Srl CILFIT and Lanificio di Gavardo SpA v Ministry of Health, European Court Reports 1982-03415, ECLI:EU:C:1982:335, point 20.

11 Cf, T Gizbert-Studnicki, Wykładnia celowościowa, 3 1 *Studia Prawnicze* (1985) 51–52.

12 I Kant, *Metafizyka moralności* (Ewa Nowak trans., Wydawnictwo Naukowe PWN 2007) 243–244.

competence, it is possible to initiate the Rule of Law procedure referred to in Article 7 TEU. On the other hand, in the areas covered by the competence of the Union, the European Commission initiates an infringement procedure against a [Member] State pursuant to Article 258 TFEU. Irrespective of the proceedings addressed directly against a State, the Court of Justice has exclusive competence to make binding interpretations of EU law by answering the questions raised by national courts. Since 2015, the Polish courts have been referring questions for a preliminary ruling relating to the infringement of the Rule of Law by the Polish authorities, including mainly the legislative authority adopting legislation contrary to the European Rule of Law principle within the meaning of the Polish Constitution,[13] but also EU law.[14] National judges seek assistance in facing domestic legislation, which is contrary to EU law, by references for a preliminary ruling.

8.3. Article 7 TEU procedure against Poland

As far as serious Rule of Law failings in a Member State are concerned, Article 7 TEU remains both an exceptional and the most emblematic tool for the EU to take action against a Member State. This tool provides a staged process of dialogue with a Member State, structured with the Commission's opinions and recommendations presented hereinafter. Article 7(1) TEU procedure has been triggered in two cases so far. For the first time in December 2017 by the Commission in respect of Poland, and in September 2018 by the European Parliament in respect of Hungary.[15] The Treaty on the European Union lists separately the values on which the Union is founded and the objectives pursued by it. At the same time, those drafting the EU Treaties have decided that one of the Union's objectives is to support its values. Despite the substantive closeness of the values and objectives, the division adopted in the Treaty is reflected in respective Treaty provisions, including the Treaty norms providing for the aforementioned specific type of procedure in case of an infringement of the Union's values. Facing the systemic threats to the Rule of Law, the European Commission developed *A new EU Framework to strengthen the Rule of Law*,[16] which was adopted in 2014. It is addressed to all Member States and aims to ensure the effective and coherent

13 W Sadurski, *Poland's Constitutional Breakdown* (Oxford University Press 2019).

14 S Biernat and M Kawczyńska, The Role of the Polish Constitution (Pre-2016): Development of a Liberal Democracy in the European and International Context, in A Albi and S Bardutzky, eds, *National Constitutions in European and Global Governance: Democracy, Rights, the Rule of Law* (T.M.C. Asser Press 2019) 745–793, aaccessible at https://doi.org/10.1007/978-94-6265-273-6_16.

15 European Commission, Communication from the Commission to the European Parliament, the European Council and the Council, Further strengthening the Rule of Law within the Union State of play and possible next steps, Brussels, 3.4.2019, COM/2019/163 final, 3.

16 European Commission, Communication from the Commission to the European Parliament and the Council, A new EU Framework to strengthen the Rule of Law, COM/2014/0158 final.

protection of the European Rule of Law in all Member States.[17] The reason for the adoption of the new Rule of Law framework was the absence of effective instruments for monitoring and sanctioning the compliance with the EU's values by the respective Member States of the Union.[18] In legal terms, this document does not constitute a major breakthrough as it specifies the existing mechanisms. However, recent events in Poland show the need to reinforce the existing cooperation procedures between EU institutions to better safeguard the Rule of Law in the EU. The new EU Framework to strengthen the Rule of Law introduces an early warning instrument giving the European Commission the opportunity to initiate a dialogue with the Member State concerned in order to prevent the escalation of systemic threats to the Rule of Law.

In turn, by virtue of Article 7 TEU, two mechanisms to ensure that the conduct of Member States complies with the values on which the European Union is founded have been introduced. They are the prevention mechanism and the sanctions mechanism; however, the conditions for the application of both mechanisms are related to a breach of the Union's values referred to in Article 2 TEU.[19] The prevention mechanism is applicable if 'there is a clear risk of a serious breach by a Member State of the values referred to in Article 2', whereas the sanctions mechanism is applicable in the situation of 'the existence of a serious and persistent breach by a Member State of the values referred to in Article 2'.[20]

On 1 June 2016, the European Commission adopted an opinion on the Rule of Law in Poland[21] making reference to the Rule of Law procedure. The concerns of the EU Commissioners have been raised by such events in Poland as the appointment of judges of the Constitutional Tribunal, the functioning of the Constitutional Tribunal, and the effectiveness of the constitutional review of new legislation (media law and other laws). The *Sejm* [the chamber of the Polish Parliament], elected in 2015, amended the Law on the Constitutional Tribunal, by an accelerated procedure, enabling to annul the judicial nominations made by the previous legislature and to appoint five new judges. The terms of office of the President and Vice President of the Tribunal was shortened to three years, whereas the current terms of office were to finish automatically within three months of the date of adopting that amendment. Before the entry into force of the amendment, the term of office of the President and Vice President of the Tribunal was not specified, thus it could last a maximum of nine years, because judges of the Constitutional Tribunal were appointed for a term of office of nine years. On 25 November 2015, the newly elected *Sejm* annulled the five

17 D Kochenov and L Pech, 'Better Late than Never? On the European Commission's Rule of Law Framework and its First Activation: Commission's Rule of Law Framework', 54 *JCMS: Journal of Common Market Studies* (2016) 1062–1074.

18 D Kochenov and L Pech, 'Monitoring and Enforcement of the Rule of Law in the EU: Rhetoric and Reality', 11(3) *European Constitutional Law Review* (2015) 512–540.

19 Article 7 (1) TEU.

20 Article 7 (2) TEU.

21 European Commission, Opinion on the Rule of Law in Poland and the Rule of Law Framework. Questions and Answers, Brussels, 1 June 2016, MEMO/16/2017.

nominations made by the previous legislature and on 2 December 2015, it nominated five new judges. The Constitutional Tribunal received requests for a ruling on the decisions of the *Sejm*, both the previous and the new legislature. On 3 December 2015, the Constitutional Tribunal ruled that the previous legislature had been entitled to nominate three judges for seats vacated during its term of office, but it was not entitled to appoint two candidates for posts vacated during the term of office of the new legislature. In addition, the Tribunal held that the President of the Republic of Poland was obliged to take the oath of three validly elected judges immediately. On 9 December 2015 the Constitutional Tribunal held that the new legislature was not entitled to annul the nominations of three judges that had been made under the previous legislature, nonetheless, it was entitled to appoint two judges whose term of office began under the new legislature. In addition, it declared shortening the term of office of the President and Vice President of the Constitutional Tribunal invalid. Meanwhile, the President of the Republic of Poland received the oath from all five judges nominated by the new legislature, thus acting against the aforementioned rulings. Consequently, the judgments of the Constitutional Tribunal had not been implemented and therefore concerns with respect to the Rule of Law were raised.[22]

Concurrently, the European Commission substantiated its grave concerns on the planned reform of the judiciary in Poland. In view of the Commission's concerns, President Jean-Claude Juncker said that an independent judiciary was an essential precondition for membership in the European Union. Therefore, the EU could not accept a system which allows dismissing judges at will. Moreover, the President has reminded that independent courts are the basis of mutual trust between Member States and their judicial systems. Consequently, as the Polish government went ahead with undermining the independence of the judiciary and the Rule of Law in Poland, the Commission had no other choice than to trigger Article 7.[23] Subsequently, on 27 July 2016, the European Commission sent to Poland a recommendation on the Rule of Law in Poland, in which it presented its concerns and the recommended ways to solve the issues which those objections referred to[24] (i.e., the first recommendation on that issue). That recommendation was complemented by the recommendation of 21 December 2016, issued after the European Commission's discussion on the latest developments in Poland,[25]

22 Ibid.; L Pech, 'Systemic Threat to the Rule of Law in Poland: What should the Commission do next?', *VerfBlog*, 2016/10/31, https://verfassungsblog.de/systemic-threat-to-the-rule-of-law-in-poland-what-should-the-commission-do-next/.

23 European Commission – Press release, European Commission acts to preserve the Rule of Law in Poland, Brussels, 26 July 2017, IP/17/2161.

24 European Commission – Press release, Rule of Law: Commission issues recommendation to Poland, Brussels, 27 July 2016, IP/16/2643.

25 European Commission – Press release, Rule of Law: Commission discusses latest developments and issues complementary Recommendation to Poland, Brussels, 21 December 2016, IP/16/4476. On this topic: L Pech and KL Scheppele, 'Poland and the European Commission, Part III: Requiem for the Rule of Law', *VerfBlog*, 2017/3/03, https://verfassungsblog.de/poland-and-the-european-commission-part-iii-requiem-for-the-rule-of-law/.

in particular, because of the prospect of appointing a new President of the Constitutional Tribunal.[26] On 26 July 2017, the European Commission called upon the Polish authorities to solve the problems identified within one month (the third recommendation to Poland under the Rule of Law framework).[27] On 29 July 2017, concurrently to the Rule of Law procedure, the European Commission launched an infringement procedure against Poland, on the basis of Article 258 TFEU, by sending a Letter of Formal Notice, following the publication in the Polish Official Journal of the Law on the Ordinary Courts Organisation. (*PL: Ustawa – Prawo o ustroju sądów powszechnych*).[28] On 20 December 2017, the European Commission officially held that there was a clear risk of a serious infringement of the Rule of Law in Poland, although for almost two years the Commission had made numerous attempts to start a constructive dialogue with Polish authorities in the context of the Rule of Law framework. At the same time, the Commission proposed to the Council to adopt a decision under Article 7 (1) TEU, according to which the Council, acting by a majority of four-fifths of its members, was entitled to determine that there was a clear risk of serious breach by a Member State of the values referred to in Article 2 TEU.[29] On the same day, the College of Commissioners decided to bring the case against the Polish government to the Court of Justice for an infringement of EU law following the adoption of the Law on the Ordinary Courts Organisation (*PL: Prawo o ustroju sądów powszechnych*), in particular, its provisions providing for the different retirement ages of judges. The case was presented in the following paragraph. That decision was at times considered as a step backwards because it gave the Court of Justice the opportunity to comment on the Rule of Law in Poland under Article 258 TFEU and not under Article 7 TEU.[30] The European Parliament supported the European Commission's decision to launch the procedure under Article 7 TEU on 1 March 2018.[31] The achievements of the Polish authorities after 2015 are treated as a sign of authoritarian trends, which threaten the European Union

26 European Commission – Fact Sheet, Commission Recommendation regarding the Rule of Law in Poland: Questions and Answers, Brussels, 21 December 2016, MEMO/16/4479. On this topic: L Pech and KL Scheppele, 'Poland and the European Commission, Part II: Hearing the Siren Song of the Rule of Law', *VerfBlog*, 2017/1/06, https://verfassungsblog.de/poland-and-the-european-commission-part-ii-hearing-the-siren-song-of-the-rule-of-law/.

27 European Commission – Press release, European Commission acts to preserve the Rule of Law in Poland, Brussels, 26 July 2017, IP/17/2161.

28 European Commission – Press release, European Commission launches infringement against Poland over measures affecting the judiciary, Brussels, 29 July 2017, IP/17/2205.

29 European Commission – Fact Sheet: Commission action on the Rule of Law in Poland: Questions and Answers, Brussels, 20 December 2017, IP/17/5367.

30 M Taborowski, The Commission takes a step back in the fight for the Rule of Law, *VerfBlog*, 2018/1/03, https://verfassungsblog.de/the-commission-takes-a-step-back-in-the-fight-for-the-rule-of-law/.

31 European Parliament resolution of 1 March 2018 on the Commission's decision to activate Article 7(1) TEU as regards the situation in Poland (2018/2541(RSP)), OJ C 129, 5.4.2019, p. 13–13.

much more than the withdrawal of the United Kingdom[32] since they undermine the fundamental values and legal bases of European integration.[33]

From the Commission's perspective, the progress by the Council in these two cases 'could have been more meaningful'.[34] In the meantime, it turned out that the Council had to establish new procedures to apply Article 7 TEU in practice because it still needed to prove to be fully effective. Experience gained so far from the application of Article 7 TEU can justify a few conclusions. On the one hand, the dialogue indisputably helped identify the problems and frame the discussion. On the other hand, it had not solved the detected Rule of Law deficiencies so that the Commission triggered Article 7(1) TEU procedure against Poland in December 2017. As a result, some other ideas came into light. One of the ideas is the Commission's proposal to help protect the EU's financial interests if there are generalised deficiencies related to the Rule of Law. The proposal for a regulation on the protection of the Union's budget in case of generalised deficiencies as regards the Rule of Law in the Member States is under the legislative procedure after its first reading in the European Parliament.[35] Another idea is related to the establishment of a European Public Prosecutor's Office which should also assist in promoting a coordinated judicial response to such risks across the Member States. It is being set up to become operational at the end of 2020 and will have its seat in Luxembourg.

Significantly, the Hungarian government rejected joining the European Public Prosecutor's Office. In response, more than 500,000 Hungarian citizens have signed a petition demanding that the country join the institution.[36] The European Public Prosecutor Office appears to be a major breakthrough in particular in the process of strengthening the protection of EU finances against fraud,[37] but it can also be granted an important role in protecting the EU values. At first glance, these ideas appear to be effective, although it is hard to predict its effectiveness in terms of measures undertaken within the Article 7 TEU procedure. It is indisputable that Article 7 TEU, for its full effectiveness, requires additional instruments based on the common understanding of what is meant by the Rule of Law, what its key features are, and where deficiencies might arise.[38]

32 T Tridimas, 'BREXIT Means BREXIT. Article 50: An Endgame Without an End?', 3 *King's Law Journal* (2016) 297–313.

33 H Grabbe and S Lehne, Defending EU Values in Poland and Hungary, September 04 *Carnegie Europe – Carnegie Endowment for International Peace* (2017) 1.

34 European Commission, Communication from the Commission to the European Parliament, the European Council and the Council, Further strengthening the Rule of Law within the Union State of play and possible next steps, COM/2019/163 final, 3.

35 Proposal for a Regulation of the European Parliament and of the Council on the protection of the Union's budget in case of generalised deficiencies as regards the rule of law in the Member States, COM/2018/324 final - 2018/0136 (COD).

36 D Istrate, 'Half a million Hungarians sign petition to join EU prosecutor's office', November 15 *Emerging Europe* (2019).

37 W Geelhoed, LH Erkelens and AWH Meij, *Shifting Perspectives on the European Public Prosecutor's Office* (Springer 2017) 1.

38 European Commission, Communication from the Commission to the European Parliament, the European Council and the Council, Further strengthening the Rule of Law within the Union State of play and possible next steps, COM/2019/163 final, 3.

8.4. Infringement proceedings initiated by the Commission against Poland for the breach of the Rule of Law

The shortcomings of Article 7 TEU do not preclude the application of Article 258 TFEU in an effective and efficient way. In each case where the Commission considers that a Member State has failed to fulfil an obligation under the Treaties, the Commission may bring the matter before the Court of Justice of the European Union.[39] Before submitting the complaint to the Court of Justice, the Commission undertakes a preliminary investigation sending a 'warning letter' to the Member State concerned, and then the Member State has the opportunity to submit its observations. After giving the possibility to explain the Member State's position, the Commission delivers a reasoned opinion on the matter. Finally, if the Member State concerned does not comply with the Commission's opinion within the period laid down, the Commission brings the case before the Court of Justice of the European Union. As a consequence, each proceeding against a Member State is preceded by a dialogue that gives the possibility to cease the infringement proceeding at the stage of the initial administrative procedure. However, if the dialogue does not lead to any agreement, the Court of Justice shall decide as to the matter at stake.

Even though the Commission initiated the Article 7(1) TEU procedure against Poland in July 2018, the Commission sent Poland a letter of formal notice regarding the conformity of the Law of 8 December 2017 on the Supreme Court[40] and the Amending Law of 10 May 2018[41] with the second subparagraph of Article 19(1) TEU, and Article 47 of the Charter of Fundamental Rights of the European Union (Charter), and invited Poland to submit its observations. Poland contested the Commission's arguments. On 14 August 2018, the Commission addressed a reasoned opinion to Poland, alleging that it had failed to fulfil its obligations under the combined provisions mentioned above. Then, the Commission invited Poland to comply with that reasoned opinion. In response, Poland reiterated that the alleged failure to fulfil obligations was unfounded. As a result, the Commission brought an action before the Court under Article 258 TFEU on 2 October 2018 claiming that the Court should declare that, by lowering the retirement age of the judges of Polish Supreme Court and applying it to judges appointed to that court before 3 April 2018, and by granting the President of the Republic the discretion to extend the period of judicial activity of Supreme Court judges, the Republic of Poland failed to fulfil its obligations under the combined provisions of the second subparagraph of Article 19(1) TEU and Article 47 of the Charter. Significantly, Poland was supported by Hungary within the proceeding. They both submitted that national rules such as those challenged in the action could not make an object of a review in the light of the second subparagraph of Article 19(1) TEU and Article 47 of the

39 D Adamski, 'The Social Contract of Democratic Backsliding in the "New EU" Countries', 56(3) *Common Market Law Review* (2019) 623–665.

40 PL: *Ustawa z dnia 8 grudnia 2017 r. o Sądzie Najwyższym, Dz. U. 2018 poz. 5.*

41 PL: *Ustawa z dnia 10 maja 2018 r. o zmianie ustawy – Prawo o ustroju sądów powszechnych, ustawy o Sądzie Najwyższym oraz niektórych innych ustaw, Dz. U. 2018 poz. 1045.*

Charter.[42] The Court (Grand Chamber) recalled that these provisions, like general principles of EU law such as the principle of judicial independence, are applicable only in situations governed under EU law.[43] Consequently, the Court stated that Article 47 of the Charter was not applicable in the given case, having regard to the absence of any situation in which EU law is being implemented, within the meaning of Article 51(1) of the Charter. Moreover, it follows from Article 6(1) TEU, Article 51(2) of the Charter and Protocol No 30 on the application of the Charter to Poland and to the United Kingdom[44] that the Charter does not extend the scope of application of EU law beyond the European Union's competences.[45] However, the Court declared that, on the one hand, by providing that the measure consisting in lowering the retirement age of the judges of Polish Supreme Court was to apply to judges in post who had been appointed to that court before 3 April 2018 and, on the other hand, by granting the President of the Republic the discretion to extend the period of judicial activity of judges of that court beyond the newly fixed retirement age, the Republic of Poland had failed to fulfil its obligations under the second subparagraph of Article 19(1) TEU.[46]

The judgment proves that in the case of an alleged breach of the Rule of Law (a foundational value of the Union that is also reflected in Article 19 TEU), the Commission can institute proceedings under Article 258 TFEU against a Member State, even when that Member State is not implementing EU law under Article 51(1) of the Charter. Actually, the Court has highlighted that Article 19 TEU gives a concrete expression to the value of the Rule of Law in Article 2 TEU and that the second subparagraph of Article 19(1) TEU obliges every Member State to ensure that the bodies, which as 'courts and tribunals' defined by EU law come within its judicial system in the fields covered by EU law, meet the requirements of effective judicial protection including judicial independence. To the extent that such a court may rule on questions concerning the application or interpretation of EU law, the Member State concerned must ensure that that court meets those requirements.[47] The Polish experience is worth studying since it offers examples of legislative techniques which are capable of application in other countries.[48]

In the meantime, the Commission put an application for interim measures on the basis of Article 279 TFEU. The Court of Justice declared that Poland should immediately suspend the application of the contested provisions of Polish Law of

42 Judgment of the Court (Grand Chamber) of 24 June 2019 in case C-619/18 European Commission v Republic of Poland, ECLI:EU:C:2019:531, point 37.

43 Ibid., point 39.

44 OJ 2010 C 83, 313.

45 Ibid., point 41.

46 Ibid., operative part. The Court of Justice accepted the Opinion of Advocate General Tanchev delivered on 11 April 2019 in case C-619/18 European Commission v Republic of Poland, ECLI:EU:C:2019:325.

47 Opinion of Advocate General Tanchev delivered on 11 April 2019 in case C-619/18 European Commission v Republic of Poland, points 61 and 63.

48 M Bernatt and M Ziółkowski, 'Statutory Anti-Constitutionalism', 28 *Washington International Law Journal* (2019) 526.

10 May 2018 on the Amendment of the Law on the Organization of Common Law Courts, the Law on the Supreme Court and certain other laws, as well as of any measure taken according to these provisions. Moreover, Poland shall take all necessary steps to ensure that the judges of the Polish Supreme Court concerned by those provisions can perform their duties in the same post, while enjoying the same status and the same rights and conditions of employment as they benefited until 3 April 2018 (the date of entry into force of the Supreme Court Act). Furthermore, Poland was obliged to refrain from any measure aimed at the appointment of judges to the Polish Supreme Court in place of those concerned by the provisions which are at the basis of the breach and which make subject of the main action, as well as of any measure to appoint the new first president of that court, or to indicate the person responsible for directing that court in place of its first president until the appointment of the new first president. After all, Poland was required to communicate to the Commission, at the latest one month after the notification of the order on interim measures and then regularly every month, all of the measures that Poland had adopted to comply fully with the order.[49] Following the interim order of the Court of Justice, the first president of the Polish Supreme Court has summoned judges who are older than 65 years of age to come back to work.[50] Simultaneously, the interim order applied to 42 judges of the Supreme Administrative Court, including Vice President of the Supreme Administrative Court, president of one of the voivodship administrative courts, two vice presidents of the voivodship administrative courts, and two chairpersons of the departments.[51]

A few months after the presented judgment, the Court of Justice issued a judgment in another case initiated by the action for failure to fulfil obligations under Article 258 TFEU, brought on 15 March 2018 by the Commission against Poland.[52] This time the infringement proceeding was based on two grounds. Firstly, the Commission contended that by introducing a retirement age of 60 for women and 65 for men, when it was previously 67 for both sexes, judges of the ordinary courts, public prosecutors, and judges of Polish Supreme Court in July 2017,[53] Poland had breached its obligations under Article 157 TFEU, as well

49 Ordonnance de la vice-présidente de la Cour du 19 octobre 2018 dans l'affaire C-619/18 R Commission contre Pologne, ECLI:EU:C:2018:852. The only available official language versions are French and Polish.

50 Z Kmieciak, 'Ochrona tymczasowa w sprawie ze skargi Komisji przeciwko Polsce dotyczącej przepisów ustawy obniżającej wiek przejścia w stan spoczynku sędziów SN. Glosa do postanowienia TS z dnia 19 października 2018 r., C-619/18 R', 1 *Państwo i Prawo* (2019) 143–150 [PL].

51 Communication of 22 October 2018 of the Supreme Administrative Court (Poland) regarding the CJEU order of 19 October 2018 on interim measures (PL: Komunikat NSA z dnia 22 października 2018 r. dotyczący postanowienia TSUE z dnia 19 października 2018 r.).

52 Judgment of the Court (Grand Chamber) of 5 November 2019 in case C-192/18 European Commission v Republic of Poland, ECLI:EU:C:2019:924.

53 PL: Ustawa z dnia 12 lipca 2017 r. o zmianie ustawy – Prawo o ustroju sądów powszechnych oraz niektórych innych ustaw, Dz. U. 2017 poz. 1452.

as the Directive on the implementation of the principle of equal opportunities and equal treatment between men and women in matters of employment and work.[54] The first complaint was new, in the sense that discrimination on the basis of sex was yet to feature in the cases that have been presented above. Secondly, the Commission contended that Poland had failed to fulfil its obligations under the combined provisions of the second subparagraph of Article 19(1) TEU and Article 47 of the Charter by lowering the retirement age of judges of the ordinary courts, while at the same time vesting the Minister for Justice with the discretion to prolong the period of active service of individual ordinary court judges.

Finally, the Court of Justice (Grand Chamber) decided that the Commission's action must be upheld in its entirety. Therefore, the Court declared that Poland had failed to fulfil its obligations under Article 157 TFEU and Articles 5(a) and 9(1)(f) of Directive 2006/54/EC, and also failed to fulfil its obligations under the second subparagraph of Article 19(1) TEU. It is worth mentioning that the reforms to the retirement rules of Polish judges put in place in 2017 have attracted a raft of international criticism. Advocate General Tanchev, in its opinion in case C-192/18, enumerated a few examples of the criticism from the side of different international organizations.[55] Facing such strong criticism from all over the world, the European Commission was obliged to act in the public interest[56] and fulfilled its duty properly.

8.5. Preliminary ruling procedure in case of the breach of the Rule of Law

On the one hand, the way the Polish authorities have governed after 2015 is seen as a manifestation of authoritarian trends that may threaten the European Union and cause its fragmentation. On the other hand, there are EU institutions, in particular the Commission, which are working on safeguarding EU values. Simultaneously, the role of [domestic] judges [of Member States] referring

54 Directive 2006/54/EC of the European Parliament and of the Council of 5 July 2006 on the implementation of the principle of equal opportunities and equal treatment of men and women in matters of employment and occupation (recast), OJ L 204, 26.7.2006, p. 23–36.

55 The Venice Commission Opinion on the Draft Act amending the Act on the National Council of the Judiciary, on the Draft Act amending the Act on the Supreme Court, proposed by the President of Poland, and on the Act on the Organisation of Ordinary Courts; United Nations Human Rights Council, Report of the Special Rapporteur on the independence of judges and lawyers on his mission to Poland; the Organisation for Security and Cooperation in Europe Office for Democratic Institutions and Human Rights, the Opinion on Certain Provisions of the Draft Act on the Supreme Court of Poland. Opinion of Advocate General Tanchev delivered on 20 June 2019 in case C-192/18 European Commission v Republic of Poland, ECLI:EU:C:2019:529, point 3.

56 V Kosta and B de Witte, Human Rights in the Court of Justice of the European Union, in M Scheinin, *Human Rights Norms in 'Other' International Courts* (Cambridge University Press 2019) 265.

questions for a preliminary ruling to the Court of Justice, in case of any suspected breach of EU values by national authorities, can hardly be overstated.

Indeed, it did not take long to see the consequences of breaking the Union's values on the occasion of the judiciary reform in Poland. On 12 March 2018, the Irish High Court decided to refer to the Court of Justice a request for a preliminary ruling relating to the extradition of Arthur Celmer, arrested in May 2017 in Ireland under the European Arrest Warrant, due to allegations of drug trafficking. The words of A Celmer's lawyer, quoted by the media, show that Polish legislative reforms 'fundamentally undermine the basis of mutual trust and recognition between Poland and the executive judicial authority', which means that the European Arrest Warrant system is 'seriously jeopardized'.[57]

In response to the Irish High Court's doubts, the Court of Justice ruled that Article 1(3) of Council Framework Decision on the European arrest warrant[58] must be interpreted as follows. Where the executing judicial authority, called upon to decide whether a person in respect of whom a European Arrest Warrant has been issued, has material, such as that set out in a reasoned proposal of the European Commission adopted pursuant to Article 7(1) TEU, indicating that there is a real risk of breach of the fundamental right to a fair trial guaranteed by the Charter, on account of systemic or generalised deficiencies so far as concerns the independence of the issuing Member State's judiciary, that authority must determine, specifically and precisely, whether having regard to his personal situation, as well as to the nature of the offence for which he is being prosecuted, and the factual context that forms the basis of the European Arrest Warrant, there are substantial grounds for believing that that person will run such a risk if he is surrendered to that State.[59] The judgment of the Court of Justice in the above-mentioned case, initiated by the Irish High Court, is binding not only in that particular case but also in any case where there are doubts related to the issuing of a European Arrest Warrant, about ensuring a fair trial in Poland before an independent court.

Besides, between 2015–2019, the Polish courts of different instances referred the questions for a preliminary ruling to the Court of Justice, raising doubts relating to the observance of the Rule of Law by the Polish legislative and executive powers. Joined Cases C-585/18, C-624/18 and C-625/18[60] are worth

57 Judgment of Ms. Justice Donnelly delivered on 12 March 2018, Record No. 2013 EXT 295, Record No. 2014 EXT 8, Record No. 2017 EXT 291. In addition, the words of the attorney quoted after 'Politico': www.politico.eu/article/ireland-poland-extradition-case-referred-to-europe-top-court-ecj/.

58 2002/584/JHA: Council Framework Decision of 13 June 2002 on the European arrest warrant and the surrender procedures between Member States – Statements made by certain Member States on the adoption of the Framework Decision, OJ L 190, 18.7.2002, p. 1–20.

59 Judgment of the Court (Grand Chamber) of 25 July 2018 in case C-216/18 PPU LM., ECLI:EU:C:2018:586, operative part.

60 Joined cases C-585/18, C-624/18 and C-625/18 AK (C-585/18) v Krajowa Rada Sądownictwa and CP (C-624/18), DO (C-625/18) v Sąd Najwyższy (C-624/18 and C-625/18), joined party: Prokurator Generalny zastępowany przez Prokuraturę Krajową.

mentioning as they relate to problems presented above concerning the independence of the Polish Supreme Court (C-619/18) and the independence of the ordinary courts (C-192/18). All these issues are situated within the context of the reform of the Polish justice system instituted by measures adopted in 2017 and which have been the subject of the Commission's reasoned proposal in accordance with Article 7(1) TEU regarding the Rule of Law in Poland. The actions at stake were brought before the Chamber of Labour Law and Social Security of Polish Supreme Court by judges affected by Polish measures lowering the judicial retirement age. Those measures were already held by the Court of Justice to be incompatible with Poland's obligations under the second subparagraph of Article 19(1) TEU,[61] given that they are inconsistent with the principles of the irremovability of judges and judicial independence, both of which are protected under EU law. Furthermore, the newly created Disciplinary Chamber of the Supreme Court has been designated to adjudicate the actions, but the referring court queries whether the Chamber offers sufficient guarantees of independence under EU law to hear such claims as the group of judges eligible for appointment by the President of the Republic to the Disciplinary Chamber are selected by the National Council of the Judiciary.[62] It is the body charged with safeguarding judicial independence in Poland. However, its independence has been put in doubt by Polish legislation modifying the manner in which its judicial members are appointed. In addition, its composition is now primarily determined by the legislative and executive authorities.[63]

The establishment of the National Council of the Judiciary in 1989, as well as the empowerment of the general assemblies of judges in courts, gave rise to the idea of judicial self-government in Poland. This idea implied that judges hold important decision-making roles or veto power on matters concerning the judiciary in Poland. At that time, it was regarded as a precondition of the separation of powers and judicial independence, none of which existed under Communist rule. Thus, the judicial 'reform' introduced in 2017 in Poland marks the end of judicial self-government as it undermined the independence of the National Council of the Judiciary by altering the mode of election of its judicial members and it also concentrated the power over the judiciary within the competence of the executive power.[64]

In light of the considerations mentioned above, Advocate General Tanchev proposed in his opinion to answer that national provisions conferring jurisdiction to rule in a dispute involving EU law to a chamber of a national last instance court which does not meet the requirements of judicial independence laid down

61 Judgment of 24 June 2019, Commission v Poland (Independence of the Supreme Court) (C-619/18).

62 *PL: Krajowa Rada Sądownictwa.*

63 Opinion of Advocate General Tanchev delivered on 27 June 2019 in joined cases C-585/18, C-624/18 and C-625/18, ECLI:EU:C:2019:551, points 1–3.

64 A Śledzińska-Simon, 'The Rise and Fall of Judicial Self-Government in Poland: On Judicial Reform Reversing Democratic Transition', 7 *German Law Journal* (2018) 1839–1870.

in Article 47 of the Charter and/or the second subparagraph of Article 19(1) TEU must be disapplied. As indicated by the Commission, in the light of the importance of judicial independence for ensuring effective judicial protection for individuals under EU law, another chamber of a national last instance court, such as the referring court in the main proceedings, must be able, of its own initiative, to disapply national provisions which are incompatible with that principle. National courts are obliged to supply an effective remedy to enforce EU law when it is otherwise unavailable under national law.[65] Adopting such a reform, Poland has been held to violate European judicial standards, thereby placing the Rule of Law at risk.[66]

The Court of Justice has agreed with the Advocate General's opinion and maintained the Court's established case-law regarding the requirement for the independence of national courts.[67] First of all, objections against the admissibility of the reference were rejected by the Court,[68] as well as the arguments put forward by the Polish Public Prosecutor General. Finally, the Court of Justice has stated that the referring court must ascertain whether the new Disciplinary Chamber of the Polish Supreme Court is independent in order to determine whether that chamber has jurisdiction to rule on cases where judges of the Supreme Court have been retired, or in order to determine whether such cases must be examined by another court which meets the requirement that courts must be independent.[69] This means that the Court of Justice concluded that it is up to the referring court to ascertain whether the framework of the new Disciplinary Chamber fulfils these requirements but, at the same time, the Court has pointed out the conditions that must be met in order to fulfil the criterion of independence. The factors to be taken into consideration by referring court are enumerated in paragraphs 143 to 151 of the judgment. Undoubtedly, they give rise to legitimate doubts, in the minds of subjects of the law, as to the imperviousness of the Disciplinary Chamber to external factors, and, in particular, to the direct or indirect influence of the legislature and the executive, and as to its neutrality with respect to the interests before it. The analysis of these factors taken together leads to the conclusion that the Chamber is not seen to be independent or impartial.[70] As a

65 Opinion of Advocate General Tanchev delivered on 27 June 2019 in joined cases C-585/18, C-624/18 and C-625/18, ECLI:EU:C:2019:551, point 156.

66 U Müßig, *Reason and Fairness: Constituting Justice in Europe, from Medieval Canon Law to ECHR* (BRILL 2019) IX.

67 Judgment of the Court (Grand Chamber) of 19 November 2019 in Joined Cases C-585/18, C-624/18 and C-625/18 AK and Others v Sąd Najwyższy, ECLI: EU:C:2019:982.

68 Judgment of the Court (Grand Chamber) of 19 November 2019 in Joined Cases C-585/18, C-624/18 and C-625/18 AK and Others v Sąd Najwyższy, points 73–86.

69 Court of Justice of the European Union, Press Release No. 145/19, Luxembourg, 19 November 2019, Judgment in Joined Cases C-585/18, C-624/18 and C-625/18 AK v Krajowa Rada Sądownictwa, and CP and DO v Sąd Najwyższy.

70 It is a direct reference to the paragraph 153 of the judgment of the Court (Grand Chamber) of 19 November 2019 in Joined Cases C-585/18, C-624/18 and C-625/18 AK and Others v Sąd Najwyższy.

consequence, the Polish Supreme Court concluded that the National Council of the Judiciary in its current formation is neither impartial nor independent of the legislature or the executive. Moreover, the Supreme Court stated that the conclusion is clear and unambiguous: the Disciplinary Chamber of the Supreme Court is not a court within the meaning of Article 47 CFR, Article 6 of the Convention for the Protection of Human Rights and Fundamental Freedoms, and Article 45(1) of the Constitution of the Republic of Poland.[71]

8.6. Conclusion

The analysis of the case-law of the Court of Justice confirms that nationals of Member States and national judges seek assistance at the Court of Justice in case of infringements of the Rule of Law principles. The examples provided illustrate why all Member States need to be concerned about not fully respecting the Rule of Law by one of the Member States. Following the violation of the Union's values by the Polish authorities, the European Commission, acting as the guardian of the Treaties, has taken up and dealt with Polish law. The consequences of the breach of the Union's values will be severe, irrespective of whether the Court of Justice considers the actions of the Polish authorities to be in non-compliance with European Union law pursuant to Article 7 TEU or Article 258 TFEU. The presented analysis justifies the thesis that systematic infringements of EU law (in the sense of Article 258 TFEU) contribute to the statement of systemic threat of the Union's values, the legal consequences of which are set out in Article 7 TEU. Undoubtedly, the sanction of the suspension of certain of the rights deriving from the application of the Treaties to the Member State in question, including the voting rights of the representative of the government of that Member State in the Council, has not only political consequences but above all serious legal effects. Poland is the first Member State against which the Rule of Law procedure under Article 7 TEU not only has gone so far, but (in regards to which) it has been applied for the first time at all. Over time, the speed of legislative changes in Poland have given the impression that Poland has overtaken Hungary in adopting legal regulations incompatible with European Union law, even if initially it seemed that Hungary was an 'unsurpassed model' for Poland. The number and, what is more important, the subject of the complaints against Poland, as well as the continuation of the procedure under Article 7 TEU against Poland proves that this was not just an impression. The authoritarian trends in Poland are considered as a serious threat to the integrity of the European Union, as they undermine the legal foundations of European integration, threatening the proper functioning of the European Union law system, where individuals are the subjects and the largest

71 Judgment of the Supreme Court of December 5th, 2019 (case III PO 7/18), available in English on the Supreme Court website: www.sn.pl/aktualnosci/SiteAssets/Lists/Komunikaty_o_sprawach/AllItems/III-PO-0007_18_English.pdf.

beneficiaries. Given the importance of the Rule of Law for the confidence of citizens in the Union and the effective delivery of its policies, the Commission's declaration that the Rule of Law is of central relevance to the future of Europe deserves appreciation.[72]

Bibliography

Dariusz Adamski, 'The Social Contract of Democratic Backsliding in the "New EU" countries', 56 *Common Market Law Review* (2019), 623–666.

Maciej Bernatt and Michał Ziółkowski, 'Statutory anti-constitutionalism', 28 *Washington International Law Journal* (2019), 487–526.

Stanisław Biernat and Monika Kawczyńska, 'The role of the Polish constitution (Pre-2016): Development of a liberal democracy in the European and international context', in A Albi and S Bardutzky, eds, *National constitutions in European and global governance: Democracy, rights, the Rule of Law* (The Hague, T.M.C. Asser Press 2019), 745–793.

Lóránt Csink, 'Rule of Law in Hungary. What can law and politics do?', Chapter 7 of this book.

Tímea Drinóczi, 'Temporal effects of decisions of the Hungarian Constitutional Court', in Patricia Popelier, Sarah Verstraelen, Dirk Vanheule, and Beatrix Vanlerberghe, eds, *The effects of judicial decisions in time* (Intersentia 2014), 87–106.

Tímea Drinóczi, 'The Rule of Law: The Hungarian perspective', Chapter 5 of this book.

Willem Geelhoed, Leendert Hendrik Erkelens, and Arjen Meij, *Shifting Perspectives on the European Public Prosecutor's Office* (Springer 2017), 1–97.

Tomasz Gizbert-Studnicki, 'Wykładnia celowościowa', 3–4 *Studia Prawnicze* (1985), 51–69.

Heather Grabbe and Stefan Lehne, *Defending EU values in Poland and Hungary* (Carnegie Europe – Carnegie Endowment for International Peace September 04, 2017), 1–7, https://carnegieeurope.eu/2017/09/04/defending-eu-values-in-poland-and-hungary-pub-72988 (accessed May 17, 2020].

John Harrison Watts and Cliff Roberson, *Law and Society: An Introduction* (CRC Press 2013), 1–350.

Dominik Istrate, 'Half a million Hungarians sign petition to join EU prosecutor's office', *Emerging Europe*, November 15 (2019), https://emerging-europe.com/news/half-a-million-hungarians-sign-petition-to-join-eu-prosecutors-office/.

András Jakab and Eszter Bodnár, 'The Rule of Law, democracy and human rights in Hungary: Tendencies from 1989 until 2019', Chapter 4 of this book.

Immanuel Kant, *Metafizyka moralności* (Ewa Nowak tr., Wydawnictwo Naukowe PWN 2007), 1–385.

Zbigniew Kmieciak, 'Ochrona tymczasowa w sprawie ze skargi Komisji przeciwko Polsce dotyczącej przepisów ustawy obniżającej wiek przejścia w stan spoczynku sędziów SN. Glosa do postanowienia TS z dnia 19 października 2018 r., C-619/18 R', 1 *Państwo i Prawo* (2019), 143–150.

72 European Commission, Communication from the Commission to the European Parliament, the European Council and the Council, Further strengthening the Rule of Law within the Union State of play and possible next steps, COM/2019/163 final, 1.

Dimitry Kochenov and Laurent Pech, 'Better Late than Never? On the European Commission's Rule of Law Framework and its First Activation: Commission's Rule of Law Framework', 54 *JCMS: Journal of Common Market Studies* (2016), 1062–1074.

Dimitry Kochenov and Laurent Pech, 'Monitoring and Enforcement of the Rule of Law in the EU: Rhetoric and Reality', 11(3) *European Constitutional Law Review* (2015), 512–540.

Vasiliki Kosta and Bruno de Witte, 'Human rights in the court of justice of the European Union', in M. Scheinin, ed, *Human rights norms in 'other' international courts* (Cambridge University Press 2019), 263–286.

Ronan McCrea, 'Hungary and Poland pose worse threat to EU than Brexit. Mutual recognition and trust among member states around legal systems vital to EU', *The Irish Times*, November 4, (2019), https://www.irishtimes.com/opinion/hungary-and-poland-pose-worse-threat-to-eu-than-brexit-1.3628355.

Ulrike Müßig, *Reason and Fairness: Constituting Justice in Europe, from Medieval Canon Law to ECHR* (BRILL 2019) IX, 1–629.

Laurent Pech and Kim Lane Scheppele, 'Poland and the European Commission, Part II: Hearing the Siren Song of the Rule of Law', *VerfBlog*, 2017/1/06, https://verfassungsblog.de/poland-and-the-european-commission-part-ii-hearing-the-siren-song-of-the-rule-of-law/.

Laurent Pech and Kim Lane Scheppele, 'Poland and the European Commission, Part III: Requiem for the Rule of Law', *VerfBlog*, 2017/3/03, https://verfassungsblog.de/poland-and-the-european-commission-part-iii-requiem-for-the-rule-of-law/.

Laurent Pech, 'Systemic threat to the Rule of Law in Poland: What should the commission do next?', *VerfBlog*, 2016/10/31, https://verfassungsblog.de/systemic-threat-to-the-rule-of-law-in-poland-what-should-the-commission-do-next.

Wojciech Sadurski, *Poland's Constitutional Breakdown* (Oxford University Press 2019), 1–304.

Anna Śledzińska-Simon, 'The Rise and Fall of Judicial Self-Government in Poland: On Judicial Reform Reversing Democratic Transition', 7 *German Law Journal* (2018), 1839–1870.

Maciej Taborowski, *The Commission takes a step back in the fight for the Rule of Law*, *VerfBlog*, 2018/1/03, https://verfassungsblog.de/the-commission-takes-a-step-back-in-the-fight-for-the-rule-of-law/.

Takis Tridimas, 'BREXIT Means BREXIT. Article 50: An Endgame Without an End?', 3 *King's Law Journal* (2016), 297–313.

Zygmunt Ziembiński, *Wstęp do aksjologii dla prawników* (Wydawnictwo Prawnicze 1990), 1–253.

Jurisprudence of the CJEU

Joined cases C-585/18, C-624/18 and C-625/18 AK (C-585/18) v Krajowa Rada Sądownictwa and CP (C-624/18), DO (C-625/18) v Sąd Najwyższy (C-624/18 and C-625/18), joined party: Prokurator Generalny zastępowany przez Prokuraturę Krajową.

Judgment of 24 June 2019, Commission v Poland (Independence of the Supreme Court) (C-619/18).

Judgment of the Court (First Chamber) of 6 November 2012 in case C-286/12 European Commission v Hungary, ECLI:EU:C:2012:687.

Judgment of the Court (Grand Chamber) of 24 June 2019 in case C-619/18 European Commission v Republic of Poland, ECLI:EU:C:2019:531.

Judgment of the Court (Grand Chamber) of 24 June 2019 in case C-619/18 European Commission v Republic of Poland, ECLI:EU:C:2019:531, point 37.

Judgment of the Court (Grand Chamber) of 25 July 2018 in case C-216/18 PPU LM., ECLI:EU:C:2018:586, operative part.

Judgment of the Court (Grand Chamber) of 5 November 2019 in case C-192/18 European Commission v Republic of Poland, ECLI:EU:C:2019:924.

Judgment of the Court (Grand Chamber), 5 February 2014 in in case C-385/12 Hervis Sport- és Divatkereskedelmi Kft. v Nemzeti Adó- és Vámhivatal Közép-dunántúli Regionális Adó Főigazgatósága, ECLI:EU:C:2014:47.

Judgment of the Court of 6 October 1982 in case 283/81 Srl CILFIT and Lanificio di Gavardo SpA v Ministry of Health, European Court Reports 1982-03415, ECLI:EU:C:1982:335, point 20.

Judgment of the General Court (Ninth Chamber, Extended Composition) of 16 May 2019 in joined cases T-836/16 and T-624/17 Republic of Poland v European Commission, ECLI:EU:T:2019:338.

Opinion of Advocate General Tanchev delivered on 11 April 2019 in case C-619/18 European Commission v Republic of Poland.

Opinion of Advocate General Tanchev delivered on 27 June 2019 in joined cases C-585/18, C-624/18 and C-625/18, ECLI:EU:C:2019:551.

National jurisprudence

Judgment of Ms. Justice Donnelly delivered on the 12 March 2018, Record No. 2013 EXT 295, Record No. 2014 EXT 8, Record No. 2017 EXT 291. In addition, the words of the attorney quoted after 'Politico': www.politico.eu/article/ireland-pol and-extradition-case-referred-to-europe-top-court-ecj/.

9 Are the EU Member States still masters of the Treaties? The European Rule of Law concept as a means of limiting national authorities

Agnieszka Grzelak

9.1. Introduction

From 2015 onwards, Poland is in a situation where its relations with the European Union are continuously being tested in the context of the application of the standards of the European Rule of Law. The undermining of the independence of the Constitutional Tribunal, allowing for further steps towards a system in which the executive has a significant impact on the independence of the judiciary, the subordination of public media or civil service,[1] has led to this extraordinary situation. The EU institutions, particularly the Commission and the Court of Justice, but also the Council and the European Parliament, in various procedures, have to assess the situation in Poland, having regard to the provisions of the Treaties, in particular Article 2 TEU, but also Article 19 TEU and Article 47 of the Charter of Fundamental Rights (CFR). It can be said that Poland has, in recent years, become a 'testing court' for the use of the various procedures provided for in the Treaties, as well as for the testing of the scope of EU law in this context.[2]

However, Poland is not the only Member State in which problems related to the functioning of the judiciary or, more generally, the Rule of Law, have become the subject of analyses in various legal procedures in the CJEU or other EU institutions, in accordance with EU law. In recent years, Hungary and Romania have also faced very similar problems. Moreover, in France or Germany, i.e., in countries with established democracies, not everything is acceptable – in these cases, however, the problems are incomparable with the systemic threats in Poland or Hungary.[3]

1 W Sadurski, *Poland's Constitutional Breakdown* (Oxford University Press 2019).

2 M Taborowski, *Mechanizmy ochrony praworządności państw członkowskich w prawie Unii Europejskiej. Studium przebudzenia systemu ponadnarodowego* (Wolters Kluwer 2019) 22, 23.

3 Cases in the CJEU: 1) regarding Germany: Joined Cases C-508/18 and C-82/19 *Minister for Justice and Equality v. OG and PI* EU:C:2019:456, 2) regarding Romania – pending cases: Case C-547/19 *Asociația 'Forumul Judecătorilor din România'*; Case C-83/19 *Asociația 'Forumul Judecătorilor Din România'*, 3) regarding Hungary – pending case: C-564/19 *IS*. Cf. also European Parliament resolution of 12 September 2018 on a proposal calling on

In the established democracy, the judicial system should be able to respond to all threats to the Rule of Law. However, this is the judicial system of the European Union that is designed to ensure the coherence and uniformity of EU law. Within this framework, Article 19 TEU entrusts the Court of Justice, but also the national courts, with the task of ensuring judicial control in the EU legal order. The very existence of the effective judicial review to ensure respect for Union law is an inherent feature of the Rule of Law within the meaning of Article 2 TEU.[4] The EU legal system is based on the premise that Member States respect all the principles set out in Article 2 TEU, including the Rule of Law principle. It is a necessary and essential condition for preserving the autonomy of EU law in relation to national law.[5] It is clear from the *Van Gend* judgment that the legal construction of the Community system (now the EU legal system) is based on the assumption that Member States share many of the common values on which the EU legal system is based. In the early stages of the European integration, the acquis did not explicitly include any of these principles, and the procedures for breaching Treaty obligations primarily concerned the infringement of the acquis. This system, when one analyses the recently decided and still-pending cases, is the most influential one, but this is not the only legal procedure and possibility to control the Member States with regard to the Rule of Law. The problem of assessing compliance of Member States' actions with the principles of democracy, the Rule of Law, or human rights became only a matter of time with the growing importance of loyal cooperation and mutual trust.[6] The above-mentioned assumption was therefore linked to a system of mutual trust between the EU Member States.[7]

The European Communities, in their early stages of existence, did not contain provisions that explicitly referred to their values and principles. Gradually, with the successive enlargements of the Communities, and later of the EU, the values expressed in the Schuman Declaration became more and more important.[8]

the Council to determine, pursuant to Article 7(1) of the Treaty on European Union, the existence of a clear risk of a serious breach by Hungary of the values on which the Union is founded (2017/2131(INL)).

4 Case C-64/16 *Associação Sindical dos Juízes Portugueses v. Tribunal de Contas* EU:C:2018:117, paragraph 36; Case C-72/15 *PJSC Rosneft Oil Company v. Her Majesty's Treasury and Others*, EU:C:2017:236.

5 Case C-284/16 *Slowakische Republik v. Achmea BV*, EU:C:2018:158. See also Bruno de Witte 'European Union Law: How Autonomous is the Legal Order?' 65 *Zeitschrift für öffentliches Recht* (2010) 141; JW van Rossem 'The Autonomy of EU Law: More is Less?', in RA Wessel and S Blockmans, eds, *Between Autonomy and Dependence. The EU Legal Order under the Influence of International Organisations* (Springer 2013) 13.

6 D Kochenov, 'Busting the myths nuclear: A commentary on Article 7 TEU', 10 *EUI Working Papers* (2017) 11.

7 Case 2/13, Opinion of the Court, EU:C:2014:2454, paragraph 168.

8 D Kochenov, 'EU Enlargement Law: History and Recent Developments: Treaty–Custom Concubinage?' 9 (6) *European Integration Online Papers* (2005).

Already in its judgment in *Les Verts* in the 1980s,[9] the Court of Justice held that the then European Economic Community was a community based on the Rule of Law, but that there was no need to develop or approximate that concept in the case-law of the Court of Justice in subsequent years. Only in recent years, it became entirely clear that the EU Member States have not respected the values expressed in this principle.[10] Poland is a specific case in this context due to the use of all legal options: for the first time, the Commission has decided not only to launch a political dialogue based on its Communication from 2014,[11] but also to initiate the procedure under Article 7(1) TEU, and to bring actions for breach of Treaty obligations before the Court of Justice on the basis of Article 258 TFEU. Finally, Polish courts have decided to refer questions to the Court for preliminary rulings (Article 267 TFEU) which also concern the verification of legislative acts adopted in recent years in Poland for compliance with the Rule of Law. The number of various legal proceedings initiated on the EU level is at its largest in the case of Poland; however, as indicated in the introduction, legal procedures are also used in relation to other countries.

The purpose of this text is not to deal with the systemic problem of the relationship between EU law and national law, especially in the context of the growing role of the Court of Justice. The author intends to note the importance and role of the EU institutions, as well as the role of the Member States, in the process of safeguarding the value of the Rule of Law in the EU, taking into account the community of values. Naturally, the examples will refer mostly to the situation in Poland for the reasons mentioned above.[12] The author intends to deny the views (expressed, e.g., by the governments) which argue that the procedures used are not of a legal nature, that they are merely an expression of the political will of other countries, and that Member States have lost control over which direction EU law is interpreted by the CJEU. On the contrary, the author intends to say that the professionalism of the CJEU judges, as well as the legal conditions of the Treaty, contribute to the depoliticisation of procedures.

9.2. The European Rule of Law and protection of the national identities of the Member States

The Rule of Law, as a value referred to in Article 2 TEU, is certainly not a standalone standard on the basis of which it is possible to require the fulfilment of specific obligations by the Member States. Instead, it is a meta-principle made up

9 Case 294/83 *Parti écologiste 'Les Verts' v. European Parliament*, EU:C:1986:166.

10 See Taborowski, n 2, 21.

11 COM(2014) 158 final: Communication from the Commission to the European Parliament and the Council: A new EU Framework to strengthen the Rule of Law

12 For some general remarks on the EU Rule of Law mission in Poland, see Chapter 8 of this book by S Majkowska-Szulc. On the Polish perspective of the Rule of Law, see Chapter 6 by I Wróblewska, who analyses the understanding of the Rule of Law in the Polish jurisprudence and doctrine.

of other elements with an independent normative meaning, e.g., the effectiveness of judicial protection in the EU stemming from the second sentence of Article 19 paragraph 1 TEU.[13] Since the Rule of Law was present in the Community legal system as a value common to the constitutional systems of the Member States long before it was incorporated into Article 2 TEU, it can be considered that codification of this principle in the Treaties rather represented an acceptance and confirmation of its importance for the Member States as a necessary element of European integration.[14] However, this does not mean that Article 2 TEU cannot be applied and interpreted by the Court of Justice, EU institutions, and national courts. In the context of the subject matter of this paper, it is only a matter of indicating that the Member States themselves have given substance to Article 2 TEU and should accept its consequences, including the fact that the Rule of Law clause obliges to a certain direction of interpretation of the principles that form its part. The Rule of Law is a founding value for the Union legal order, which means that Union courts (including national courts) must take the Rule of Law into account when exercising their judicial function.[15]

The comparison of the independent legal meaning of the Rule of Law clause in Article 2 TEU with the national identity clause in Article 4(2) TEU has been identified in the literature.[16] Article 4(2) TEU requires the European Union to respect the national identity of Member States, inherent in their fundamental political and constitutional structures. The meaning of the concept of national identity, as set out in Article 4(2) TEU, is not clearly established in EU law and the case-law of the CJEU.[17] This provision presupposes that there is an inviolable core of national competencies that can be protected against Europeanisation, excluded from harmonisation and unification measures. This allows the Member States, although to an undefined extent, to protect their most important national interests against undesirable interference from EU law.[18] The very concept of

13 See n 4.

14 T Konstadinides, *The Rule of Law in the European Union: the Internal Dimension* (Oxford and Portland, OR, 2017) 169; Taborowski, n 2, 81.

15 L Pech, 'The Rule of Law as a Constitutional Principle of the European Union' 4 *Jean Monnet Working Paper* (2009) 58. T Drinóczi and A Bień-Kacała, Illiberal constitutionalism and the European Rule of Law, Chapter 1 of this book, 13–20.

16 See Taborowski, n 2, 84.

17 M Dobbs, 'Sovereignty, Article 4(2) TEU and the Respect of National Identities: Swinging the Balance of Power in Favour of the Member States?' *Yearbook of European Law* (2014) 33; B de Witte, 'The Lisbon Treaty and National Constitutions: More or Less Europeanisation?', in C Closa, ed, *The Lisbon Treaty and National Constitutions: Europeanisation and Democratic Implications*, 3 ARENA Report (2009), 9 RECON Report (2009) <www.researchgate.net/publication/265242262_The_Lisbon_Treaty_and_National_Constitutions_Europeanisation_and_Democratic_Implications/link/5405dcb20cf23d9765a774fd/download> (accessed 11 January 2020).

18 M Laskowska and M Taborowski, 'Obowiązek wykładni przyjaznej prawu Unii Europejskiej – między otwartością na proces integracji a ochroną tożsamości konstytucyjnej', in S Dudzik and N Półtorak, eds, *Prawo Unii Europejskiej a prawo konstytucyjne państw członkowskich* (Wolters Kluwer 2013) 80.

national identity specific to a particular state can only be defined in the context of the legal system of that state, whereas the core of the values resulting from Article 2 TEU should be defined by the Court of Justice and may lead to the creation of the concept of European identity.[19]

It may be questioned whether Member States can invoke Article 4(2) TEU in the context of an attempt to ensure that national legislation is considered compatible with EU law. Such attempts are currently being made by the Polish or Hungarian government to show that reforms of the judiciary do not fall within the competence of the European Union. The analysis of the Court of Justice case-law and the doctrine[20] leads to the conclusion that the Court of Justice may completely reject arguments relating to Article 4(2) TEU if the method of reference in a specific situation is not reliable and appropriate. This argument was rejected, *inter alia*, with regard to the working time of judges,[21] or the rules on access to the profession of lawyer.[22]

In Case C-619/18, the Court of Justice clearly summarised and further explained:

> Furthermore, although, as the Republic of Poland and Hungary point out, the organisation of justice in the Member States falls within the competence of those Member States, the fact remains that, when exercising that competence, the Member States are required to comply with their obligations deriving from EU law (see, by analogy, judgments of 13 November 2018, Raugevicius, C-247/17, EU:C:2018:898, paragraph 45, and of 26 February 2019, Rimšēvičs and ECB v Latvia, C-202/18 and C-238/18, EU:C:2019:139, paragraph 57) and, in particular, from the second subparagraph of Article 19(1) TEU (see, to that effect, judgment of 27 February 2018, Associação Sindical dos Juízes Portugueses, C-64/16, EU:C:2018:117, paragraph 40). Moreover, by requiring the Member States thus to comply with those obligations, the European Union is not in any way claiming to exercise that competence itself nor is it, therefore, contrary to what is alleged by the Republic of Poland, arrogating that competence.[23]

There is no doubt that Article 4(2) TEU has a specific normative function in terms of the interpretation of the law by strengthening the arguments of the Member States when assessing the compatibility of national law with EU law, while being subject to review by the Court of Justice, allowing the Court to react flexibly in specific cases. Therefore, both the Rule of Law clause and the national

19 W Sadurski, 'European Constitutional Identity', 33 *EUI Working Papers* (2006) 1.

20 See Taborowski, n 2, 86.

21 Case C-393/10 *Dermod Patrick O'Brien v. Ministry of Justice* EU:C:2012:110 or Case C-192/18 *Commission v. Poland*, EU:C:2019:924.

22 Joined Cases C-58/13 and C-59/13 *Angelo Alberto Torresi and Pierfrancesco Torresi v. Consiglio dell'Ordine degli Avvocati di Macerata* EU:C:2014:2088.

23 Case C-619/18 *Commission v. Poland*, EU:C:2019:531, paragraph 52.

identity clause are similarly structured and bear a similar burden, although in case of a breach of Article 2 TEU, it should be more difficult for a Member State to justify a systemic breach of this principle by using the arguments stemming from Article 4(2) TEU. There is no doubt, however, that the national identity clause allows for a dialogue between the Court and the national courts on its content and the limits it sets. This dialogue is of a clear legal character, although politically sensitive. On the potential abuse of the argument of the necessity to protect constitutional/national identity, the Advocate General Maduro pointed out in his opinion in Case C-213/07:[24]

> [R]espect owed to the constitutional identity of the Member States cannot be understood as an absolute obligation to defer to all national constitutional rules. Were that the case, national constitutions could become instruments allowing Member States to avoid Community law in given fields. Furthermore, it could lead to discrimination between Member States based on the contents of their respective national constitutions. Just as Community law takes the national constitutional identity of the Member States into consideration, national constitutional law must be adapted to the requirements of the Community legal order.

In another case, the Advocate General Pedro Cruz Villallón pointed out:[25]

> Specifically, the Court of Justice has given preference to those constitutional traditions when establishing a particular culture of rights, namely that of the Union. The Union has thus acquired the character, not just of a community governed by the Rule of Law, but also of a "community [...] with a constitutional culture". That common constitutional culture can be seen as part of the common identity of the Union, with the important consequence, to my mind, that the constitutional identity of each Member State, which of course is specific to the extent necessary, cannot be regarded, to state matters cautiously, as light years away from that common constitutional culture. Rather, a clearly understood, open attitude to EU law should in the medium and long term give rise, as a principle, to basic convergence between the constitutional identity of the Union and that of each of the Member States.

However, in some Member States, the problem is that authoritarian tendencies are on the increase, so mutual trust and any attempt to engage in a dialogue-based discussion cannot be assumed.[26] In such a situation, the national identity

24 Opinion of the Advocate General in case C-213/07, 8 October 2008, *Michaniki AE v. Ethniko Symvoulio Radiotileorasis and Ypourgos Epikrateias*, ECLI:EU:C:2008:544, paragraph 31.

25 Case C-62/14 *Peter Gauweiler* EU:C:2015:7, Opinion of AG Poiares Maduro, paragraph 61; emphasis added.

26 RD Kelemen and L Pech 'Why autocrats love constitutional identity and constitutional pluralism: Lessons from Hungary and Poland', 2 *Reconnect Working Paper* (2018).

clause may serve as a basis for the argument that EU law cannot interfere in key elements of the national legal order, which are very closely linked to the Rule of Law. Some Member States, including Poland,[27] therefore try to invoke the principle of national identity on issues such as the independence of the judiciary where there are serious concerns about Poland's violation of the values set out in Article 2 TEU.[28]

One may, therefore, wonder whether the national identity clause should not be invoked only by Member States that respect the values of Article 2 TEU. The national identity of states should be built as the identity of EU Member States that joined the organisation of states sharing the same values. Constitutional pluralism recognises the legitimacy of parallel legal systems. Pluralism, however, cannot provide answers when it comes to the design and enforcement of founding values, which require homogeneous acceptance throughout the Union. Deficiencies affect the entire Union legal order.[29]

The wording of Article 2 TEU requires that the Union is founded on these values and that they are common to the Member States. It does not require that the values are binding in law. Yet, the normativity of values will depend on the extent at which their compliance can be enforced. In Opinion 2/13, the Court of Justice made it clear that the legal structure of the EU is based on the assumption that each Member State shares with all other Member States a number of the common values on which the Union is founded (Article 2 TEU).[30] This premise justifies the existence of mutual trust between the Member States, implies that values will be recognised, and that Union law implementing them will be respected. The Rule of Law is, therefore, a feature of the supranational system of EU law, which is both autonomous of and complementary to the legal systems of the Member States. The Rule of Law has a protective function for the effective application of EU law in the internal legal order, including the need to ensure effective judicial protection. The elements of the Rule of Law stemming from Article 2 TEU could be the beginning of a European identity clause, which, when examining the compatibility of national law with EU law, requires a move towards the protection of supranational law. It would be consistent with the protective function of the values of the Rule of Law.

27 As for the use of the concept of national identity in other Members States, see e.g., T Drinóczi, 'Constitutional identity in Europe: the identity of the constitution. A regional approach', 2 *German Law Journal* 2020, 105–130.

28 The Chancellery of the Prime Minister, White Paper on the Reform of the Polish Judiciary, Warsaw, 7 March 2018 <www.premier.gov.pl/en/news/news/the-government-presents-a-white-paper-on-the-reforms-ofthe-polish-justice-system.html> (accessed 11 February 2020).

29 O Mader, 'Enforcement of EU Values as a Political Endeavour: Constitutional Pluralism and Value Homogeneity in Times of Persistent Challenges to the Rule of Law', 11 *Hague Journal on the Rule of Law* (2019) 133.

30 See n 7, paragraph 168.

The above means that, although it is a Member State that identifies its national identity, it must take into account European values – the values of the community to which it has accessed independently and in accordance with its national identity. European identity and the competences of the European Union are by no means conferred top-down, but their scope depends solely on the Member States, which have jointly committed themselves to respect them.

9.3. Political dialogue between the Commission and the Member State on the basis of the Communication from 2014

In 2014 the Commission presented a Communication[31] aimed at ensuring effective and consistent protection of the Rule of Law in all Member States. The aim of the new mechanism was firstly to ensure the protection of the fundamental values of the EU, and secondly to achieve a higher level of mutual trust. The mechanism described in the Communication is intended to serve a preventive function – to prevent the emergence of a systemic threat to the Rule of Law, while allowing the European Commission to prepare itself to submit a proposal in accordance with its competences under Article 7 TEU. The procedure described in it creates a framework within which the Commission establishes contact with the authorities of a Member State while allowing it to communicate its position and to exchange arguments. It also allows the other Member States to prepare their position in the longer term. It is worth recalling that in its Communication, the Commission included an autonomous definition of the Rule of Law, setting out the core of its elements, taking into account the case-law of the CJEU, the case-law of the ECHR, and the Council of Europe acquis – again, components of the common legal tradition of the Member States.

In the context of the question asked in the title of the study, it may be recalled that, following the adoption of the Communication, reservations have arisen regarding the Commission's competence to conduct such proceedings.[32] Indeed, some commentators assumed that an infringement of the values set out in Article 2 TEU could only be dealt with under Article 7 TEU, without any preceding procedure. Even in the view of the Council Legal Services, there is no legal basis in the Treaty for the creation of a new supervisory mechanism for the Rule of Law. In the end, however, the Council itself, i.e., the representatives of the Member States, took note of the conclusions of the opinion of the Legal Service, but did not express a position that clearly called into question the Commission's competence. The Council only stressed that the dialogue must be conducted in

31 Commission, Communication from the Commission to the European Parliament and the Council. A new EU Framework to strengthen the Rule of Law, COM (2014) 158 final.

32 Legal Service of the Council of the EU, Opinion 10296/14 on the Commission's Communication on a new EU Framework to strengthen the Rule of Law: Compatibility with the Treaties, 27 May 2014, not published.

such a way as to complement the work of other EU institutions and international organisations.[33] Nor has the Council, in the context of the Commission's dialogue with Poland, ever questioned this competence of the Commission before. In addition, in December 2014, the Member States agreed to hold an annual dialogue among themselves in the framework of the Council of the EU in order to promote and protect the Rule of Law,[34] which is to be based on the principles of objectivity, non-discrimination, and equal treatment of Member States, using an impartial, evidence-based approach.

It can, therefore, be concluded that, in principle, the States accepted this procedure, as in case of the EU-Pilot procedure,[35] a kind of informal dialogue between the Commission and the State on a potential breach of EU law, preceding the opening of a procedure under Article 258 TFEU.[36] Finally, as Taborowski rightly points out,[37] the Court of Justice has also accepted the Commission's competence, using in its ongoing proceedings information collected in the course of proceedings conducted based on the provisions of the Communication.[38]

When comparing the theoretical assumptions of the Communication with the reality and the first case of Poland, it should be recalled that, after an intensive two years of political dialogue and four recommendations presented by the Commission,[39] the Commission eventually submitted a reasoned proposal to the Council.[40] Problems with the Rule of Law in Poland have also revealed the need to clarify the scope of national competences and the relationship between the principle of effective judicial protection and the state's competence to organise the judiciary in the state. The core of the recommendations concerned important systemic issues: the first two focused mainly on the problem of legitimacy and functioning of the Constitutional Tribunal, while the other two were mainly related to the so-called reform of the judiciary in Poland.[41] It is worth noting that not all the specific issues which were the subject of the Commission's assessment were unconditionally considered by the Commission as falling within the scope of EU law. For example, the European Commission itself had doubts as to whether

33 See outcome of the Council meeting, 3362. Council meeting, General Affairs 16936/14, Brussel 16 December 2014.

34 Council Conclusions 17014/14, Brussels 16 December 2014.

35 The concept was presented for the first time in COM(2007) 502.

36 A Grzelak, 'Ramy prawne UE na rzecz umacniania praworządności. Uwagi na tle wniosku Komisji Europejskiej z 20 grudnia 2017 r.', 2 *Sprawy Międzynarodowe* (2018) 213.

37 See Taborowski, n 2, 137.

38 Cf. Case C-216/18PPU *LM* EU:C:2018:586 or Case C-619/18R Commission v. Poland, order of the Court, EU:C:2018:1021.

39 Commission Recommendations (EU) 2016/13743, (EU) 2017/1464, (EU) 2017/1520 and (EU) 2018/103.

40 Commission, Proposal for a Council decision on the determination of a clear risk of a serious breach of the Rule of Law by the Republic of Poland – reasoned proposal in accordance with Article 7(1) of the Treaty on European Union regarding the Rule of Law in Poland, COM(2017) 835 final.

41 Cf. S Majkowska-Szulc, 'Safeguarding the European Union's core values: The EU Rule of Law mission in Poland', Chapter 8 of this book, 178–186.

the issue of appointing and dismissing presidents of common courts by the Minister of Justice fell within the scope of EU law. While this problem was raised in the recommendations, it was the subject of communications before the initiation of the procedure under Article 258 TFEU,[42] and ultimately the Commission did not file a complaint to the CJEU on this issue.[43] The Commission also set certain limits to its actions – the issue of the independence of the Constitutional Tribunal was not a sufficient reason to immediately initiate proceedings under Article 7 TEU or Article 258 TFEU, while the independence of the Supreme Court, which under EU law is the so-called court of the last instance, obliged the Commission to act.[44] Generally, the idea of the Commission's proceeding on the basis of the Communication is based on the assumption that the mechanism introduced in Article 7 TEU requires prior monitoring of the situation in the Member States – therefore, EU institutions are authorised to take action in a situation where Member States display behaviours threatening EU values, and the Member States must accept such actions.[45]

Finally, Taborowski rightly points out that the greatest challenge in the future is to apply the Communication in a manner that excludes allegations of double standards and arbitrariness. In this respect, it is important that proceedings against other Member States prove that the use of this procedure against Poland was not a one-off experiment, which would be an argument for those who point to a reduction in the powers of Member States in this procedure.

9.4. Article 7 TEU mechanism

The Article 7 TEU mechanism, first activated in relation to Poland by the above-mentioned Commission proposal of 20 December 2017 and then by the European Parliament in relation to Hungary,[46] is designed to monitor Member States' compliance with the values set out in Article 2 TEU.[47] Since the early 1990s, the clause on respect for the Rule of Law and human rights has been part of the enlargement strategy and the subject of association agreements. One of the

42 See press releases IP/17/2205 and IP/17/3186.

43 See press release IP/17/5367; P Bogdanowicz and M Taborowski, 'Brak niezależności sądów krajowych jako uchybienie zobowiązaniu w rozumieniu art. 258 TFUE (cz. II)', 2 *Europejski Przegląd Sądowy* (2018) 22.

44 See Taborowski, n 2, 129.

45 The European Parliament has not yet established its own mechanism for monitoring the Rule of Law, although in 2016 an inter-institutional agreement the EU Pact for Democracy, Rule of Law and Fundamental Rights – has been proposed, see EP Resolution 2015/2254(INL). See also P Oliver and J Stefanelli, 'Strengthening the Rule of Law in the EU: The Council's Inaction', 54 *Journal of Common Market Studies* (2016) 1075.

46 European Parliament resolution of 12 September 2018 on a proposal calling on the Council to determine, pursuant to Article 7(1) of the Treaty on European Union, the existence of a clear risk of a serious breach by Hungary of the values on which the Union is founded (2017/2131(INL))

47 For details of the proceedings in Poland, see Majkowska-Szulc, n 11, 178–186.

sanctions for non-compliance with these standards was the prolongation of the accession procedure. However, these consequences, after the accession, were no longer relevant. Member States were not formally assessed for compliance with the Rule of Law anymore.[48] The situation has changed with the planned major enlargement of the EU following the adoption of the Treaty of Amsterdam. The Treaty of Amsterdam introduced Article 7 in the TEU, which referred to Article 6 TEU expressing the founding values of the EU.[49]

The expected EU enlargement was not the only reason. The situation regarding the participation of the extreme right-wing FPÖ in the Austrian government, and the imposition of sanctions by the 14 Member States that operated outside the EU legal framework on a bilateral basis, made everyone aware of the weakness of the system and the necessity to change it.[50] In reality, however, neither the Commission nor any other body of the then Communities initiated any proceedings against Austria. Therefore, the changes were agreed by the EU Member States, first accepting the Treaty of Nice and then the Treaty of Lisbon.[51] An Intergovernmental Conference, which was held in 2000, resulted in the Treaty of Nice. Lessons from the crisis in Austria were already learned during the Conference. They expressed themselves in an agreement aimed at supplementing the procedure of Article 7 TEU with a mechanism of 'monitoring' and 'early warning' in the event of a situation in one of the EU Member States threatening to respect the principles set out in Article 6(1) TEU at the time. As a consequence, a new paragraph 1 (corresponding in principle to the current paragraph 1 of Article 7 TEU) was added to Article 7 TEU, establishing such an 'initial' mechanism. It also added the possibility for the Court of Justice to review the legality of decisions taken by the Council (now also by the European Council) under the procedure of Article 7 TEU, but 'only with regard to compliance with the purely procedural provisions of that Article'. The Court must rule on such a case within one month of the date of the proposal (now Article 269 TFEU). The Lisbon Treaty did not substantially modify Article 7 TEU in this way.

It is clear that the Member States themselves, accepting the changes introduced by the Treaty of Amsterdam, later Nice, and confirming their findings in Lisbon, wanted to establish a sanction mechanism. The Article 7 TEU procedure is entirely conceived as a procedure in which the Member States

48 With some exception concerning Bulgaria and Romania, see: MA Vachudova and A Spendzharova, 'The EU's Cooperation and Verification Mechanism: Fighting Corruption in Bulgaria and Romania after EU Accession', European Policy Analysis (SIEPS 2012).

49 W Sadurski, 'Adding Bite to a Bark: the Story of Article 7, EU Enlargement, and Jörg Haider' 16 *The Columbia Journal of European Law* (2010) 385.

50 S Schmahl, 'Die Reaktionen auf den Einzug der Freiheitlichen Partei Österreichs in das österreichische Regierungskabiett. Eine europa- und vökerrechtliche Analyse', 5 *EuR* (2000) 819.

51 It should be remembered, however, that the first plans to create such a mechanism appeared back in the 1980s, as part of the work on the new Treaty on European Union, Twelve Spinelli Draft. See OJ C 77, 14 February 1984.

themselves, acting within the Council or the European Council, make an assessment of the actions of one of the Member States. This assessment should be based on the legal findings and evidence; however, as far as the final voting is concerned, this procedure leaves ample room for diplomatic action and political actions. It is also confirmed by Article 269 TFEU, which excludes the jurisdiction of the Court of Justice to review the substance of acts adopted within the framework of Article 7 TEU.

The introduction of the procedure in Article 7 TEU was, therefore, a decision of the Member States who agreed on the current wording of this provision. The Article 7 TEU procedure aimed to close the gap between a situation where all Member States were considered to meet the same high initial standards and a reality where this was not the case. Not only should the procedure be based on legal evidence, but – independently from this – the procedure of Article 7 TEU may lead to negative legal consequences for the Member State. Moreover, the submission of an application in itself has image implications, followed by political consequences, which may put pressure on the Member State to take action to ensure the proper functioning of the EU legal system. Kochenov is right to point out that the scope of Article 7 TEU is key for understanding the whole instrument.[52] From the outset, Article 7 TEU was intended to apply to all Member States and not, as in the case of the Cooperation and Verification Mechanism (CVM), to only some of them.

Indeed, Article 7 TEU regulates three stages of the procedure designed to safeguard the values of Article 2 TEU:

- a procedure to declare the existence of a 'clear risk of a serious breach' of the values referred to in Article 2 TEU and the adoption of recommendations how to remedy the situation addressed to the Member States in breach (Art. 7(1) TEU);
- a procedure to state the existence of a serious and persistent breach of values (Art. 7(2) TEU);
- a sanctioning mechanism following the statement of a serious and persistent breach (Art. 7(3) TEU).

The Article 7 TEU procedure leaves the decision to start investigating the legality of EU Member States' actions in light of EU values entirely in the hands of a political decision by Parliament, the European Commission, or a majority of Member States.[53] However, this political decision should be based on the legal assessment. From the perspective of the procedure of Article 7 TEU, the

52 See Kochenov, n 6, 12.

53 S Carrera and P Bárd, 'The European Parliament vote on Article 7 TEU against the Hungarian government. Too late, too little, too political?' [2018] CEPS Commentary <www.ceps.eu/wp-content/uploads/2018/09/EP%20vote%20on%20Article7_0.pdf> (accessed 13 January 2020).

procedure followed by the Commission on the basis of the Communication of 2014 is all the more relevant since a request under Article 7(1) TEU must be justified using legal arguments. It also justifies action by the Commission – after all, it is necessary to carry out appropriate factual and legal analyses. The role of the Member State under scrutiny is to cooperate and conduct effective dialogue, presenting the position and trying to find solutions.

The Commission's proposal for Poland highlights the strictly legal dimension of the perceived problem with the Rule of Law, eventually presenting a discretionary assessment on the basis of legal analysis. The Council is now to carry out the assessment with a wide margin of discretion and political discretion. Ultimately, the procedure under Article 7 TEU can play a role from the perspective of the protective function of the Rule of Law. It can also have a long-term impact on a Member State to restore the Rule of Law, leading to its isolation.[54] Again, Taborowski rightly points out that the Council's behaviour towards Poland (no more decisive action) is in line with the approach of the Member States to the procedure under Article 259 TFEU, as well as with the nature of the mechanism established by the Member States within the Council, which consists mainly of discussion and exchange of views. Therefore, states expect that threats to the supranational character of the EU will be controlled by institutions established for this purpose, especially the Commission and the Court, while the procedure under Article 7 TEU will be used when other mechanisms become ineffective.[55] All in all, the protection of the values, although legal in its assumptions, is a predominantly political task that calls in the end again for legal solutions (changes in the legal system of the Member States).

9.5. Mechanisms for the protection of the European Rule of Law in judicial procedures

9.5.1. Action brought by the Commission against a Member State – Articles 258 TFEU to 260 TFEU

In several documents on mechanisms for protecting the Rule of Law, both the Commission and the Council (de facto the Member States themselves) have stated that the Rule of Law within the meaning of Article 2 TEU can be protected under the procedures of Articles 258 to 260 TFEU when a Member State violates its obligations under Treaties which fall within the scope of EU law.[56] In practice, the procedure laid down in Article 258 TFEU allows the Commission, as the guardian of the Treaties, to oversee the application of Union law by the Member States. This procedure is also an important determinant of the supranational

54 J Barcz, 'Unia Europejska wobec niepraworządnego państwa', 1 *Państwo i Prawo* (2019) 3.

55 See Taborowski, n 2, 210.

56 Commission, Communication from the Commission to the European Parliament and the Council. A new EU Framework to strengthen the Rule of Law, COM(2014) 158, 6 or Council conclusions of 16 December 2014, 22.

character of the European Union and is accepted, with all its consequences, by the states that are members and by those acceding to the EU.[57]

The growing role of the Court of Justice in the light of the 'spirit of the Treaties' can, of course, be considered. It should be recalled that there are two perspectives on the evolution and operation of the EU legal system. According to the proponents of the legal autonomy approach, the Court of Justice has been able to push forward its European integration agenda against the interests of some Member States.[58] That could mean that national governments paid insufficient attention to the Court's decisions and competences during the 1960s and 1970s when the Court developed its milestone rulings with the support of national courts.[59] Nowadays, Member States realise that the Court of Justice has become a very serious player, with a significant impact on the development of the direction of the European Union as a whole.

In contrast to an approach based on political power, national governments are not passive and reluctant victims of European law. In most cases, the CJEU is supported by Member State governments. After all, the states themselves have granted the Court autonomy in order to make it more efficient, even when the Treaties themselves did not fully address procedures or competences. In turn, the judges of the Court of Justice realise that their power is ultimately dependent on the consent of the Member States and is rather reluctant to take decisions that governments do not approve. Whatever the characteristics of the Court, it is probably true that the Court is a strategic entity that is also sensitive to the expectations of Member State governments.[60] It should be stressed, however, that the purpose of the procedure under Article 258 TFEU is to objectively establish an infringement of Union law by a Member State, and therefore the Court of Justice cannot be required to take into account the principle of reciprocity, difficulties in the legislative process, or problems arising from the division of competences under national law as factors justifying the infringement of Treaty obligations. Nor can the argumentation that the problem lies within the exclusive competence of a Member State be accepted when the problem presented by the Commission falls within the scope of EU law.

In the case of complaints from the European Commission in relation to Poland in the context of the Rule of Law, attention should be paid to the evolution of the position of the European Commission in the light of the parallel development of the case-law of the Court of Justice. The Commission's traditional approach

57 In case K 32/09 Polish Constitutional Tribunal stated, inter alia, that '[t]he Constitutional Tribunal shares the view, expressed in the doctrine that accession to an international organisation entails conferring competences for the exercise of power necessary to carry out the activities of the organisation, by relevant national bodies, on the bodies of the organisation'.

58 See e.g., J Weiler, 'The Transformation of Europe', 100 *Yale Law Journal* (1991) 2403.

59 G Garrett, RD Kelemen, and Heiner Schulz, 'The European Court of Justice, National Governments, and Legal Integration in the European Union', 52 *International Organization* (1998) 149.

60 Ibid., 168.

to understanding effective judicial protection is evidenced by the fact that, when bringing an action against Poland in Case C-192/18,[61] the Commission dropped the part of the objections it intended to raise concerning the appointment and dismissal of court presidents. The Commission limited its application to the problem, which was based not only on Article 19(1) of the TEU in connection with Article 2 TEU and Article 47 CFR, but also on Directive 2006/54/EC.[62] In order to justify the link between the procedure for appointing court presidents and EU law, the Commission would need to draw on an innovative approach to the role of national courts in the EU legal protection system. This possibility was only confirmed by the Court of Justice in its judgment C-64/16 on Portuguese judges.[63] In fact, the Court also considered the area covered by EU law to be covered by the rules governing the institutional statute of national judges[64]. National courts, whose institutional status will be protected from interference by other Member State authorities, will be able to carry out their functions smoothly and ensure effective protection of the rights of individuals deriving from EU law. This new approach – a broader understanding of the issue of independence of judges in the context of the Rule of Law in EU law – is clearly visible in the case initiated by the Commission against Poland in relation to disciplinary measures (C-791/19).

Analysing the subject of this chapter, it is also necessary to point out that in the judgment in Case C-619/18, the Court found that under Article 40 of the Treaty on European Union, the Union is composed of states which have freely and voluntarily committed themselves to the common values referred to in Article 2 TEU. According to the Court of Justice, the EU law is based on a fundamental assumption that each Member State shares with all the other Member States and recognises that those Member States share those same values. It means that the Member States themselves had decided, when they joined the EU, to respect those values. It cannot, therefore, be argued that, by upholding these values, the Commission or the Court is depriving the Member States of the possibility of pursuing their own plans for judicial reform. The Court of Justice has also repeated that a vital element of the judicial system is the preliminary ruling procedure which ensures the uniform application and autonomy of EU law. The Court also stressed that the EU is 'a union base on the Rule of Law in which individuals have the right to challenge before the courts the legality of any decision or other national measure concerning the application to them of an EU act'. The Member States, by joining the EU, are obliged to establish the system

61 Case C-192/18 *Commission v. Poland* EU:C:2019:924. Cf. the pending Case C-791/19 *Commission v. Poland.*

62 Directive 2006/54/EC of the European Parliament and of the Council of 5 July 2006 on the implementation of the principle of equal opportunities and equal treatment of men and women in matters of employment and occupation (recast) [2006] OJ L204/23.

63 Judgment of the Court (Grand Chamber) of 27 February 2018, *Associação Sindical dos Juízes Portugueses v. Tribunal de Contas*, ECLI:EU:C:2018:117.

64 See Taborowski, n 2, 230.

of legal remedies and procedures ensuring effective judicial review in fields covered by EU law. Moreover, one should remember that the principle of effective judicial protection of individuals' rights stems from the constitutional traditions common to the Member States and is enshrined in Articles 6 and 13 of the European Convention on Human Rights, to which all Member States are parties. No one can, therefore, say that these principles are unknown to the Member States or 'invented' by judges of the CJEU or the European Commission. In case C-619/118, the Court held that, although the organisation of the justice system in the Member States lies within the competence of those states when exercising that competence, the Member States are required to comply with their obligations deriving from EU law.

In the second case against Poland, the Commission analysed the adoption of amendments to the Supreme Court Act.[65] In this case, it is not only the decision taken on 24 June 2019 that is important but the order for interim measures addressed to the Polish State. The legal effects were related to the suspension of the legal effects of the national provisions covered by the freezing and the return to the previous regulation. Such a far-reaching safeguard measure was intended to protect the interest of the Union in preserving the value of the Rule of Law and the effective implementation of a possible future CJEU judgment. The Member State is not in a position to interfere with the way in which the provisional measure is to be implemented and to undermine its effectiveness. Finally, the Court assessed national law and left no doubt as to the compatibility of the national provisions requiring Supreme Court's judges to retire on the basis of a statutory reduction in the age at which they are to retire. The national authorities are therefore not in a position to interpret that provision differently.

Moreover, the European Commission brought the case before the Court against Poland concerning disciplinary proceedings and violations of the principles of judicial independence and judicial independence in legislation adopted in recent years.[66] In January 2020, the Commission decided to apply for interim measures. In all cases, the position of the Polish government expressed both at the hearing at the Tribunal in the first case (C-192/18) and other documents (e.g., the White Paper), pointed to the exclusive competence of the Member States to organise the judiciary and implement reforms as planned by the government and lack of competence of the EU to interfere in domestic matters.

These arguments of the Polish government must be rejected and was rejected by the Court of Justice in case C-619/18. Article 19 TEU, in fact, imposes on the Member States a positive obligation to provide sufficient remedies in the fields covered by EU law – a violation of the right to effective judicial protection can only be assessed with regard to Article 47 CFR. However, Article 19 TEU may be invoked by private parties as a parameter of judicial review for assessing the compatibility

65 Judgment of the Court of Justice of 24 June 2019 in case C-619/18 Commission v. Poland, ECLI:EU:C:2019:531.

66 Case C-791/19, https://europa.eu/rapid/press-release_IP-19-6033_en.htm.

with EU law of the guarantees provided by national law for judicial independence. The judgment actually intends to place judicial independence at the core of the EU constitutional order. The Court emphasised that being the 'concrete expression' of the Rule of Law values enshrined at Article 2 TEU – on which the Union is founded – Article 19 TEU ensures the continuous respect by the Member States of its common foundational values (paragraphs 42, 47). That clearly means that Articles 47 CFR and Article 19 TEU read together, the principle of effective judicial protection, and in particular judicial independence, becomes something more than another general principle of EU law since it has been capable of shaping Member States' discretionally as to the organisation of their judiciaries.[67]

9.5.2. Protection of the European Rule of Law by national courts – preliminary ruling procedure

Many of the comments made above are also valid in relation to the preliminary ruling procedure, where national courts ask the Court of Justice, under Article 267 TFEU, to interpret EU law or to assess the validity of EU law acts. In the case of Polish courts, this procedure has been used frequently in recent months. In the case of other states, this possibility, with regard to the problems with the Rule of Law, has not been used so often.[68] In the context of these cases, a wider problem arises as to the extent to which national courts have the power to refer questions for a preliminary ruling to the Court of Justice. The executive authorities in Poland, Hungary, or Romania are trying to push through the thesis that it is inadmissible to refer questions for a preliminary ruling on matters relating to fundamental aspects of the functioning of the justice system in the Member States as falling within the exclusive competence of the Member States. In particular, one should note the Polish Prosecutor General's request to the Constitutional Tribunal[69] in which the Prosecutor General (who is also the Minister of Justice) argues that

67 A Simonelli, *Thickening up judicial independence the ECJ ruling in Commmission v. Poland (C-619/18)*<europeanlawblog.eu/2019/07/08/thickening-up-judicial-independence-the-ecj-ruling-in-commission-v-poland-c-619-18/> (accessed 13 January 2020).

68 See, however, pending cases from Romania: C-547/19 Asociaţia 'Forumul Judecătorilor din România'; case C-83/19 Asociaţia 'Forumul Judecătorilor Din România' or Hungarian case C-564/19 IS. Cf. the Polish cases: 1) asked by the common courts: pending Joined Cases C-558/18 (City of Łowicz) and C-563/18 (Prokuratura Okręgowa w Płocku), concerning disciplinary proceedings against judges (Opinion of the Advocate General of 24 September 2019); pending Case C-623/18 (Prokuratura Rejonowa w Słubicach); pending Cases C-763/19 and C-764/19 – both from the Court of Appeal of Krakow and other, 2) cases before the Supreme Court: pending Case C-522/18 Social Insurance Institution (ZUS); pending Case C-537/18 National Council of the Judiciary; Joined Cases C-585/18, C-624/18 and C-625/18, EU:C:2019:982, C-668/18 Uniparts, EU:C:2019:1093; pending Case C-487/19 WŻ, pending Case C-508/19 Prokurator Generalny and 3) cases before the Supreme Administrative Court: pending Case C-824/18, in which the original questions were extended by order of 26 June 2019 (II GOK 2/18).

69 Pending case K 7/18.

> although Article 267 TFEU is a provision adopted by Poland by way of ratification of an international agreement pursuant to Article 90(1) of the Constitution of the Republic of Poland, one cannot agree with the claim that the Republic of Poland has agreed to include in the jurisdiction of the Court of Justice of the European Union matters which are constitutionally reserved for national authorities by means of competence provisions specified directly in the Constitution of the Republic of Poland and in the references to the regulation of given matters in the Act contained in the Basic Law.

The case has not yet been settled by the Constitutional Court, but the argument put forward which, if accepted by the Constitutional Tribunal, would mean that the power of national courts would be limited, must be rejected.

In this context, it is necessary to recall certain basic findings, since the essence of the question referred for a preliminary ruling has been repeatedly explained in the case-law of the CJEU. In particular, in its judgment of 6 March 2018 in Case C-284/16 *Achmea*,[70] the Court of Justice made clear that a judicial system aimed at ensuring consistency and uniformity in the interpretation of EU law was established by the Treaties in order to ensure that the specific features and autonomy of the Union's law order were preserved. This system aims at ensuring consistency and uniformity in the interpretation of Union law.[71] The Court of Justice of the EU in the *Achmea* judgment stressed that

> the key element of the judicial system thus constituted is the preliminary ruling procedure provided for in Article 267 TFEU, which, by establishing a dialogue between the different courts, in particular between the Court and the courts of the Member States, is intended to ensure a uniform interpretation of Union law, thus making it possible to ensure its consistency, full effectiveness and autonomy and, lastly, the specific nature of the law laid down in the Treaties.[72]

The Polish General Prosecutor in his proposal mentioned above also completely ignored this argument, which relates to the link between the independence of national courts and the effectiveness of EU law.[73] National courts, when applying judicial procedures, are bound by the principles of equivalence and effectiveness in cases where there is an element of EU law.[74] Finally, the General Prosecutor's request enters into the competence of the Court of Justice, which itself assesses in each case the admissibility of a question referred for a preliminary ruling.

70 Judgment of 6 March 2018 in Case C-284/16 Slovakia v. Achmea BV, ECLI:EU:C:2018:158.

71 See n 7, paragraph 171.

72 See n 7, paragraph 176 and the case-law cited therein.

73 This was also made clear by the Court of Justice of the EU in its judgments in Case C-64/16 *Associação Sindical dos Juízes Portugueses* EU:C:2018:117, Case C-284/16 *Achmea* (ECLI:EU:C:2018:158) or Case C-216/18 LM (ECLI:EU:C:2018:586).

74 See also Joined Cases C-392/04 and C-422/04 *Arcor*, EU:C:2006:586.

It may also be added that pursuant to Article 53(2) of the Rules of Procedure of the Court of Justice of the European Union,[75] where it is clear that the Court has no jurisdiction to hear and determine a case or where a request or an application is manifestly inadmissible, the Court may, after hearing the Advocate General, at any time decide to give a decision by reasoned order without taking further steps in the proceedings. This example shows that the Prosecutor General in Poland, as well as a team of politicians and government officials, completely do not understand the position of a Member State, as well as the relationship between the law of a Member State and EU law. They also forget that it is the Member States themselves that shaped this system and are now obliged to implement the Treaty that they have concluded – in accordance with their own constitutional provisions.

Of course, the questions referred for a preliminary ruling must meet the formal requirements laid down in Article 94 of the Rules of Procedure of the CJEU. The national court cannot expect that the CJEU will answer every question formulated outside of the scope of the Treaty. Therefore, it is not surprising that the CJEU sometimes refuses to reply, indicating the lack of its own competence. In the Opinion of the Advocate General in Cases C-558/18 and C-563/18 of 24 September 2019,[76] the inadmissibility of the Polish courts' questions in the cases in question follows from the fact that, pursuant to Article 267 TFEU, the CJEU may not issue advisory opinions on general or hypothetical questions and that the referring decisions or the case file do not contain sufficient explanations as to the relationship between the Polish provisions at issue and the relevant provisions of Union law. In this case, the judgment of the Court of Justice is not yet known, but there is no doubt that the answer to the questions referred for a preliminary ruling in joined cases C-558/18 and C-563/18 will require the development of the existing case-law of the CJEU on the admissibility of questions for a preliminary ruling, and the scope of application of EU law in the aspect of the guarantee of judicial independence in the light of Article 19(1) TEU. The CJEU must, however, act within its own legal limits.[77]

Regardless of the final outcome of the above-mentioned cases, it should be remembered that national courts are the guarantor of the proper functioning of the supranational system of EU law and constitute an important link in the cooperation with the CJ in the preliminary ruling procedure. This situation was accepted by the Member States during the accession process or the process of ratification of the Treaties. Analysis of the mechanisms associated with proceedings before the CJEU, which are clearly based on the Treaty rules, undoubtedly leads to the conclusion that the Rule of Law as a value under Article 2 TEU is also

75 Consolidated version of the Rules of Procedure of the Court of Justice of 25 September 2012 [2012] OJ L265, as amended on 18 June 2013 ([2013] OJ L173/65), on 19 July 2016 ([2016] OJ L217/69) and on 9 April 2019 ([2019] OJ L111/73).

76 Opinion of AG Tanchev, EU:C:2019:775.

77 See also Majkowska-Szulc n 41, 178–186.

protected by judicial mechanisms that allow for the effectiveness of EU law in the legal systems of the Member States and protect the rights of individuals derived from EU law. The protection of the Rule of Law by national courts must take place in a way that is appropriate to their functioning, i.e., by protecting parties to proceedings in cases involving elements of the Rule of Law. EU law gives national courts the possibility to enforce EU law in their internal legal order, while other authorities in a Member State have no right to intervene in the jurisprudence of judicial authorities, guaranteeing their independence.

9.6. Conclusion

The question asked in the title of the chapter must be answered in the affirmative: yes, the Member States are still masters of the Treaties. They are the ones who negotiate the content of the Treaties, including the amending Treaties, the Treaty of Amsterdam, and the Treaty of Lisbon, which gave Article 7 of the TEU its current form. These are the Member States that gave the Court of Justice of the EU jurisdiction to rule on matters relating to the Rule of Law as well. These are the Member States that conduct the political dialogue within the EU Council. Finally, these are the Member States that should adopt the regulation that could link access to EU funds to respect for the Rule of Law.[78] All these procedures for the protection of the Rule of Law fully show the role that Member States play in the European Union. All these procedures are of a legal nature and are based on legal premises – from the Treaties and constitutional provisions of the Member States. Also, the Article 7 TEU procedure, which ends with a political decision by the Member States, is only initiated if it is certain that the state will not fulfil its legal obligations. This EU legal system was shaped by the Member States themselves, which, based on their sovereign decision, created or joined the European Union. Any decision by state authorities that leads to a limitation on the application of EU law, including above all violating the fundamental values of the EU (Rule of Law), must be understood as a lack of will to continue cooperation in this form, with all the consequences of such a decision.

It became clear that strengthening the Rule of Law – and in particular judicial independence – has been on the EU agenda for several years. Obviously, with the new Commission of the Van der Leyen, it is still a high priority. The situation in Poland and Hungary has confirmed that the measures provided in the Treaties are not sufficient to effectively counteract certain risks or infringements of the Rule of Law that may occur in the Member States. If the judicial protection

78 Commission, Proposal for a regulation of the European Parliament and of the Council on the protection of the Union's budget in case of generalised deficiencies in regard to the Rule of Law in the Member States, COM (2018) 324 final. The proposed Regulation allows activation of a system to block access to EU funds in order to protect the Union's financial interests from the risk of financial loss in the event of detection of generalised deficiencies with regard to the Rule of Law.

mechanisms cannot reverse the negative trends that may jeopardise the essence of European integration, then it will be necessary to continue the proceedings within the framework of the political mechanisms. There is no doubt that the refusal to respect the Rule of Law, the refusal to comply with possible judgments of the Court of Justice, the attempt to question the legitimacy of the EU institutions and their power to take action against states that do not comply with the agreed rules, must be seen as calling into question the country's participation in the process of European integration.

Enabling the protection of elements of the Rule of Law through judicial mechanisms means that the value of the Rule of Law is protected in a way that is appropriate to the EU's supranational legal system. In addition, there are still present political evaluation mechanisms, although there is a lack of significant activity by the EU Member States, both in terms of the possibility to act on the basis of Article 259 TFEU and in terms of initiatives within the EU Council leading to the creation of a mutual evaluation mechanism.

Some authors claim that, at the moment, we may even witness a constitutional moment that will have a fundamental impact on the future development of constitutional order, with no formal changes of the Treaties.[79] Only now it will turn out whether the Rule of Law as a principle defined in Article 2 TEU in the form in which this concept has been understood so far in the jurisprudence of the CJEU and international documents will be accepted as a current part of the EU legal order, or whether the states – Poland, Hungary, or others – will be able to introduce changes in the understanding of this principle and thus change the EU law in the form in which we know it so far. Homogeneity of values is a condition for the legitimacy of the EU's cohesion and effectiveness.[80] Therefore, on the one hand, the Member States, as 'masters of Treaties', have an influence on the competences of the EU and its scope of action, but on the other hand, as – again – 'masters of Treaties', they must also collectively uphold the values that build the European Union. It is, therefore, necessary for the Commission or the Court of Justice, but also perhaps the Council or the European Council, to draw a 'red line', which, if crossed by some Member States, would mean that cooperation within a transnational European legal area would no longer be possible.[81]

A systemic breach of the Rule of Law may undermine the effectiveness of Union law in the internal legal orders of the Member States. It forms the basis for determining the normative meaning of Article 2 TEU. The Rule of Law clause should have a protective function, aimed at achieving a unifying effect

79 See Taborowski, n 2, 23, also A von Bogdandy and others, 'Guest Editorial: A potential constitutional moment for the European rule of law – The importance of red lines', 55 *CMLRev* (2018) 983.

80 K Lenaerts, 'Die Werte der Europäischen Union in der Rechtsprechung des Gerichtshofs der Europäischen Union: Eine Annäherung', 44 *Europäische Grundrechte Zeitschrift* (2017) 640.

81 See n 76, 983.

of the European Union and guaranteeing the stability of the EU values and legal system. From the perspective of the EU order, it should be important that in the event of a conflict of interests protected by a national identity clause and the Rule of Law, the Rule of Law should take precedence in this respect, given the objectives of the EU and the values attached to membership of the organisation.

Bibliography

Jan Barcz, 'Unia Europejska wobec niepraworządnego państwa', 1 *Państwo i Prawo* (2019), p. 3–23.

Armin von Bogdandy, Piotr Bogdanowicz, Iris Canor, Maciej Taborowski and Matthias Schmidt, 'Guest Editorial: A potential constitutional moment for the European Rule of Law – The importance of red lines', 55 *CMLRev* (2018), pp. 1–14.

Piotr Bogdanowicz and Maciej Taborowski, 'Brak niezależności sądów krajowych jako uchybienie zobowiązaniu w rozumieniu art. 258 TFUE (cz. II)', 2 *Europejski Przegląd Sądowy* (2018), p. 15-24.

Sergio Carrera and Petra Bárd, 'The European Parliament vote on Article 7 TEU against the Hungarian government. Too late, too little, too political?' *CEPS Commentary* (2018), www.ceps.eu/wp-content/uploads/2018/09/EP%20vote%20on%20Article7_0.pdf (accessed 13 January 2020).

Mary Dobbs, 'Sovereignty, Article 4(2) TEU and the respect of national identities: Swinging the balance of power in favour of the member states?', 33(1) *Yearbook of European Law* (2014), p. 298–334.

Drinóczi, Tímea and Bien-Kacala, Agnieszka, 'Illiberal constitutionalism and the European Rule of Law,' Chapter 1 of this book, 3–41.

Geoffrey Garrett, R Daniel Kelemen, and Heiner Schulz, 'The European Court of Justice, national governments, and legal integration in the European Union', 52 *International Organization* (1998), p. 149–176.

Agnieszka Grzelak, 'Ramy prawne UE na rzecz umacniania praworządności. Uwagi na tle wniosku Komisji Europejskiej z 20 grudnia 2017 r.', 2 *Sprawy Międzynarodowe* (2018), p. 213–230.

R Daniel Kelemen and Laurent Pech, 'Why autocrats love constitutional identity and constitutional pluralism: Lessons from Hungary and Poland', 2 *Reconnect Working Paper* (2018).

Dimitry Kochenov, 'EU Enlargement Law: History and Recent Developments: Treaty–Custom Concubinage?', 9(6) *European Integration Online Papers* (2005).

Dimitry Kochenov, 'Busting the myths nuclear: A commentary on Article 7 TEU', 10 *EUI Working Papers* (2017).

Theodore Konstadinides, '*The Rule of Law in the European Union: The Internal Dimension* (Hart Publishing, Portland, OR/Oxford 2017).

Marzena Laskowska and Maciej Taborowski, 'Obowiązek wykładni przyjaznej prawu Unii Europejskiej – między otwartością na proces integracji a ochroną tożsamości konstytucyjnej', in Sawomir Dudzik and Nina Półtorak, eds, *Prawo Unii Europejskiej a prawo konstytucyjne państw członkowskich* (Wolters Kluwer 2013), p. 79–108.

Koen Lenaerts, 'Die Werte der Europäischen Union in der Rechtsprechung des Gerichtshofs der Europäischen Union: Eine Annäherung', 44 *Europäische Grundrechte Zeitschrift* (2017).

Oliver Mader, 'Enforcement of EU Values as a Political Endeavour: Constitutional Pluralism and Value Homogeneity in Times of Persistent Challenges to the Rule of Law', 11 *Hague Journal on the Rule of Law* (2019), p. 133–170.

Peter John Oliver and Justine Stefanelli, 'Strengthening the Rule of Law in the EU: The Council's Inaction', 54 *Journal of Common Market Studies* (2016), p. 1075–1084.

Laurent Pech, 'The Rule of Law as a Constitutional Principle of the European Union',4 *Jean Monnet Working Paper* (2009).

Jan Willem van Rossem, 'The Autonomy of EU Law: More is Less?', in Ramses Wessel and Steven Blockmans, eds, *Between autonomy and dependence: The EU legal order under the influence of international organisations* (Springer 2013), p. 13–46.

Wojciech Sadurski, 'Adding Bite to a Bark: The Story of Article 7, EU Enlargement, and Jörg Haider', 16 *The Columbia Journal of European Law* (2010).

Wojciech Sadurski, 'European Constitutional Identity', *EUI Working Papers* (2006), p. 33.

Wojciech Sadurski, *Poland's Constitutional Breakdown* (Oxford University Press 2019).

Stefanie Schmahl, 'Die Reaktionen auf den Einzug der Freiheitlichen Partei Österreichs in das österreichische Regierungskabiett. Eine europa- und vökerrechtliche Analyse', 5 *EuR* (2000), p. 819–835.

Maciej Taborowski, *Mechanizmy ochrony praworządności państw członkowskich w prawie Unii Europejskiej. Studium przebudzenia systemu ponadnarodowego* (Wolters Kluwer 2019).

Milada Vachudova and Aneta Spendzharova, 'The EU's Cooperation and Verification Mechanism: Fighting Corruption in Bulgaria and Romania After EU Accession', *European Policy Analysis* (SIEPS 2012), http://www.sieps.se/en/publications/2012/the-eus-cooperation-and-verification-mechanism-fighting-corruption-in-bulgaria-and-romania-after-eu-accession-20121epa/Sieps_2012_1epa?

Joseph Weiler, 'The transformation of Europe', 100 *Yale Law Journal* (1991), p. 2403–2483.

Bruno de Witte, 'The Lisbon Treaty and national constitutions: More or less Europeanisation?', in Carlos Closa, ed, *The Lisbon Treaty and National Constitutions: Europeanisation and Democratic Implications*, (2009) 3 ARENA Report (2009), (2009) 9 RECON Report, www.researchgate.net/publication/265242262_The_Lisbon_Treaty_and_National_Constitutions_Europeanisation_and_Democratic_Implications/link/5405dcb20cf23d9765a774fd/download (accessed 11 January 2020).

Bruno Witte de, 'European union law: How autonomous is the legal order?', 65 *Zeitschrift für öffentliches Recht* (2010), p. 141–155.

Part V

Illiberal legality vs. European Rule of Law

10 Illiberal legality

Tímea Drinóczi and Agnieszka Bień-Kacała

10.1. Introduction

By now, it is evident that both the Hungarian and the Polish Rule of Law concepts, since 2010 and 2015, have shown significant and visible unorthodoxy, which have affected its understanding as a value and a legal concept. The review of the value-level non-compliance with the European Rule of Law, the way the EU acquis have been complied with, and what difficulties have emerged during the years in the previous chapters substantiates the theory of illiberal legality. As opposed to the term of the European Rule of Law, we have proposed to call its Hungarian and Polish version illiberal legality, which is not only partially different from the European Rule of Law but, paradoxically, forms its perverted inversion and, as such, is similar to it. It has two twin sides, too, i.e., a European and a domestic one. Within the context of illiberal constitutionalism, this term can best express the partial hollowed-outness of the concept of the European Rule of Law, express how it features the Hungarian and Polish constitutional system, and contribute to our understanding of whether the European Rule of Law is still a common value in Europe.

In this chapter, against the background that has been explored in this book so far, we first conceptualise illiberal legality by overviewing its construction and connection to the European Rule of Law (Section 10.2). A normative account of its legal features and attributes as a value and value-origins in the Hungarian and Polish society follow in Sections 10.3 and 10.4. We conclude in the last section by listing the consequences of the existence of illiberal legality on the European project in general, and offer an assessment of the European Rule of Law as a universal value in particular.

10.2. Construction of illiberal legality and the European Rule of Law

Illiberal legality is a nationalistic and overpoliticised conceptualisation of the European Rule of Law, which, in the political narrative, is used to protect the sovereignty of the state that is under attack by external factors, such as the supra- and international (legal) community, or social and economic challenges. Politicisation of the term of the European Rule of Law detaches it from its legally binding nature and takes it out of context, which serves the purposes of illiberal populism. The detaching exercise from, and the nationalistic redesign of, the European Rule of Law is always opportunistic: depending on whether it is in the interest of the populist leader, the European Rule of Law is either respected or ignored to a certain extent.

The voters in both Hungary and Poland care little about the realisation, implementation, and especially the value-content of the Rule of Law, which is quite unfortunate. As the Venice Commission noted, '[t]he Rule of Law can only flourish in a country whose inhabitants feel collectively responsible for the implementation of the concept, making it an integral part of their own legal, political and social culture.'[1] Collective responsibility can hardly be nurtured when the Rule of Law is surrounded by nationalistic and political interpretations. It takes the concept out of context, especially when this narrative claims that the Rule of Law is a fluid, mainly political concept, itself being ill-fitted or inadequate for use as an objective measure in an official legal procedure (such as on Article 7 TEU). It disregards the co-existence of two considerations, and, thus, misguides the debate: even though legal procedures can politically be assessed, criticised, or even praised, they still stay at the realm of the law informed by legal approaches, guarantees, processes, and legal arguments. The official legal Rule of Law procedures reflect a legal design and content and are drawn on the need for cooperation, dialogue, mutual understanding, and comparison, and, like many other aspects of the law, are pervaded by political considerations. The err thus is there when legal arguments are rebutted based on exclusively political and populist arguments, and, at the same time, the legal context is simply disregarded.

This context is provided by the fact that Hungary and Poland are Member States of the EU, a community whose fundamental and commonly shared values, i.e., the Rule of Law, democracy, and human rights, among others, form parts of legal documents, such as the TEU and national constitutions. The enforcement of the legal provisions is the task of the legally established bodies of the national and supranational community. At the same time, all of the above, and the success of the enforcement activity can later be used for political assessments that are made by political bodies through a legal process which can and will be designed to make a political decision on the membership of the community. Membership of a community is always a political decision that, in a community that follows the principles of the Rule of Law, should be supported and guided by legal rules and processes. This decision may be based on an assessment of how a member observes common value when the trust in the member is tilted. In the EU, Member States are trusted to follow the shared values and commonly agreed principles and rules.[2]

1 Rule of Law Checklist [Adopted by the Venice Commission at its 106th Plenary Session (Venice, 11–12 March 2016)].

2 Opinion of the Court (Full Court) of 18 December 2014 In case 2/13; ECLI:EU:C:2014:2454, paragraph 168, Commission v Poland, C-619/18.

In the Member States, people trust their politicians and state institutions to follow the legally binding rules, including the national constitution, EU law, and international obligations. In the huge pool of political ideologies, people are free to choose; politicians and parties are free to pursue different political visions in so far as the end result fits the actual and current state of the European project. It seems, however, that in Hungary and Poland, the political atmosphere is different from the other Member States as the majority of the people still trust in illiberal and populist politicians, even if they have seen the results of their political and party activities.

The term 'illiberal legality' is, thus, offered to characterise the 'Rule of Law situation' in illiberal constitutionalism. Illiberal legality indicates the hollowed-out meaning of the European Rule of Law in Hungary and Poland. It does not respect the basic tenets of constitutionalism but, due to the membership in the EU (and other international organisations), it is legally – and politically – forced to recognise some constraint over its exercise of public power. Illiberal legality is the logical consequence and necessary component of a constitutional remodelling that is designed and performed by a populist or authoritarian leader who is leading the country into an authoritarian regime within the framework of the EU. Therefore, illiberal legality is the antithesis of the European Rule of Law, in terms of values, the role of a constitution, and the components of the European Rule of Law, which, as it is normatively claimed in Chapter 1,[3] represents a thick version of the Rule of Law. Illiberal legality retains formal legality, which is part of each thin concept of the Rule of Law, and extends to the application and enforcement of the enforceable EU law. This effect shall be viewed as a weak internal constraint on the domestic powers.

In Hungary and Poland, however, not only the Rule of Law but other ideals have been fading away as well: the individual liberty and responsibility based on which not only a person but a nation can emerge, and the respect for other people just because they are human beings, an attitude and worldview without which there are no human rights. The value-orientations of Hungarians and Poles in the second decade of the 21st century seem to be at odds with the values that can comfortably accommodate constitutionalism, constitutional democracy, and assist in the implementation of their components, including the European Rule of Law. It is a strange development if we consider how the transition took place both in Hungary and Poland at the beginning of the 1990s. Let us, however, explore it after discussing the legal features of illiberal legality.

3 See it in T Drinóczi and A Bień-Kacała, 'Illiberal constitutionalism and the European Rule of Law', Chapter 1 of this book, 13–20. For the implementation of the European Rule of Law' in Hungary, see T Drinóczi, 'The European Rule of Law and illiberal legality in illiberal constitutionalism: The case of Hungary', 16 MTA Law Working Papers (2019), https://jog.tk.mta.hu/uploads/files/2019_16_Drinoczi.pdf.

10.3. Legal features of illiberal legality

Illiberal legality emphasises the instrumental and opportunistic use of the law in both legislation and law-application and adjudication. It simply views and uses the law as a tool of political power (rule by law) to achieve its mission at any cost, without any understanding of the ideal that no one is above the law, i.e., the constitution-amending, legislative power, and constitutional review competences cannot be abused to the advantage of a selected group of people. Thus, it also can be argued that neither the equality (non-discrimination), the prevention of the abuse (misuse) of power, nor the other elements of the benchmark of the Checklist are realised in Hungary and Poland to a sufficient extent. Each segment of the Rule of Law is compromised, and the failure to adhere to the European Rule of Law requirements is systematic, politically induced and supported, and widespread in the legal systems. It does not mean, however, that the European Rule of Law as a legal norm is not observed, to a certain extent, along with the other Member States. It features the opportunistic approach of illiberal constitutionalism towards this concept. The practice of the implementation and everyday application of the EU law is, among others, appreciated as a constraint on domestic public power. Here, we just recall these findings from the end of Chapter 1 and remind how the European Rule of Law has been conceptualised in the same chapter (Figure 10.1).[4]

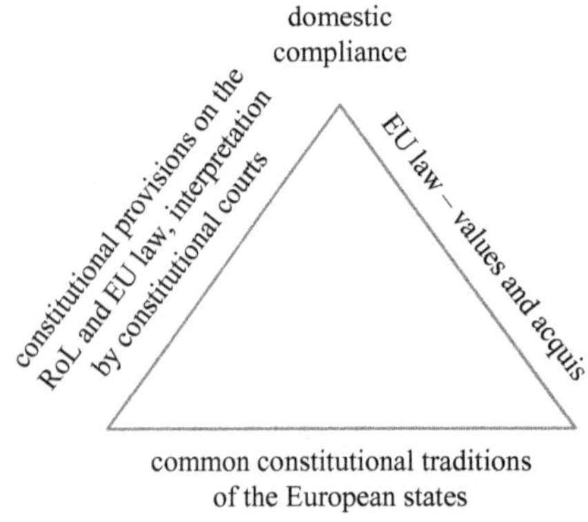

Figure 10.1 The European Rule of Law from Chapter 1. Source: Drinóczi and Bień-Kacała, n 3, 17, and Drinóczi, n 3, 12.

4 See e.g., T Drinóczi, F Gárdos-Orosz, and Z Pozsár-Szentmiklósy, 'Formal and informal constitutional amendments in Hungary', MTA Law Working Papers 2019/18, https://jog.tk.mta.hu/uploads/files/2019_18_Drinoczi_GardosOrosz_PozsarSzentmiklosy.pdf; https://hclu.hu/en/articles/hclus-analysis-of-the-seventh-amendment-of-the-fundamental-law. The wider context and implications are discussed in T Drinóczi, 'Constitutional politics in contemporary Hungary' 1 *Vienna Journal of International Constitutional Law* (2016) 63–98; T Drinóczi, 'Hungarian Constitutional Court: The Limits of EU Law in the Hungarian Legal System', 1 *Vienna Journal of International Constitutional Law* (2017) 139–151.

The Fundamental Law (FL) and the 1997 Polish Constitution are the fundamental laws of the land, which are at the top of the legal hierarchy. Laws are usually adopted by observing procedural rules and their content is in harmony with the constitution, regardless of how symbolic, ineffective, and defective it is in terms of the requirement of modern constitutionalism. The FL does not necessarily observe the principles of constitutionalism and, for instance, human rights. If the constitution cannot be considered as a modern constitution and the Constitutional Court (CC) is packed, the body of laws that are adopted will be in harmony to the FL but might not satisfy the requirements of modern constitutionalism. Thus, legality may be formally but not substantially observed; consequently, the law would reflect the illiberal content of the constitution. In Poland, the systemic illiberal changes have been adopted by parliamentary legislation through which some laws and the interpretations of the otherwise liberal constitution have received illiberal content. Besides the apparent unconstitutional legislation and governmental actions, legal opportunism is also present when the Polish Constitution is referred to as the basic and enforceable document of the land against the actions of the European Law. Therefore, the constitution cannot utterly serve as a fundamental norm of the legal systems of Hungary and Poland, nor can the law curb the arbitrary use of power. It simply assists those in power to achieve their political goals and guides the society according to some selected, overemphasised, and oversimplified ideologies and political ideas that are preferred by (and are pleasing to) the political decision-makers. In Hungary, the role of Christianity with all of its presumed implications in a society that is not famous for its religious nature, paternalism, and communitarianism can be mentioned, among others. The FL itself is used as a political instrument; this was evident during its adoption process, which made it a partisan constitution, and when, e.g., the Fourth and the Seventh Amendment with their contested content[4] were adopted. In Poland, the 1997 Constitution was disregarded, and then informally changed by parliamentary legislation on the Consitutional Tribunal (CT), judiciary, the Supreme Court, and the National Council for Judiciary with support of the CT.[5] After the 2019 election, as, again, PiS did not gain a constitutional majority, the 1997 Constitution with its new illiberal interpretation is still rhetorically used as a base for further changes. According to the speech that Marshal-Senior Antoni Macierewicz delivered during the first sitting of the *Sejm* (12 November 2019), the primary 'legal, social and moral basis of our state order' are the independence of Poland, the legal recognition of the relations between a man and a woman only, and the protection of life in its prenatal phase.[6] This means that, if it will not be formally changed, the Constitution could neither ultimately limit the political

5 A Bień-Kacała, Informal constitutional change: The case of Poland, 6 *Przegląd Prawa Konstytucyjnego* (2017) 199–218; A Bień-Kacała, Verfassungsdurchbrechung or informal constitutional change. Polish experience, *Przegląd Prawa Konstytucyjnego*, 2020 (forthcoming).

6 www.wprost.pl/kraj/10269223/macierewicz-wyglosil-przemowienie-marszalek-senior-mowil-o-katastrofie-smolenskiej-gender-i-konstytucji.html.

power nor adequately guarantee human rights, which makes it a partly symbolic and ineffective constitution. In the unlikely event that the Polish Constitution will formally be changed, it could receive an illiberal content that is similar to the Hungarian FL. At the same time, we expect that the Constitution might further be changed informally, and in such a way filled up with illiberal content.

Under the FL and the Polish Constitution, the legislative power is separated from the executive power; they are supposed to cooperate in the field of legislation – as they usually do in a parliamentary system. In practice, this is not the case; the parliament sometimes is just the necessary evil in the decision-making process, and parliamentary rules and positions are used to prevent expressing opposing views. The drafting and legislative process is characterised by formalism, disregard of substantive considerations of legisprudence[7] and the components of legislative quality.[8] It is also overwhelmed by political will. In Hungary, the generally accepted trends[9] in legislation, such as impact assessment, consultation, parliamentary deliberations, evidence-based legislation, and use of ICT and transparency have not been followed, and even the barely noteworthy achievements of the 20 years between 1990 and 2010 have significantly been corroded. The packed CC is unable and unwilling to conduct a semi-procedural review of legislation.[10] In Poland, a similar tendency can be noticed.[11]

There is a firm reliance on the judicial system, no matter how its independence has intentionally been curbed. What matters are as follows: first, the usual procedural and control mechanisms are in place, i.e., the constitutional and, in the majority of cases, statutory rules; this, from a merely formal and positivist perspective, and in the context of the thin concept of the Rule of Law, cannot be criticised. Second, justice can be provided by courts, but it is, quite contrary to the principle of equality before the law, limited due to its delayed nature, its incapacity to restore the previous and constitutional status quo, the personal reconvergence between a public office holder and political decision-makers, and, lately the refusal of the government to execute final court decisions.[12]

7 See lately e.g., H Xanthaki and U Karpen, eds, *Legislation and Legisprudence in Europe. A Comprehensive Guide for Scholars and Legislative Practitioners* (Oxford Hart 2017); M Bernatt and M Ziółkowski, 'Statutory Anti-Constitutionalism', 28 *Washington International Law Journal* (2019) 499–501.

8 T Drinóczi, Legislation in Hungary, in U Karpen and H Xanthaki, eds, *Legislation in Europe. A country by country guide* (Hart, forthcoming), https://ssrn.com/abstract=3447792.

9 See e.g., Drinóczi, 'Concept of quality in legislation – Revisited: Matter of perspective and a general overview' 3 *Statute Law Review* (2015) 225–227.

10 See e.g., I Bar-Siman-Tov, Semiprocedural Judicial Review, 3 Legisprudence (2012).

11 See the 2018 report of the Supreme Audit Office assessing a drafting process www.nik.gov.pl/plik/id,16190,vp,18712.pdf and one of the XII reports on legislation, the reports are cyclically delivered by NGO www.batory.org.pl/upload/files/Programy%20operacyjne/Forum%20Idei/XII_Komunikat_OFL.pdf.

12 The Debrecen Court of Appeals found that from 2004 to 2017, Roma students were taught separately at the Gyöngyöspata Primary School. This segregation violated their rights and they ordered the payment of 100 million forints (EUR 300,000) as compensation. The

The constitutional interpretation and application of the principle of the Rule of Law have also changed. In Hungary, the scope of application of the Rule of Law has been reduced; the thinnest possible concept is enforced, while its Western value-content is disregarded, due to the new FL. Its instrumental use and an authoritarian attitude of the majority of CC judges are both emerging phenomena. In Poland, the situation is similar: the scope of irregularities amount to a degradation of the Rule of Law, especially in the field of judicial independence, and impartiality and human rights. The distinctive difference is, as said, the content of the Constitution that has been informally changed towards an illiberal one.[13]

These considerations are collected and visualised in Table 10.1. In the context of this book and, especially, this chapter, when we assess the Rule of Law and the degree of its implementation in Hungary and Poland, we can refer to its thin version as described in Chapter 1 and illustrated in Table 10.1. That is, the thin version of the Rule of Law equals formal legality, i.e., a power exercised via law (rule by law), the state actions to be subjected to law, equality before the law, and certain characteristics of the law as defined by Raz and Fuller. It can form a basis for measurements and be an object of constitutional review and interpretation process. When it is about the thick concept of the Rule of Law, the formal legality is expanded, and certain substantive elements are added, mainly those that are constitutionally related to the term: they are mentioned in the same constitutional provision, appear in the jurisprudence of the constitutional courts, and ensure the enforcement of (any) constitutional rules.

Given the fact that the realisation of the European Rule of Law or, as a matter of fact, any of its concepts (similarly to that of democracy and human rights) is a matter of degree, we cannot confidently state that there is no Rule of Law in Hungary and Poland. What we can assertively claim, however, is that these states employ a different understanding of the Rule of Law when compared to the concept of the European Rule of Law. What we have in Hungary and Poland is something different: it does not equate with what it used to mean between 1990 and 2010 to 2015, but it has not yet been reduced to the mere rule by law (power exercised via the law) without considering other components that different authors and judicial actors attach to the concept. They employ illiberal legality.

The illiberal legality and its connection to the European Rule of Law are depicted in Figure 10.2.

Prime Minster said that the Government would not pay the compensation because it is unacceptable to 'give money for nothing', i.e., money earned without working for it. https://hungarytoday.hu/govt-finds-court-ruling-on-school-segregation-of-romas-unfortunate-refuses-to-pay-compensation/.

13 The report of Helsinki Foundation for Human Rights entitled 'Instead of the Rule of Law there is the Rule by Law', www.hfhr.pl/wp-content/uploads/2019/09/Rz%C4%85dy-prawem-FIN-web.pdf

Table 10.1 Overview on the versions of the Rule of Law in Hungary and Poland

Version	*Content*	*Hungary – realisation*	*Poland – realisation*
Thin/Formal	reasonably clear, reasonably stable, publicly available general rules and standards that are applied prospectively and not retrospectively (Raz) generality, publicity, stability, prosperity, clarity, consistency of the law, the possibility of compliance with the law, and congruence between rules announced and their actual administration (Fuller)	rather yes than no Note the retroactive taxation in the constitution in 2010	rather yes than no, stability is partly defective due to hasty changes of the judicial system and other legislation
	predictability (May)	rather yes than no the constitution can easily be changed	rather yes than no the constitution has been changed informally
Formal legality	power exercised via law (rule by law) the state actions to be subjected to the law	yes – yes but the constitution can easily be changed (abusive constitutionalism) – the content of the constitution can be challenged – CC is packed	yes – yes but the interpretation of the constitution is selective and arbitrary – unconstitutional interpretations and legal measures are declared constitutional – CT is packed
	equality before the law	challenged; constitutional/legal inequality	challenged; accountability depends sometimes on political agenda
	characteristics of the law	– rather yes than no – see above	– rather yes than no – see above

(*Continued*)

Table 10.1 (Continued) Overview on the versions of the Rule of Law in Hungary and Poland

Version	*Content*		*Hungary – realisation*	*Poland – realisation*
Rule of Law Checklist of the Venice Commission	Mixed in each element	constitutional supremacy, legtality, legal certainty	– constitution and the laws can easily be changed – plus see above	– constitution can be changed informally – laws can easily be changed – plus see above
		equality, non-discrimination	challenged	challenged
		prevention of abuse (misuse) power	challenged	challenged
		an independent judiciary	challenged	highly challenged
		access to justice	rather yes that no	rather yes that no

Source: authors

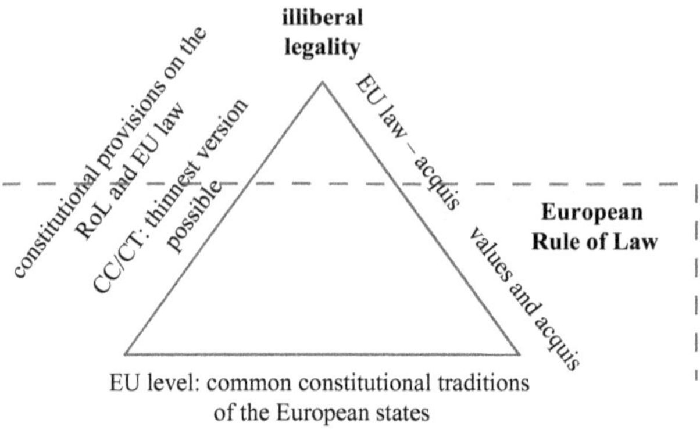

Figure 10.2 Illiberal legality and the European Rule of Law – Hungary and Poland. Source: Drinóczi, n 3, 26.

The extent of non-compliance with the benchmark of the Rule of Law by the political decision-makers, in terms of quality and quantity, goes far beyond the innocent claim that honest mistakes have been made. Neither political nor constitutional dialogue have managed to resolve differences in views between the Hungarian and Polish governments and political and judicial bodies of the supranational and international community: constitutional (adopting the FL and its major, most contested amendments) or legislative reforms (e.g., on the judiciary) have been completed in the majority of cases in a manner which did not consider the opinions (or did so *ex post facto*) of the Venice Commission, the Commission and Parliament of the EU, and many other actors, including NGOs and judicial bodies, such as the European Court of Human Rights and the Court of Justice of the European Union. The reason for the deafness may be found in different worldviews. As formulated by László Trócsányi, former Minister of Justice of Hungary: 'In Europe today, we witness the clash between individualism and a mind-set prioritising community interests and the public good.'[14] This position is also present in the constitutional courts of Hungary and Poland.[15]

The political decision-makers posit Hungary and Poland as defenders of 'community interests and the public good', as they interpret them, which include the vigorous defence of the nation-state and national identity against any 'foreign' concern. Each criticised step of the Government finds its justification in existing (but often deliberately misinterpreted and misused) political, philosophical,

14 L Trócsányi, 'New challenges facing democracy and the rule of law', 3 *Hungarian Review* (2017), http://hungarianreview.com/article/20171117_new_challenges_facing_democracy_and_the_rule_of_law.

15 25/2013 (X. 4) CC decision, concurring opinion of Béla Pokol. The CT judgement of 16 March 2017 on the Law on Assemblies suggests the subordination of the individual to the state, see I Wróblewska in this volume.

human rights, and legal considerations. When invoking these thoughts the European, Hungarian, and Polish political decision-makers, and occasionally judicial actors, talk at cross purposes, making it harder to resolve difficulties. When addressing these ideas in communication with the citizenry, they use a smoothly comprehensive, manipulative, and oversimplified language. The population does not have any 'vaccination' against this political and legal 'fake news', and, apparently, it does not need one.

As far as politicians are using similar political means to achieve the very same goal of building illiberal constitutionalism in Poland and Hungary, based on a strong and effective state governed by a populist leader who also governs a homogenous nation, differences stemming from current constitutional and political contexts do not matter. What seems to be more important here is the specific mind-set and value-orientation of the ordinary citizen, who remains an enthusiastic supporter of the Hungarian or Polish populist leaders, notwithstanding the controversial national politics and explicit xenophobia instigated towards fellow human beings.

10.4. Illiberal legality and values

This continuous support might have something to do with the fact that Polish and Hungarian voters show similar value-attitudes: a majoritarian understanding of democracy[16] and a strong desire for stability, which is the reason why they are willing to trade off liberal and democratic values; a tendency towards conservativism and authoritarianism; and the prioritisation of hierarchy as a value, as opposed to egalitarianism, intellectual and affective autonomy, and mastery.[17] Therefore, it is still the people who tolerate, accept, and even support the changes of populist politics. It seems that people want, or at least do not substantially oppose, the remodelling of constitutionalism in Hungary and Poland. The recent election results of autumn 2019 in Poland and Hungary[18] could bring

16 See the summary of the Value Research: J Eichhorn, et al., '*How European publics and Policy actors values an open society. Key insight across countries*' (Open Society European Policy Institute 2019), http://voicesonvalues.dpart.org/images/finalreports/OSI-019-18-Key-Insights_v5.pdf. The reports on Hungary (by Bulcsú Hunyadi, Csaba Molnár, Veszna Wessenauer), Poland (by Filip Pazderski), Italy, Germany, and France are available at http://voicesonvalues.dpart.org/. It is of interest that, Italians, who dealt with a populist governmental crisis in August 2019, share similar value-attitudes to Hungarians and Poles towards an open society. Additionally, Zygmunt Bauman opines that it is rather the pluralism of moral rules put the people into the feelings and fears of uncertainty and ambivalence. Thus, pluralism has brought chaos among moral values; the world full of almost non-limited freedom and overwhelming responsibility for peoples' own choices created the crisis of morality. Therefore, a strong need of stable, solid and firm values provided by authority arises. Z Bauman, *Etyka ponowoczesna* [The late modern ethics] (Warszawa 2012).

17 SH Schwartz and A Bardi, 'Influences of adaptation to communist rule on value-priorities in Eastern Europe', 2 *Political Pscychology* (1997) 398.

18 The PiS lost a majority in the *Senat*, and during the Hungarian local elections, opposition candidates won control in 11 of Hungary's 23 larger cities, including Budapest. B Novak,

a more healthy vertical division of power and a higher quality of legislation[19] to Hungarian and Polish illiberalism, which could recalibrate the degree of the Rule of Law compliance.

These election results showed that, first, the Hungarian opposition could organise itself (it had one common candidate against a Fidesz candidate), and that people appreciated this at the local level. Second, that Poles still support the illiberal turn of PiS but, at the same time, they do not fully accept any further reduction of pluralism.[20] Nevertheless, the foundations of the illiberal regime are still intact. The local level's autonomy is limited; Hungarian local governments and the Polish *Senat*, which cannot significantly influence legislative content and avert any informal (and usually unconstitutional) constitutional change, still need to work within the national, and thus illiberal, framework, which can easily be changed if needed.

However, this result also shows what most probably did not change: the value-attitude of the people. People can indeed gradually acclimate their values to changed circumstances, upgrade the importance of values that become attainable, and downgrade the importance of those whose pursuit is no longer adaptive.[21] The question is how long this acclimation takes and whether it can happen at all in society. It is intriguing especially in the eastern part of Europe because scholars can identify distinctive Western European values[22] when they compare them with the ones more commonly shared in Eastern Europe. These are as follows: low importance to mastery values; most importance to affective autonomy values and least importance to conservative values; more appreciation of initiative and achievement; more tolerance towards outgroups and post-material values, such as freedom and social responsibility.[23] This, and the results of scientific narrative psychology and other social-psychological empirical studies support our presumption: the emotional attitudes of the people and the community can be found behind the illiberal transformation, as well as the degree of tolerance for the disrespect of the Rule of Law. Regardless of the 20 or 25 years of liberal constitutionalism in Hungary and Poland, what we seem to have had (to possibly differing

'Setback for Orban as Opposition in Hungary Gains Ground in Elections', (14 October 2019) www.nytimes.com/2019/10/14/world/europe/hungary-elections-orban.html.

19 On the quality of legislation, see Drinóczi, n 10.

20 They do support other political groups that are consolidated on the left (SLD, Wiosna, Razem) and those on the far-right side (Konfederacja Wolność i Niepodległość) of the political palette. https://poledialogu.org.pl/wp-content/uploads/2019/09/Political-cynicism-Resume-in-English.pdf, 16.

21 Schwartz and Bardi, n 18, 394.

22 From a different perspective, see M Weber, *The Protestant Ethic and the Spirit of Capitalism* (Routledge 1930), W Wrzesiński, *Charakter narodowy Polaków. Z rozważań historyka* [National character of Poles. From the historian's reflections] (Uniwersytet Wrocławski 2004).

23 In Eastern Europe, mastery values are even less important; conservativism and hierarchy are more important. Schwartz and Bardi, n 18, 406. Similarly, see e.g., M Krygier,'The Challenge of Institutionalisation', 3 *European Constitutional Law Review* (2019) 557.

degrees) are as follows: lack of respect for others; compromised self-confidence; the feeling of being a victim, and all the attached sensations of inferiority; the need for a strong leader; prioritising values of conservativism and hierarchy; and reluctance regarding, or controversial attitudes towards, the values of liberal constitutional democracy or open society, such as intellectual autonomy, individual liberty, and responsibility. All of these identity-related phenomena, which have apparently already been internalised, eventually combine to form a national and constitutional identity. This type of group identity, at certain historical moments, seemed and still seems to be fertile soil for populist leaders who have an illiberal vision of society and state. Nevertheless, it does not offer the best conditions for developing the civic virtues necessary for upholding a substantive constitutional democracy.

Reasons, most probably, are rooted in the past. The third wave of democratisation in Poland and Hungary was based on the naïve belief that the Western European development of values could be implemented overnight by the use of institutional implants, disregarding the necessity of the long-lasting process of transformation and the still-evident existence of the communist or socialist past.[24] By using different approaches towards constitution-making, Poland and Hungary created new constitutional regimes,[25] which were based on the Rule of Law, democracy, and human rights.[26] The Western concept of the Rule of Law was needed for a new legal design after over 40 years of communism. It, however, had to go hand in hand with the newly established democracy, which, again, was formed based on Western experiences. In the emerging democracies of the region, the Rule of Law had to be viewed as a necessary safeguard from a descent into illiberalism – what happened in Russia and Romania.[27] In 1989, it was believed that Eastern Europe was able to implement a constitutional democracy embracing and featuring all of the Western values. After almost 30 years since the fall of communism, the opinion is shared that only an imitation and a longing for a (Western type of) 'normality' could be observed, instead of an

24 G Skąpska, 'Law and society in a natural laboratory: The case of Poland in the broader context of East-Central Europe', in M Kaase, V Sparschuh, and A Wenninger, ed, *Three social science disciplines in Central and Eastern Europe: handbook on economics, political science and sociology (1989–2001)* (Berlin 2002) 597.

25 Poland adopted the so-called Small (Interim) Constitution in 1992 and started to work on the new one that was finally approved in 1997. Hungary, mainly due to the features of the transition, decided not to adopt a new constitution but almost entirely changed the socialist one during a series of constitutional amendments.

26 Both states had a catalogue of fundamental rights in their respective constitutions. They joined the Council of Europe – Hungary in 1990, Poland in 1991 – and ratified the European Convention of Human Rights. Hungary joined in 1992, and the ECHR entered into force in Hungary in 1993. Poland joined in 1993, and the ECHR entered into force in 1993.

27 For more on this, see T Humphrey, 'Democracy and the rule of law: Founding liberal democracy in post-Communist Europe', 2 *Colum J. E Eur. L* 94 (2008) 116.

actual implementation.[28] During the last 30 years, the Western 'normality' has, however, changed, which has been left unnoticed in Eastern Europe. This region has stuck somehow at the beginning of the transition period in the 1990s with the demand for a strong 'national normality',[29] which is now translated into constitutional identity, mainly in Hungary, and the demand for independence and sovereignty, most dominantly in Poland.

Both Hungarians and Poles seem to create a specific understanding of values, including the Rule of law – despite similarities and differences in their constitutional history, historical particularities, and emotional trajectory. Studies from various fields of social sciences[30] support the assertion that the Hungarian historical trajectory – collective victimhood caused primarily by the Trianon peace treaty in 1918,[31] citizens having been abandoned in their disappointment by all regimes throughout Hungarian history[32] – is not a favourable ground to build

28 I Krastev and S Holmes, 'Explaining Eastern Europe: Imitation and Its Discontents', 3 *Journal of Democracy* (2018) 118–122.

29 See more in P Lendvai, *The Hungarians: A Thousand Years of Victory in Defeat* (Princeton University Press 2004); A Zamoyski, *The Polish Way: A Thousand-Year History of the Poles and Their Culture* (Hippocrene Books 2012); A Bień-Kacała, A Tarnowska and W Włoch, 'Nation – delegation – constitution: Reconsidering role of religion in Polish identity development', 1 *Bratislava Law Review* (2019) 6–25; A Bień-Kacała, A Tarnowska and W Włoch, 'The nation, delegation, and constitutional change in Poland', 4 *Hungarian Journal of Legal Studies* (2018) 355–377; T Drinóczi and A Bień-Kacała, 'Extra-legal particularities and illiberal constitutionalism : the case of Hungary and Poland', 4 *Hungarian Journal of Legal Studies* (2018) 338–354.

30 See e.g., narrative psychological studies and findings of historians, societal psychologists, sociologists, and philosophers. É Fülöp, et al., Emotional Elaboration of Collective Traumas in Historical Narratives (2014) http://real.mtak.hu/20201/3/emotional_elaboration_of_collective_traumas.pdf; J László, 'Narratív pszichológia', 28 *Pszichológia* (2008), http://real.mtak.hu/2385/1/49413_ZJ1.pdf; M Murray, 'Narrative psychology and narrative analysis', in PM Camic, et al., eds, *Qualitative Research in Psychology: Expanding Perspectives in Methodology and Design* (2003), www.researchgate.net/publication/274889276_Chapter_6_Narrative_psychology_and_narrative_analysis 95; A Tarnowska, 'The Sovereignty Issue in the Public Discussion in the Era of the Polish 3rd May Constitution (1788–1792)', in U Müßig, ed, *Reconsidering Constitutional Formation I National Sovereignty* (Springer Open 2016) 215; W Wrzesiński, n 23; A Zajenkowska, *Polska na kozetce. Siła obywatelskiej refleksyjności* [Poland on the couch. The power of civic reflexivity] (Sopot 2016); D Doliński and T Grzyb, *Posłuszni do bólu. O uległości wobec autorytetu w 50 lat po eksperymencie Milgrama*, [Painfully obedient. On the submission to authority 50 years after Milgram's experiment] (Sopot 2017); A Leszczyński, *No dno po prostu jest Polska. Dlaczego Polacy tak bardzo nie lubią swojego kraju i innych Polaków* [Poland hit the rock bottom. Why Poles do not like their country and other Poles] (Warszawa 2017); P Augustyniak, *Homo Polacus. Eseje o polskiej duszy* [Homo Polacus. Essays about 'the Polish soul'] (Znak 2015).

31 The Treaty of Trianon was the peace agreement of 1920 to formally end World War I between most of the Allies of World War I and the Kingdom of Hungary, which was at that time, a 'monarchy without a monarch.' Around two-thirds of the territory of the country was allocated to neighbouring countries, along with its population. One-third of Hungarians were left outside of post-Trianon Hungary.

32 Gy Spiró, *Két középkelet-európai mentalitás az államiság szempontjából*, 2000 Irodalmi és Társadalmi havi lap 6 (2007); Fülöp et al., n 31, 7, 19.

an emotionally stable identity upon.[33] Poles are characterised as a traumatised nation because of the loss of statehood and independence. These particularities were strengthened during the Soviet era in both states. Schwartz and Bardi's findings from 1997 on the value-priorities in the region after the communist rule seem to be supported by the value research results published in 2019. They concluded that the value-profile common in Eastern European countries, which lacks the commitment to egalitarianism and the values autonomy, is ill-suited for the development of democracy.[34]

Recent research on collective narcissism has shown that a connection can be identified between this kind of value-orientation (nationalism, authoritarianism, hierarchy, social dominance orientation, homogeneity) and populism. These values and attitudes overlap with collective narcissism.[35] Collective narcissism is defined as

> a belief that one's own group (the ingroup) is exceptional and entitled to privileged treatment, but others do not sufficiently recognize it. Thus, central to collective narcissism is resentment that the ingroup's exceptionality is not sufficiently externally appreciated.[36]

As such, collective narcissism is a core source of political choices that undermine liberal democracy. In particular, it is linked to intergroup hostility and aggression, voting behaviour, political conservatism, and conspiratorial thinking. It is related to the biased perception of intergroup reality, in which events are selectively seen and remembered in the service of the ingroup's image, and linked to a divisive social identity.[37] It is also linked to collective victimhood. As a result, the assumed victimised past that has remained unresolved, and the intense feeling of exceptionality shared by Poles and Hungarians create an environment that is friendly towards illiberal transformation and the building of a particular understanding of the Rule of Law – illiberal legality.

10.5. Consequences of illiberal legality on the European project

As it has been said repeatedly, the ambition of this book was to answer a simple question: given the severe Rule of Law deterioration in Hungary and Poland, can the Rule of Law still be viewed as a common or universal European value? Based

33 Fülöp, et al., n 31, 11
34 Schwartz and Bardi, n 18, 407–408. Similarly, Skąpska, n 25, 597.
35 A Golec de Zavala, K Dyduch-Hazar, and D Lantos, 'Collective Narcissism: Political Consequences of Investing Self-Worth in the Ingroup's Image', 40 *Advances in Political Psychology* (2019) 46; A Cichocka and A Cislak, Nationalism as collective narcissism, 34 *ScienceDirect Current Opinion in Behavioral Sciences* (2020) 69–74.
36 A Golec de Zavala, K Dyduch-Hazar, and D Lantos, n 36, 37–38.
37 Ibid., 39, 42, 44.

on the chapters of this book, and after briefly summarising the main observations on illiberal legality and its connection to illiberal constitutionalism and the European Rule of Law, we will conclude with two points.

10.5.1. Illiberal legality – Context

For us, the value-judgment on the Rule of Law assessment in a country does not only depend on the existence of the principles of the Rule of Law, but also on the extent to which they are implemented. The manifestation of the Rule of Law is a matter of degree; neither of its elements can present an absolute value, the lack of which results in the complete elimination or non-existence of the Rule of Law. Given this, and against the background explored in the book, this chapter confirms that the Rule of Law does not have the same meaning in the ingroup, i.e., the legal and cultural community we call the EU,[38] and the states examined. Illiberal constitutionalism features, amongst other things, illiberal legality. Illiberal legality emphasises the instrumental and opportunistic use of domestic law in both the legislation and the application of the law. Another characteristic is the weak constraint that the European Rule of Law poses on the domestic public power because it requires the implementation and application of the EU law, i.e., both the values and the acquis. It entails also a special and distinct set of societal and value-oriented bedrocks, which are different from those of the (more advanced) Western societies that are still able to maintain their substantive constitutional democracy regardless of the challenges they face, such as the rise of populism.

10.5.2. Illiberal legality – Effects

The Rule of Law could be viewed as a (partially) shared European value. We do not emphasise the 'partially' in the brackets when we consider the Rule of Law in its thin version. The thin understanding of the Rule of Law requires only a few efforts: it is to be shown that there is a normative concern for order. We do emphases the 'partially' in the brackets, however, when we locate the Rule of Law in the European context, in which both Hungary and Poland are located. In this sense, we still maintain the observation on the European Rule of Law and the Hungarian and Polish illiberal legality – which entails that the thicker components of the European Rule of Law are heavily challenged. We have reached a similar conclusion when we studied the Rule of Law from the perspective of axiology and culture.

It is a fact that the EU cannot resolve its legal differences with Hungary and Poland. There are two alternative implications of a situation in which a legal and cultural community is not able to maintain and enforce its legal regime. It

38 In sociology and social psychology, an ingroup, is a social group to which a person psychologically identifies as being a member.

is either the fact that the shared nature of its legal values, political ideals, and principles can be justifiably questioned, or that the country whose actions raise doubts about the universality of this principle has already ceased to be a part of that community. In this latter case, the Rule of Law cannot have the same meaning in the ingroup, i.e., legal and cultural community mentioned above and in the state examined. That is why the Rule of Law, as it is implemented in Hungary and Poland, is suggested to be called illiberal legality.

Therefore, supported by other considerations as well,[39] it is also concluded that legal mechanisms from the 'outside group' cannot be effective as illiberalism, and that all of its implications are also the symptoms of that society, which not only does not revolt but actually supports the regime and applauds its actions.

In the most pessimistic assessment of the above and the context of the European Rule of Law as a value and political ideal, Hungary and Poland seem to be already outside of the 'group'. The only withdrawal force is the weak constraint power of the remnants of the European Rule of Law on the Hungarian and Polish public power. The question is when the European legal community, i.e., the EU and Hungary and Poland, will realise it, and what measures they will take. Wielders of the political power of Hungary and Poland cannot be disciplined by the usual 'ingroup' measures (i.e., European), because these are the resolution methods of another 'reality.' The sooner the European political community and leaders realise this,[40] the better they can promote the universality of the principle of the Rule of Law within the European Union, as a European Rule of Law, and productively advance the European project further.

An optimistic version would propose or refer an enforcement mechanism through which the EU could successfully enforce its values. This chapter and volume have not aimed at any of this, however, and it shall be noted that the EU is still in the process of finding an adequate mechanism. Regrettably, prevention seems to be more important than dealing with the renegade states – which, on the other hand, is understandable as the actors do not speak the same language. This approach does not help to resolve the differences at all but, instead, either brings us back to the most pessimistic scenario or demands a more realistic one.

A more realistically appealing assessment would project a formation of a longer-term game between the EU and Hungary and Poland, until the point when the illiberal constitutionalism is overturned, or when the EU membership of Hungary and Poland will politically, economically, and emotionally be undesirable for both the other Member States and the EU herself. The synergy of this three-factor is, however, improbable to occur at the same time, and the overturning of the regimes does not seem feasible. This democratic component of illiberal constitutionalism, however, still needs to be further researched.

39 Drinóczi and Bień-Kacała, n 30.

40 See also the warning of Renata Uitz in R Uitz, 'The Perils of Defending the Rule of Law Through Dialogue', 1 *European Constitutional Law Review* (2019) 15.

To be absolutely clear: there are two alternative implications of a situation in which a legal and cultural community is not able to maintain and enforce its legal regime; either the universality of its legal values and principles can justifiably be questioned, even if there is no common understanding concerning the definition of the Rule of Law; or the country whose actions challenge the universality of a principle and value has already ceased to be the part of that community. It is an 'either/or' issue; there should be no in-between. If there is, we call it illiberal constitutionalism and, in the field of the Rule of Law, illiberal legality.

Bibliography

Piotr Augustyniak, *Homo Polacus. Eseje o polskiej duszy* [Homo Polacus. Essays about 'the Polish soul'] (Znak 2015).

Ittai Bar-Siman-Tov, 'Semiprocedural judicial review', 3 *Legisprudence* (2012) 271–300.

Zygmunt Bauman, *Etyka ponowoczesna* [The late modern ethics] (Wydawnictwo Aletheia: Warszawa 2012).

Maciej Bernatt and Michał Ziółkowski, 'Statutory anti-constitutionalism', 28 *Washington International Law Journal* (2019) 487–526.

Agnieszka Bień-Kacała, Anna Tarnowska, and Wojciech Włoch, 'Nation – delegation – constitution: Reconsidering role of religion in Polish identity development', 1 *Bratislava Law Review* (2019) 6–25.

Agnieszka Bień-Kacała, Anna Tarnowska, and Wojciech Włoch, 'The nation, delegation, and constitutional change in Poland', 4 *Hungarian Journal of Legal Studies* (2018) 355–377.

Agnieszka Bień-Kacała, 'Informal constitutional change: The case of Poland', 6 *Przegląd Prawa Konstytucyjnego* (2017) 199–218.

Agnieszka Bień-Kacała, 'Verfassungsdurchbrechung or informal constitutional change. Polish experience', 4 *Przegląd Prawa Konstytucyjnego* (2020) (forthcoming).

Aleksandra Cichocka and Aleksandra Cislak, 'Nationalism as collective narcissism', 34 *ScienceDirect Current Opinion in Behavioral Sciences* (2020).

Dariusz Doliński and Tomasz Grzyb, *Posłuszni do bólu. O uległości wobec autorytetu w 50 lat po eksperymencie Milgrama* [Painfully obedient. On the submission to authority 50 years after Milgram's experiment] (Smak Słowa: Sopot 2017).

Tímea Drinóczi, 'Concept of quality in legislation – Revisited: Matter of perspective and a general overview', 3 *Statute Law Review* (2015) 211–227.

Tímea Drinóczi, 'Constitutional politics in contemporary Hungary', 1 *Vienna Journal of International Constitutional Law* (2016) 63–98.

Tímea Drinóczi, 'Hungarian Constitutional Court: The limits of EU Law in the Hungarian legal system', 1 *Vienna Journal of International Constitutional Law* (2017) 139–151.

Tímea Drinóczi, 'Legislation in Hungary', in U Karpen and H Xanthaki, eds, *Legislation in Europe. A country by country guide* (Bloomsburry 2020), https://ssrn.com/abstract=3447792.

Tímea Drinóczi, 'The European Rule of Law and illiberal legality in illiberal constitutionalism: The case of Hungary', *16 MTA Law Working Papers* (2019), https://jog.tk.mta.hu/uploads/files/2019_16_Drinoczi.pdf.

Tímea Drinóczi and Agnieszka Bień-Kacała, 'Extra-legal particularities and illiberal constitutionalism: The case of Hungary and Poland', 4 *Hungarian Journal of Legal Studies* (2018) 338–354.
Tímea Drinóczi and Agnieszka Bień-Kacała, 'Illiberal constitutionalism and the European Rule of Law', see Chapter 1 of this book.
Tímea Drinóczi, Fruzsina Gárdos-Orosz, and Zoltán Pozsár-Szentmiklósy, 'Formal and informal constitutional amendments in Hungary', *MTA Law Working Papers* 2019/18, https://jog.tk.mta.hu/uploads/files/2019_18_Drinoczi_GardosOrosz_PozsarSzentmiklosy.pdf.
HCLU's analysis of the seventh amendment of the Fundamental Law, 2018. August 27. https://hclu.hu/en/articles/hclus-analysis-of-the-seventh amendment-of-the-fundamental-law (accessed December 2018).
Jan Eichhorn, Victoria Kupsch, Luuk Molthof, Magali Mohr, *'How European publics and Policy actors values an open society. Key insight across countries'* (Open Society European Policy Institute 2019).
Éva Fülöp, István Csertő, Barbara Ilg, Zsolt Szabó, Ben Slugoski and János László, 'Emotional Elaboration of Collective Traumas in Historical Narratives', (2014) http://real.mtak.hu/20201/3/emotional_elaboration_of_collective_traumas.pdf.
Agnieszka Golec de Zavala, Karolina Dyduch-Hazar, and Dorottya Lantos, 'Collective narcissism: Political Consequences of Investing Self-Worth in the Ingroup's Image', 40 *Advances in Political Psychology* (2019).
Thomas Humphrey, 'Democracy and the rule of law: Founding liberal democracy in post-Communist Europe', 2 *Columbia Journal of East European Law* 94 (2008) 94–127.
Ivan Krastev and Stephen Holmes, 'Explaining Eastern Europe: Imitation and its Discontents', 3 *Journal of Democracy* (2018) 118–122.
Martin Krygier, 'The Challenge of Institutionalisation', 3 *European Constitutional Law Review* (2019) 544–573.
János László, 'Narratív pszichológia', 28 *Pszichológia* (2008), http://real.mtak.hu/2385/1/49413_ZJ1.pdf.
Paul Lendvai, *The Hungarians: A thousand years of victory in defeat* (Princeton University Press 2004).
Adam Leszczyński, *No dno po prostu jest Polska. Dlaczego Polacy tak bardzo nie lubią swojego kraju i innych Polaków* [Poland hit the rock bottom. Why Poles do not like their country and other Poles] (W.A.B: Warszawa 2017).
Michael Murray, 'Narrative psychology and narrative analysis', in Paul Camic, et al., eds, *Qualitative research in psychology: Expanding perspectives in methodology and design* (2003), American Psychological Association, www.researchgate.net/publication/274889276_Chapter_6_Narrative_psychology_and_narrative_analysis.
Benjamin Novak, 'Setback for orban as opposition in Hungary gains ground in elections', (14 October 2019), *New York Times*, www.nytimes.com/2019/10/14/world/europe/hungary-elections-orban.html.
Shalom H Schwartz and Anat Bardi, 'Influences of adaptation to communist rule on value priorities in Eastern Europe', 2 *Political Pscychology* (1997) 385–410.
Grażyna Skąpska, 'Law and society in a natural laboratory: The case of Poland in the broader context of East-Central Europe', in Max Kaase, Vera Sparschuh, and Agnieszka Wenninger, eds, *Three social science disciplines in Central and Eastern Europe: Handbook on economics, political science and sociology (1989–2001)* (Berlin 2002) 588–603.

György Spiró, *Két középkelet-európai mentalitás az államiság szempontjából, 2000 Irodalmi és Társadalmi havi lap* 6 (2007).

Anna Tarnowska, 'The Sovereignty Issue in the Public Discussion in the Era of the Polish 3rd May Constitution (1788–1792)', in Ulrike Müßig, ed, *Reconsidering constitutional formation I national sovereignty* (Springer Open 2016) 215–264.

László Trócsányi, 'New challenges facing democracy and the rule of law', 3 *Hungarian Review* (2017).

Renáta Uitz, 'The Perils of Defending the Rule of Law Through Dialogue', 1 *European Constitutional Law Review* (2019) 1–16.

Max Weber, *The protestant ethic and the spirit of capitalism* (Routledge 1930).

Wojciech Wrzesiński, *Charakter narodowy Polaków. Z rozważań historyka* [National character of Poles. From the historian's reflections] (Uniwersytet Wrocławski 2004).

Helen Xanthaki and Karpen Ulrich, eds, *Legislation and Legisprudence in Europe. A Comprehensive Guide for Scholars and Legislative Practitioners* (Oxford: Hart 2017).

Anna Zajenkowska, *Polska na kozetce. Siła obywatelskiej refleksyjności* [Poland on the couch. The power of civic reflexivity] (Smak Słowa: Sopot 2016).

Adam Zamoyski, *The Polish Way: A Thousand-Year History of the Poles and Their Culture* (Hippocrene Books 2012).

Index

Advocate General 186, 188–189, 199, 212
Amendment: Fourth 108, 109, 111, 114–115, 128–129, 161–164, 223; Seventh 109, 113, 114, 125, 161, 223
anti-principle of improper law-making 142–143
arbitrary 3, 8–9, 19, 81, 87, 126, 141, 142, 154, 160, 177, 223, **226**
Aristotle 77–81, 83, 86–87, 94–97
Article 2 TEU 18, 20, 117, 155, 162, 165–166, 170, 172, 174, 179, 181, 184, 194–201, 203, 205, 206, 208, 210, 212, 214
Article 4 TEU 197–199
Article 7 procedure 26, 33, 36, 117, 144, 153, 158, 162, 164–168, 170–172, 178–183, 187–188, 190, 196, 201, 203–206, 213, 220
authoritarian: government 8; regime 4, 8, 11, 20–21, *22*, 31, 36, 144, 221; state 11, 24–25, 30; system *see* regime authoritarian
authoritarianism 22, 25–28, 36, 229, 233
autocratic *22*, 31
autonomy 8, 50, 59, 60, 93, 145, 195, 207, 208, 211, 229–231, 233

Bedner, Adrian 7, 10, **14–15**
Bingham, Tom 7, **15**, 154
Bogdandy, Armin von 172

CEU 115
Charter *see* Charter of Fundamental Rights of the European Union
Charter of Fundamental Rights of the European Union 114, 145, 183–184, 186–187, 189, 194, 208
Christianity 47, 53, 54, 57, 223
civic virtues 77, 231
CJEU 117, 124, 144–145, 170, 172–175, 177, 183, 194, 196–197, 201, 203, 207, 209, 211–212, 214, 228
collective: consciousness 49–51; narcissism 233; victimhood 232–233
common good 79, 88, 98
communism 231
conservatism 233
constitution: façade 7, 31; *republican* 88–89; symbolic 223, 224
constitutional: culture 106, 199; dialogue 228; law 19, 89, 105, 109–110, 153–154, 161–162, 166, 170, 199; supremacy 13, **16**, 119, **227**; theory 89, 94; violence 140
Constitutional Court: Germany 12; Hungary 12, 106–115, 117, 119, 120, 122, 128, 162–163, 165, 211, 228
constitutional democracy: substantive *22*, 28, 31, 231, 234
constitutionalism: abusive 28, 31, **226**; authoritarian 28, 30–31; illiberal 4–5, 20–23, 25, 31, 121, 129, 148, 219, 221–222, 229–230, 234–236; legal 22, 138; liberal 13, *22*, 26, 28, 119; modern 77, 88–89, 92, 94, 99, 117, 223; multilevel 13, 25; political 22, 138
constitutionalist 20, 27
Constitutional Tribunal: Poland 12, *25*, 133, 135, 138–140, 179–181, 194, 202–203, 210–211, 228
constraint 4, 20, *22*, 22–23, 25, 27–28, **29**, 30–32, 36, 120–121, 146, 177, 221–222, 234–235
consultation 121, 140, 143, 145, 224
cooperation: judicial 176
Cormacain, Ronan 9, **16**

Council of Europe 21, 23, 107, 113, 117, 157, 201
Court of Justice of the European Union *see* CJEU
cyclical assemblies 147

data protection: Commissioner 112, 163; National Agency 112
democracy: constitutional *see* constitutional democracy; illiberal 21, 155; liberal 21, 106, 117, 155, 233
democratic: development 21; state 13, 126, 129, 133, 134, 137, 142, 146
deterioration: Rule of Law 4, 36, 233
disciplinary: measures 208, 209; tribunal 124
Dreier, Horst 94
Dworkin, Ronald 12, 93

ECHR *see* European Convention on Human Rights
elections: European 113n27, 123; local 229n18; national 109, 113, 125, 133, 137, 166
emergency: crisis situation caused by mass migration 122; Special Legal Order 122
EPP 123n20, 164, 172
equality 6, 13, **14**, **16**, 17, 21, 59–61, 81n20, 85, 88, 119, 125, 129, 155, 176, 222, 224–225, **226–227**
EU law: acquis *17*, 18–19, 119, 195, 219, *222*, *228*, 234; enforcement 18–19, 32–33, 36, 63, 65, 130, 200, 220–221; implementation 19, 28, 32–33, 67, 222, 234; infringement 25, 32–34, **35**, 170, 172, 178, 181, 183, 185, 190, 195, 201, 207, 213
eunomía 78, 81–83, 87, 91
European Arrest Warrant 187
European Commission 26, 65n62, 112, 141, 144–145, 166, 178–181, 186, 187, 190, 201–202, 205, 207, 209
European Convention on Human Rights 106, 209
European Judges Association 144
European Parliament 107, 113n27, 117, 123, 162, 164–168, 170–171, 173, 178, 181–182, 194, 203
European People's Party *see* EPP
European Public Prosecutor Office 182
European Rule of Law 13, 19–21, 32, 36, 119–120, 129, 130, 174, 178–179, 194, 196, 206, 210, 219–222, 225, *228*, 234–235
European Union: Treaty 63–64, 144–145, 155, 164, 167, 175–178, 195–196, 201, 207, 208, 212–213

Fidesz 24n93, 32n122, 107, 123n20, 125, 128n45, 157, 164, 172, 230
freedom: academic 115, 165; assembly 113, 115, 125, 147; association 115, 159, 165; expression 91, 123, 125, 159–160, 165; information 115, 121, 125; media 30n114; religion 164–165; speech *see* expression
Fuller, Lon 6, 8, 10, **14**, 91, 225, **226**
Fundamental Law 13, 107–115, 120, 125, 128, 161–164, 223
fundamental rights *see* human rights

Gesetzesstaat 61
The Good Change 137–138
Greek philosophy 53, 54, 57
Grimm, Dieter 89

Habermas, Jürgen 80n14, 83n34, 92n84, 93
harmonisation 197
Hegel, Georg 95
hierarchy 17, 59–60, 64, 89, 110, 127, 129, 223, 229, 230n23, 231, 233
history: Hungarian 105, 231, 232; Polish 231, 233
Hobbes, Thomas 78, 79, 82–83, 98
hollowing out 120, 126n34, 144, 219, 221
hostile takeover: constitutional order 140
human rights 3, 5, 7, 9, 10, 12, **15**, **16**, 17n68, 18, 21–24, 27, 30–31, 57, 60, 85, 90, 92n84, 94, 105, 108–110, 114–115, 117, 125, 146, 154, 155–157, 162, 164–165, 169, 172, 176, 195, 203, 220–225, 229, 231
Hungarian Soviet Republic 105

idealism 45, 47, 50, 52–53, 66, 68
identity: constitutional 22, 109, 199, 231–232; national 22, *23*, 59, 148, 156–157, 197–201, 215, 228, 231
illiberal 3, 4, 8, 10, 20–23, 25, 28, 31, 36, 116, 120–121, 129, 148, 153, 155–157, 219, 220–225, *228*, 229–231, 233–236

illiberalism 153, 155–157, 230, 235
impact assessment 121, 124
inclusion 10, 21, 92n84, 136
inferiority 58, 231
infringement procedure 33, 164, 170, 172, 178, 181
ingroup 233–235
ius 84, 90, 93
iustum 84, 90–93

Jogállam: demokratikus 5, 13, 120, 126, 129
judicial: cooperation *see* cooperation judicial; independence 13n61, 112–113, 119, 122–125, 184, 188–189, 209, 210, 212–213, 225; power *see* power judicial; reform 208

Kaczyński, Jarosław 21, 147n76
Kant, Immanuel 80n14, 86, 88, 94, 97, 156
Kelsen, Hans 23, 80n14, 84, 85n43, 86
Kúria 112, 114, 122, 124, 128
Krygier, Martin 3, 8, 82n28

Law and Justice Party *see* PiS
lawfulness 85, 91, 134
law-making 9, 19, 32–33, 82, 84, 87, 90n73, 92–94, 110, 121, 133, 136, 142–143, 145, 169
legal: certainty 7, 13, **16**, 110–111, 119–121, 126–127, 136, 140, **227**; community 21, 65, 143, 219, 235
legality: formal 6–7, **14**, 17, 36, 130, 221, 225, **226**; illiberal 21, 36, 219, 221–222, 225, *228*, 229, 233–236
legislation: accelerated 121, 179; exclusive 121; instrumentalisation 110; quality 111, 224, 230
l'État de droit 5, 154
Locke, John 87–88

MacIntyre, Alasdair 96
majoritarianism 121
Maslow, Abraham 52
masters of treaties 214
materialism 45, 47–48, 50–52
migration: migrants 165; quota 114
Minister of Justice 113, 144, 203, 210, 228
mutual understanding 220

narrative psychology 230
National Council of Judiciary 25n102, 223
national courts 19, 178, 189, 195, 197, 199, 207, 208, 210–213
National Judicial Office: President 109, 112, 121, 123n16, 163
New EU Framework to strengthen the Rule of Law 18n70, 178–179
NGO 115, 122n13, 159, 160, 228
nomos 78, 81n20, 87, 91
non-discrimination 119, 130, 155, 176, 202, 222, **227**

objectivism 47, 53n28
Orbán, Viktor 20–21, 121, 125, 156
outside group 230, 235
overconstitutionalisation 163

packing: constitutional courts 120, 121, 223, 224, **226**
Palombella, Gianluigi 19
państwo prawa: demokratyczne 5, 13
PiS 21, 24n93, 25n102, 137, 141n43, 146, 223, 229n18, 230
pluralism 30n115, 59, 116, 155, 163, 178, 200, 229n16, 230
populism 156, 220, 233–234
populist: agenda 31, 133; leader 19, 22, 32, 220, 229, 231; nationalism 18, 22, 25
power: abuse and misuse 13, **16**, 19, 21, 80n16, 119, 124n22, 125, 130, 157, 222, **227**; executive 88, 111, 141, 187, 224; judicial 119, 122; legislative 128, 222, 224
predictability 7, 8, 10, 12, **14**, 17, 59, **226**
preliminary ruling procedure 20, 33, 124, 186, 208, 210–212
prime minister: Hungarian *see* Orbán, Viktor; Polish 141–142, 147
process: drafting 9; law-making 19, 32, 121
Prosecutor: European Public Prosecutor Office 182; General 121, 124, 128, 189, 210, 212

Rawls, John 79n10, 80n17, 92, 95
Raz, Joseph 6, 8–10, 13n59, **14**, 85–86, 225, **226**
Rechtsstaat 5, 12, 61, 84n36, 96, 120, 134, 154
regime: anti-democratic 4; authoritarian *see* authoritarian regime; hybrid *22*, 30n115, 117; totalitarian *22*, 52

remodelling: constitutional 21, 27, 122, 221, 229
retirement: judges 32n123, 123, 144, 163, 174, 181, 183–186, 188
right: access to justice 13, **16**, 119, 122, **227**; assigned judge 123; asylum seekers 165; economic and social 165, 168; equal treatment 81, 123n17, 165, 186, 202; migrants 165; minorities 137, 145, 155, 163, 165, 176; refugees 165
Romania 194, 210, 231
Roman law 53–54, 57
Rule of Law: enforcement 18, 127; English 154; European *see* European Rule of Law; formal 5–12, **14–15**, 85–86, 90, 91n76, 92, 127, 129, 130, 136–137, 221; material 5–13, **14–15**, 91n76, 127–128, 133; narrow *see* formal; substantial *see* material; thick *see* material; thin *see* formal
Russia 27–28, **29–30**, 31, 231

Sargentini report 26, 164–165, 168, 173
Sartori, Giovanni 90, 91
Sejm 26n103, 140n34, 142, 144, 179–180, 223
Senat 140, 229n18, 230
separation of powers 87, 110–111, 115, 117, 121, 127, 133, 135, 137, 143–146, 148, 161, 188
Singapore 28, **29**, **30**, 31
solidarity 59, 63–64, 79n8, 155, 176
Sorokin, Pitirim 45, 55
Soros, György 165
sovereign 83, 98, 138, 140, 145, 148
sovereignty: people 89, 94, 95; state 139, 219
state of law 59, 134–135, 137, 143, 146–148
subsidiarity 59
super-culture 45, 55–57, 61, 63–64, 66–68
Supreme Administrative Court 185
Supreme Court: Disciplinary Chamber 188–190; Hungary 32n122, 112, 122, 128; Poland 32n123, 123n17, 141, 144, 174, 183–185, 188–190, 203, 223

Tavares report 162
transformation: democratic 117, 134, 136, 139, 145, 231; illiberal 230, 233
transition: democratic 24, 105, 107; political 106
Transitory Provisions 108, 163
trust: mutual 18, 64, 164, 174, 180, 187, 195, 199–201
Turkey 27–28, **29**, **30**, 31

UN Human Rights Council 144
use of law: instrumental 130, 222, 234; opportunistic 222, 234

value: common 10, 63–64, 96, 130, 153–154, 162, 164, 171, 195, 200, 208, 219, 220; cultural 61–62; democratic 229; EU 18, 64–65, 67, 174–177, 182, 186–187, 203, 205, 215; European 45, 48, 52–53, 56–60, 63–67, 69, 117, 130, 154, 201, 230, 233–234, legal 61–62, 64–65, 67, 235–236; liberal 5; orientation 221, 229, 233; system 18, 96
Van Gend judgment 195
Venice Commission: Rule of Law Checklist 13, **16**, 119, 122
Verfassungsstaat 12

xenophobia 229

Zakaria, Fareed 21, 155

For Product Safety Concerns and Information please contact our EU representative GPSR@taylorandfrancis.com
Taylor & Francis Verlag GmbH, Kaufingerstraße 24, 80331 München, Germany

www.ingramcontent.com/pod-product-compliance
Lightning Source LLC
LaVergne TN
LVHW011123300926
849160LV00008B/495
* 9 7 8 0 3 6 7 5 1 2 1 3 2 *